Tales of God's Friends

Sultān Sulaymān the Magnificent visits the tomb-shrine of Eyüp Ansari in Istanbul. Ottoman Turkish, Trustees of the Chester Beatty Library, Dublin, T. 413 f. 38a.

Tales of God's Friends

Islamic Hagiography in Translation

EDITED BY JOHN RENARD

University of California Press

BERKELEY   LOS ANGELES   LONDON

University of California Press, one of the most distinguished university presses in the United States, enriches lives around the world by advancing scholarship in the humanities, social sciences, and natural sciences. Its activities are supported by the UC Press Foundation and by philanthropic contributions from individuals and institutions. For more information, visit www.ucpress.edu.

University of California Press
Berkeley and Los Angeles, California

University of California Press, Ltd.
London, England

Library of Congress Cataloging-in-Publication Data

Tales of God's friends: Islamic hagiography in translation / edited by John Renard.
    p.   cm.
  Includes bibliographical references and index.
   ISBN 978-0-520-25322-3 (cloth : alk. paper)—ISBN 978-0-520-25896-9 (pbk. : alk. paper)
   1. Muslim saints—Biography. 2. Sufis—Biography. 3. Islamic literature—Translations into English. I. Renard, John, 1944–.
BP189.4.T35 2009
297.092'2—dc22
[B]
                                          2008046836

Manufactured in the United States of America

18 17 16 15 14 13 12 11 10 09
10 9 8 7 6 5 4 3 2 1

This book is printed on Natures Book, which contains 30% post-consumer waste and meets the minimum requirements of ANSI/NISO z39.48–1992 (R 1997) (*Permanence of Paper*).

Contents

Illustrations

Preface

You hold in your hand, dear reader, a collection of some of the world's most marvelous narratives of exemplary Muslim piety. Translated from seventeen languages of origin, most of the stories appear here for the first time in English, and many for the first time in any European language. This gathering is also, to my knowledge, the first truly global anthology of Islamic hagiography in translation in any language. In the interest of maximum coverage, both historically and geographically, I was privileged to enlist the generous and enthusiastic collaboration of more than two dozen Islamic studies scholars specializing in a broad spectrum of languages and Islamicate cultures and literatures. Of the twenty-seven individual translated sections, several have appeared previously in published form, and I have included them here because they contribute unique and otherwise hard-to-find material.

SELECTION AND METHOD

Designed as a companion volume to *Friends of God: Islamic Images of Piety, Commitment, and Servanthood*, the present anthology seeks to provide through primary sources a sense of the multiple facets and expansive dimensions of Islamic hagiography. A deeper and more thorough survey would, of course, require many volumes like this. In making selections, my overriding concerns have been to include samples that represent as many important languages of origin as possible while maintaining a balance among regions; feature a variety of major figures and literary genres, along with examples of lesser-known Friends of God; and draw equally from classical, medieval, and modern times. I have arranged the material to facilitate a global appreciation of the vast topic. Emphasis is on the primary source in translation; sufficient introductory comment is offered to provide religious and literary context, along with adequate annotation to assist nonspecialist readers through the material.

Some selections translate texts about a single important figure from more than one source or language of origin. These are included to provide readers and teachers convenient opportunities for diachronic (12, 19) (parenthetical numbers refer to translations as numbered in the table of contents and synoptic/comparative chart) or cross-cultural synchronic (1, 5) comparisons as to how the figure in question has "developed" as evidenced by changing perceptions. In addition, a concern for gender inclusiveness has led to the presentation of several texts by or about important female Friends of God (e.g., 14, 16, 23).

TECHNICALITIES

Synoptic/comparative chart: To facilitate an integrated overview of the material gathered here, a synoptic/comparative chart assembles basic data about the main figures featured in the texts and about the texts themselves, including reference to author, dates, place and language of origin, and literary form. (See the appendix, pages 372–76.)

Annotation: In order to facilitate reading for nonspecialists, the in-text raised numbers indicate notes that supply either identification and related commentary or bibliographic or other scholarly apparatus or more technical information. Readers can, of course, read the texts in any order; but I have edited with a view to both an economy and minimal continuity of notes such that an item or person identified in a text appearing earlier will not receive a similar note on later appearance.

In-text apparatus: Parentheses ( ) are used within a translated text to set off dates not included in the original and to indicate the English-language equivalent of a foreign technical term. Brackets [ ] in a text are used to indicate either an interpolation (i.e., a translator's addition not specifically included in the original but inserted for the sake of clarification) or a translation of text not found in the original text itself but as a marginal addition to the original. Distinctions between these latter two usages are specified in backnotes to texts in question.

References to Qur'ānic texts appear in parentheses, giving only *sura* and verse numbers as in (24:35). Unless otherwise noted, single dates given in parentheses for individual figures are death dates. I have included Hijrī/ lunar as well as Shamsī/solar dates, but in many cases the equivalences are approximate rather than based on exact calculation by lunar or solar month in order to arrive at the precise year. In cases of contexts not explicitly regarded as "Islamic," such as modern Turkey, I have not used dual dating.

Glossary: To assist readers with random identification of concepts or technical terms, a multilingual glossary includes most important non-English terms essential to Islamic hagiography, along with a sample of language-specific variants. For greater utility, many terms used in *Friends of God* are also included here.

Transliteration: Transliteration of major Islamicate languages, especially those that use the Arabic alphabet (e.g., Persian, medieval and early modern Turkic, Siraiki, and Urdu), already presents challenges in that standard conventions often apply only to a single language. Such difficulties multiply when a book like this encompasses material translated from several or more of those languages. But the problems of consistency expand almost exponentially when a project also deals with texts from non-Arabic script languages, including some that use variations on Roman script (such as modern Turkish, Wolof, and Indonesian), or languages that use very different systems (such as Bengali, written in Devanagari script, and Chinese). Knowing full well that thorough consistency under such circumstances is virtually impossible, I have attempted to strike something of a happy medium in the interest of minimizing reader confusion and assisting nonspecialists toward some semblance of accurate pronunciation. In many cases I have included in parentheses the Arabic "original" of certain technical religious terms spelled differently in a given text's language of origin—so for example, [Indonesian] *marepat* (*maʿrifa*), and, in hopes of aiding pronunciation, have opted to provide long vowels in instances of names and terms traceable ultimately to Arabic. I thank the reader in advance for patience with my less than entirely satisfying attempts at compromise in this regard.

ACKNOWLEDGMENTS

I am indebted first of all to the contributing scholars without whose generosity and expertise in a host of languages and cultures this anthology would have been simply impossible. It has been a privilege and a pleasure to experience the expansive feeling of a "community of scholarship" among so many talented specialists in so many areas of Islamic religious studies, many of whom I had not known personally before I solicited their participation in this project. Several contributors also kindly made available photographs from their collections to be used as illustrations. Thanks in abundance to them all, with special appreciation to Tony Stewart for his invaluable assistance with various technical matters.

As to the matter of permission and fair use of materials presented here in translation: Every effort has been made to identify and locate the rightful copyright holders of all material not specifically commissioned for use in this publication and to secure permission, where applicable, for reuse of all such material. Credit, if and as available, has been provided for all borrowed material either on-page, on the copyright page, or in an acknowledgement section of the book. Errors, omissions, or failure to obtain authorization with respect to material copyrighted by other sources has been either unavoidable or unintentional. The editor and publisher welcome any information that would allow them to correct future reprints.

My thanks also go to Robert Porwoll of Saint Louis University for his editorial assistance through two years' work on this two-volume project on *Friends of God* and their stories, and Ben O'Connor also of Saint Louis University for his reading of earlier materials for this anthology. I thank also Annie Chen of Saint Louis University for her assistance in proofreading final pages and indexing. For assistance in procuring illustrations, my thanks to Richard Blurton, Jamal Elias, Alan Godlas, Ken H. Honerkamp, Nahla Nassar, Tony Stewart, Sufia Mendez Uddin, and Elaine Wright. Thanks also to Reed Malcolm, Kalicia Pivirotto, Kate Warne, and Steven Baker, all of University of California Press, for their support and invaluable expertise in bringing this project to completion. Finally, my deepest gratitude to Mary Pat for her constant good humor, wisdom, and unfailing support over the course of this two-volume project.

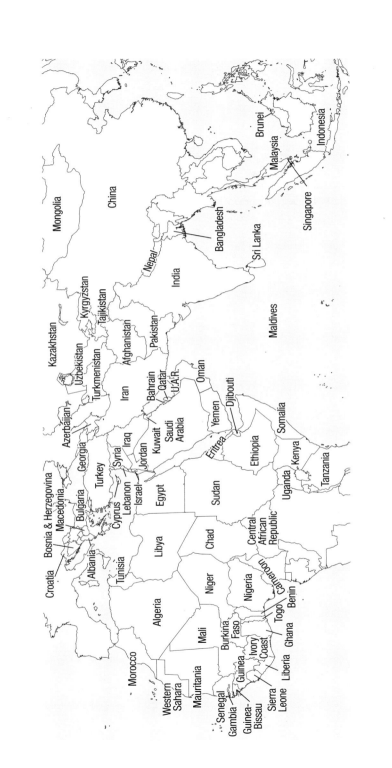

Islamic Hagiography

Sources and Contexts

.   .   .   .   .

Travelers who venture across the broad terrain of Islamic hagiography need a map that shows major landmarks in time as well as space. Negotiating the landscapes of this global subject requires some familiarity with the many signs of diversity in the sources and their subjects. To relate these materials, whether textual or visual, more precisely to their unique histories, one needs at least a general awareness of the particular geographical *regions* and *cultural milieux* in which the various sources are rooted. Second, one needs to locate each source *chronologically* and then within a specific historical framework or cultural context. In this instance, it is also helpful, if not downright necessary, to locate the major characters who are the featured players in these documents. Finally, it is important to note the wide diversity of *languages* and literatures of origin represented in these documents.

The table of contents provides a general map along these lines. More than two dozen translated texts, contributed by as many specialists working in some seventeen languages, are organized here using two overlapping principles. First, six main sections divide the material by geographic region; second, within each region, stories are further arranged more or less chronologically according to the periods in which the main characters lived or, in the case of texts about either multiple figures or thematic rather than narrative material, by the date of the text. There is some instructive overlap in languages of origin, in that Arabic texts come from outside the region identified here as the Arab Middle East and North Africa, just as Persian texts might originate beyond the regional category labeled Iran and Afghanistan.

If this first set of broad categories—regions/cultures, history/chronology, and language of origin—tend to sort out and *separate* the individual examples of hagiography, four dimensions can just as often *connect* them. Those features are medium, form or genre, theme and narrative device, and function. By "medium" I mean any specific mode of communication, whether textual, visual/nonverbal, or more recently, electronic combinations of text, image, and sound, by which Friends and their stories have been disseminated. "Form and genre" refer here principally to modes and styles of verbal and visual communication. Islamic hagiographical literature embraces a striking breadth of literary forms, from brief sayings to extended narratives, from lyric poetry to the modern novel. A third useful category, "themes and narrative devices," encompasses a host of motifs or tropes, character types, and plots or story formulae that make up the apparently universal stock-in-trade of the hagiographer. Finally, "function" is a rubric under which to suggest briefly something of the manifold roles that our sources, whether textual or nonverbal, and the main characters in the narratives have played in their cultural, political, and religious contexts.

In the next few pages, I describe the contents of the present volume from the two perspectives—divergent and convergent—to better assist readers in benefiting from the introductions to each of the texts in translation.

MAPPING THE WORLD OF ISLAMIC HAGIOGRAPHY

Here I suggest ways of understanding the diversity and breadth of materials collected in this anthology through the filters of geography and culture, chronology and history, and languages and literatures of origin.

Geography and Culture

As the six parts of this collection acknowledge, material and main characters originate across a vast swath of the globe. That swath begins at Senegal and North Africa, moves through Central and East Africa, and continues on through the Central Middle East and into Central Asia, across the Indian Subcontinent, and as far east as China and southeast to Malaysia and Indonesia. For nearly a millennium and a half, the faith tradition of Islam has flourished in and been expressed through the multiple cultural matrices now often coextensive with nation-states. In virtually all of those contexts, exemplars of piety, devotion, and servanthood (including prophets) known as Friends of God have been and remain major carriers of tradition and symbols of living Islamic faith.

Friends of God come in at least four sizes: global, transregional, regional, and purely local. Globally renowned figures include (in addition to the prophets) Abū Bakr, 'Abd al-Qādir al-Jīlānī, Bāyazīd al-Bistāmī, Hallāj, and

Junayd. Some Friends enjoy a celebrity status that, while less than global, crosses the imaginary boundaries of two or more major regions roughly commensurate with the Arabicate, Persianate, Turkic, sub-Saharan African, or Malay literary-linguistic worlds (or the regions where any of these smaller worlds overlap significantly). Among these transregional figures one might name Hacı Bektaş Veli, Saʿdī and the founders of several transregional Sufi orders, such as the Tījānīya and Wafāʾīya. Regionally important figures include Friends belonging to specific Sufi orders widely influential in regions such as West and North Africa (the Tījānī Shaykh ʿAbbās Sall of Senegal, and the Shādhilī Abū Yaʿzā), Central and East Africa (Nana Asmaʾu; her father, Usman dan Fodiyo; and Shaykh Uways), Egypt (Muhammad Wafāʾ), Turkey and Central Asia (Yūnus Emre, Sarı Saltık, Sarı İsmail, and Hakīm Ata), South Asia (historical figures like the Ismāʿīlī Pīr Sadr ad-Dīn, Ahmad Sirhindī, Sadr ad-Dīn Sadr-i Jahān, as well as mythic figures like the wondrous Bonbībī and Mānik Pīr), and Indonesia (Sunan Ampel and the Walī Songo). In addition hundreds, perhaps even thousands, of intriguing characters function as patron saints of cities, villages, and remote tribal areas across the globe. Although this last category includes countless minor characters who rarely merit the attention of hagiographers and generally remain of local stature, some, such as Bonbībī, have attained regional celebrity.

As an aid to a more concrete orientation to the geographical expanse of Islamic hagiography, the table presented on pages 372–76 summarizes and compares basic information about both the main Friends of God featured in the texts and the texts themselves.

Chronology and History

Texts translated here were selected with a view to representing as many of the major periods of Islamic history as feasible in a single volume on this subject. In soliciting the contributions of this remarkable cohort of specialists, I considered the historical contexts of the works excerpted as well as the lifetimes of the figures whose stories those excerpts recount. The individuals who are the subjects of these accounts are represented in the following diachronic scheme. Textual sources run a wide gamut, from first/seventh-century Hadith (1), to medieval prose accounts (1–6, 9–12) and early modern traditional written and oral hagiographical texts (7, 8, 13–16, 18, 21, 24, 25, 27), to more recent hagiographical and autobiographical accounts (12, 17, 19, 20, 22, 23, 26).

As for specific personalities, pre-Islamic figures include most prominently the prophet Job (Ayyūb) and his wife, Rehema. Making appearances in brief Chinese narratives we find Mary (Yuhala) and her son, the second-to-last prophet, Jesus (Ersa), with occasional references to the prophet Ilyās and his soul-brother, Khidr. From the time of Muhammad we have the Prophet himself; the great Companion and first caliph, Abū Bakr (13 AH/634 CE); Uways al-Qaranī (37/657), noted for his intimate spiritual relationship to Muhammad; and Sa'd ibn Abī Waqqās (55/674), credited with introducing Islam into China. Another early figure represented here is Shī'ī personality Muhammad ibn al-Hanafīya. Representative exemplary figures from late antiquity and early medieval times include Junayd of Baghdad (298/910) and assorted colorful early Sufis who appear in brief anecdotes from Sa'dī (see also 26, 1, 25, 5, 6, 13, and 14).

Among individuals from mid- to later medieval times are Abū Ya'zā (572/1177); seventh/thirteenth- and eighth/fourteenth-century notables such as Hacı Bektaş Veli, Sarı İsmail, Sarı Saltık, Yūnus Emre (720/1321), Hakīm Ata, Muhammad Wafā' (765/1363); and ninth/fifteenth–tenth/sixteenth-century figures such as Sunan Ampel (c. 875/1470) (with mention of his near-contemporary the Wali Songo), Sadr ad-Dīn Sadri Jahān (921/1515), and Ahmad Sirhindī (1034/1624) (see 9–12, 26, 17, 18).

From early modern times come such diverse characters as Ma (Muhammad Sāhib, 1089/1678), Wang Daiyu (1090/1679), Usman dan Fodiyo (1233/1817) and his daughter Nana Asma'u (1281/1864), and the Mulla of Hadda (see 27, 14, 8)

Fourteenth/twentieth-century personalities Khwāja Hasan Nizāmī (1375/1955), Somali Shaykh Uways (1327/1909), and Nūr 'Alī Ilāhī (1394/1974) (see 22, 16, 7). Finally, escaping easy chronological identification, are the "mythic" Bonbībī, Mānik Pīr, and Khidr (see 23, 24, and various other stories with Khidr in cameo appearances).

Languages and Literatures of Origin

Contributions to this anthology represent some seventeen languages of origin: Arabic, representing North Africa and the Arab Middle East; Persian, Turkic tongues of three varieties (early Ottoman, Chaghatay, and modern), and Pashtu, representing parts of the Central Middle East and Central Asia; Wolof, Hausa, Fulfulde, Swahili, and Arabic again, from various regions of Africa; Gujarati (an important language of northwestern India), Siraiki (a major language spoken in the Pakistani province of Sindh), Urdu (the "national" language of Pakistan), Bengali, and Persian again, from the South Asian subcontinent; and Malay, Chinese, and modern Indonesian, representing Southeast and East Asia. As the following sections describe further, nearly as many literary forms—and even more hagiographical and other themes—bridge the linguistic gaps. The synoptic-comparative chart identifies the languages of origin of the principal texts translated here.

DISCERNING THE COMMON ELEMENTS

In addition to the great color and profusion into which the sources of our knowledge about Friends of God fan out, one can also discern important common threads in medium; genre and form; theme and narrative device; and function of character and source.

Medium

This anthology and its companion thematic overview monograph, *Friends of God: Islamic Images of Piety, Commitment, and Servanthood,* acknowledge, in varying degrees, both textual and nontextual modes of hagiographical communication. It goes (almost) without saying that the texts receive the bulk of that attention. Numerous as are the verbal varieties and literary textures of Islamic hagiography, a remarkable proliferation of visual imagery enriches the whole subject. The most common, and ancient, genre of visual hagiographical is the narrative illustration. Although these images typically illustrate important scenes in traditional stories, they are not always located in direct physical proximity to the texts they visualize. Book-size manuscript paintings, often called miniatures, of hagiographical themes appear in greatest numbers after the ninth/fifteenth century, especially under the patronage of Turkic, Persian, and Mughal Indian royalty. A sample of some two dozen such miniatures appears in *Friends of God,* taken from illustrated manuscripts of major hagiographical texts, showing scenes featuring major Friends of God in action. The additional images that appear in the present volume include items of that genre as well. The cover photo of the paperback edition, for example, is a vibrant depiction of Shaykh Ahmad-i Jām (also figure 9 in *Friends of God*) riding a lion and using serpents for rein and whip. In connection with the stories of Saʿdī's Saints, we have an illustration of Saʿdī himself visiting an idol temple in a teaching occasion (Fig. 4). A remarkable image featuring an Indonesian Friend of God called Nūr Sayyid Kiai shows a member of the royal family, depicted in the style of *wayang kulit* shadow figures, seeking spiritual counsel from the saint in his wilderness haunt (Fig. 19). "The Tales of Mānik Pīr," in the South Asian section of this anthology, notably contributes to readers' appreciation of the interrelationships of text and image, as it incorporates a set of eight delightful narrative images from an illustrated manuscript of the story (Figs. 11–18). Like the legendary Mānik Pīr, the mysterious Khidr (Fig. 5) floats free, unencumbered by historical moorings. Shrine-tombs of early Companions of the Prophet, such as that of Eyüp (Ayyūb) al-Ansārī (frontispiece), have inspired a number of visual depictions. A second small-scale visual medium, of more recent vintage, is the under-glass painting that has become widely popular in parts of North and West Africa since the latter half of the fourteenth/twentieth century. I was unable to procure examples of the medium for illustrations in either of the companion volumes. On a slightly larger scale, a sample of sculpture appears in a Bengali context (Fig. 10).

On a still larger scale, however, are the numerous and often spectacular architectural expressions of reverence for the Friends of God that have been erected across the globe. Most such structures are funerary enclosures, many of which have expanded into sprawling complexes encompassing a host of facilities for social and ritual functions. Both volumes include photographs of architectural sites associated with prophets and Friends from Abraham to the more recent Nizām ad-Dīn Awliyā'. Thanks to photos taken by several of our contributors, a number of these foundations are represented visually in these volumes (Figs. 1–3, 6–10).

Form and Genre

The twenty-seven texts offered here, along with twenty visual images, represent a variety of literary forms, functions, and hermeneutical presuppositions. In addition, by including not only "classical" illustrations typically associated with some manuscripts but also a variety of more recent images and "new media" whose relationships to text are only beginning to be explored, this volume's contents broaden the traditional spectrum of media and forms about which scholars of Islam have customarily discussed the subject of hagiography. Following is an overview of the principal literary forms represented in this volume.

Many of the texts translated here exemplify the major subgenres of hagiography. Indeed, this exceptionally diverse collection of texts offers a rare opportunity for showcasing the variety of literary forms. These include, for example, the *tabaqāt* ("classifications, generations," as in 1D, 5A, and 5B); the *tadhkira* (remembrances, recollections, as in 17); the *manāqib* (marvelous deeds or feats, as in 2, 4, 11, and 12A); and the *sīra* (life story, as in 9). Lan Zixi's "Epitaphs of the Real Humans" (27) shares formal characteristics with these more traditional hagiographic forms but is sui generis in that it very pointedly explains the spiritual qualities (*fadā'il;* see 1A and 1B) of the figures described (both prophets and Friends of God) in terms of the major ancient-Chinese non-Muslim cultural and belief systems Confucianism and Daoism.

Not all data on Friends of God come to us from literary forms that are hagiographical in the narrower, more intentional sense of the term. In addition, the anthology embraces a variety of other genres that contribute to the vast repertory of hagiographical lore. For example, stories of Abū Bakr (1) begin with the foundational genre of Hadith, and many hagiographers have made extensive use of Hadith, often weaving these ancient sayings into their narratives as a way of connecting their main characters to the life and times of the Prophet and major Companions like Abū Bakr and Muḥammad's cousin and son-in-law, ʿAlī. Since the teachings of the great ones have frequently been enshrined in briefer *apophthegmata* or *logia*, some of the present texts feature brief sayings of a Friend of God arranged thematically (as in 5B).

Some Friends of God, such as Sarı Saltık (10), feature in literary forms akin to the popular, romantic, or mystical "epic," replete with fantastic tales that highlight the central figure's divinely protected exploits. Likewise the prophet Job (Ayyub) and his wife, Rehema, appear here in an excerpt from the East African *Epic of Job* (15), whose literary form is explicitly identified as part of the Swahili *tendi* "epic" tradition. Other accounts, such as the one about the Mulla of Hadda (8), share the fantastic/romantic aura of these "epic" tales and survive largely in oral tradition preserved and handed down in written form after being told to anthropologists.

Elements of the "fantastic" may also be found in the phenomenon of "marvelous deeds" or "saintly miracles" that play roles of varying importance in hagiographical texts. A related literary genre designed to deal with the creedal and theological implications of miracles includes, for example, the *fatwā* (legal advisory) and *radd* (technical response to inquiry about religious theory or practice, as in 3). Yet another genre addresses pilgrims' need for assistance in making visitations to the shrine-tombs of great Friends (21). Such works provide information on the ritual expectations attendant on visitation, as well as *radd*-like explanations of background issues such as intercession and marvels. Finally, among prose genres, even the modern novel makes a cameo appearance in a latter-day look at the story of Yūnus Emre as contrasted with a more traditional medieval account (12B).

An important large category of texts often enlisted in the service of hagiography includes poetry of several types—didactic, lyric love poetry, and panegyric—all represented here in various texts. Of the first type we have an example in the mixed prose and poetry of Saʿdī, widely understood as a kind of sage counsel or "wisdom" literature (6). So important is this understanding of Saʿdī's works that one commentator on the didactic qualities of Khwāja Hasan Nizāmī's autobiography (22) calls it a *"Gulistān* [a major work of Sa'dī] in Urdu." In the second thematic type, lyric love poetry, we have examples from South Asia in the form of *qawwālī* (19); several texts also incorporate bits of lyric poetry attributed to the figure to whom the text is dedicated (4, 16, 18, 20). Nana Asma'u's works fit generally in the third category of panegyric (14), as do the Siraiki *na't* (19) and the Gujarati poem (20) and Wolof encomium of great Tījānī Sufis (13). Finally, from Bangladesh comes the unique Bengali panegyric form called *puthi* (23).

Autobiographical accounts also contribute considerable hagiographical data and from a unique, often idiosyncratic perspective. Examples of such narratives here include the diary-like text of Ostād Elāhī (7) and Hasan Nizāmī's recollections of his younger life (22). Also in this category are portions of the texts by Ahmad Sirhindī (18).

See the synoptic chart for a comparative view of the various subgenres of the texts translated here.

Themes and Narrative Devices

Among the most prominent themes are a wide variety of saintly marvels (*karāmāt*). Virtually every text translated here describes "custom-shattering" events, either of prophets (*mu'jizāt*) or Friends of God (*karāmāt*). On this important theological topic, we have here the treatise of Yāfi'ī (3) as well as many narrative accounts. Miracles and marvels run the gamut from less remarkable phenomena such as talking animals or mind-reading humans to much more spectacular feats of power. In some cases, a central figure (such as Sarı Saltık in 10) prominently demonstrates submiraculous abilities that result more from heightened native cleverness than powers clearly of divine origin. In that respect, such figures embody strong residual "heroic" characteristics onto which distinctly "saintly" prerogatives have been grafted. Some of our stories recount unusual avenues by which protagonists receive communications from the unseen world. These include dreams and visions, messages from disembodied "calling voices" from offstage, and sudden unexpected visitations by mysterious emissaries such as Khidr. Readers will encounter in these varied tales other, often engaging and delightful instances of an extraordinary degree of holiness and piety.

Conflict with or polemic against non-Muslims appears as a major motif in several accounts, and conversion to Islam is a major feature within that larger theme (as in the Sarı Saltık and Hacı Bektaş Veli tales (10, 11). Gender roles and relations feature in several of the texts. These include relational roles such as those of wife, mother, and sister. On the other hand, texts about regionally prominent figures such as Bonbībī (23) accord their subjects primary stature independent of their relationships to any male figure. In the unique case of our Nigerian texts, the author was a notable woman, Nana Asma'u, who penned a *tabaqāt*-like panegyric poem dedicated to major female Sufis (14C). Gender takes on particularly interesting dimensions in the *Tales of Mānik Pīr* (24) and in the *Epic of Job* (15), which features a role for the Job's wife, Rehema, far more prominent than she plays in scriptural or later traditional accounts of the prophet.

Narrative themes incorporate larger-scale shared features, such as plot or scene structures and story types. Marvel stories showcase major figures effecting a host of extraordinary deeds, such as traveling instantaneously, taking the form of nonhuman beings or assuming other sorts of remarkable disguise, and transforming matter into new substances, to name only a few of the principal themes. Stories of family conflict, struggle between ethnic and religious communities, and the evolution of organizations such as Sufi orders provide additional material for the storyteller. On a smaller scale, a favorite narrative device is mistaken or mysterious identity, whether effected through deliberate disguise or the result of long separation (as in a father's not recognizing the son he left when the child was very young or as yet unborn). Sarı Saltık, a master of disguise, dresses as a priest, and the Hacı Bektaş Veli story makes pointed references to identifying Christians by their garb. A device occasionally related to identity and especially prominent in the story of Hakīm Ata is conflict between father and son, sometimes in turn associated by extension with struggle for authority. A common device employed to define a sense of place is the use of archetypal natural features, such as the tree in the Hakīm Ata narrative. Birds also sometimes function as metaphors for an individual's soul or as a vehicle of revelation or for a message from the unseen world.

Function: Characters and Sources

Individual figures play a wide range of roles. Nearly all the Friends of God stand out as paragons of virtue and high-mindedness, with an occasional nod to quick-witted deviousness. As a very early and especially prominent Companion of Muhammad, Abū Bakr is doubly important in this context. Junayd of Baghdad is widely described as a leading figure in the "Baghdad school" of mysticism, and countless Sufi genealogies include him prominently in their lineages. Such later figures as Usman dan Fodiyo enjoy, according to their hagiographers, enhanced stature precisely because of their spiritual kinship with the Prophet. The Prophet is said to have promised that God would raise up a "renewer" at the outset of every lunar century, and sources excerpted here explain how one such *mujaddid* (Ahmad Sirhindī) and his supporters believed he fulfilled a role even greater than that, as millennial renewer. Friends like Yūnus Emre whose reputations include their important contributions to Sufi organizations such as the Mawlawīya (Rūmī's order) are also celebrated for their gifts as mystical poets. Among the more colorful figures in our narratives are those who were not historical personages at all. These include Mānik Pīr, Bonbībī, and Khidr, the last of whom appears in cameo roles in several of our texts.

Whatever their form or genre, hagiographical narratives arise from a variety of motives and are designed to play various roles. One of the more important functions of the earlier hagiographical anthologies was to provide concrete data on major Sufis in defense against the charge that Sufism tended toward heterodoxy in its teachings and practices. Such is the case with works by Sarrāj and Hujwīrī excerpted here (1). As hagiography developed and as extended lives of individual figures became more common, motives for writing included the desire to preserve the teachings and wisdom of the great Friends of God in times of spiritual drought, as a help to seekers of God after the death of the Friend. Several authors of free-standing hagiographical anthologies (as distinct from the hagiographical selections incorporated into larger works), such as those of Isfahānī and Jāmī (5), for example, combine motives like these. Many hagiographical anthologies of a more limited scope feature the stories of Friends associated with one specific organization, as in the case of the Shādhilīya, Wafā'īya, Bektāshīya, or Tījānīya orders (2, 4, 11, 13).

Some works were produced out of a desire to legitimize a region or country's Islamic pedigree by focusing on the stature of the individuals credited with first introducing the faith there. Stories of Indonesia's Walī Songo (26), the tale of Sarı Saltık (10), and the Chinese text by Lan Zixi (27) suggest such functions. In some instances, there is evidence of other social and political motivation as well, such as Khwāja Hasan Nizāmī's experience in pre-Partition India/Pakistan (22) and the story of Sadr ad-Dīn Sadr-i Jahān's role in post-Partition times (17).

Last but by no means least, these narratives have long been treasured as immensely entertaining, full of warmth, wit, and insight into human foibles of every kind. Even in this light, however, tales of God's Friends are always a great deal more than just stories or neutral data. The accounts, like the characters of whom they tell, are much more complex and multilayered than they may at first appear. Beneath their appealing simplicity lies a depth of experience, profound reflection, and vivid imagination, without which they would not have survived and grown richer as they have. Taken together, this amazing collection of tales and personalities makes accessible far-flung, largely untapped resources in Islamic religious literatures that offer entrée to a score of major Islamicate cultures. Their genius for showcasing the human and humane dimensions of one of the world's great faith traditions is, in the end, what makes tales of God's Friends so important now, as through centuries past.

PART I

The Arab Middle East and North Africa

.   .   .   .   .

The four selections of Part 1 introduce major figures from North Africa and the Arab Middle East as presented in several important literary genres. Abū Bakr, Muhammad's father-in-law, Companion, and first successor (caliph), appears from the perspectives of four different sources—three Arabic and one Persian. Readers will notice a distinct progression in the treatment of this important figure from earlier to later sources. We begin with reports from one of the central Hadith collectors and move to slightly more extended accounts from three early hagiographical anthologies—two included in larger manuals of Sufi spirituality and the third a free-standing work of hagiography. Three texts dedicated to more detailed free-standing Arabic hagiographic themes and purposes come from three different major areas of the Arabophone world. In an "eyewitness account," an influential North African hagiographer offers a selection of scenes from the life of a medieval Maghribī Sufi spiritual leader. From an author who lived in the Arabian Peninsula comes another literary form, a theoretical "response" to concerns about the often contested matter of saintly marvels. Finally, a selection from a hagiographical text presents accounts concerning the founding figures of an Egyptian Sufi order.

1 Abū Bakr in Tradition and Early Hagiography

John Renard

Among the Companions of the Prophet, none has attained a loftier status in tradition and lore than Muhammad's first successor, and father-in-law, Abū Bakr (c. 570–13/634). Sources place him among the staunchest of the early converts to Islam and describe him as enjoying an especially intimate relationship to the Prophet. From the first authoritative collections of Hadith (sayings attributed ultimately to Muhammad) through the beginnings of more explicitly hagiographical literature, Abū Bakr stands out as an instructive example of how the representation of one embodiment of holiness developed across several centuries of Islamic traditional sources. Excerpts of important texts about this major figure are included here for two reasons. First, among the Islamic tradition's central paradigmatic figures, Abū Bakr is among the least well known outside Islamic circles. Second, his story well exemplifies the broad continuity of Islamic hagiography that is one of the larger premises of this volume. We begin here with Muslim's collection of Hadith and trace the evolution of this towering figure in three of the most influential Sufi hagiographies.

ABŪ BAKR IN THE HADITH LITERATURE

Nearly all of the major Hadith collections include sections on the "virtues" or "excellent qualities" (*faḍā'il*) of Muhammad's Companions. First and foremost among the Companions in all these collections stands Muhammad's dear friend, father-in-law, and first successor (*khalīfa*) to leadership of the Muslim community, Abū Bakr. In the Hadith collection (*saḥīḥ*) of Muslim (262/875), one of the earliest and most authoritative major traditionist works, the lengthy chapter on the virtues of the Prophet's Companions includes entries on some forty individuals, among whom are nine women of Muhammad's family. Muslim's traditions also spotlight the lofty qualities of various groups or categories of people, including the Helpers (*ansār*), who assisted Muhammad upon his migration to Medina, those who engaged in the Battle of Badr (3/624) on the Prophet's side, and the members of several specific Arab tribes.

Muslim situates his chapter on the merits of the Companions immediately after a shorter section dedicated to the noble qualities of Muhammad. That chapter concludes with entries on several major pre-Islamic prophetic figures. Muslim does not specify his motives for adding material on Jesus, Abraham, Moses, Joseph, and Khidr. But the Traditions cited feature the Prophet's own, often subtle associations of himself with these earlier prophets in various ways. In the present anthology, as in *Friends of God*, a fundamental premise is that one cannot truly appreciate the function of spiritual paradigms in the Islamic tradition without understanding the continuity between the prophetic and post-prophetic eras.

From the perspective of literary form, hagiographically significant Hadiths include a wide variety of types. Materials run the gamut from quasi-aphoristic sayings of a line or two; to brief anecdotes about Muhammad, previous prophets, and the Prophet's contemporaries; to more extended narratives. Abū Bakr is a pivotal figure in the evolution of traditional Muslim convictions about this cloud of witnesses who model faith, values, and commitment. A series of traditions excerpted below (without full chains of transmission) provides a sense of the qualities so long prized and acknowledged as exemplary.[1] Note how consistently Abū Bakr's stature is described in relation to the opinion and person of Muhammad.

TRANSLATION

(2381) Anas ibn Mālik passed along the tradition that Abū Bakr the Authentic had communicated to him, namely: While we were in the cave, I spied the feet of the pagans at our very heads. I [later] said, "Messenger of God, if one of them had glanced down at his feet, he would have spotted us just there!" At that he replied, "Abū Bakr, what is one to think about two people whose third person is God?"[2]

(2382) Abū Saʿīd passed along the tradition that God's Messenger seated himself on the *minbar* and said, "God gives his servant the alternative of preferring either worldly splendor or that which is in God's presence, so the servant elected that which is in God's presence." Abū Bakr then wept copiously, and said, "May our fathers and mothers be your ransom." [I.e., we would surrender our parents to ransom you, if that were ever necessary.] [Abū Saʿīd said that] God's Messenger was the one so chosen, and Abū Bakr was more fully aware of that than we were. God's Messenger said, "The person most gracious of all toward me with both his possessions and his presence is Abū Bakr. If I were to seek out anyone as an intimate confidant, I would choose Abū Bakr as a dear friend; but Islam is brotherhood. Let no window be left open in the mosque but the window of Abū Bakr."[3]

(2384) ʿAmr ibn al-ʿĀs passed along the report that God's Messenger had dispatched him in charge of a military detachment to [a reservoir in Syria called] Dhāt as-Salāsil. [The General said:] "When I came to [the Prophet], I asked, 'Which of the people do you love the most?' He replied, 'Āʾisha.' I asked, 'And among the men?' 'Her father [Abū Bakr],' he replied. I then asked 'After that, whom?' He answered, 'Umar' and then added [the names of other] men.'"

Ibn Abī Mulayka handed down a report in which he said, "I heard ʿĀʾisha say that someone had asked her, 'Whom would God's messenger have delegated as successor, had he delegated a successor?' Her reply had been, 'Abū Bakr.' 'And after that, whom?' And she had replied, 'Umar.' 'And who then, after ʿUmar?' the inquirer had continued. She had replied, 'Abū ʿUbayda ibn al-Jarrāh.'" At that point, she stopped.

(2386) Muhammad ibn Jubayr ibn Mutʿim passed along an account from his father that a woman asked God's Messenger a question, but he instructed her to return later. [When she came back, s]he asked, "Messenger of God, what do you think [I should do] if I were to come and not find you?" [The reporter then observes that his father had said that] it was as if the woman were alluding to [the Prophet's] death. [Muhammad said:] "If you don't find me, then go to Abū Bakr."[4]

(2387) ʿĀʾisha reported: "During his [terminal] illness, God's Messenger said to me, 'Summon Abū Bakr to me, along with your brother, so that I might write a statement [about succession to leadership]. For I am afraid that someone might assert a claim [to the right of succession], saying "I am the most qualified," when [in fact] God and the believers support only [lit., reject all but] Abū Bakr.'"

(1028) Abū Hurayra is reported to have said, "God's Messenger said, 'Who among you began the day fasting?' Abū Bakr replied, 'I did.' [Muhammad] then asked, 'And who among you has followed a funeral procession today?' Abū Bakr responded, 'I have.' [The Prophet] inquired further, 'Who among you has provided sustenance today for the poor?' Abū Bakr answered, 'I have.' [Muhammad] then asked, 'And who among you has visited the sick today?' Abū Bakr said, 'I have.' 'No individual,' said God's Messenger, 'who embodies all these [deeds] will fail to enter the Garden.'"

(2388) According to Abū Hurayra, God's Messenger said: "As a man was leading an ox of his bearing a load, the ox turned toward him and said, 'I was created not for this, but for plowing the earth.' People [who heard this] said, 'Glory to God! Did the ox talk?' God's Messenger commented, 'I believe so, as do Abū Bakr and 'Umar.'" Abū Hurayra quoted God's Messenger as saying, "While a shepherd guarded his herd, a wolf attacked and snatched a goat from among them. The shepherd went looking for it until he retrieved it from [the wolf]. So the wolf turned toward [the shepherd] and said, 'Who would look after it on the day of the wild beast,[5] when none but me would be its shepherd?' So the people exclaimed, 'Glory be to God!' And God's Messenger commented, 'I believe that, as do Abū Bakr and 'Umar.'"[6]

·　·　·　·　·

SARRĀJ ON ABŪ BAKR

A century or so after Muslim's death, a fellow Central Asian produced one of the first major manuals of Sufi spirituality. The *Book of Light Flashes* (*Kitāb al-lumaʿ*), by Abū Nasr as-Sarrāj (378/988), is among the earliest of such works to offer a section devoted to Abū Bakr the Authentic One.[7] A distinctive feature of Sarrāj's treatment of his subject is his interest in Abū Bakr's unique spiritual qualities and penetrating insight. Like Muslim and other Hadith authorities, Sarrāj devotes separate sections to Abū Bakr's successors among the "Rightly Guided Caliphs," 'Umar, 'Uthmān and 'Alī. Unlike Muslim, Sarrāj situates his section on Abū Bakr's "excellent qualities" just after a discussion of Sufi interpretations of the Hadith. Unlike the Hadith themselves (whether of Muslim or the other authorities), with their suggestion that Abū Bakr's greatness and influence derives in a way from his relationship with Muhammad, Sarrāj's observations shift the emphasis markedly, delving into the psychological dimensions and implications of Abū Bakr's privileged spiritual status. However famous and oft cited the anecdote he chooses to comment on (such as Abū Bakr's celebrated comment to the crowd gathered when the Prophet died), Sarrāj takes an unusual approach and manages to offer a thoughtful and arresting interpretation. His chapter heading provides an important clue to his unique point of view.

TRANSLATION

Chapter discussing Abū Bakr the Authentic One (God be pleased with him) and his distinction from the other Companions of God's Messenger by way of spiritual states that the Sufis of this religious community imitate and seek for guidance.

Abū Bakr the Authentic One said,[8] "If a caller announced from the heavens that only a single man would enter Paradise, I would hope to be that one; and if a caller announced from the heavens that only a single man would enter Hell, I would fear that I was that man." Mutarrif said, "By God, this is the ultimate in fear and the ultimate in hope!" We have a report from Abū 'l-'Abbās ibn 'Aṭā' that, upon being asked about God's word, "Be you [pl.] learned in matters of your Lord" (3:79), he answered, "That means 'Be you like Abū Bakr the Authentic One'; for when God's Messenger died, the inmost thoughts of all the believers were reduced to confusion, but no such effect occurred in Abū Bakr's thinking. He went outside and said to the people, "O people, for anyone who worshipped Muhammad, know that Muhammad has died; for anyone who has worshipped God, know that God lives and does not die." One who is learned in matters of the Lord must share this feature, that ephemeral experiences leave no mark on the inmost thought processes, even if the event were to bring about a cataclysm.

Abū Bakr al-Wāsiṭī said, "The first Sufi expression occurred, in this context, on the tongue of Abū Bakr by way of an allusion, from which the people of deeper understanding have derived the subtle indications that cause anxiety for those endowed [only] with conventional knowledge." The shaykh [Sarrāj] said: What al-Wāsiṭī was referring to when he said "The first Sufi expression occurred on the tongue of Abū Bakr" is the word "God."[9] When [Abū Bakr] had forsaken his possessions, the Prophet asked him, "What have you bequeathed to your family?" He replied, "God and his Messenger." That is, he said "God," then he said "and His Messenger." Most assuredly, that is a splendid allusion for the proponents of the absolute realities of the divine transcendent unity. However, Abū Bakr the Authentic One made other allusions whose implications include other subtle realities. These are known to those endowed with spiritual truths and understood through devotion and by being formed through them.

Among them is what [Abū Bakr] said when he ascended the *minbar* after the Messenger of God had died, thus troubling the hearts of the Companions of the Messenger of God. They feared that Islam would vanish with his death and his departure from among them. So [Abū Bakr] said,

"For those who worshipped Muhammad, know that Muhammad is dead. And for those who worshipped God, know that God lives and does not die." Now the subtle insight in that is his affirmation of the divine transcendent unity and that which the hearts of the assembly of the Companions had affirmed.

Another of {these spiritual truths} is what he said to the Prophet on the Day of {the Battle of} Badr. When the Prophet said, "O God, if you wipe out this tribe, none on earth will worship you thereafter." Then Abū Bakr said, "Don't make such a statement to your Lord, for by God, He will bring it about for you as he promised you!"—or words to that effect. For, in the word of God Most High, "Recall that your Lord revealed to the angels, 'I am with you all, so strengthen those who believe. I will strike terror in the hearts of those who disbelieve'" (8:12). [Abū Bakr] was thereby set apart from the rest of the Companions, after their hearts had been troubled, on the grounds of the reality of his affirmation of what God promised them in the way of victory; and he was guided by the reality of his faith and his being singled out. What if someone were to inquire, "Then what does it mean that the Prophet experienced a change while Abū Bakr remained steadfast, if the Prophet is more perfect than Abū Bakr in all his spiritual states?" The answer is that the Prophet is more knowledgeable about God than Abū Bakr, and Abū Bakr is the strongest in faith among the Companions of God's Messenger. Therefore, Abū Bakr's steadfastness has to do with the reality of his faith in what God Most High has promised. The change in the Prophet, on the other hand, has to do with the increase of his knowledge of God Most High, in that he knows from God what Abū Bakr knows not [as yet]. Do you not see that when the gusts of the wind wax strong, the Prophet's status [lit., hue] alters {while that of none of his Companions changes}? And he said, "If you knew what I know, you would laugh little and weep copiously, and you would go out to the highroads and call out to God Most High and tarry no longer in your beds."

Abū Bakr the Authentic One was also distinguished, among the Companions of God's Messenger whose hearts had been troubled, for inspiration and clairvoyance in three contexts. The first occurred when the Companions of God's Messenger agreed unanimously to avoid fighting against the rebels[10] over their refusal to pay the prescribed alms tax (*zakāt*). Abū Bakr, however, remained resolved to fight them, saying, "By God, if they refuse {even so small an injunction} among what they had {previously} performed for God's Messenger as tethering the camel, I would fight them over it {with the sword}." And his opinion was correct. {And people said that the correctness was in his opinion, even in his opposition to what they [the other Companions] indicated.} The group came around to his view when they saw that he had it right.

The second situation occurred when he disagreed with the opinion of the collectivity of the Companions concerning the rebellion of Usāma's troops. [Abū Bakr] said, "By God, I will not loosen any knot that the Messenger of God tied." Thirdly, there is what Abū Bakr said to [his daughter and wife of the Prophet,] ʿĀʾisha: "I gave you a gift, and it is your two brothers and two sisters." But {ʿĀʾisha} knew of only two brothers and a single sister. Abū Bakr, however, had a pregnant serving maid, and he said, "It has entered my mind that [the child] is a little girl." And [the servant] bore a little girl. This, then, completes the matter of inspiration and clairvoyance. The Prophet said, "Beware the clairvoyance of the believer, for he sees with the light of God."

Abū Bakr also possessed other significant dimensions that the proponents of spiritual realities and those who possess hearts value highly. If I were to mention all of them, the book would go on and on. Tradition has it that Bakr ibn ʿAbd Allāh al-Muzanī said, "Abū Bakr outstripped the rest of God's Messenger's Companions not in the amount of [his] fasting and ritual prayer, but with respect to the content of his heart." Someone else commented that what was in his heart was love for God, glorious and majestic, and sincere good faith toward Him. People say that at ritual prayer time, Abū Bakr would say, "Children of Adam, go to your fire, which you have kindled, and extinguish it." It is reported that he ate some [religiously] questionable food; and when he realized it, he vomited and said, "By God, even if what came out had done so only together with my very spirit, I would have ejected it. I heard God's Messenger say, 'When a body is nourished by what is forbidden, the Fire is more appropriate for it.'"

{He used to say, for fear of punishment and terror of the day of reckoning, "I wish that I were verdure on which animals would feed and that I had never been created." It is related that Abū Bakr said, "I have concerned myself most of all with three verses of the Book of God, exalted and glorified. One of them is the saying, 'If God allows harm to touch you, none can assuage it but He. And if He wishes some good for you, no one can deflect his graciousness' (10:107). I know, therefore, that if He desires good for me, no one but He can lift it from me, and if He desires evil for me, no one but He can deflect it from me. The second is the saying, 'So keep Me in mind, and I will be mindful of you' (2:152), so that I occupy myself with the recollection of God Most High over anything that can be recalled beside God. And third is the saying, 'There is no living creature on earth whose sustenance does not depend on God' (11:6). By God, I have given no thought to my means of sustenance once I have recited this verse!"}

{They say the following poetic lines are those} of Abū Bakr the Authentic One:

> You who consider yourself above the world and its adornments,
>   Transcendence is more than the aggrandizement of clay by means
>   of clay.
> If you are looking for the noblest of all humankind,
>   Look to the king decked out in a pauper's garb.
> That is the person whose compassion is magnified among humankind,
>   And that is beneficial for both this world and the religion.

{It is reported that Junayd said, "The most exalted saying about the acknowledgement of God's transcendent unity is that of Abū Bakr, 'Glory be to the One who provided no path for created beings to intimate knowledge of Him apart from the inability to know Him intimately.'"}

·   ·   ·   ·   ·

ABŪ BAKR IN ISFAHĀNĪ'S 'ORNAMENT OF GOD'S FRIENDS'

In ten volumes, *The Ornament of God's Friends* (*Hilyat al-awliyā'*), by Abū Nuʿaym al-Isfahānī (430/1038), is among the most comprehensive of the early medieval hagiographical anthologies.[11] A word about Abū Nuʿaym's overall method in his gathering of well more than six hundred holy lives is helpful here. Like many earlier hagiographers, he builds his entries on individual spiritual exemplars around the model of traditionists such as Muslim. He records anecdotes and sayings about each Friend of God, careful to list the complete "chain of transmitters" (*isnād*) at the head of each report. Abū Nuʿaym frequently inserts his own comments after these attested reports, offering brief but important insights into his own interpretation of the individual's deeper significance.

Isfahānī places his treatment of Abū Bakr at the very beginning of the whole work. As the first and foremost of the initial generation of Muslims, Abū Bakr heads up the specific category of some four dozen Companions among those who made the Hijra (the *muhājirūn*). To that list, Isfahānī appends a roughly equal number of much shorter notices concerning individuals counted among the "People of the Bench," a select group of devout individuals associated with a portico of the Prophet's house in Medina. Abū Nuʿaym's entry on Abū Bakr consists of two sections, one mostly anecdotes about the Friend, and another entitled "Some individual sayings of his in relation to his spiritual states." Abū Nuʿaym is keenly interested in Abū Bakr's manifold connections with Sufism. As a result, the comments he inserts after nearly every individual report are typically about its relevance to Sufism. Here is a sampling of Abū Nuʿaym's portrait of Abū Bakr, excerpted from the beginning of a much longer piece.

Abū Nuʿaym clearly amplifies his subject beyond the relatively spare characterizations of many earlier sources. From a literary perspective, his use of a type of rhymed prose, in which as many as five or six successive clauses end in the same sounds, elevates his treatment above the ordinary. He opens with a lovely, even lyrical, encomium of the great Companion and follows up with the kind of Hadith-like citation that characterizes the great bulk of *The Ornament of God's Friends.*

TRANSLATION

Abū Bakr the Authentic One, foremost in assent [to belief in Muhammad's experience of the Night Journey and Ascension] and known as the "freed slave" [i.e., freed from hell by his faith], confirmed by God with success; Companion of the Prophet both when at home and while on journeys, his solicitous friend in all circumstances, and his comrade after death in the burial garden suffused with light [in Medina]; singled out in the wise recollection [i.e., the Qurʾān] for the pride of place by which he surpasses the collectivity of the best [people] and the generality of the devout. His nobility has endured through succeeding ages, and the aspirations of those with hands and eyes have failed to attain his summit. So says the One who Knows the Mysteries in (Qurʾān, 9:40), "The second of two when they were in the Cave," as well as in other scriptural verses and Traditions and the widely known expressions occurring there and in the traditional reports. Like the morning sun, [their meaning] spreads abroad, excelling all candidates for excellence and overcoming all who contend and dispute. And [the scripture] refers to "Those among you who gave of themselves and fought before the victory are on a higher level [than those who did so afterward]" (57:10), [among whom] the Authentic One stands alone in his spiritual states and in the realization of the truth. The best of those chosen by God and called to the Path, he was liberated from [the love of] possessions and the trappings of fame. Firmly established in setting out acknowledgment of the divine transcendent unity as ultimate purpose and goal, he became a benchmark for [those who endure] tribulation and a model for [those who] are put to the test. The renunciation that set him apart from the crowd became a much-sought jewel,[12] focused entirely on the Truth [God] as he was, and inclined away from Creation. It is said that Sufism is firm adherence to spiritual truths amid the confusion of competing options.[13]

According to Ibn ʿAbbās, Abū Bakr went out when God's Messenger had died, while ʿUmar was talking to the people. He said, "Sit down, ʿUmar." But ʿUmar refused to sit down, so he said, "Sit down, ʿUmar," and pronounced the confession of faith. Then he said, "Now hear me, those among you who worship Muhammad: Muhammad is dead; and those among you who worship God: God lives and does not die. God the Exalted has said, 'Muhammad is only a messenger, before whom there were [other] messengers who died. If he dies or is killed, will you reverse your course?'" (3:144). By God, if the people had not known that God, the mighty and glorious, had revealed this verse that Abū Bakr would eventually recite, none of them would have accepted it from him. And we hear no announcement from the people except what they follow. Ibn Shihāb said that Saʿīd ibn al-Musayyib quoted ʿUmar ibn al-Khattāb as saying, "By God, it was only after I had heard Abū Bakr say it that I was so stunned that my feet burned and I fell to the ground, and I knew [for sure] when I heard him say it that God's Messenger had indeed died."

The shaykh [Abū Nuʿaym] said that [Abū Bakr] attained the glory of fulfillment in the most resplendent stations of purity. It is said [accordingly] that Sufism sets the servant apart in everlasting singularity.

ʿĀʾisha said, "When the Quraysh implemented the guardianship of Ibn ad-Dughunna,[14] they said to him, 'Leave Abū Bakr and let him worship his Lord in his house. And let him perform ritual prayer as he wishes and recite Qurʾān as he wishes there; for he neither offends us nor performs ritual prayer or scriptural recitation in public anywhere but his house.' So Abū Bakr did so and then it seemed good to him that a mosque be built in the courtyard of his house. He used to perform ritual prayer there and recite Qurʾān, so that the women of the unbelievers and their children gathered around him in amazement and watched him. Now Abū Bakr was a man who wept freely and did not hold back his tears when he recited Qurʾān. That frightened the leaders of the Quraysh, so they sent for Ibn ad-Dughunna and he came to them. Then Ibn ad-Dughunna went to Abū Bakr and said, 'O Abū Bakr, you know the terms under which I made a pact with you [i.e., that he would perform his religious devotions in private]; so either renege on that or return to my protection, for I do not want the Arabs to hear that I am shirking my duty to a man with whom I have made a pact.' So Abū Bakr said, 'In that case, I return your guardianship to you, for I prefer the guardianship of God and his Messenger.'"

. . . . .

ABŪ BAKR IN HUJWĪRĪ'S 'REVELATION OF REALITIES VEILED'

Hujwīrī (c. 465/1072) composed the first major Persian work on Sufi spirituality, *Kashf al-Mahjūb,* and included a hagiographical section to support his understanding of the history and significance of Sufism. He begins his segment on the Companions of the Prophet with a biographical sketch of Abū Bakr.[15] He discusses only the four Rightly Guided Caliphs—unlike Sarrāj, who appends brief notices about lesser figures among the Companions. Hujwīrī follows up with a chapter on the "Family of the Prophet," as represented by the first five Shī'ī imāms after 'Alī; after that, he dedicates a short chapter to the "People of the Bench," on whom Sarrāj also includes an entry.

Hujwīrī's observations about Abū Bakr are particularly instructive in that he organizes his remarks around specific virtues that make his subject a model for Sufis. These crucial qualities include Abū Bakr's contemplative capacity, ascetical discipline in renouncing this world, steadfastness, consistent option for spiritual as well as material poverty, and reticence to assume the role of authority figure in the community of believers. Like many other Sufi authors, Hujwīrī also emphasizes Abū Bakr's preeminence as the finest human being after God's prophets. The author offers the example of Muhammad's first successor as a means by which readers might reaffirm and refine their own spiritual motivations.

TRANSLATION

Abū Bakr 'Abd Allāh ibn 'Uthmān the Authentic One (*siddīq*) (God be pleased with him) was the shaykh of Islam and, after the prophets, the finest human being. He was the Prophet's successor, foremost master of the proponents of complete dedication, and exemplar of the practitioners of self-discipline. He was widely known for his marvelous deeds (*karāmāt*), and even in his own time he was said to have manifest signs and intimations concerning spiritual relationships, as well as concerning the subtle realities of the subject of Sufism. The shaykhs considered him the paragon of the masters of the contemplative life (*mushāhada*) because of the paucity of his narratives and of the traditions he passed along. 'Umar, on the other hand, they regarded as the preeminent master of inner spiritual combat (*mujāhada*) because of his austerity and diligence. As is widely attested in sound reports and well known among religious scholars, Abū Bakr usually recited Qurʾān quietly when he prayed at night, whereas when ʿUmar prayed, he did so more audibly. The Messenger [of God] asked Abū Bakr why he recited in silence, and he answered, "The one to whom I speak hears, since I know that he is not absent from me and is nearby. His attentiveness to a call, whether silent or audible, is all one and the same." When asked [why he recited aloud], ʿUmar replied, "I rouse the somnolent and scare off Satan." The latter is an indication of active spiritual combat, the former of a contemplative approach. Compared to the station of contemplation, the station of active spiritual combat is like a drop in the ocean. That is why the Prophet said to ʿUmar, "Yours is only a fraction of the good effects of Abū Bakr." If ʿUmar, the glory of Islam, could claim only a single portion of Abū Bakr's good results, consider how the [rest of] creation would measure up.

According to tradition, Abū Bakr said, "Our abode is fleeting, the circumstances of our life are on loan, our very breaths are counted, and our sloth is evident."[16] In other words, constructing a transitory palace is a result of folly, relying on a condition that is [merely] borrowed arises from vanity, investing one's heart in numbered breaths stems from heedlessness, and calling indolence religion is fraudulent. For that which is on loan must be returned, that which passes does not remain, that which can be enumerated comes to an end, and for torpor there is no medicine. [Abū Bakr] was referring to this when he said, "The world and mundane concerns deserve no attention, and one who attends to them becomes enthralled endlessly. For whenever one is engaged with the ephemeral, one is veiled from the eternal, since the ego-soul and the world are a veil between the seeker and God." [God's] Friends (*dūstān*) turn away from both when they realize that they are borrowed. What is borrowed by them belongs to another, and they quickly turn away from the property of others.

It is also reported that [Abū Bakr] said in his prayers of supplication, "O God, expand the world for me, and let me reject it." First, he said, "Make the world wide for me," and then, "Guard me from its evils." The underlying meaning here is that he first [asked,] "Give me the world so that I might give thanks for it," and then, "Give me the ability to handle the world so that, for your sake, I might withdraw my hand from it and turn away from it. I might thereby combine the levels of gratitude and giving [to the poor] with the station of patience, without becoming poor willy-nilly but opting deliberately for poverty." This runs counter to that spiritual guide who said, "An individual whose poverty is imposed is more perfect than one whose poverty is chosen. Imposed poverty is the result of the destitution itself, whereas chosen poverty is brought about by the individual. Since one's acquisition [of wealth] is limited by the impetus of [imposed] poverty, it is better than that of one who advances through individual initiative."

I say that the individual more clearly shaped by poverty is the one who in the midst of financial security conceives in his heart a desire for poverty, and acts in such a way as to wrest it from what humankind values most—that is, the world; not the one who [already] in impoverished circumstances conceives in his heart a desire for wealth and goes after gold in the courts of tyrants and sultans. [In other words,] the person [authentically] formed by poverty is the one who descends from financial security into actual need, not the one who from a state of actual need goes in search of high authority. The supremely Authentic One [Abū Bakr] is, second only to the prophets, in the forefront of all created beings. No one may set foot ahead of him, in that he gave optional poverty priority over imposed penury. All of the shaykhs of Sufism, apart from the one spiritual guide I mentioned, concur on this. I have provided [that shaykh's] opposing proofs and argumentation and my refutation thereof, and the supreme Authentic One [himself] corroborated this and provided a cogent argument [to the same effect] in this tradition about [himself] passed down by Zuhrī: When they gave allegiance to [Abū Bakr] as Caliph, he ascended the pulpit and gave an address. In the course of his address he said, "By God, I have never, for even one day or night, had any ambition to exercise governance, nor have I been eager to do so. I have never asked God for this, either privately or in public, nor have I any delight in assuming leadership."[17] When God, exalted and majestic, brings a servant to the perfection of authenticity and elevates him to the condition of steadfastness (*tamkīn*), he waits expectantly for the infusion of thoughts from God, so that he might turn toward whatever quality comes to him by that means. If he is so commanded, he becomes a pauper; if otherwise commanded, he becomes a prince, without inclining either way of his own volition. The Authentic One, God be pleased with him, from start to finish conducted himself with single-minded surrender to such a degree that this band [of Sufis] consider him the model of renunciation, stability, zeal for poverty, and alacrity in renouncing worldly authority. As a result, he is the religious leader of the collectivity of Muslims and especially of the adherents of this [Sufi] Path.

NOTES

1. Translation of texts excerpted from *Sahīh Muslim*, 5 vols. (Beirut: Dār Ibn Hazm, 1995), 4:1478–81, traditions 2381–88.

2. During the Hijra, the two had taken refuge in a cave to escape from pursuing Quraysh tribesmen. The implication of the final statement is that with God present to them, they have nothing to worry about.

3. When Muhammad was ill toward the end of his life, he required some silence. He ordered all whose houses abutted the mosque where the Prophet stayed to close their doors and windows—everyone but Abū Bakr. Muslim follows this tradition with five variant versions.

4. This may be a reference to Muhammad's final illness in 632. Muslim inserts here a note about a variant version of the tradition.

5. Translating *yawm as-sabu'i*, possibly a reference to the eschatological circumstance in which all humankind will be unmindful of their immediate responsibilities.

6. Here Muslim concludes this section by referring to two variant versions of the tradition and one variant chain of transmission.

7. Text in straight brackets [ ] is the translator's interpolation; that in curled brackets { } is indicated as a marginal variant in R. A. Nicholson, ed., *Kitāb al-Luma' fi'l-Tasawwuf of Abū Nasr Al-Sarrāj* (London: Luzac, 1963), Arabic text, 121–24. Translated with permission of the Gibb Memorial Trust.

8. As reported by Mutarrif ibn 'Abd Allāh.

9. Following Richard Gramlich's reading in his *Schlaglichter über das Sufitum* (Stuttgart: Franz Steiner Verlag, 1990), 205.

10. I.e., the Arab tribes that reverted to their pre-Islamic ways after Muhammad's death.

11. Arabic text translated here is from Abū Nu'aym al-Isfahānī, *Hilyat al-awliyā' wa tabaqāt al-asfiyā'*, ed. Sa'īd ibn Sa'd ad-Dīn Khalīl al-Iskandarānī (Beirut: Dār Ihyā' at-Turāth al-'Arabī, 2001), 1:34–42, excerpted from 34–36.

12. The beginning of this rather elliptical construction could also be taken to mean, "The renunciation that he practiced and that involved withdrawal from the public. . . ." Abū Nu'aym seems to be getting at the apparent contradiction between Abū Bakr's choice of a private spiritual life and the emergence of that very choice as the most publicly desirable of spiritual options.

13. Literally, "the disparity of paths" (*ikhtilāf at-tarā'iq*).

14. According to Ibn Ishāq, Abū Bakr had asked Muhammad's permission to leave Mecca because of increasing antagonism from the Quraysh. Two days' journey from Mecca, Abū Bakr encountered a prominent member of the Quraysh named Ibn ad-Dughunna, who was shocked to hear the reason for Abū Bakr's departure from Mecca. Ibn ad-Dughunna offered to be Abū Bakr's patron and protector if he wanted to return to Mecca. Abū Bakr agreed to go back with the assurance of guardianship. Ibn Ishāq, *The Life of Muhammad*, trans. A. Guillaume (Lahore: Oxford University Press, 1955), 171.

15. Translated from the Persian text of *Kashf al-Mahjub*, ed. V. A. Zhukovskij (Leningrad: Dar al-'ulum, 1926): 78–81. For other English translations, see *The Kashf al-Mahjub, The Oldest Persian Treatise on Sufism*, trans. R. A. Nicholson, Gibb Memorial Series no. 17 (1911; repr., London: Luzac, 1970),

70–72; and *The Kashf al-Mahjub: "Unveiling the Veiled,"* trans. with commentary by Maulana Wahid Bakhsh Rabbani (Kuala Lumpur: A. S. Noordeen, 1997), 79–81.

16. Here Hujwīrī inserts a Persian gloss of the Arabic saying of Abū Bakr.

17. Here again, Hujwīrī inserts a Persian gloss of the Arabic.

2 Tamīmī's Eyewitness Account of Abū Ya'zā Yallanūr (572/1177)

Kenneth Honerkamp

Abū Ya'zā Yallanūr ibn Maymūn[1] (572/1177) was the archetype of the Moroccan Friend of God. He is a major figure in a hagiographical work entitled *A Beneficial Rendition of the Lives of the Saints of the City of Fes and its Surrounding Regions* (*Al-Mustafād fī manāqib al-'ubbād bi madīnat Fās wa mā yalīhā min al-bilād*) by Abū 'Abd Allāh Muhammad ibn Qāsim at-Tamīmī al-Fāsī (c. 603/1207).[2] Abū Ya'zā's reputation as an unlettered reclusive Berber ascetic and Friend of God whose supplication was heard and answered by God has permeated the lore of Moroccan spirituality from his own lifetime until today.[3] He lived during the first of the great Berber empires that consolidated the Maghrib under a single ruling power, the Almoravids (ad-Dawlat al-Murābitīya). This period witnessed the encounter of the Moroccan rural Sufi tradition represented by Abū Ya'zā himself with the urban Sufi tradition of Andalusia, influenced by the mystical teachings of the eastern lands of Iraq and Persia. Abū Ya'zā's principal disciple, Abū Madyan (594/1198),[4] later known as the Shaykh of Shaykhs and the "Junayd of the West," would be the touchstone that united the two traditions culminating in such figures as Abū l-Hasan ash-Shādhilī (656/1258), Ibn 'Abbād of Ronda (792/1390), Ahmad Zarrūq (899/1494), Mulay al-'Arabī ad-Darqāwī (1239/1823), and many more.

Abū Ya'zā himself lived an ascetical existence. He reports that in his youth he spent over twenty years in the High Atlas Mountains in the region of Tinmil, where he was known by the name Abū Wagartīl, or "the one who wears a palm fiber mat," because that was all he used to cover his body. He sustained himself on the herbs and plants that naturally occurred in the mountains there. He then spent eighteen years in the region of Azemmour, near the Atlantic coast of Morocco, where he was known as Abū Nalkūt, because all he ate was an herb (*nalkūt*) used by poor people

Figure 1. Mulay Bu Azza (Abū Yaʿzā) tomb, in a remote region of
Morocco's Middle Atlas mountains; a *Muqaddam* greets visitors.
Photograph by Alan Godlas.

during times of drought.[5] In Azemmour he met Abū Shuʿayb Ayyūb ibn
Saʿīd as-Sanhājī (561/1166) and became his disciple and lifelong servant. It
was from Abū Shuʿayb that he received the initiatic cloak (*khirqa*) of the
Sufi path. Abū Yaʿzā reports that during his lifetime he served over forty
Friends of God, some itinerant and others sedentary. Eventually he took up
residence in the Middle Atlas Mountains in the region known as Arujjān,
better known today as the pilgrimage center of Mulay Bouazza, where his
shrine is located in the region of Khouribga, in the province of Meknes.

Figure 2. Main entry archway of Mulay Bu Azza (Abū Yaʿzā) tomb.
Photograph by Alan Godlas.

The accounts from at-Tamīmī narrated here take place for the most part in
the mosque that Abū Yaʿzā had built in Arujjān. Abū Yaʿzā was more than
130 years old when he died in 572/1177.[6]

To understand at-Tamīmī's account of Abū Yaʿzā and the miracles he
relates, it is necessary to comprehend the manner in which at-Tamīmī

perceived Abū Ya'zā's role in the world he inhabited. The miracles that at-Tamīmī ascribes to Abū Ya'zā seem more within the realm of "extreme piety" or "severe asceticism" than within that of miracles as we consider them today. How are we to grasp, then, that these accounts, which at-Tamīmī evidently accepted at face value, indicate an elevated spiritual state of intimate knowledge of God, or *ma'rifa*? How should we understand the relationship between the accounts of at-Tamīmī and the role of Abū Ya'zā, an illiterate Berber ascetic, as an exemplar and spiritual mentor for the most eminent personalities of his day?

Tawhīd, the metaphysically essential oneness of all manifestation, is the essence of Islamic spirituality and the substance behind all formal existence. And yet few would deny that we live in a world of multiplicity and diversity. Knowing that "the Real" was ultimately one, aspirants on the path of knowledge of God sought to actualize the knowledge of the ultimate oneness of God that was at once veiled and yet manifest in multiplicity. The Sufis sought therefore to actualize the knowledge of this oneness through a total commitment to God, or in Sufi terminology, the Real. This commitment to God entailed submission to the Law (Sharia), application of spiritual disciplines (*riyāda*), and spiritual education (*ādāb*). The totality of this commitment, submission, and education was referred to as "traveling the Path" (*sulūk*). A tripartite division of Law, Path, and Divine Reality—or Sharia, *Tarīqa*, and *Haqīqa*—gave expression to the essential elements of Sufism that from the earliest times of the community had defined Islamic spirituality until the triad eventually came to be seen as the cultural heritage of the Islamic peoples wherever they might be found.

The term *'ārif*, or "possessor of experiential knowledge," refers to a person who has actualized in his or her person the essential oneness of the Real through the perfection of these three elements of the Path and who mirrors them in his or her comportment. *Walī*, synonymous with the term *'ārif*, has a twofold connotation: the "intimate" or "Friend of God" and the guardian, protector, or intercessor.[7] Both of these meanings are relevant to our discussion of Abū Ya'zā's role as exemplar and spiritual mentor. Knowledge of God implies intimacy or closeness to God, and this intimacy bestows authority that is the substance of the educational process itself. Vincent Cornell has pointed out the integral link between the perceived proximity of the Friend of God to God and his teaching authority:

> When this logic is applied to the Muslim saint, the following argument pertains: Allāh is the source of all power and authority. Since the *walī* of Allāh is Allāh's "friend" he must be close to Allāh. Therefore he is

seen by others as Allāh's protégé, just as the friend of the king is seen as the protégé of that king.[8]

The relationship of the Walī to God was thus the key to his or her authority within the relationship of teacher and disciple. In fact, the active element of the relationship was the transfer of this authority from the master to the disciple through the spiritual education the master imparted.

The most basic characteristic of this educational process was and is compliance with the legal foundations of Islamic society, the Qurʾān and the Sunna. For this is the foundation of all knowledge and the key to the direct and intimate knowledge of God. Submission to the religious law implied striving for perfect servanthood, in which perfect sincerity was the key to actualizing the unity of form and substance. This meant in practice inner and outer conformity with the Law, the inner dimension of which entailed utter dependence on God and inner and outer conformity with the exemplar par excellence, the Prophet. Abū ʿAbd ar-Rahmān as-Sulamī (d. 412/1021) stresses this aspect of the spiritual journey in his work dealing with the early mystics of Nishapur:

> Among their tenets is that the state of servanthood is founded upon two essential things: the perfect awareness of one's total dependence upon God–Most High, and perfect imitation of the Messenger of God. It is in this that the soul finds neither respite nor rest.[9]

Sharia and adherence to the Sunna were thus more than a code of comportment; they were a means of conformity with divine reality, with the Real. The model for this conformance was the saint exemplar, for as a reflection of the Real he or she represented that which was most central to the spiritual life of the community. Peter Brown, writing on the role of the saint exemplar in late antiquity, finds this same centrality within the context of Christianity. He defines the saint exemplar as a "'carrier of Christ,' . . . a figure who distilled in concrete and accessible form 'central' values and expectations," and he characterizes, as well, the fundamental relationship that bound the holy man as exemplar and his disciples as being one of "esteem and love."[10] These views of sanctity in the Christianity of late antiquity ring true, are applicable within the Islamic context, and provide a common ground for understanding realities and relationships so central to at-Tamīmī's account of the sanctity of Abū Yaʿzā as he perceived it. Abū Yaʿzā, though illiterate, followed the Sharia scrupulously. He depended on God and gave little consideration to his own comforts, and he followed the example of the Prophet in his humble comportment and generosity. In a telling narrative from *Kitāb at-tashawwuf*, at-Tādilī narrates that Abū Yaʿzā was seen in a dream flying though the air soon after his death. Asked how he had attained that state, he responded, "By giving away food."[11] All of these attributes led at-Tamīmī and others to see Abū Yaʿzā as a teacher who exemplified the highest degrees of intimate knowledge of the divine. Which brings us back to at-Tamīmī, who himself was among the foremost representatives of his day of the path of Abū Yaʿzā and his disciple Abū Madyan.

Abū ʿAbd Allāh Muhammad ibn Qāsim at-Tamīmī al-Fāsī was born in Fes, Morocco, between 535/1140 and 540/1145. Little is known of his early life and education other than what can be gleaned from *Al-Mustafād*. This work makes apparent that even as a child, at-Tamīmī had a close rapport with earliest representatives of the Sufi tradition in Morocco. When at-Tamīmī was a child, his father took him to be blessed by Abū Yaʿzā, who prayed over him and stroked his head. As a youth he met and frequently visited ʿAlī ibn Hirzihim (559/1162)[12] in his *zāwiya* and attended his lessons on the *Book of Self-Scrutiny (Kitāb ar-Riʿāya)* of al-Muhāsibī (243/857). As a student he met and often met with Shuʿayb Abū Madyan,[13] also known as the One Who Responds to Needs (al-Ghawth). At-Tamīmī relates that when he asked to study the *Risālat al-Qushayrīya* with Abū Madyan, he taught him instead the Hadith "The essence of all error is love of the world." At-Tamīmī, through his associations with these key personalities, became in his own right an exemplar of the formative Moroccan Sufi tradition.

We know more of his later life as a student and traveler from a written account of his studies (*fahrasa*), *The Resplendent Star (An-Najm al-mushriqa)*,[14] in which he records the names of his teachers and the works he studied under them. He left Fes at an early age, traveling to Sebta (Ceuta), in northern Morocco, and then the Middle East, where he spent sixteen years among the greatest scholars of his time. He met and studied under Abū Tāhir as-Silafī (578/1182). By the time he had returned to Fes, he had gained a reputation as a scholar of Hadith in both the Middle East and Morocco. In Fes he assumed the position of imam of the al-Azhar Mosque, in the neighborhood of ʿAyn Khayl. This mosque remains to this day not far from the Shrine of Mulay Idrīs, just off the Talʿa Kabīra, and is currently being restored. At-Tamīmī died in 603/1207.

At-Tamīmī's dual role as spiritual exemplar and scholar of Hadith is testified to in the multiple references to him in the works of Ibn al-ʿArabī (638/1240), the Andalusian mystic known as the Greatest of Spiritual Masters (ash-Shaykh al-Akbar).[15] In these references, Ibn al-ʿArabī refers to at-Tamīmī as "my shaykh." This is for two reasons. Ibn al-ʿArabī reports that in 593/1197 he came to Fes and studied and heard *al-Mustafād* from at-Tamīmī himself in the al-Azhar Mosque of ʿAyn Khayl.[16] He also narrates from at-Tamīmī numerous Hadith in his *Niche for Lights* (*Mishkāt al-anwār*).[17] Then in 594/1197 at-Tamīmī invested Ibn ʿArabī with the *khirqa*, thus becoming his spiritual mentor.[18]

Until recently, *al-Mustafād* was considered a lost text, known only through its citations in other works. It is the earliest extant work of Moroccan hagiography and must have been completed by 593/1197, when Ibn al-ʿArabī heard it from at-Tamīmī. Every work of Moroccan hagiography that followed *al-Mustafād* benefited from at-Tamīmī. Some have cited him explicitly, while some have not. *Al-Mustafād* is particularly important in that many of at-Tamīmī's accounts are eyewitness accounts, like the account translated here of Abu Yaʿzā. The published edition was edited from one manuscript dating from 813/1410. The manuscript is missing the first pages and the title page. The Moroccan edition of *al-Mustafād* has no introduction and begins directly with the biographies of at-Tamīmī's principal mentors, Abū al-Hasan ibn Hirzihim, Abū Yaʿzā, and Abū Madyan. The work comprises eighty-one biographies in all.

TRANSLATION

At-Tamīmī's accounts of Abū Yaʿzā Yallanūr (572/1177)

Among them is the venerated elder (shaykh) Abū Yaʿzā, whose family name was Yallanūr. It is said that he lived to be well more than one hundred years old. His renown in Morocco (*al-maghrib*) for his asceticism, the acceptance of his supplications, and the acuity of his insight (*firāsa*)[19] free us of any need to recount all the qualities he is known for and the miracles attributed to him. Instead, in all but two vignettes related to me by others, what I will recount here is only what I myself saw while in his presence.

He was the Shaykh of the Shaykhs of the Maghrib [Abū Madyan] and, though God knows best, one of the *abdāl*.[20] He would eat nothing that the generality of people ate and lived mostly on the wild plants found in the mountainous regions of Morocco known as Arujjān where he and his family and children lived, distant from other settlements.[21]

I saw him in the city of Fes, where he came when I was still a small child. My father brought me to him in his arms, and Abū Yaʿzā blessed me with supplications and passed his hand over my head. Once I was older, I journeyed with a group of disciples to the region where he lived, three day's travel from the city of Fes, may God protect it. Whenever we passed a village or a home or encampment along the way, the folk there called out to us, "Guests of the Shaykh!" If it was the end of the day, we rested there and spent the night as guests, and if it was early in the day, we were given milk to drink. Thus was our journeying until we reached him, may God bless him.

I witnessed from him miraculous deeds and acts of beneficence. The narratives of his miracles, passed down by people through multiple channels (*mutawātir*), are more numerous than what I will mention here, for his fame has spread far and wide. What I will cite, however, in keeping with the conditions I specified earlier, is what I myself witnessed with the exception of two vignettes, which were related to me by others.

One of the things I saw was that the house in which his family dwelled had neither door nor lock. The mosque in which he prayed faced the entrance of this house, and just adjacent to it was a thick brush-filled forest (*shaʿrāʾ*).[22]

The visitors who would congregate there were numerous. It was his habit in his mosque, when he prayed the late-evening prayer,[23] to enter the prayer niche (*miḥrāb*). Some of those present prayed in congregation in the mosque already full of people, while those who could not fit into the mosque would pray outside for a portion of the night. Then the imam would leave and the people would disperse, some of them to sleep in the mosque, others outside the mosque, either right around it or at some distance from it.

The Shaykh used to make his way to the top of the mountain and enter the forest. My companions and I would rest on the path that the Shaykh would follow as he descended from the mountain. Whoever was there also had with them their mounts and pack animals that they would tie up wherever they wished outside the precincts of the Shaykh's house. When night fell, we would see lions come so close that the people at the mosque could see them and be seen by them, but they never came any closer than that, nor was anyone afraid of them.[24]

Muhammad [at-Tamīmī] relates: One of [the miraculous things] I witnessed happened once when I was with him in the mosque, awaiting the *maghrib* [evening] prayer. When the mosque was completely full, he turned back toward the people and told them, "Arise and go out to meet a devout servant of God (*ʿābid*) from Sebta." So people left the mosque, I among them. The mosque was on a high rise and overlooked the path and the forest, and [I watched] the people go down to a level clearing and then enter the forest. They were there only a brief time before they returned with a man. When I looked at him, I recognized him as our friend the *faqīh* Abū 's-Sabr Ayyūb ibn ʿAbd Allāh al-Fihrī.[25]

[Another time] I was present for the prayer of *maghrib* in the mosque just mentioned, sitting by his side awaiting the prayer. He had a small raised area for himself on the eastern side of the mosque in the southern corner of the first row[26] just large enough for him to sit and perform his prayers upon; and at this moment I was beside him on the ground. A man arrived with branches of green oleander (*diflā*)[27] that the Shaykh took from him and placed beside him. As soon as he heard the call to *maghrib* prayer, he took up a branch and began to eat the leaves as I watched.[28] Since his face showed not the least sign of discomfort, I thought that this oleander must be sweet, and when a leaf from the branch in his hand fell to the ground, I picked it up and put it beneath my clothing, then stood to offer the prayer. When we had completed the prayer and had retired to his house for the evening meal, as was the habit there, I took out the leaf and put it in my mouth, only to find it was [as bitter as] I had always known oleander to be. I then knew what I had seen the Shaykh do was miraculous.

Muhammad said: I walked with him one day to the Friday prayer in a nearby encampment. When we reached the congregational mosque, everyone inside stood up for him and complained to him of the famine and drought that had beset them and how their barley crop was in dire need of water. This was during the spring season. The Shaykh said nothing. After the people had completed the prayer and were leaving the mosque, they [again] stood up for him and addressed him as a group. He went outside the mosque and stood there. He was wearing an old patched black burnoose that reached only to above his knees, an old ragged cloak (*jubba*) of coarse goat hair (*tallīs*), and upon his head a cap (*shāshīya*) made of palm fiber. That was all he ever wore, may God show him mercy. He removed his burnoose and *shāshīya*—the hair of his head was pure white—and lifted his hands [in prayer] with the people behind him. He did not speak Arabic well, but I understood from his speech that he said, "O my Lord, these companions (*mawālī*) have asked this servant to ask You for rain. But how could one such as I ask such a thing?" Tears filled his eyes and he abased himself and wept copiously. We had not yet returned from that place nor had we gone very far before rain began to fall so hard we had to remove the shoes and sandals on our feet [in order to walk in] the flood water, and the blessing of the Shaykh reached everyone, may God have mercy on him.

Muhammad said: As to his intuitive utterances and his perspicacity where the affairs of people are concerned, they are so well known and recounted that I have no need to mention them here.

He had veiled his lower-self (*nafs*) from passion and denied himself the pleasures of worldly life even while able to pursue and attain them.[29] He provided people with meat and honey and sustained himself with what it was his habit to eat. I saw what he lived on and I saw his servant prepare it for him. She would take a small earthen cooking pot like the ones made for young children and put in it a small amount of black beans (*al-lalblāb*). When they were cooked, she would scoop up a handful of acorn meal and barley flour and mix it all together. This she would give him when he came after the prayer of *maghrib,* and he would take a spoon in his hand and ladle out what was in the pot. This would suffice him, and by my life, its totality did not come to even half a *ritl.*[30]

Muhammad said: I was also with him in the city of Marrakech. He had been sent there and took up residence in the minaret of the congregational mosque,[31] and there I would visit him and sit in his company. With him he had wafers of roasted acorn meal, resembling those used in making *mūrī.*[32] And these are what he lived on. When time came for his return to his own region, I asked him for one of those wafers and he gave me one. I arrived with it to the city of Fes, may God protect it from all affliction, and it proved to have curative properties. Anyone suffering from stomach pains or fever to whom I gave a portion the size of a quarter dirham would be cured by God the instant it reached his stomach.

[Another thing] I witnessed while I stayed with him in the place he lived was that after praying the early-morning prayer in his mosque, the people would gather to recite a portion of the Qur'ān.[33] When they had finished, he would invite everyone to gather near and then ask whoever was on his right to make a supplication, then the one next to him, and so forth. Should one of them be not so gifted, it would pass to the next, then the next, until the turn came back to the Shaykh Abū Ya'zā, may God have mercy upon him. There would be in attendance in these gatherings people of distinction and scholars of repute (*ashyākh*) from many regions, but no one would move during the supplication of anyone there. When the turn came back to the Shaykh and he would begin to supplicate in the language of the West (*al-gharbī*),[34] I mean, a non-Arabic language (*'ajamī*), a sense of awe would descend upon everyone in the mosque. Some would begin to cry and be overtaken by a lofty state, a presence of the heart, and an intimacy with God that was not to be found during anyone else's supplication. Even though I did not understand much of what he was saying, I myself experienced this state. It was the self-effacement, humility, and sincerity in his supplication that would elevate hearts and bring forth the purest intentions. The following verses remind me of my own state [during these moments] and that of the Shaykh:

A dove cooing in the early dawn
  Plaintive, chanting artfully
Stirred in me the memory of a companion lost
  Such a frail being, yet she aroused sorrow in me
When she began [her lament] I moved her to joy
  When she gave expression to it I found joy
She complained and I understood her not
  I complained and she understood me not
It is only through love's ardor that I understand her
  While she too through love's ardor understands me
It was only my weeping that moved her heart
  While only her weeping moved mine.

Muhammad said: One day I prayed the pre-dawn prayer (*al-fajr*) with him in the mosque, and then I sat with him until the dawn prayer (*as-subh*). When we were exiting through the door of the mosque, a woman appeared who had been possessed by jinn and was in the midst of a seizure, rolling on the ground. He said to her what I understood to be, "You seize her in this place? Go out from this place!" Then the woman got up and left the sacred precinct of the mosque only to fall to the earth and begin to roll on the ground in a seizure as she had at the door of the mosque. Then he went to her and spoke again to her, upon which she got up—no sign of any pain upon her—and covered her face out of shyness before the people.

Muhammad said: During the time I stayed with him, I saw that he would customarily come to the mosque during the last part of the night, when there remained of the night but a third or less. The people there would congregate around him, and he would wake anyone he passed by on his way. He would then put forward the imam, or someone else who was there, to pray with the people whatever [number of prostrations] was possible. Then the Shaykh would say in his language what we understood to mean, "Enough. The dawn draws near," and the imam would shorten his recitation and give the final salutation. Immediately following the supplication, the muezzin would go outside the mosque [where he could see the sky] and find that the beginning of the time for the dawn prayer was apparent. I witnessed this from him for many days and used to think that the Shaykh was being informed [about the time] from someone else surveying [the sky]. So I asked about that and was told, "That is something common for him. Even in the darkest gloom or clouds, the beginning of the time for the dawn prayer appears to him."[35] The Shaykh during all this never moves from his place, nor has this been known of anyone else.

In respect to humility, forbearance, tolerance, patience, and his willing-ness to descend among the general folk and answer their needs, I witnessed in him, beyond any doubt, that which is not to be found in anyone else. An example of this was on a day when I was going to travel away from him. It was his custom that no one who had stayed with him should leave without first seeking his permission. If one did not, his path would be beset with obstacles such as illness, or lions, or being stung by a scorpion or being overcome by fear, such that they would retrace their steps.

So [on that day] some of those present who had journeyed to him—and we were from many different regions—had asked his permission to return, and he had had a great quantity of food prepared and invited everyone there to partake of it. The people were entering the house where he lived, one group after another, eating, giving the Shaykh their parting salutations (*yusallimūn*), and then departing. I was sitting to one side of the house, watching them take their leave, and saw how he greeted each of them in a manner suitable to his state and station. I saw, too, that among them someone brought a vessel of olive oil and asked the Shaykh to bless it by blowing upon it (*yarqī*), and this he did, and someone asked him to knot a thread, and this he did for one group; and some came with wild herbs and asked him to bless them, and this he did. Then some of them took up the remaining food and asked him to bless it for them, and this he did. They continued in this manner until all the food before him was gone. Then someone said, "Perhaps a bit of the hair from your head?" and he removed the palm fiber hat from his head—his hair was white like cotton—and he inclined his head toward him. The man then took some scissors and cut [a lock of] his hair, and all who were there began to do likewise until the hair from his head was practically gone, and then they continued to cut nearer and nearer to the scalp until they were down to his skin in many places and cut some of it as well! And all the while he merely sat there, neither complaining nor twisting about, as still as a rock, may God bless him, and not trying to defend himself in any way. It continued thusly, until those who were present prevented anyone else [from approaching the Shaykh]. This was from their part, not from his.

I saw a man in his house who had been afflicted with an illness that was eating his face away, may God protect us from that, so that one of his cheeks was gone. When I asked him about his situation, he said, "When what you see afflicted me, I was told about the Shaykh and I came to him. I have been here for some time, and every morning he blesses me by his breath, then chews an olive leaf and spits it upon the afflicted area. Now the illness has stopped spreading, and I am hoping, God willing, to regain my health." When I set out from the Shaykh's home, the man was still there.

Figure 3.   Mulay Bu Azza (Abū Yaʿzā) tomb, cenotaph at center of shrine. Photograph by Alan Godlas.

Muhammad said: During the time that I was staying with him, I was overtaken by a state. I began to loathe mundane existence (*ad-dunyā*), and [the notion of] returning to my home became abhorrent to me. I said [to myself], "I will not enter a place where I have been disobedient to God," and that is what I resolved to do. Then the Shaykh said to me, "That is not possible for you: you have a mother. Staying with her and caring for her is better for you." So I gave up my plan and wept, and then made my decision to return.

Muhammad said: That [which I have related above] was from the river of his miraculous deeds and states (*wādī 'ajā'ibihi*). Reflections of excellence (*fadā'il*) shine forth and then disperse. O what a grief-ridden existence.[36]

I was informed by Shaykh Abū Isḥāq Ibrāhīm ibn 'Alī, may God have mercy upon him, that he heard Shaykh Abū Ya'zā say, "I have served nearly forty Friends of God. Among them were those who wandered from place to place and among them were those who lived among the people until they passed away."

And Abū 'Alī Hasan ibn Muhammad said to me, "I saw him [Abū Ya'zā] in a mosque in Fes and greeted him with greetings of peace and sat with him. When the prayer was over, I said to him, 'O my respected sir (*yā sayyidī*), what happened to your feet?' He said, 'Snow cut into them.' [Concerning Abū Ya'ā's physical description, Abū 'Alī Hasan] said, "He was dark-skinned. Then he [Abū Ya'zā] left and I did not hear any news of him after that."

Abū Ya'zā passed away in the beginning of Shawwāl in the year five hundred and seventy-two after the Hijra.[37]

NOTES

1. *Yallanūr* is a Berber term made up of two words, *īlā* and *al-nūr*, meaning "the possessor of light" or "a fortunate one." *Ī'zā* means "the beloved one" (*al-'azīz* or *al-mahbūb*). Abū Ya'qūb at-Tādilī (627/1229–30), *Kitāb at-tashawwuf ilā rijāl at-tasawwuf*, ed. Ahmed Toufiq (Rabat, Morocco: Université Mohammed V, Faculté des Lettres et des Science Humanities, 1984), 213 n. 475.

2. This translation is based on Muhammad al-Sharīf's critical edition of *Al-Mustafād*, with the permission of the editor. See Muhammad ibn 'Abd Allāh at-Tamīmī al-Fāsī (572/1177), *Al-Mustafād: fī manāqib al-'ubbād bi madīnat Fās wa mā yalīhā min al-bilād* (Tétouan, Morocco: Université 'Abd al-Mālik as-Sa'dī, Faculté des Lettres et des Science Humaines, 2002), hereafter *al-Mustafād*. Special thanks to Michael Fitzgerald, my friend and research colleague, who proofread the translation, suggested changes, and provided background material.

3. Abū Ya'zā is mentioned in all the major Moroccan hagiographies. Of

these I have employed the following: *Kitāb at-tashawwuf,* 222–23; Ibn Qun-
fud al-Qustantīnī, *Uns al-faqīr wa 'izz al-haqīr,* ed. M. al-Fāsī and A. Faure
(Rabat, Morocco: al-Markaz al-Jāmi'ī li'l-Ba'th al-'Ilmī, 1965), 15, 16, 21, 25; Ibn
al-Qāḍī, *Jadhwat al-iqtibās* (Rabat, Morocco: Dār al-Mansūr li 't-Tibā'a wa'-
l-Warāqa, 1973), 564; Muhammad b. Ja'far al-Kittānī (1927), *Salwat al-anfās,*
ed. 'Abd Allāh al-Kāmil al-Kittānī, Hamza Muhammad al-Tayyib al-Kittānī,
and Muhammad Hamza ibn 'Alī al-Kittānī (Casablanca: Dār al-Thaqāfa, 2004),
1:186–89. Two works in particular are dedicated to the life and miracles of
Abū Ya'zā: Abū al-'Abbās al-'Azafī (633/1235), *Da'āmat al-yaqīn fī za'āmat
al-muttaqīn,* ed. Ahmed at-Toufiq (Rabat, Morocco: Maktaba Khidmat al-
Kutub, 1989), and Ahmad at-Tādlī as-Sawma'ī (1013/1604), *Kitāb al-mu'zā fī
manāqib ash-Shaykh Abī Ya'zā,* ed. 'Alī al-Jāwī (Agadir, Morocco: Université
Ibn Zuhra, Faculté des Lettres et des Science Humaines, 1996). Of all these
works, *Al-Mustafād* is the earliest. The most comprehensive work in English
that deals with the life and times of Abū Ya'zā is Vincent Cornell, comp. and
trans., *The Way of Abū Madyan: The Works of Abū Madyan Shu'ayb* (Cambridge: Islamic Text Society, 1996), 8–10, 13–14, 22–23, 25–29, 33, 138 n. 36,
142 n. 43. This work also includes the only treatise on Sufism attributed to
Abū Ya'zā, 180–186.

4. At-Tamīmī, *al-Mustafād,* 41–45.

5. At-Tādilī, *Kitāb at-tashawwuf,* 217.

6. With the exception of one treatise in Arabic, Abū Ya'zā left no written
record of his teachings. For a discussion of the teachings of Abū Ya'zā, see
Cornell, *The Way of Abū Madyan,* 26; translation of this text, 181–87.

7. Vincent Cornell, *Realm of the Saint: Power and Authority in Moroccan
Sufism* (Austin: University of Texas Press, 1998), xviii.

8. Ibid., xix–xx.

9. Abū 'Abd ar-Rahmān al-Sulamī, *Risālat al-malāmatīya,* ed. Abū al-
'Alā al-'Afīfī (Cairo: Dār Ihyā' al-Kutub al-'Arabīya, 1945), 111.

10. Peter Brown, "The Saint as Exemplar in Late Antiquity," in *Saints and
Virtues,* ed. John Stratton Hawley (Berkeley: University of California Press:
1987), 9.

11. At-Tādilī, *Kitāb at-tashawwuf,* 222.

12. At-Tamīmī, *al-Mustafād,* 15–28.

13. Ibid., 41–45.

14. This work remains unpublished and is found only in private manuscript collections.

15. For a list of references, see Claude Addas, *Quest for the Red Sulfur:
The Life of Ibn 'Arabī,* trans. Peter Kingsley (Cambridge: Islamic Text Society,
1993), 313.

16. Ibn 'Arabī, *Al-Futūhāt al-Makkīya* (Cairo: Dār Sādir, 1329H), 4:503.
It was while leading the afternoon prayer (*al-'asr*) at the al-Azhar Mosque
that Ibn 'Arabī attained the Abode, where he became light and became "a face
without a nape" (*wajh bi lā qafā*). *Al-Futūhāt al-Makkīya,* 2:486. Also see
Addas, *Quest for the Red Sulfur,* 149.

17. Ibn ʿArabī, *Mishkāt al-anwār* (Cairo: n.p., 1329H), Hadith nos. 1, 6, 28, and 36.

18. Ibn ʿArabī, *Kitāb nasab al-khirqa*, cited in Addas, *Quest for the Red Sulfur*, 143.

19. *Firāsa* is generally understood to be the ability possessed of certain of the Friends of God to "see into" a person's state. It is reported in a Hadith found in the collections of at-Tirmidhī, at-Tabarānī, and others that the Prophet Muhammad said, "Beware of the insight (*firāsa*) of the believer, for verily he sees by the light of God."

20. The *abdāl*, literally "substitutes," form part of the essential elements of the Sufi cosmological hierarchy. They are believed to be certain Friends of God who live in different parts of the world, variously numbered at four, seven, or seventy, whose presence carries an essential blessing for creation. They are so named because whenever one of them dies, God substitutes (*istabdala*) him or her with another. John Renard, *Historical Dictionary of Sufism* (Lanham, MD: Scarecrow Press, 2005), 229.

21. In a note in *at-Tashawwuf*, its editor, Ahmed Toufiq, explains that the name *Arujjān* relates to the Berber word *īrūjān*, which means "vapor" or "steam" (*al-bukhār*). The name thus refers to the Berber tribe of Bahzmīra in the region where the shrine of Abū Yaʿzā is located. See *at-Tashawwuf*, 213 n. 476.

22. *Shaʿrāʾ*, according to Dozy, is a forest or place planted with trees. R. Dozy, *Supplément aux Dictionnaires Arabes* (Beirut: Librarie du Liban, 1981), 1:763. My translation reflects the topography of the region as it appears today.

23. This refers to the prayer of al-ʿishāʾ, the first ʿishāʾ prayer being the prayer of *maghrib*.

24. The wooded regions of Morocco were the principal habitat of the Atlas lion, also known as the Barbary or Nubian lion, *Panthera leo leo*, a species that has been extinct in the wilds of Morocco since the 1920s.

25. Abū ʾs-Sabr Ayyūb al-Fihrī as-Sebtī (609/1212) was a well-known ascetic from Sebta who had taken up residence in Marrakech. He frequented Abū Yaʿzā, Abū Madyan, and Ibn Ghālib (568/1172–73). *At-Tashawwuf*, 415–16. Ibn ʿArabī cites him among his teachers; he studied with him in Ceuta. Abū ʾs-Sabr died on the field in the Battle of al-ʿIqāb in Andalusia.

26. The text reads, "wa kān lahu dukkān bi gharbī al-masjid fī ar-rukn al-qabalī fī ʾs-saff al-awwal"; if what the text claims were the case, however, it would be impossible for this place to be on the western side of the mosque in the southern corner in the first row, because mosques in Morocco are oriented toward the east. I have adjusted the translation to fit the orientation of mosques in Morocco.

27. *Nerium oleander* L., a poisonous plant that abounds in the region where Abū Yaʿzā resided. The bitterness of the plant is so well known that it informs the Moroccan proverb "As bitter as oleander" (*murr ka diflā*).

28. We can assume from the fact that the Shaykh ate just after the sunset

call to prayer that he was fasting that day and used the oleander leaves to break his fast.

29. That is, the Shaykh did not live ascetically because he was too poor to have anything, but rather renounced what he could have.

30. A *ritl* is a measure decided more by regional custom than by a uniform standard of weights and measures. Given the size of the pot, the amount was most likely less than eight to ten ounces.

31. This was most likely the well-known Kutubīya Mosque, where according to Ahmād at-Tādlī as-Sawmaʿī, Abu Yaʿzā was imprisoned by the sultan ʿAbd al-Muʾmin ibn ʿAlī in 540/1145. The sultan later released him and ordered him to be left alone. He was brought to Marrakech due to the following he had attracted from all over Morocco. See Ahmād at-Tādlī as-Sawmaʿī, *Kitāb al-muʿzā*, 68–69.

32. A food made from roasted honey and bread. Although this food is unknown in Morocco today, a common breakfast in the countryside, especially if guests are present, consists of large flat breads, browned in butter or olive oil, over which honey is poured.

33. Group recitation aloud of one *hizb* (one sixtieth) of the Qurʾān after the dawn and sunset prayers is a practice still followed in Morocco today.

34. Meaning here the language of the Berber (al-Amāzīghiyīn).

35. At-Tādilī reports a similar story in *at-Tashawwuf* from a Muhammad ibn ʿAlī (not at-Tamīmī, who is ibn Qāsim), who witnessed this same phenomenon and said, "Certain of those present thought that he saw the rise of the dawn from a small opening (*kuwwa*) before him in the mosque, so they looked at the walls and there was no opening." *At-Tashawwuf*, 216.

36. Nonliteral translation for *fayā tūl kadāh ʿalā tūl*. I take the phrase to be an expression of at-Tamīmī's grief at the memory of Abū Yaʿzāʾs passing.

37. This would place his death in April of 1177 CE.

3 'Abd Allāh ibn As'ad al-Yāfi'ī's Defense of Saintly Marvels

Erik S. Ohlander

'Afīf ad-Dīn 'Abd Allāh ibn As'ad al-Yāfi'ī (768/1367) was one of the most famous Sufi scholars of eighth/fourteenth-century Arabia. A native of Yemen, he eventually settled in Mecca, where he enjoyed great prestige as an expert in the religious sciences, in particular for his vast knowledge of Hadith and history. A Shāfi'ite by legal training and an Ash'arite by theological conviction, not only was al-Yāfi'ī known as a vigorous opponent of both Mu'tazilite rationalism and the fideism of Ibn Taymīya (728/1328) and his school, but he was also renowned as a spiritual director. As a Sufi, his main allegiance lay with the Qādirīya, of which he himself is considered to have founded a subbranch (the so-called Yāfi'īya). Given the frequency with which his name is mentioned in connection with various Sufi luminaries with whom he crossed paths in the most international of cities in the entire Muslim world, his teachings, works, and ideas seem to have been widely spread among his contemporaries.

An indefatigable champion of Sufism, al-Yāfi'ī penned a number of works in which he defended its teachings and traditions from its detractors, in particular his *Diffusion of Perfumed Merits: On the Favor of the Sufi Masters, Possessors of Lofty Spiritual Stations (Nashr al-mahāsin al-ghāliya fī fadl al-mashāyikh as-sūfīya ashāb al-maqāmāt al-'āliya)* and his *Gardens of Sweet Herbs: On Tales of the Righteous (Rawd al-rayāhīn fī hikāyāt as-sālihīn)*. It is the former text from which the following selection is taken.[1]

In the introduction to the *Diffusion of Perfumed Merits,* al-Yāfi'ī explains that he was asked to clarify, once and for all, his thoughts on the oft debated issue of the marvels (*karāmāt*) of the Friends of God in response to a long-running discussion he had been having on the subject with various learned individuals. As the author makes clear, both the

47

intent and the style of the treatise are those of a "solicited legal opinion" (*fatwā*), which per tradition is typically organized as an explicative
response "issued" (*iftā'*) to a question or series of questions submitted by
a "petitioner" (*mustaftī*). Using the language and style of one giving such
a *fatwā* (*muftī*), in the *Diffusion of Perfumed Merits* al-Yāfiʿī responds to
a total of ten questions submitted by his petitioners, namely: (1) Are the
marvels of the Friends of God real or not? (2) If real, are they of the same
type and significance as the evidentiary miracles (*muʿjizāt*) of the prophets? (3) What is the difference between a saintly marvel and an evidentiary
miracle? (4) What is the difference between miracle and magic? (5) Why
are more saintly marvels recorded for later ages than for the age of the
Prophet and his Companions? (6) If there was a paucity of saintly marvels
in the time of the Companions of the Prophet, why is theirs considered the
best generation of the Muslim community? (7) Can a believer who claims
knowledge of the unseen be called an unbeliever? (8) Who are better: the
Friends of God who perform marvels or those who do not? (9) Who are
better among the corporate body of the learned scholars of religion: those
specializing in esoteric knowledge (*ʿulamāʾ al-bātin*) or those specializing
in exoteric knowledge (*ʿulamāʾ al-zāhir*)? And (10) what is the difference
between the specialty of the latter, the "divine law" (Sharia), and the specialty of the former, the "really real" (Haqīqa)?

The following translation contains al-Yāfiʿī's response to the first two
questions, as well as an abridgement of his oft cited "catalog" of ten types
of saintly marvels appended to the end of his response to question two.[2]

TRANSLATION

The First Section: On Responding to the First Question

I say,[3] and all success lies with God, that the occurrence of marvels to the
Friends of God is both intellectually conceivable and evinced by tradition.
As for its intellectual conceivability—and it is not impossible in the face of
the power of God Most High—it belongs to the same category of possibilities as the occurrence of the evidentiary miracles of the prophets. This is
the doctrine of the Sunnis among the Sufi masters, the religious scholars,
jurists, and Hadith transmitters. Their written works testify to this, east
and west, among Persian and Arab alike, and, God willing, in the second
section of this treatise I will furnish complete rational proof against the
inconsistencies of those who completely proscribe their admissibility and
those who reject the admissibility of their significance.

As for their presence in tradition, I have in mind the occurrence of saintly marvels as found in the Noble Qurʾān as well as in well-authenticated reports of the sayings and doings of the Prophet and those concerning his Companions.

Regarding this subject in the Mighty Qurʾān, there is what God has related about Mary in his saying, "Whenever Zakarīya entered her chamber to see her, he found her supplied with sustenance. He said, 'O' Mary, from whence did this sustenance come?' to which she replied, 'It is from God'" (3:37); and she was supplied with winter fruits in the summer and summer fruits in the winter, just as it is mentioned in the interpretation of this verse. Also, the words of the Most High in the *Chapter of Mary:* "Shake toward yourself the trunk of the palm tree, it will rain fresh ripe dates upon you" (19:25), and as is mentioned in the interpretation of this verse, these dates were out of season. Likewise the divine inspiration sent to the mother of Moses regarding his affair (20:37–39, 28:7), as well as what God has related about the wonders worked by al-Khadir[4] with Moses (18:65–82). Similarly in the story of Dhū 'l-Qarnayn,[5] whom God strengthened to do what was impossible for anyone else to do but him (18:83–98), and again in the story of the Companions of the Cave[6] and the wonders manifest to them, such as a talking dog among them (18:9–26). In the story of Āsāf ibn Barakhyā with Solomon and the throne of Bilqīs, there is the saying of the Most High, "But one of them who had knowledge of the book said, 'I will bring it to you in the blink of an eye'" (27:40).[7] All of these episodes were not effected by prophets, but rather by Friends of God.

As for such things in reports of the sayings and doings of the Prophet, there is the Hadith of the monk Jurayj and the child who spoke from the cradle, which is a sound Hadith found in the two Sahīhs (of al-Bukhārī and Muslim).[8] In addition, the Hadith of the Companions of the Cave, whose exit was blocked by a boulder that was then opened for them, is also mentioned in the two Sahīhs and its soundness is well authenticated.[9] Then we have the sound, widely transmitted Hadith about the cow who spoke to her owner,[10] and the well-authenticated and widely transmitted Hadith mentioned in the two Sahīhs regarding Abū Bakr and his guest, in which after eating it was discovered that the amount of food had grown three times larger than it been before the meal began.[11] The report that Abū Bakr foresaw that his expectant wife was carrying a girl is also one widely disseminated.[12] Yet another sound and well-authenticated Hadith found in the two Sahīhs identifies ʿUmar [ibn al-Khattāb; d. 23/644] as among those gifted with supernatural inspirations;[13] as well as the sound report that when he called out, "O' Sāriya, the mountain!" during his Friday sermon, his voice reached all the way to Sāriya [ibn Zunaym ad-Duʾilī; d. c.

30/650].[14] Here, 'Umar experienced two saintly marvels: first, the situation of Sāriya and his Muslim companions and that of the enemy was revealed to him; and second, his voice reached a far-off country. There are, further-more, well-authenticated and sound Hadiths, one regarding Sa'd and Sa'īd about each responding to the call of the other; another cited in al-Bukhārī about Khubayb (c. 3/625) eating picked grapes that were out of season;[15] another in al-Bukhārī regarding Usayd ibn Hudayr (20/640–21/642) and 'Abbād ibn Bishr (12/633), in which they are reported to have left the com-pany of the Prophet on a particularly dark night as if there were two lamps in their hands;[16] and yet another about the man who heard a voice from the clouds saying, "Water the garden of so-and-so."[17] In addition, [there are the reports that] Ibn 'Umar (73/693) said "step aside!" to a lion that was blocking people from continuing along the road and immediately turned tail and left;[18] or that when the Prophet sent al-'Alā' ibn al-Hadramī (c. 21/641–42) on a raid when a marsh separated him from his enemies, he called upon God by his greatest name and then walked across the water;[19] or that a large wooden serving bowl sitting between Salmān [al-Fārisī; d. c. 35–36/655–57] and Abū 'd-Dardā' (32/652) was heard by both to be praising God.[20] It is also widely related that 'Imrān ibn Husayn (52/672) was able to hear the angels' salutations to him [at the end of each ritual prayer] until he was cauterized [for hemorrhoids]. [Thereafter] he no longer heard their greetings until God restored [that favor] to him.[21] Then there is the sound Hadith of Muslim in which God's Messenger says, "Many a person with disheveled hair is turned away from the gates, yet if he were to swear by God, it would be fulfilled."[22]

If this Hadith has not furnished sufficient proof, then consider what is mentioned about the pious forbears among the Companions of the Prophet and the generation following, and after them the Sufi masters, the vera-cious jurists, and the rest of the righteous Friends of God regarding the plenteous marvels witnessed everywhere, from the remotest regions to the most populated areas in each and every land, whose sheer number cannot be recorded on paper. I have mentioned a fraction of these in the book *Gardens of Sweet Herbs: On Tales of the Righteous* as well as in *The Guidance (al-Irshād)*, and, God willing, I will also mention something about them in the second section of this book.

Now, although people have composed many books on this subject, a single marvel is sufficient for one with discernment, because it suffuses reality. Its lights have so glittered as to tantalize the gaze of the faithful with the sheer verdancy of its glimmering, and the fragrance of its stories has wafted forth to perfume the ears of those who hear it. How the gaze of liars has become blinded from even seeing it due to all manner of illicit things, and how their ears have been deafened from even hearing its tales! Indeed, upon smelling its sweet scent, every one of them seems to have come down with a cold. Regarding this figurative expression, I say:

The light luxuriously emerged from the lovers' quarter,
  rising to illuminate near and far alike.
And a luxurious perfume wafted from the boudoir,
  with a scent so sweet to arouse my distress.
The dim-sighted cannot see that light,
  and the congested are deprived of smelling that scent.
But the one who has seen or smelt it awakes enamored
  by the sheer headiness of sweet and delicate delights.
If the wine of its intimate encounter were poured forth,
  for the folk of passion by one wholly enamored by it,
they'd bathe in the lovely scent of a private rendezvous,
  in paradisiacal gardens, and the refreshing scent of sweet herbs.
A life of ease under the cooling shade of heavenly favor,
  you'd see them as royalty in paradises of divine knowledge.
Oh, how wonderful are these gifts and blessings;
  so weep over them, my companions and brothers!

The Second Section: On Responding to the Second Question

On the basis of an unquestionably sound, certain, and well-selected doctrine, it is admissible to say that the saintly marvel can reach the same degree as the evidentiary miracle in both type and significance. I have concluded this through reason as well as on the basis of what has been transmitted on the authority of the masters of the basic sources of religion and the many soundly authenticated reports regarding such occurrences among the Friends of God.

As for its rationality, this is not immune to rejection, with respect to either tradition or reason. The first [type of counterargument] would be false since there is no rejecting what is found in tradition, but rather, as I will show, tradition patently confirms its admissibility. As for the second, either [the possibility of lofty marvels] is rejected on the face of it, or by something that is other than it; the first would be false since an absolute breaking of the natural order of things,[23] large or small, by the prophet, the Friend of God, or others, either noble or base, is not logically impossible given the power of the Lord of Power. In the second instance, [the argument] would be based on some obscurity in the prophet's professing himself to be a prophet or something of that sort. The latter [of these] would be false since there is no putting off [the miracle's] source nor any contesting of an evidentiary miracle. As to the first, [a breach of nature] is not coupled with the proclamation of a prophet, or it is. The first is false since there is no obscurity, while the second is publicly witnessed; and he who objects to a breaking of the natural order of things coupled with the proclamation of a prophet is himself constrained by a restrictive obscurity since there is no obscurity without the breaking [of the natural order], that is to say, its being coupled with a previously mentioned proclamation, by which I mean that there is no rejecting any breaking [of natural order] that is connected with the proclamation of a prophet when it is already expected as a result of the prior proclamation, praise be to God!

This confirmation that I have established for admitting the significance of saintly marvels must necessarily be rejected by the Muʿtazilites since they categorically deny their admissibility, inasmuch as recognizing the admissibility of the greatest of them leads one to recognize the admissibility of the least of them. In addition, the doctrines of some of those who make weak arguments concerning the admissibility of saintly marvels should also be considered suspect, and God willing, I will mention these momentarily.

As for tradition, in the first section we have already furnished proof from the Qurʾān, the reports of the sayings and doings of the Prophet, and from reports concerning his Companions, against the Muʿtazilites' categorical rejection of saintly marvels. So now we will mention some proof from the teachings of the veracious and exacting scholars of the basic sources of religion against those who maintain weak arguments in asserting their admissibility.

In his book *The Guidance* (*al-Irshād*), an-Najīb Abū 'l-Maʿālī [al-Juwaynī; d. 478/1085],[24] the Imam of the Two Sanctuaries, said:

> The Ashʿarites do not logically conclude the breaking of the natural order of things with respect to the Friends of God, and the Muʿtazilites are unanimous in rejecting it. The eminent doctor Abū Ishāq (ash-Shīrāzī; d. 476/1083) was inclined toward their teachings, but then came to admit saintly marvels, and so the parties took sides. There were those who concluded that the saintly marvel does indeed break the natural order of things if it occurs without the volition of the Friend of God, and in this respect they concluded that the saintly marvel is of the same category as the evidentiary miracle, but this is not sound, as we will mention. There were those who logically concluded the admissibility of the freely chosen saintly marvel, but they rejected its occurrence in the case of a public proclamation [of sainthood], saying, 'If the Friend of God proclaims his sainthood, then he is supported in confirming his

proclamation by a breaking of the natural order,' and this is prohibited because they reckoned this to be what distinguishes a saintly marvel from an evidentiary miracle. This line of argument is also unsatisfying. We, on the other hand, do not reject the occurrence of breakings of the natural order of things that occur in connection with a prescribed proclamation, but some of our companions have concluded that what is manifest through the prophet as an evidentiary miracle is not admissible as a saintly marvel to a Friend of God. Those who maintain this reject the parting of the sea, the transmutation of a staff into a snake, and the revivification of the dead as possible marvels for the Friend of God, and so forth among the miracles of the prophets. This is not correct either. The correct view, in our opinion, is the admission of the entire gamut of breakings of the natural order of things on the occasion of their occurrence.

This is how his stipulation is worded, and following this he said:

> If it is said: but what is your proof for the admissibility of the saintly marvel? We say: no one effects a breaking of the natural order of things unless he is empowered by the Lord, glory be to Him, first, and something that appears repellent to the intellect is not prohibited, as we have already settled previously. The occurrence of a saintly marvel does not overshadow the evidentiary miracle, for the evidentiary miracle does not serve as a proof by its mere essence but rather by its connection with the public proclamation of a prophet, so as to confirm the sincerity of his message. It is not prohibited that the subjects of a king whose sincerity is proven by the proclamation of a royal edict do not act just as generously as him, and this does not belittle the purpose or sincerity of his generosity in the first place. There is no doubt about this consideration.

This is the end of his discourse and it appears here verbatim.

It is not lost on one with any comprehension that the sum of [Juwaynī's] discourse, both the former and the latter, is beautifully executed, exacting, and eloquent. He goes on to say that there is no difference between the saintly marvel and the evidentiary miracle except that the evidentiary miracle occurs in connection with a proclamation of prophethood and the saintly marvel without an assertion of prophethood, just as, God willing, I will discuss in the third section of this work. Thus, just as with evidentiary miracles, the admissibility of all breakings of the natural order of things by saintly marvels is to be affirmed, for the essences of the two do not differ save in the challenge of prophethood,[25] as affirmed by the veracious, reliable, and celebrated scholars of the basic sources of religion.

Abū Bakr al-Bāqillānī (403/1013),[26] writing on the authority of what was transmitted to him by the learned religious scholars and, in turn, transmitted to us on their authority, said:

> Evidentiary miracles are reserved for the prophets and saintly marvels for the Friends of God. There is no evidentiary miracle for the Friends of God because of the condition that an evidentiary miracle must be connected with a public proclamation of prophethood, and since the Friend of God does not proclaim prophethood, no evidentiary miracle is manifest through him.

In what he transmitted to the religious scholars and what was then transmitted from them to us, Abū Bakr ibn Fūrak (406/1015)[27] said:

> Evidentiary miracles are proofs of sincerity, and if its possessor makes a claim to prophethood, then the evidentiary miracle is a proof of the sincerity of his message. If, however, its possessor makes a claim to sainthood, then the evidentiary miracle serves as a proof of the sincerity of his spiritual state. It is then called a "saintly marvel" rather than an "evidentiary miracle" even though it is of the same category.

Likewise, in his *Sanctified Epistle (ar-Risālat al-qudsīya)*, Abū Hāmid al-Ghazālī (505/1111)[28] stated that the act of breaking the natural order of things is essentially the same as an evidentiary miracle connected with the prophet's offering of a challenge [to his opponents to prove him wrong], the presence of such a challenge being what necessarily distinguishes between the saintly marvel and the evidentiary miracle. So too in his book *The Just Mean in Belief (al-Iqtisād fī 'l-i'tiqād)*, in which he mentions saintly marvels breaking the natural order of things, he says:

> This is not inconceivable in itself because it is a logical possibility, nor is it simply disregarded because it does not necessarily imply the falsity of the evidentiary miracle. That is because the term "saintly marvel" is an expression for a breaking of the natural order that occurs without the issuance of a challenge, for if it were so connected [with such an issuance], then we would simply call it an "evidentiary miracle."

Fakhr ad-Dīn ar-Rāzī (606/1209)[29] said in his *Précis (al-Muhassal)* that the saintly marvel is distinguished from the evidentiary miracle by a prophet presenting a challenge [to his opponents to prove him wrong]. Nāsir ad-Dīn al-Baydāwī (c. 685/1286),[30] too, in his book *The Lamps (al-Masābīh)*, argues that saintly marvels were admissible both to him and the Mu'tazilites, divergence of opinion notwithstanding, on the condition that the saintly marvel is kept distinct from the evidentiary miracle inasmuch as it occurs without the issuance of a challenge.

In addition, Muhammad ibn 'Abd al-Mālik at-Tabarī[31] said in his book *The Tutor in the Necessities of Religion (al-Mu'īn 'alā muqtadā ad-dīn)*:

> Saintly marvels are of the same category as evidentiary miracles in light of the fact that both serve as proofs of sincerity. They are, however, differentiated by name because the evidentiary miracle evinces the sincerity of the one who claims prophethood and the soundness of his claim. Since it proves the sincerity of the message of the claimant to prophethood, it is termed an "evidentiary miracle." On the other hand, one who makes a claim to sainthood proves, through the category of the evidentiary miracle, the sincerity of his spiritual state, so that the action is termed a "saintly marvel" and not an "evidentiary miracle."

And, Nasīr ad-Dīn at-Tūsī (672/1274)[32] said in his book *The Fundamentals of Belief (Qawā'id al-'aqā'id)* that the act of breaking the natural order of things that occurs without a challenge is called a "saintly marvel" and is reserved for the Friends of God. Likewise, Hāfiz ad-Dīn an-Nasafī (710/1310)[33] said in his *Creed ('Aqīda)*:

> On the basis of widespread reports and plenteous tales of the chosen ones, the Mu'tazilites considered marvels of the Friends of God admissible, though [in fact] their views varied. But if the admission of saintly marvels had the effect of truncating the knowledge of the prophet—the evidentiary miracle is, after all, connected with the claim of prophethood—and if the Friend of God were to claim [that prerogative], then he would be guilty of unbelief.

And, Abū 'l-Qāsim al-Qushayrī (465/1072)[34] said in his *Epistle (Risāla)*, "The occurrence of saintly marvels is an outward indication of the sincerity of inward spiritual states." He then continues, "And the conditions of all evidentiary miracles, or at least most of them, are also found in regard to the saintly marvel, with the sole exception of the public proclamation of prophethood."

These ten Sunni imams whose veridical works and esteemed words on matters of belief I have abridged here—and there is no need to introduce more, because those already mentioned are sufficient, especially the first six—all agree that the difference between the saintly marvel and the evidentiary miracle is only the [unbelievers'] challenge to the prophet, and not one of them makes it a condition that the essence of the saintly marvel be different from that of the evidentiary miracle in either category or significance. This proves the admissibility of equating the two, with the sole exception of the previously mentioned challenge, as the illustrious Imam of the Two Sanctuaries has made clear.

In admitting their essential identity, and even while they are the same, it is still incumbent to note this difference: the saintly marvel and the evidentiary miracle are one and the same except for the previously mentioned challenge. As such, their identity is admissible in regard to things such as the revival of the dead and other things in the category of disruption of the natural order of things.

Another witness to the soundness of this is his [Muhammad's] saying in the sound Hadith, "Yet if he were to swear by God it would be fulfilled." Now, if the previously mentioned response were to be common to every case, and the oath be to raise the dead or such like—and indeed this has occurred to many of the Friends of God—I would consider it the greatest of saintly marvels. Yet this exceeds the limit, so I will abstain from further counsel and simply mention ten types.[35]

The First Type: Raising the Dead   In my view, some of the righteous from Yemen informed me that the great master of experiential knowledge known as al-Ahdal,[36] the master of Shaykh Abū 'l-Ghayyith (651/1253), had a cat named Pearl whom the shaykh's servant struck because it was eating his dinner. The cat died later that night, and the servant tossed it aside somewhere (or he said in some ruins, something which only the shaykh knows for certain), and when the shaykh returned, he said nothing to him for two, perhaps three nights, until finally he asked, "Where is Pearl?" The servant responded, "I do not know." The shaykh replied, "You don't know?" He then called out to her, "Pearl! Pearl!" and she came to him straightaway and he fed her.

Also, some of the folk of knowledge and prayer, whom I believe were from the Maghrib, informed me on their own authority that one of the companions of Yūsuf ad-Dahmānī [mid-seventh/thirteenth century] had passed away and his family was mourning for him. When the shaykh saw the intensity of their mourning, he said to [the deceased], "By the leave of God Most High, arise!" He arose and lived for as long a time afterwards as God desired.

Now, about including the raising of the dead among their marvels: even though it is a stupendous act, it is still admissible in view of the choice and sound sayings of the recognized authorities of the past, like those well-known and reliable authorities of the basic sources of religion I have already introduced. Nevertheless, the fact remains that whatever is admissible as an evidentiary miracle for a prophet is admissible as a saintly marvel for the Friend of God, so long as he does not claim prophethood.

The Second Type: The Speech of the Dead   In this context, some righteous masters of Yemen informed me that one day the great jurist Ismā'īl al-Hadramī (c. 676/1277) was passing through a cemetery with a large crowd, and out of nowhere great wailing and laughter were heard. He was asked about this, and said, "I saw the people of this cemetery being tortured and I grieved for them, so I implored God that I be allowed to intercede on their behalf, and so I interceded. The inhabitant of this particular grave here (and he pointed to a grave near a new plot) said, 'O' jurisconsult Ismā'īl, I am one of them, being so-and-so the songstress,' and then she laughed, and I said, 'You are among them.' He said, 'Then I sent for the grave digger and asked him, "Whose grave is this here?" and he replied, "The grave of so-and-so the songstress."'"

In the case of the aforementioned master, there were four saintly marvels: first, the condition of the dead being revealed to him; second, the dead speaking to him, by which I mean the aforementioned songstress; third, the acceptance of his intercession on their behalf; and fourth, his knowledge that his intercession had been accepted. How great are these four saintly marvels, especially the third: his being able to intercede for so many and lift away their sins through his saintly blessing!

The Third Type: Splitting and Drying the Sea   As for this, there is what has been transmitted to us on the authority of al-Qushayrī in his *Epistle* regarding some Sufis on a ship. The narrator says:

> We were sailing on a ship when a man who had been ill died, so we conducted his funeral service and then got ready to cast his body into the sea, but lo and behold, the sea had become dry and the ship had come to rest upon the ground, so we dug a grave and buried him. As soon as we had finished, the water rose back up to its normal level, the boat was raised, and we were gladdened.

The Fourth Type: The Transmutation of Matter   Know that this type is among the most common and well known of all saintly marvels, such as the transmutation of stones into gems or gold, or the transmutation of salt water into fresh, or for some of them, water into poison; the transmutation of sand into flour or sugar, earthenware into silver or gold, or eggplant seeds into gold; or for some of them, sawdust into fine timber or firewood into gold and so forth, things that are readily found in books dealing with the marvels of the Friends of God such as the Epistle of al-Qushayrī and such like.

Know that this type is extensive, and because it is not necessary to mention it here, God willing, we will furnish a brief synopsis in the sixth section because it is better dealt with in response to the sixth question.

The Sixth Type: Instantaneous Travel   Know that they are well known for this "wrinkling the surface of the earth"[37] and that it is better than either flying in the air, walking upon the water, or traversing the world at an incredible pace.

A related report was transmitted to me at the congregational mosque of Tarsus concerning someone who desired to visit the Holy Sanctuary, and as soon as the thought entered his head, he was there. Likewise, there is the report of a group from a far-off county who, on the Day of 'Arafāt, performed the major ablution, prayed, donned the pilgrims garb, and then made a lingering prostration, and when they lifted their heads, they found themselves gazing upon the camels making their way from Minā to 'Arafāt.[38]

The Seventh Type: The Pouring Forth of Water   On this subject there is what is related by al-Qushayrī in his *Epistle*, on the authority of the chain of transmission [of this book] as it has been related to me:

> While on the road to Mecca one of Abū Turāb an-Nakhshabī's (245/860) companions told him, "I am thirsty," so he struck the ground with his foot and a bubbling spring of water burst forth. The young man said, "I would like to drink it from a glass," and so [an-Nakhshabī] struck the ground with his hand and delivered him the finest white drinking glass he had ever seen, and he drank and was quenched. He said, "We took that drinking glass with us all the way to Mecca."

The Eighth Type: Inanimate Objects and Animals Speaking to Them   In this context, there is the well-known tale from Muhammad ibn Mubārak (as-Sūrī) (215/830) about the pomegranate tree that addressed Ibrāhīm ibn Adham (160/777) while on the road to Jerusalem, saying to him, "O' Abū Ishāq, honor us by eating our fruits," and it said this thrice. It was a stunted tree with sour pomegranates, bearing fruit but once a year, but when he ate from it, however, it shot up and its pomegranates became sweet, and it bore fruit twice per year. They named it the "pomegranate tree of the godservants" because godservants sheltered in its shade.

Abū 'Abd Allāh al-Qurashī (599/1203) said, "One time I was traveling along the shore when all of a sudden an herb addressed me, saying, 'I am the cure to that sickness you have,' but I did not take or apply it." It was also transmitted to me that he said, "While [I was] on the road to Mecca, a camel spoke to me. I saw camels who had been carrying loads stretching out their necks at night, and one of them said, 'Praise be to the one who bears upon her back what is put there,' and then that camel turned to me and said, 'Say: may God be exalted,' and so I said, 'May God be exalted.'"

The Ninth Type: Healing by Benediction   On this matter, some people of knowledge informed me that some folks came to the great jurist and Friend of God, Ahmad ibn Mūsā al-Yamānī (665/1267) with a man suffering from an oozing wound on his hand. He said to him, "Since in my opinion there is no one better than one of the righteous, please call upon God to stop this leaking wound." He said to him, "There is no power nor strength save by God," and he then wiped his hand and wrapped it in his Sufi cloak, saying, "Do not remove it until you reach home," and he left him straightaway because of the long night's journey that lay ahead. When he finally arrived, he uncovered his hand so as to eat, and his right palm bore no mark whatsoever.

It seems, and God only knows, that the aforementioned master desired to conceal his saintly marvel by covering the hand with his Sufi cloak so that it would not be made known at that moment, perhaps because there were other people around, for seeing its occurrence later is easier and less public.

The Tenth Type: Things Being under Their Command   Among the many well-known examples of this is their taming predatory beasts, and many of them have ridden on their backs, had them carry their provisions, or gather firewood. Among them is Shaykh Abū 'l-Ghayyith, who commanded a lion who ravished his donkey to carry firewood upon its back, saying to him, "By the power of the one who is worshipped, I will not carry firewood except on your back," and the lion submitted to him and carried the wood on its back. He drove him to the city gate where he set it down and then fled.

Although we have exceeded all appropriate moderation in this section, such was necessary on account of the denial [of the reality of marvels]. In fact, in proportion to the current fashion of embellishing such discussions beyond all reasonable measure, we have cut it quite short, and those endowed with reason will understand its brevity and will guide the perplexed.

NOTES

1. The edition used here is that of Ibrāhīm 'Atwah 'Awad (Cairo: Mus-tafā al-Bābī al-Halabī, 1961), as reprinted with notes by Khalīl 'Imrān al-

Mansūr (Beirut: Dār al-Kutub al-ʿIlmīya, 2000) (cited hereafter as *Nashr al-mahāsin*).

2. *Nashr al-mahāsin*, 11–36.

3. Later occurrences of this and similar conventional rhetorical devices are not translated (ed.).

4. Or, al-Khidr, the "green man," traditionally understood to be the mysterious servant of God (ʿabd) who in the above-cited passage is said to have led Moses on an incredible and perplexing journey (see A. J. Wensinck, "al-Khadir," in *Encyclopedia of Islam*, new ed., ed. B. Lewis, C. Pellat, J. Schacht, et al. [Leiden: Brill, 1965–c. 2000] [hereafter, *EI²*], 4:902).

5. Or "he of the two horns," traditionally understood to refer to Alexander the Great.

6. That is, the Qurʾānic account of the eastern Christian legend of the Seven Sleepers of Ephesus (see R. Paret, "Ashāb al-kahf," in *EI²*, 1:691).

7. A reference to the legend of the romance between King Solomon and the Queen of Sheba (see E. Ullendorf, "Bilkīs," in *EI²*, 1:1219).

8. *Sahīh al-Bukhārī*, 4th rev. ed., trans. Muhammad Muhsin Khan (Chicago: Kazi, 1976), vol. 4, bk. 55, no. 645; and *Sahīh Muslim*, trans. Abdul Hamid Siddiqui (Lahore: Sh. Muhammad Ashraf, 1971), bk. 32, no. 6188.

9. *Sahīh al-Bukhārī*, vol. 8, bk. 75, no. 5; and *Sahīh Muslim*, bk. 36, no. 6607.

10. *Sahīh al-Bukhārī*, vol. 3, bk. 39, no. 517; and *Sahīh Muslim*, bk. 31, no. 5881.

11. *Sahīh al-Bukhārī*, vol. 1, bk. 10, no. 576; and *Sahīh Muslim*, bk. 23, no. 5106.

12. Mālik ibn Anas, *al-Muwattā*, trans. Aisha Abdurrahman Bewley (London: Kegan Paul, 1989), bk. 36.33(1), no. 40 (p. 310).

13. *Sahīh al-Bukhārī*, vol. 5, bk. 57, no. 38; and *Sahīh Muslim*, bk. 39, no. 5901.

14. On the source of this report, see R. Gramlich, *Die Wunder der Freunde Gottes* (Wiesbaden: Harrassowitz, 1987), 87–89.

15. *Sahīh al-Bukhārī*, vol. 4, bk. 52, no. 281.

16. *Sahīh al-Bukhārī*, vol. 1, bk. 8, no. 454.

17. *Sahīh Muslim*, bk. 42, no. 7112.

18. On this report, see Gramlich, *Die Wunder*, 93.

19. On this, see ibid., 94.

20. On this, see ibid., 341.

21. This episode, or a version of it, is sometimes cited in discussions of dispensations allowed to the infirm during *salat*, such as the permission (*rukhsa*) to stand for the whole prayer when one is unable to perform the *sajda/julus* because of extreme physical discomfort.

22. *Sahīh Muslim*, bk. 32, no. 6351.

23. The Arabic expression used in this context is *kharq al-ʿāda* (pl. *khawāriq al-ʿādāt*)—literally, a "breach" or "disruption" of "habit" or "custom" in the

sense of an extraordinary or preternatural occurrence that transcends that which is expected or usual.

24. Among the most famous and important Sunni theologians of all time; on him, see the introduction to P. Walker's translation of al-Juwaynī, *The Guidance: A Guide to Conclusive Proofs for the Principles of Beliefs* (Reading, UK: Garnet, 2000).

25. That is, a "challenge" (*tahaddī*) posed by a prophet to his opponents to work a similar miracle, something that God will render them incapable of doing.

26. An early Ash'arite theologian who, in addition to many other works, devoted an entire treatise to the issue of prophetic miracles and saintly marvels; on him, see W. Montgomery Watt, *Islamic Philosophy and Theology*, 2nd ed. (Edinburgh: Edinburgh University Press, 1985), 76–79.

27. Another influential Ash'arite theologian whose ideas were amenable to al-Yāfi'ī's position; on him, see W. Montgomery Watt, "Ibn Fūrak," in *EI²* 3:766.

28. Celebrated student of the aforementioned al-Juwaynī who has often been credited with a reconciliation between Sufi piety and normative Sunnism; on him, see A. Knysh, *Islamic Mysticism* (Leiden, Netherlands: Brill, 2000), 140–49.

29. On this most celebrated of medieval Muslim theologians and Qur'ānic exegetes, see G. C. Anawati, "Fakhr al-Dīn al-Rāzī," in *EI²* 2:751ff.

30. Another well-known Shāfi'ī scholar whose works, usually culled from others, were often quoted by later scholars; on him, see J. Robson, "al-Baydāwī," in *EI²* 1:1129.

31. That is, Abū Khalaf Muhammad ibn 'Abd al-Malik ibn Khalaf as-Salmī at-Tabarī, a Sufi and Shāfi'ī jurist who died c. 470/1077; none of his works have been published to date.

32. On this celebrated and influential polymath, who despite al-Yāfi'ī's statement to the contrary was a Shi'ite, see H. Daiber, "al-Tūsī," *EI²* 10:744ff.

33. An important Hanafī jurist and theologian, on whom see Watt, *Islamic Philosophy and Theology*, 137.

34. Among the most influential of the Sufi systematizers of the fifth/eleventh century, whose apologetic *Epistle*, as can be seen here, secured a preeminent position as the authoritative standard on the subject; on him and this work, see Knysh, *Islamic Mysticism*, 130–32. In this section of the *Diffusion of Perfumed Merits*, al-Yāfi'ī relies heavily on al-Qushayrī's text (cf. al-Qushayrī, *The Risalah*, trans. Rabia Harris [Chicago: Great Books of the Islamic World, 2002], 423–59).

35. The following section has been abridged.

36. That is, the celebrated sixth/twelfth-century Sufi master, the "Pole of Yemen" (*qutb al-yaman*), 'Alī ibn 'Umar ibn Muhammad al-Ahdal, the eponym of the al-Ahdal family of *sayyids*, from whom sprang a long line of Sufi scholars (see O. Löfgren, "al-Ahdal," in *EI²* 1:255–56).

37. Here, al-Yāfiʿī uses the Arabic expression "zawā wajh al-ard la-hum ghayr harakat min-hum" ("the earth wrinkling up for them without them moving"; more commonly, *tayy al-ard,* "rolling up the earth," or *tayy az-zamān wa-l-makān,* "rolling up time and space"), a commonly cited saintly marvel that connotes the idea that the Friend of God stays put while space itself is literally "folded up" and brought to him, strangely similar to the idea in contemporary science fiction of interstellar propulsion though "spatial warping."

38. The Day of ʿArafāt occurs during the Hajj when pilgrims leave Mecca to perform rituals on the plain of ʿArafāt, east of the city.

4 The Wafāʾīya of Cairo

Richard McGregor

The Sādāt al-Wafāʾīya of Mamluk Egypt was a family-based Sufi order that played a dominant role in the social and spiritual life of Cairo for more than five hundred years. Originally from Tunisia, the family immigrated to Alexandria in the seventh/thirteenth century. The order became known as the Wafāʾīya after Muhammad Wafāʾ (765/1363), whose name itself was part of the hagiographical legend—as is recounted in the text below. Muhammad was succeeded as head of the family, and as shaykh of the Sufi order, by his two sons, ʿAlī (807/1405) and Abū ʾl-ʿAbbās (814/1412). Leadership would continue within the family, with twenty-two shaykhs constituting a line that extended into the earliest years of the twentieth century.

The real significance of the Wafāʾīya however was established in its earliest phase. Muhammad and his son ʿAlī were famous not only as Friends of God (*awliyāʾ*) but also as profound mystical thinkers and poets. Together they composed eighteen substantial works, in addition to several lengthy devotional litany-like prayer texts (sing. *hizb*). Most of these works await proper editions and study. Their public careers as Sufi shaykhs are attested to in the biographical literature of the Mamluk period. In addition, a hagiography has survived, collected by a contemporary, a man in their service by the name of Abū ʾl-Latāʾif. This collection, sections of which are translated below for the first time, is entitled *The Divine Gifts* (*al-Minah al-ilāhīya*).[1]

Two sources fed the spiritual heritage of the Wafāʾīya, the Shādhilīya and Muhyi ʾd-Dīn Ibn ʿArabī (638/1240). The eponymous founder of the Shādhilīya order, Abū ʾl-Hasan ash-Shādhilī (658/1258), like the Sādāt al-Wafāʾīya, had left the Maghrib for Alexandria. It was in this city that Muhammad Wafāʾ's grandfather, Muhammad an-Najm, came to embrace the Shādhilī mystical way. This order was very successful in spreading throughout the Muslim world and remains prominent today. Beyond ash-Shādhilī's saintly career, the most important individual in this tradition was certainly Ibn ʿAṭāʾ Allāh al-Iskandarī (709/1309), who left, besides his hagiography of the shaykh, a substantial body of mystical poetry and advice to spiritual novices. Both of these figures appear in *The Divine Gifts*. The relationship between the Wafāʾiya and the Shādhilīya was complex. On the one hand, Muḥammad and ʿAlī recognized their affiliation with the Shādhilīya; on the other, their own success and significance led them to assert their independence. The Wafāʾiya may be considered a branch of the Shādhilīya, but it was a branch that took its own way rather dramatically and quite early on in the history of the Shādhilīya.

A second element splits the Wafāʾiya off from its Shādhilī roots, and that is the mystical tradition developed by Ibn ʿArabī. Both Muḥammad and ʿAlī were deeply influenced by this school of thought, particularly its understanding of spiritual authority (*walāya*), the existential bond between God and creation, and the emanative process of divine self-disclosure. The Wafāʾ writings, though innovative and original, were so similar to the writings of Ibn ʿArabī that later readers often confused their authors.

The following selections from *The Divine Gifts* touch on many of these elements. Claims to spiritual authority, sometimes at the expense of the Shādhilīs, are of particular concern in the text. We read of instances in which the Prophet Muḥammad himself appears and makes key statements. Also important in this collection is the role of various inspired texts. Prayers, poems, and other works, all of which are taken to be the fruit of divine inspiration, constitute evidence of sanctity. They are not only celebrated for their beauty but also championed as media for the miraculous.

TRANSLATION

1b [ʿAlī Wafāʾ] related the following story: "When I was five years old, I used to recite the Qurʾān for a teacher named Shaykh Yaʿqūb. One day, upon arriving for my lesson, I found a man reciting Sūrat ad-Duḥā to the shaykh, with several of his companions in attendance. The reciter's *a*'s were coming out sounding like *i*'s, and the crowd was laughing at him. All of a sudden I saw the Prophet, dressed in a white cotton shirt. I was fully awake, not dreaming. The white shirt he was wearing then appeared on me. He said, "Recite!" so I delivered Sūrat ad-Duḥā. I was about to comment on it, but he had already disappeared."[2]

1b "On another occasion, when I was twenty-one years of age, I had performed ablutions for the morning prayer in the Qarāfa cemetery, and looked up to see the Prophet standing in front of me. He embraced me saying, 'God bestows favor upon you'—which was true, since I took his voice [lit., tongue] from that point onward."

2b I heard ʿAlī say, "In a dream I saw a tree uprooted from the East that grew upwards, opening itself to me, saying, 'I am the Tree of the World.' It grew to the West, then it returned and set itself in my hand." Then ʿAlī heard the following: "The whole world is a tree, and your hand is the blessed earth in which it is rooted."

2b ʿAlī once related to me, "The Might of our Lord said to me, 'O' ʿAlī, your right is guaranteed by Me; it is a wondrous portion. None loves you but that I love him. As long as he does, so will I. None hates you but that I hate him. As long as he does, so will I.'"[3]

3a [Muhammad Wafāʾ once said to Shams ad-Dīn az-Zaylāʿī,] "My sons are not like others, for they are one spirit in two bodies. They partake of the essential reality of my spirit. I received a promise from God, and entered into a pact with Him, to the effect that whosoever loves them will be among those beloved by God, while whosoever hates them will be reckoned an enemy of God."

3a At one of our sessions, [in reference to his son ʿAlī, Muhammad] said, "Whoever sees us as two is blind in one eye; but whoever sees us as one, sees with both eyes."

5b While riding back to his house, ʿAlī Wafāʾ informed me that once while meditating on God, he saw himself, as in a dream, floating in midair. In this state he came across an immaculate lofty white palace. Around it were open graves, with occupants wrapped in white, sweet-smelling. ʿAlī asked them who they were, and their spokesman said, "These are the saints of every era, but the owner of these graves is their Seal.[4] They await him, for he will be their intercessor with God. This man had opened the door of the palace before and seen my master seated inside, but did not recognize him at that point. Yet once God had brought him to this noble place, ʿAlī said to him, "They have opened the door for you, and call you to your service. [So recognize me now!]"

6a ʿAlī told me of a man who related a story of the governor of Alexandria, who was celebrating his birthday in the month of Rabīʿ al-Awwal. He had invited the prominent people of the city, among them the deputy of the port. The latter had come upon ʿAlī's grandfather [Muhammad al-Najm] and had managed to immerse himself in his knowledge. Recounting the experience, the deputy related a dream, which he described saying, "I saw myself falling from the sky, plunging to the depths of the sea." At the same celebration there was also a prince who often slandered the Sufis. He overheard the deputy and mockingly said, "I too saw myself falling from the sky, to the depths of the sea." The grandfather replied, "In my case the deputy was sincere, but in the other case [the prince] has lied. The liar will only hit his mark [or speak truthfully] when he falls to the earth. He will emerge from this encounter crippled."

7a I heard 'Alī say, "Whoever recites our litany (*hizb*) with presence of heart is forgiven by what is between the two [Qur'ānic] verses found in the noble *hizb* of the *Great Opening* that read, 'Lord, we have wronged ourselves. If you do not forgive us and show mercy, we will be lost' (7:23), and 'Lord, forgive and show mercy; You are the best of those who show mercy' (23:118). I would add to this that this noble *hizb* contains the secrets of all previous litanies (*ahzāb*), for I heard 'Alī say at one of our sessions, "If you are told to not recite the *ahzāb* of the great teacher Abū 'l-Hasan ash-Shādhilī, then say, 'Nay, do recite it, or that of the great teacher Abū 'l-'Abbas [al-Mursī, d. 686/1287].' Say also, 'Or the *hizb* of Dā'ūd [ibn Bākhilā, d. 733/1332], and others!' Such should be your answer."

13a Among 'Alī's gifts was that once he ordered me to record the date of the building of the noble presence [that is, the family mosque and shrine in Cairo's al-Qarāfā cemetery]. I asked him, "My master, in what way should I record it?" He then wrote on a sheet of paper the following as a guide: "O Protector! O One! O Protector! O Everlasting! O Lofty One! O Wise One!"[5] It was the twilight for this perfected noble presence [that is, the end of his lifetime]. The notice above his lofty tomb began with the following words: "The last hour of Friday, by its divine well-kept holiness; the seventh holy month of the year 807 Hijrī. Praise be to God, the most Mighty and most Generous, Unique and Everlasting."

14a 'Alī once said [to me], "May the Holy Spirit support you. But more generous than this is the supplication carried on in the inner reality of the servant." One example of this was the occasion [my fellow] servant Abū 'l-'Atā' and I were walking with the master, and he said to him, "Recite your special *hizb*." So he recited it. My master then commanded me to recite mine, which I did. Then he said, "What wonderful gifts these are!"

15a I was once in the service of my master, at his house on Ruda Island. Gathered in the courtyard were others in attendance including Abū 'l-Bashā'ir and Abū 'sh-Shāmil. Pointing to one of the interior facing windows, my master said, "I saw, as in a dream, Jesus sitting at this window, facing a man at the next window. He said to him, 'Surely this is a place upon which the Holy Spirit has descended.'"[6]

15a Once when I was accompanying my master, he related to us a story from the *Spiritual Inrushes* (*wāridāt*) [of his father]. He said that when the great master [Muhammad Wafā'] was born, the teacher Ibn 'Atā' Allāh al-Iskandarī and some of his companions came to the house in which he had been born. Ibn 'Atā' Allāh asked to see the swaddling baby. When he saw him, he declared to his companions, 'This one has arrived already endowed with all of our [spiritual] realities!' "

15b I was told by the judge Nasr ad-Dīn ibn Fawz ash-Shāfi'ī, known as Abū 'l-Mawāhib, that his grandfather, one of the pious and a master of spiritual states and discipline, was buried in the city of Sunhūr.[7] Many made pilgrimage to his tomb, including the great teacher Abū 'l-Hasan ash-Shādhilī. On his way south for the Hajj, ash-Shādhilī's caravan made camp on the shore across from Sunhūr. In that city there was a most devout man named Ibn Hārūn. He is buried in the town. With some companions, Ibn Hārūn set out to visit ash-Shādhilī and found that he had had his pavilion tent pitched and was resting therein. Ibn Hārūn performed a full ablution and began to circumambulate the tent. This continued for a week, only stopping when he was admitted. He entered the tent and after a short while emerged. His companions disapproved of all this, and the shaykh [ash-Shādhilī] revealed that fact to Ibn Hārūn, who responded to them saying, "By God, I performed the complete ablution and circled for a week only to see the Ka'ba circumambulating him.[8] When I went in to see him, I was struck more deeply by that experience than by anything that had happened to me during my twenty-five years of following Shaykh Abū 's-Su'ūd [ibn Abī al-'Ashā'ir, d. 644/1246]." He then invited him to his home, bringing the local 'ulamā' to pay their respects. Ibn Hārūn would begin [the introductions with], "In the Name of God, O king of the saints . . ." The essential point here is that Abū 'l-Mawāhib's grandfather had been present, and he was told by ash-Shādhilī, "I am a Jesus-like man, but after me is the awaited Muhammadan."

Then Abū 'l-Mawāhib returned to Cairo and joined the service of my master [Muhammad Wafā'] on Ruda Island. I was present when he told this story to my master. Then Abū 'z-Zāhir arrived, and my master called for him and told him this story. My master then recalled the story of a man who had been a companion of Abū 'l-'Abbās al-Mursī (686/1287), who had told him the following: "You will not die without having joined the companions of the age"—and whispered the secret that had brought him there to him. He went on to live so long that he came to know my great master.

16b I once heard the noble Abū 'l-Fath (852/1448) relate the following: "It has come down to us from good sources that in the time of my great master [Muhammad Wafā'] the Nile had refused its annual inundation, rising only a fraction of what is needed. This went on into the Coptic month of Miṣrā. The people became distressed and called upon my master for help, for he was already famous at this time for the efficacy of his divine supplications. They said, 'O' master, do you not see the danger the people are in without your supplication on their part?' My master then walked to the bank of the river, performed his ablutions and prayed. He then recited a supplicatory prayer and ended it with the exhortation [to the river], "Complete! Complete! (*Wafā' wafā'*)" Obediently the river rose up to his noble feet, and in the course of that one night reached its complete height. Thus my master became known as [Muhammad] Wafā'.

17a I heard my master say, "This noble gathering is home to all the other saints. If you are searching for Abū 'l-Hasan ash-Shādhilī, he is with you in this gathering, as is Abū 'l-'Abbās al-Mursī. Many masters are numbered here, such as 'Abd al-Qādir al-Jīlānī (561/1166) and others like the shaykhs of the *Epistle* (*Risāla*) [i.e., al-Qushayrī?] and others." Then he said, "And likewise all the saints of the past nations."

17b I heard my master say, "Visiting graves reminds us of death, but visiting a spiritual master reminds us of a life that never dies."

17b I also heard him say, "By the power of our Lord, I am the beloved of God. Whoever loves me loves God; whoever is my friend is a friend of God."

19b One Friday evening a group of us were reciting the *wazīfa* [daily office] prayers with my master. We were all sitting in the small hall adjacent to his home on Ruda Island. After we had finished the *wazīfa*, our master said, "During this recitation there were present two men and a woman from the realm of the unseen. They were sitting atop that wall."

21a My master Abū 'l-Fath told me that once, near the end of Muhammad Wafā's life, he entered his room and found him in the form of his son 'Alī. Muhammad declared, "Seeing me, is seeing him!"

21a I read from our brother Abū 't-Tayyib al-Misrī of the occasion at which he was in the service of our master and he spoke of the signs of the uniqueness of this noble family. 'Alī said, "We are a tree, and whosoever takes shade under us is shaded by God."

21b My master said, "I have never been tempted by adultery, and have never committed it. I say that adultery is found only in him who has human form. However, the gentlemen [of our family] are pure and free of human attributes. Only those with human attributes see them as humans."

23b Abū 'l-Baqā' once related to me the following: "One day I was with my master, when he was on his way to the house of Akmal ad-Dīn, shaykh of the Shaykhawīya *khānqāh*.⁹ At that time this shaykh was weak and on the point of death. We reached that place and our master asked to enter, but an attendant told us that the shaykh was secluded and not receiving anyone, since for the last three days he had been in the throes of death. Nevertheless my master went in to his room and, upon seeing him, shook him and spoke eloquent words to him. I said to myself, 'How could the attendant have claimed otherwise?' Then I heard him say to my master, 'O' master, I have been visited by the angels of death. I heard them say they would hold themselves back until my master has finished with his work.' To this my master responded, 'We have done what we needed to. God willing, there will be a change.' . . . [unclear] Then he turned from him, and had just come out of the door when the attendant ran out, saying, 'May you live long my master, and the mercy of God persists over the shaykh.' "

24a I was told by some of my brethren the story of Abū Khālis, known as Ibn Nujūm. He was someone who recited the *samā'* with a particularly beautiful voice. However, he fell short in his training and instruction, and one night my master ordered him away, obliging him to leave the country. Ibn Nujūm recounted, "Though confused, I left for the land of Syria. But I did not have with me sufficient funds, so I stopped at Siryāqus [the large Sufi hospice north of Cairo]. There I recited one tenth of the Qur'ān and a poem (*qaṣīda*). The occupants were kind enough to give me some money, which I gladly took. I said to myself, 'I shall do this in every land I travel through.' When I reached Gaza, I walked through its streets and alleys and came across an impoverished man who appeared insane (*majnūn*). The local people would insult him, and the children would pelt him with stones. It crossed my mind that he might be one of those endowed with lofty spiritual states. Fearing he might be injured by their foolish acts, I stopped, and once he was comfortable with my presence, he stood up and began walking, leading me to a desolate place. He then said, 'O' 'Alī, you are displeased with my master [Abū Khālis]!' Upon hearing this, I wept. He continued, 'He is noble, and thus he disciplines you.' I then traveled to Syria with this ringing in my ears. One day I entered a public bath and was reminded of my master's home [back on Ruda Island]. Again I wept, and recited the following:

> I must burden you, so that you carry out
> By God, what is from yourselves

From that point until my return, God's heart was my heart. On my way back to Egypt, arriving in Gaza, I saw that *majdhūb* [mystic drawn to

God] again—the man who had by chance crossed my path and who would bring a resolution to my sorry state. He said to me, 'O' 'Alī, good will has prevailed! Gratitude and acknowledgement are enjoined!' Then he asked me if I knew the reason for all this, to which I replied I did not. He said that while attending the spiritual sessions of my master, he heard the great master [Muhammad Wafā'] say to my master 'Alī, 'If only Abū Khālis were present! How pleasant the gathering would be if he were here to lead the group.' Then the *majdhūb* said to me, 'When you reach Cairo, go to our great master [Muhammad Wafā']. Since he was your advocate, he will be your brotherly protector.' I did as he suggested and went to my great master [Muhammad Wafā'], who poured his beneficence upon me, allowing me to resume my service of master 'Alī in his noble precincts." Thus Abū Khālis found more and more approval. Regarding this story, Abū 's-Sālim told me that my master 'Alī explained, "Together you all helped in his discipline. So go out to plunder the treasure that is his wisdom, but remember that [spiritual] training requires instruction, just as the father, when he educates his son, might burden him with beatings, all of which are only done for the better and to benefit his son."

25a Abū 'l-Fadl ibn al-Furāt related the story of Abū 'l-Hafs az-Zaylā'ī, who served my great master [Muhammad Wafā']. One day a plate of fresh dough was donated, and Abū 'l-Hafs took it, pierced it, and laid it near the oven. He returned to my master, who then said to him, "Put it in the oven and sit with it." So he took it over to the oven, pulled his robe about him, and with the dough in his hand, prepared to enter the fire. Startled, Ibn al-Furāt asked, "What are you doing?" To which he answered, "Our teacher has ordered me to sit in the oven." Ibn al-Furāt said, "His wish is only that you sit by the oven until the bread is baked!" Some of the other men present gathered around him and took him to our master, and told him of the disaster that had almost occurred. My master replied, "If he had entered the oven it would have been for him *cool and safe.*"[10]

27a I was told by Abū 'n-Nūr that on one occasion he asked our master about Muhyī 'd-Dīn ibn 'Arabī. Specifically, he wanted to know about the mixing of "spiritual realization" (*tahqīq*) with philosophy. Some had questioned him about this before, and his answers were always appropriate to the [spiritual] states of the inquirers. Among these was one who declared, "Surely, this is one who knows God!" Abū 'l-Fadl ibn al-Furāt told me he once heard our great master [Muhammad Wafā'] say, "Ibn 'Arabī and Ibn Sab'īn (669/1269) are two kings rising together toward a heavenly sphere; however, they will return without having penetrated its depths."

27b My master told me of a man who recited poetry (*qasīda*) at several of our great master's [Muhammad Wafā's] sessions. Some of those gathered around said to him, "This is not suitable for our group." The reciter fell silent, for he was ashamed and embarrassed. My master felt sympathy for him and treated him with honor, asking, "What did they say to you?" To which the reciter responded, "O' my master, they said, 'This is not suitable for our group.'" To which he responded, "Then tell them that it is suitable for me!" Note that this was a poem popular among the people of Alexandria.

29a Once a man known as al-Balaqsī, who had met my great master [Muhammad Wafā'] at a spiritual session in honor of Shaykh 'Ajamī, asked my master for permission to recite his noble *hizb*. He answered, "I am afraid that a *zāwiya* [Sufi residence] will be built for you in Balaqs,[11] that you will be named as shaykh, and that you will use our *hizb* as part of the *wazīfa* of al-'Ajamī, and jealousy will arise." He countered, "What do you mean? How can that be?" But he agreed with my master about his wish for a *zāwiya* and being named the shaykh of Balaqs. Some people even came to follow him, God knows why! They took him as a substitute for my master, [and although others called him back to] serve God, he would not repent. He persisted and gained his desired position, but his success did not last long. Within a week his belly ripped open and his bowels fell to the ground. My master concluded this story with the declaration: "God willing, he will be eternally damned!"

29b My Sufi companion Ibn az-Zayyāt once told me the following story about 'Alī Wafā'. He said, "I fell asleep in the noble precincts [of the Wafā' home or *ribāt*], and in a dream I saw him. He was pacing back and forth, and I was asking him about his spiritual state. My master 'Alī turned to me and said, 'Leave me be!' I then saw myself laid out in my own grave. He came to me and sat upon my chest, continuing our conversation, until he revealed to me the most delicate flowers of Paradise. Then I awoke."[12]

31b One day, in the service of my master at his home on Ruda Island, I observed the following event. The sun was setting, and he was dictating his *Spiritual Inrushes*. He declared, "The sun is approaching!" Those around him found this statement puzzling and fell silent. Then my master said, "We do not say, 'The sun is setting,' since our sun will never disappear."

31b Abū 'l-Ghanā'im once told me that the great teacher 'Abd al-Qādir al-Jīlānī declared, "The suns of our forbears have set, yet ours remains in the highest heavens and never sets."

32b Abū 'l-'Atā' once related the following from our great master [Muhammad Wafā']: "You must die at first, to never die later." Upon hearing this, Abū 'l-'Atā' said to himself, "How can this be?" But before I could ask him the meaning of this, he answered, "That is life! That is life! That is life!"

34a One of our sessions was attended by the jurist Abū 'l-Fath al-Qarāfī. Sitting directly in front of him was Abū Ridwān. Abū 'l-Fath began to shift around in an effort to see my master's face. He complained loudly that he could see only my master's turban. Hearing this disruption, my master stopped and asked who was making such a noise. Abū 'l-Fath answered him, accusing Abū Ridwān of being uncooperative. My master then said, "The fronts and backs of our companions are *qiblas*.[13] Their fronts are *qiblas* for those in the session, and their backs are *qiblas* for the people of Paradise."

34a 'Alī related the following in his *Spiritual Inrushes* (*Wāridāt*): "One day I met Shaykh Sirāj ad-Dīn al-Balqīnī, who said to me, 'I used to believe in Shaykh Walī ad-Dīn al-Mawlawī,[14] but no longer.' I replied, 'Why such a change?' He answered, 'I lost faith in him because I grew weak and often despaired with life.' I said to him, 'But you continue to live just fine. And you even held the office of judge in Damascus!'" All of which was true. Then my master said, "Observe the doctor of law; when this poor Sufi [Shaykh Walī ad-Dīn] delivers the whole country to him, he believes, but when he criticizes him, belief disappears." My master then asked him, "What is the reason for your loss of faith in him?" To which he replied, "I met him one day, and he told me that he had seen the Prophet, who had told him such and such." My master noted aside that he wanted to conceal this spiritual state, so he asked, "Did he see the Prophet in his sleep?" To which his answer was, "Although I did not ask him, he did say that this occurred while he was awake." My master said, "I could not tell him that waking visions were only for the spiritual elite. Rather I said that the evidentiary miracles (*mu'jizāt*) of the Prophet are a confirmation of the marvels (*karāmāt*) of the saint. He agreed with this, so I continued, asking him if when the Prophet's eyes were closed in sleep, did his heart not remain awake? He agreed it did. So I noted that perhaps the heart of this saint remained awake and that the Prophet had appeared to it. Then he declared to me, 'By God, you have spoken truthfully! I have recovered my faith in him.'"

35a Once when we had returned to Ruda Island and my master had seated himself, we noticed that Abū 'l-Mashāhid had brought along a lute. He presented himself to my master, seeking his permission to play. At this point, Shaykh Shams ad-Dīn al-Qalyūbī took note and said to him, "What is your opinion [of the appropriateness of] the lute?" To which he replied,

"What lute are you referring to, sir?" Shams ad-Dīn declared that the lute was a stringed instrument, and wondered if everything heard at my master's sessions was lawful. My master replied, "So what do the jurists say about this matter?" He answered, "They say that listening to stringed instruments is forbidden." To this my master said, "We are in complete agreement with them on this point. Some have said, 'I do not listen for the striking of chords, but rather the meaning of the *Spiritual Inrushes* they evoke.'" My master then signaled Shams ad-Dīn to play, which he did, to the great delight of those present.

36a During one of our sessions, I heard my master comment on the Qur'ānic description of Jesus, who said, "I am bringing glad tidings of a messenger who will come after me and whose name will be Ahmad" (61:1). My master said, "The name is Ahmad, but what is its essence? This is a wonderful secret. The 'h' is taken from Noah, the 'm' from Abraham, Moses, and Solomon, and the 'd' from Adam and David. Together these seven are the lords of noble power."[15]

45a I heard him comment on [the Qur'ānic passage 24:35, which describes God as the light of a lamp lit by an oil] that is *neither from the East nor the West*, saying, "This oil is, neither from Jesus nor Moses, but rather from Muhammad the intermediary."

45a He once commented on the passage in the story of Mary [3:37] *Every time (Zakarīya) entered her room (mihrāb)* [he found her supplied with food], explaining that here *mihrāb* means a lofty "room" [and not simply a mosque niche indicating the direction of prayer]. The term is used here to signify that she was always in a state of worship.

45a He once commented on the passage [25:20] *We have sent messengers before you, all of whom ate food and walked through the markets* [like any other person], saying, "These were sent as a mercy to the people in the streets around them, not because they needed to buy anything from the market!"

45b Our master the great teacher said, "Every saint, from this moment until the end of time, borrows from me, either at his beginning or his end." On another occasion he added the following: "He who has come before me is in fact from me, and he who comes after me borrows from me. This spiritual inheritance will convey my secrets, and one of [these inheritors] will reach the Muhammadan station, at which point he will become the Seal of saints." All this the author of the *Marvelous Phoenix: on the Seal of Saints and the Western Sun* [Ibn 'Arabī] made clear, saying, "[This will occur] with the extinction of the *khā* of destiny, and the *jīm* resting on the extinction of all sequence." Further on this, [Ibn 'Arabī] said, "I am most of the saints, following the Day of Judgment."[16]

Know, my brother, that all of his [Muhammad Wafā's] *ahzāb, tawajj-uhāt, adhkār, awrād,* and *ādāb*[17] are insurmountable; that is, there is nothing past them to aim for, nothing beyond them on this path to wish for, and no higher attainment in this realm. Thus the seeker must borrow from him "at his beginning," that is, by transmission of esoteric knowledge (*isnād*), and "at his end" by the echo of substitution.[18]

And know, my brother, that the spirit of this Seal draws its substance from God and is not simply one of the created spirits. His spirit is in fact the substance of all spirits. If it does not know this of itself while it is in its elemental body, that is because of an ignorance that is peculiar to its bodily condition. It is thus an ignorant-knower. It admits of contrary descriptions by juxtaposing knowledge and ignorance; as it is said, the basis of what is described here is as the splendid is to the beautiful [within God]. It [the spirit] has abolished ignorance with knowledge and abolished you as ignorant-knowledge.[19]

NOTES

1. The manuscript can be found in Cairo, Dār al-Kutub al-Misrīya (Tārīkh, 1151), and Paris, Bibiothèque Nationale, no. 1200. For more on the Wafā'īya, see R. McGregor, *Sanctity and Mysticism in Medieval Egypt: The Wafā' Sufi Order and the Legacy of Ibn 'Arabī* (Albany: State University of New York Press, 2004).

2. Ad-Duhā is the 93rd sura of the Qur'ān. The first two verses end with *a*'s, and thus mispronouncing them would ruin the aesthetic of the entire recitation. The Prophet's command to 'Alī, that he "recite," is an allusion to the same command (96:1) from Gabriel to the Prophet, marking the beginning of the revelation of the Qur'ān.

3. This recalls a Hadith popular among Sufis in which God says, "Whosoever shows enmity toward my Friend (*walī*), I shall be at war with him. . . . When I love him, I am his hearing by which he hears, his sight by which he sees, his hand by which he strikes, and his foot with which he walks." For a full translation, see *Forty Hadith Qudsī,* trans. E. Ibrahim and D. Johnson-Davies (Cairo: Dār ash-Shurūq, n.d.), 104.

4. "Their Seal" (*khatm*) refers to the final or ultimate figure in the category of Friends of God. See also note 15 below.

5. The text provided here by 'Alī is preserved in paint on wood panels over his grave today, although it underwent restoration in the eighteenth century. One would expect this text to add up to the date of 807 AH according to Arabic *abjad* calculation [i.e., per the numerical values of the letters of the Arabic alphabet], but it does not.

6. Traditional Arab homes are built around an inner courtyard, and thus, as would have been the case of the Wafā' home, the windows face inward, opening onto the courtyard and with a view of the windows to the other rooms of the house.

7. Sunhūr is near Lake Qārūn in the Fayyoum oasis, about 100 kilometers south of Cairo.

8. On the Ka'ba circling Abū 's-Sa'īd ibn Abī 'l-Khayr (441/1049), see Ibn al-Munawwar, *The Secrets of God's Mystical Oneness (Asrār at-Tawhīd fī Maqāmāt al-Shaykh Abī 'l-Sa'īd)*, trans. J. O'Kane (Costa Mesa, Calif.: Mazda, 1992), 231.

9. A Sufi hospice built by Amir Shaykhū 'l-'Umrānī near the Ibn Tulūn mosque in 756/1355. Thanks to a large endowment, at its height it could house up to seven hundred Sufis and offered courses in all four schools of Islamic law.

10. "Cool and safe" is a quotation from the miracle story (21:69) in which Abraham is thrown into the flames by the unbelievers but emerges unharmed.

11. An area within al-Qarāfa cemetery. See al-Maqrīzī, *Al-Mawā'iz wa 'l-i'tibār*, 4 vols. (London: al-Furqān, 2003) 4/1:172.

12. This Ibn al-Zayyat (814/1412) is most likely the author of the *ziyāra* manual *Al-Kawākib as-sayyāra* and a contemporary of this Wafā' hagiography.

13. *Qiblas* is ritual orientation toward Mecca.

14. *Mawlawī* is the Arabic form of *Mevlevi*, the name of an individual of the Sufi order according to the teachings of Jalāl ad-Dīn Rūmī (672/1273).

15. For the Wafā'īya, cycles of seven are significant. Examples include the seven attributes of God, the seven oft repeated verses of the first sura of the Qur'ān, and the seven cycles associated with seven prophets. See McGregor, *Sanctity and Mysticism in Medieval Egypt*, 115–16.

16. The concept of a Seal of saints (*khatam al-awliyā'*) is well developed in the writings of Ibn 'Arabī. He distinguished between a Seal of Muhammadan sanctity and a Seal of Jesus-like sanctity. Ibn 'Arabī claimed the former position for himself, leaving the latter open, to be filled by a final apocalyptic Seal. The Wafā'īya seem to have modified this concept, focusing on a single final Seal. For more on this concept, see R. McGregor, "From Virtue to Apocalypse: The Understanding of Sainthood in a Medieval Sufi Order," in *Studies in Religion/Sciences Religieuses* (Spring 2002): 168. The passage from Ibn 'Arabī here is rather opaque. The *khā* (letter *kh*) of destiny (*zamān*) might refer to the first letter, *khā*, of *khatm* (Seal); but the *jīm* (letter *j*) and how it relates to the extinction of, literally, "the meanings of the sequences" (*madlūl al-kurūr*) is unclear to me beyond the sense of an extinction (or completion) of the line of saintly esoteric masters by its Seal. I have not been able to locate these passages in Ibn 'Arabī's *Kitāb Khatm al-Walāya*, ed. K. Abbas (Damascus: al-Mada Publishing, 2004). I take Ibn 'Arabī's subsequent claim to be "most of the saints" as a parallel to Muhammad Wafā''s claim to be the source of *walāya* (spiritual authority) for all other saints.

17. All terms for different types of personal devotional prayers: litanies, recollections, "divine office," spiritual attitude/behavior.

18. This saintly seeker is very likely 'Alī Wafā', who drew on his father's sanctity and also replaced him as shaykh.

19. I understand this entire section to be in the voice of 'Alī Wafā', and thus the "great teacher" mentioned at the outset is his father.

PART II

Iran and Afghanistan

. . . . .

Iran and its contemporary neighbor to the east Afghanistan have been home to countless Friends of God. Material on the legendary Baghdad Sufi leader Junayd offers two different perceptions of his importance: it comes from two medieval hagiographical anthologies, the fifth/eleventh-century Arabic *Ornament of God's Friends* by Abū Nuʿaym of Isfahan (in south-western Iran) and the ninth/fifteenth-century Persian *Breaths of Intimacy* by Jāmī. The seventh/thirteenth-century Iranian writer Saʿdī's brief anec-dotes about a variety of early Friends of God provides samples of a blend of poetry and wisdom literature with hagiographical interest. From the four-teenth/twentieth century comes an unusual autobiographical look at two influential "contemporary" Iranian Sufis. And finally, representing Afghanistan is a wondrous tale about a thirteenth/nineteenth-century reli-gious hero and his role in the political challenges of his time.

5 Junayd in the 'Hilyat al-awliyā" and the 'Nafahāt al-uns'

Jawid Mojaddedi

Abū 'l-Qāsim al-Junayd (297/910) was a Sufi leader of Persian origin who spent most of his life in Baghdad, where he became the most celebrated member of the Baghdad school of Sufism. He is presented in the earliest hagiographic collections, compiled by affiliates of or sympathizers with the Baghdad school, as the most highly respected Sufi of his time. The compiler of *The Generations of the Sufis* (*Tabaqāt as-Sūfīya*), Abū 'Abd ar-Rahmān as-Sulamī (412/1021), expressed this view most emphatically by positioning his biography of Junayd at the head of the "second generation" of Sufis and by choosing students of Junayd to head the subsequent generations, beginning with his immediate successor, Abū Muhammad al-Jurayrī (311/924).[1] Junayd's preeminence in the eyes of Sulamī and his contemporaries is evident also from his standing as the most frequently cited authority in the manuals of Sufism written during the same period. The high rank of Junayd as the most important leader of the ninth-century Baghdad school has been maintained by Sufis of later generations up to and including the present.

In view of his importance to posterity, it may seem surprising that Junayd left behind no major writings and that his surviving letters and sermons are not considered remarkable enough to warrant his high rank.[2] It is rather to the first biographers of Junayd that one need turn to understand his importance. Sulamī's summary of Junayd's importance tells us that he was universally accepted and that he had studied jurisprudence sufficiently under respected authorities as to give *fatwās*. Abū Nu'aym al-Isfahānī (430/1038) gives less transparent, poetic introductions to his biographies, but the introduction to that of Junayd stresses in its own way his background in the religious sciences and his ability to win acceptance. These qualities are also illustrated by many of the reports included in al-Isfahānī's biography (e.g., paragraphs H5, H6, and H12, below). From the time of the classification found in *Unveiling of the Veiled* (*Kashf al-mahjūb*), by ʿAlī Hujwīrī (c. 464/1072), Junayd has been commonly identified as the advocate of a "sober" approach to Sufism.[3] His biography in the *Ornament of the Friends of God* (*Hilyat al-awliyāʾ*) already includes material that lends support to this later classification: Junayd appears as an advocate of the "sobriety" (*sahw*) that follows after drunkenness (*sukr*) when he advises other Sufis of his own awareness of higher and less ostentatious experiences that they have yet to reach (e.g., paragraphs H5, H8, H10, and H11, but see also H7). This "sober" approach is also compatible with the image of Junayd as a cautious Sufi who managed to gain acceptance among the wider community of religious authorities. There is, however, no independent evidence to suggest that he was as accomplished in jurisprudence as the hagiographers claim; in view of their general aim to emphasize the traditionalist Sunni credentials of Sufis, their exaggeration of this aspect is unsurprising.

The *Hilyat al-awliyāʾ* is a ten-volume collection of more than 650 biographies that is traditionally presented as the compilation of Abū Nuʿaym al-Isfahānī. Abū Nuʿaym was a Hadith expert and biographer of the Prophet Muhammad whose primary link to Sufism was through his maternal grandfather, ʿAlī ibn Sahl al-Isfahānī (307/920), the most celebrated Sufi of his time from Isfahan. The *Hilya* seems in reality to have been completed by a number of Abū Nuʿaym's students without complete coordination of their efforts. Repeated biographies and breaks in the text due to interpolation are the most obvious signs of the extended history of its composition; other indications include the presence of two alternative accounts of Junayd's death, as well as variants of other anecdotes (see below). While the *Hilya* may have been started before *Generations of the Sufis*, it was certainly completed after that work of the same genre, for it cross-references that work of Sulamī's and takes many extended passages verbatim from it.[4]

Biographies in the *Hilya* are arranged in a loose chronological pattern, beginning with the first four Rightly Guided Caliphs and ending with Sufi associates of Abū Nuʿ aym's grandfather, Ibn Maʿdān. Most of the biographies of individuals remembered primarily as Sufis are found in the final volume, as would be expected for individuals living after the turn of the ninth century. Although the *Hilya* contains six times as many biographies as Sulamī's *Tabaqāt*, this alone does not account for the difference in length of the two volumes; biographies in the *Hilya* are usually several times as long as their counterparts in the other work. The bulk of the narratives in Sulamī's *Tabaqāt* consist of apophthegmata, and for this reason the *Hilya* is a much richer resource.

Abū Nuʿaym's biography of Junayd in the *Hilya* is too long to be presented here in its entirety. Therefore, a selection of significant reports, including all the narratives as well as the introduction and the Hadith transmission, are presented instead. The narratives translated here involve two of the individuals traditionally identified as the teachers of Junayd, namely al-Hārith al-Muhāsibī (243/857) and Sarī as-Saqatī (251/865), with a preference for the former unmistakably expressed. It is worth mentioning that Junayd's biography is the second-longest in the tenth volume of the *Hilya*, the longest being that devoted to al-Hārith al-Muhāsibī. The identity of the teacher of Junayd, who was to hold an important position in subsequent chains of authority, continued to be debated among Sufis, especially after Muhāsibī fell increasingly out of favor (e.g., see paragraph N4 below).

ʿAbd ar-Rahmān Jāmī (898/1492) was a prolific Sufi author based in Herat (present-day Afghanistan), where he was an active member of a branch of the Naqshbandī Sufi order. Although he is best known for his narrative poems, his most celebrated prose work is his biographical collection, the *Breaths of Intimacy* (*Nafahāt al-uns*). This work, completed circa 881/1476, contains approximately six hundred biographies, covering the period from the second/eighth century to the late ninth/fifteenth century, and ordered according to a complicated, mainly chronological arrangement.[5] Its final two groups of biographies are unusual in that they are devoted to poets and Sufi women, respectively. Jāmī used numerous written sources, which he usually identifies. The most significant of these is the work attributed to ʿAbd Allāh Ansārī Harawī (481/1089), entitled *The Generations of the Sufis* (*Tabaqāt as-Sūfiya*)—often mistaken for a Persian translation of as-Sulamī's Arabic work with the same title. Nearly half of the biographies in the *Nafahāt* are based closely on their counterparts in the work of his predecessor from Herat, and constitute about four-fifths of Jāmī's coverage of the period between the ninth and twelfth centuries.[6]

The biography of Junayd is among those based largely on Ansārī's *Tabaqāt*. Although Jāmī redacted the text from that source, he chose to include the comments attributed to Ansārī using his title, *Shaykh al-Islam* (see below). As indicated by the references given by Jāmī, his biography of Junayd also includes material from the chronicle *Mirʾāt al-janān* by ʿAbd Allāh al-Yāfiʿī (768/1367; see selection 3, this volume). The material features the miracle story about Junayd's first teaching session (paragraph N3, below), which appears to have been generated by the Hadith transmission that had become an integral part of the biographical tradition of Junayd in the early eleventh century (H17). Hadith transmissions were increasingly replaced as evidence of legitimacy in hagiographies by miracle stories, and this example epitomizes this general development. Another tendency in the development of biographical traditions that is illustrated below is the preference for extended narratives. Often what were originally separate and unrelated reports became combined in later texts to fulfill the need for longer stories (e.g., compare H2 and H9 with N2).

Junayd's continued importance for Sufis in ninth/fifteenth-century Persia is evident from the organizational framework of the *Nafahāt*, in that Jāmī links all later Sufi lineages back as far as two early common links—Junayd and Abū Yazīd al-Bistāmī (261/874). The latter, who left no writings and remains a fairly obscure historical figure (albeit with extraordinary popularity in medieval Persian literature), is often associated with Junayd; usually he is identified as the individual who represents a type of Sufism that contrasts most with Junayd's teachings. This is the most likely reason why Jāmī chose this pair to establish the authority of all the later Sufi lineages he includes.

TRANSLATION

From Hilyat al-awliyā'

H1. *Junayd ibn Muhammad Junayd*

Among them was the one well-versed in all the sciences, who was supported by the fountains of persuasiveness, illuminated by the purity of certainty, confirmed by sound faith, who possessed a scholar's knowledge of what is found written in the Holy Book, and who employed persuasive discourse that supported what has been revealed and is undoubtedly correct: Abū 'l-Qāsim Junayd ibn Muhammad Junayd. His speech was tied to divine revelation and his explanation clarified the holy guidance. This man surpassed his peers through his rift-healing explanation and his reliance on the appropriate methodology, as well as his persistence in the faithful practice of the religion.[7]

As a Disciple of Sarī as-Saqatī:

H2. Abū 'l-Qāsim Bardān al-Hāwandī[8] said that he heard Junayd say: I came to see Abū 'l-Hasan as-Sarī one day. When I knocked on his door, he asked:

"Who is it?"

I answered: "Junayd."

Then he said: "Enter!"

And so I entered and saw him sitting prepared to welcome me. I had four dirhams with me, so I gave them to him, at which point he said to me:

"Congratulations, for you will prosper! I was in need of these four dirhams and had asked God to send them to me in the hands of a man who will prosper before Him."[9]

H3. Ja'far ibn Muhammad informed us through something he wrote and Muhammad ibn Ibrāhīm related it to me, saying that he heard Abū 'l-Qāsim Junayd ibn Muhammad say: One day I entered before Sarī as-Saqatī and saw that he was unsettled. I said, "Shaykh, I see you are unsettled."

He said, "Just now there was a knock on my door and I said, 'Enter!' A youth (*shābb*) who looked as though he was about the right age for discipleship entered before me and asked me about the meaning of repentance (*tawba*), so I informed him. He then asked me about the condition of repentance so I told him."

Then he said, "That is the meaning of repentance and this is its condition, so what is its essence (*haqīqa*)?"

I said, "The essence of repentance for you is that you do not forget the reason for repentance."

He said, "It is not like that for us."

So I asked him, "What is the essence of repentance for you then?"

He said, "The essence of repentance is that you do not remember the reason for repentance." I am now contemplating his words.

Junayd said: I then responded, "How beautiful his words are!"

Then [Saqatī] said to me, "Junayd, what is the meaning of this?"

I said, "Master, if I am with you in the state of agony and you transfer me from that state to the state of purity, then my remembrance of agony while being in this state of purity would be negligence."

I entered before him on another day and saw him unsettled, so I said, "Shaykh, I notice that you are anxious."

He said, "Yesterday I was in the congregational mosque when a youth stopped before me and said to me, 'Shaykh, the slave knows that God has accepted him!'

"I said, 'He does not know.'

"He said, 'Oh yes he does.'

"And he said once again, 'Oh yes he does.'

"I said to him, 'How does he know?'

"He said, 'If I see that God has held me back from every act of disobedience and made me conform to every act of obedience, then I know that God has accepted me.'"[10]

As a Disciple of Al-Ḥārith Al-Muḥāsibī:

H4. Abū Bakr al-Khawwās[11] said that he heard Junayd ibn Muhammad say: Al-Ḥārith ibn Asad al-Muḥāsibī used to come to our house and say, "Come out for a stroll with me."

I would say to him, "And let you take me away from my seclusion and security against my carnal soul [or ego] to the streets, the realm of wretchedness and lustful sights!"

He would say, "Come out with me and don't be scared!"

So I would go out with him, and it would be as if the street were empty of everything—we would not see anything to dislike!

And whenever I came across Muhāsibī in the place where he would sit, he would say to me, "Ask me something!"

I would tell him, "I do not have a single question to ask you."

He would then say, "Ask me about anything that comes to your mind!"

Questions would then rain down upon me and I would ask him about them. He would answer them for me on the spot and then go to his house and put them into writing.

I used to say often to Hārith, "What about my seclusion and my intimacy? You want to take me out to the vileness of the vision of the people and the streets!"

He would say to me, "How often will you say, 'What about my intimacy and my seclusion!' If half of mankind were to approach me, I would not find any intimacy with them, and if the other half were to keep away from me, I would not feel lonely because of their keeping their distance!"[12]

As a Sufi Authority:

H5. 'Abd al-Wāḥid ibn 'Alwān[13] said that he heard Junayd say in a homily he was addressing to him: "O young man, cling steadfastly to knowledge even if mystical states enter into you, and then knowledge will be your companion, for the states develop within you, then fade away, because God says: *'Those versed in knowledge say, "We believed it; everything is from our Lord"'* (3:7)."[14]

H6. Abū Muhammad al-Jurayrī said that he heard Junayd speak to a man who, while mentioning experiential knowledge (*ma'rifa*), had said: "Those with intimate knowledge of God reach the abandonment of voluntary movements (*tark al-harakāt*) through piety and proximity to God." Junayd responded, "This is the talk of the people who speak of omitting good deeds, and it is a serious error to me—someone who steals and fornicates is better than someone who says this! Those with intimate knowledge of God take good deeds from God and return to Him through them.

If I were to live for another thousand years, I would not reduce my pious deeds in the slightest unless I were to be prevented from doing them. It is the most certain thing I know and the most powerful thing that I have experienced directly."[15]

H7. Ja'far ibn Muhammad informed me through something that he wrote to me, and 'Uthmān ibn Muhammad also told me, that Junayd was asked, "Which is more perfect, the drowning of knowledge ('ilm) in ecstasy (wujūd) or the drowning of ecstasy in knowledge?" He answered, "The drowning of knowledge in ecstasy; those who have knowledge of God can't be compared with those who are filled with His ecstasy."[16]

H8. Hakīm ibn Muhammad[17] said that he was present with Junayd Abū 'l-Qāsim on an occasion when a group were feigning ecstasy during a spiritual audition (samā') that they were listening to while he sat there with his head hanging down. They said to him: "O Abū 'l-Qāsim, we don't see you move at all."

He responded: *"You will see the mountains and reckon that they are firmly fixed, but they will float away like clouds"* [Qur'ān, 27:88].[18]

H9. Muhammad ibn Sa'īd[19] said that he heard Junayd ibn Muhammad, upon being asked what is the essence of gratitude (shukr), say: "Not to make use of His favors for disobedience to Him."[20]

H10. Ja'far informed us, and 'Uthmān also told me about it, saying: I [Ja'far] was walking with Junayd when Shiblī met him and said to him, "Abū 'l-Qāsim, what do you have to say about someone for whom God suffices as attribute, knowledge, and existence?"

He responded, "Abū Bakr, divinity is lofty and lordship is mighty; there are a thousand levels between the eminent of the generation and you, at the first level of which one's self-identity disappears."[21]

H11. He [Ja'far] said, Shiblī stopped before Junayd and said, "What do you have to say, Abū 'l-Qāsim, about someone whose existence is a truth, and not merely in theory?" He responded, "Abū Bakr, between the eminent people and you are seventy steps, the lowest of which is that you forget yourself."[22]

H12. Ja'far ibn Muhammad informed me in writing, and I also heard about it from Muhammad, who said that he heard Junayd ibn Muhammad say: Once, after completing my prayers and lying down to sleep, I perceived a voice saying to me: "Someone is waiting for you at the mosque." I therefore set off and indeed found someone standing in the mosque.

He asked me: "O' Abū 'l-Qāsim, when will the sickness of the soul (nafs) become its cure?"

I answered, "If it opposes its desires, then its sickness is its cure."

He said, "I had said this to my soul, but it said, 'I won't accept it from you until you ask Junayd.' "

I asked, "Who are you?"

He said, "I am one of the jinn, and I have come to you from far off in the West."[23]

H13. Ibrāhīm ibn ʿUthmān[24] said that he heard Junayd ibn Muhammad say: I went into the desert in the middle of the year as an obligation of full trust in God (*tawakkul*). After several days of walking, I reached an oasis, where I performed my ablutions and filled my flask with water. When I was about to perform the ritual prayer, I saw a youth approaching who was dressed like a merchant who has just left his house to go to the bazaar or one returning home from the bazaar. He greeted me, and so I asked the youth:

"Where have you come from?"

He answered, "From Baghdad."

So I asked, "When did you set off from Baghdad?"

He said, "Yesterday."

I was astonished at this, for I had walked for several days before reaching the same spot. He sat down and we spoke to each other. Then he took out something to eat from his sleeve.

I said, "Give me some of what you are eating." He placed in my hand a bitter gourd, and I ate it. It tasted to me instead like dates. The youth then went off while I stayed behind a bit longer.

After I entered Mecca, I started performing the circumambulation when my robe was suddenly pulled from behind. When I looked around, I saw a youth with very rough skin, wearing a loincloth around his waist and over his shoulder. I said to him:

"Increase my experiential knowledge of God (*maʿrifa*)."

He said, "I am the same youth who gave you the bitter gourd to eat."

I asked him, "What is your rank?"

He answered, "O' Abū 'l-Qāsim, they scattered us and let us fall, saying 'Cling fast!' (2:256)."[25]

H14. I heard Abū Bakr Muhammad ibn Ahmad al-Mufīd say that he was present with Junayd one day when his disciples asked him: "O master, when will God approach His slave?" He turned his attention away from them and did not answer. They pestered him about this, but he was very sensitive and did not want his answer to displease anybody, so he turned to them and said, "I am amazed at the person who stands before his Lord without realizing His presence, and demands that He approach from this position!"[26]

Junayd's Death:

H15. Abū ʿAbd Allāh ad-Dārimī[27] said that he heard Abū Bakr al-ʿAtawī say: "I was with Junayd when he died; he recited the whole of the Qurʾān, then, starting from Sūrat al-Baqara, he recited seventy verses and died."[28]

H16. Abū Saʿīd ibn al-Aʿrābī[29] said that he heard Abū Bakr al-ʿAttār say: "I was present with Junayd, Abū 'l-Qāsim, on his death, amongst a group of our companions." He said, "Junayd was praying while sitting, and he would bend his legs when he wanted to prostrate himself. He continued like this until they became numb. It became difficult for him to move his legs, so he stretched them out. One of his friends amongst those who were present at that time—he was called al-Bassāmī—saw him in that condition. Abū 'l-Qāsim's legs had swollen, so he asked, 'Abū 'l-Qāsim, what is this?'

"He replied, 'These are God's blessings; God is the greatest!'

"Once he had completed his prayer, Abū Muhammad al-Jurayrī said to him, 'Abū 'l-Qāsim, if only you would lie down.'

"So he responded, 'Abū Muhammad, this is the time of God's kindness. God is the greatest!' That remained his state until he died."[30]

Hadith Transmission:

H17. Among [Junayd's] Hadith transmissions is the following, which was related to us by Abū ʿAbd Allāh Muhammad ibn ʿAbd Allāh an-Niyāsābūrī al-Hāfiz, who said that Bukayr ibn Ahmad as-Sūfī told him in Mecca that Junayd Abū 'l-Qāsim as-Sūfī told him that al-Hasan ibn ʿArafa told him that Muhammad ibn Kathīr al-Kūfī told him on the authority of ʿAmr ibn Qays al-Mallāʾī on the authority of ʿAtiya on the authority of Abū Saʿīd al-Khudrī [74/693], who said:

The Messenger of God said: "Beware of the miraculous insight (*firāsa*) of the believer, for he sees by the light of God." He then read the Qurʾanic verse "There are indeed signs in that for those who can read them (al-mutawassimīn)" (15:75), saying instead, "those who have insight (al-mutafarrisīn)."

Something similar to this was related to us by Muhammad ibn ʿAbd Allāh ibn Saʿīd, who said that ʿAbdān ibn Ahmad told him that ʿAbd al-Hamīd ibn Bayān told him that Muhammad ibn Kathīr told him that ʿAmr ibn Qays told him on the authority of ʿAtiya on the authority of Abū Saʿīd al-Khudrī, who heard it from the Messenger of God.[31]

From the Nafahāt al-uns

Introduction:

N1. The chief of the sect (*sayyid at-tāʾifa*), Junayd al-Baghdādī.

He belongs to the second generation. His *kunya* [family name] is Abū 'l-Qāsim, while his *laqab*s ["trade names" or nicknames] are Qawārīrī, Zajjāj, and Khazzāz. He was called Qawārīrī and Zajjāj because his father used to sell glassware. According to Yāfiʿī's *Tā'rīkh, Khazzāz* is written with a dotted khā' and a doubled and repeated zā'. He was called Khazzāz because he traded in silk. His family origins are from Nihavand, and the place where he was born and brought up is Baghdad.

He followed the law school of Abū Thawr, Shāfiʿī's foremost student. It has also been said that he followed the law school of Sufyān Thawrī. He was a companion and student of Sarī Saqatī, Hārith Muhāsibī, and Muhammad Qassāb. He is one of the leaders and chiefs of this group [the Sufis]. Everyone links himself back to [Junayd], such as Kharrāz, Ruwaym, Shiblī, and others. Abū 'l-ʿAbbās ʿAtā says, "Our leader in this science, and the authority to whom we refer and whom we imitate, is Junayd."

The caliph of Baghdad said to Ruwaym, "Hey, ill-mannered one!" He responded, "How can I be ill mannered if I have spent half a day in the company of Junayd?" This means that anyone who has spent half a day in his company cannot be ill mannered—how then for longer.

Shaykh Abū Jaʿfar Haddād said, "If intellect were a man it would be in the form of Junayd."

The following has been said: "There have been three peerless ones from that generation: Junayd in Baghdad, Abū ʿAbd Allāh Jallā' in Syria, and Abū ʿUthmān Hīrī in Nishapur."

[Junayd] passed away in the year 297/909, according to the *Kitāb at-Tabaqāt* and *ar-Risālat al-Qushayrīya*, but according to Yāfiʿī's *Tā'rīkh*, he died in the year 298/910. It has also been said that it was in the year 299/911. God knows best.[32]

N2. One day in his childhood, Junayd was playing with children. Sarī Saqatī said, "Hey lad, what do you have to say about thankfulness (*shukr*)?"

He said, "Thankfulness is that you do not make use of his favors in acts of disobedience against him."

Sarī said, "I fear very much that your share of fortune lies only in your tongue."

Junayd said, "I was always frightened of that remark until I went before him one day, having brought something that [Sarī] needed; he said, 'Rejoice, for I had requested from God that he send this to me in the hands of someone who would be successful!'"[33]

N3. Junayd said: Sarī told me, "Hold a session and speak to the people!"

I doubted my carnal soul (*nafs*) and did not consider it worthy enough until I saw the Messenger of God in a dream on a Thursday night. He said, "Speak to the people!"

I woke up and went to the door of Sarī's house before dawn. I knocked on the door. He said, "You did not judge me to be correct until you were told directly."

Then, at the break of day, I held a session and started to speak. News spread that "Junayd is speaking." A Christian youth, who was not wearing the usual clothing of Christians, stood at the periphery of the meeting. He asked, "Shaykh, what is the meaning of the saying of the Messenger of God, 'Beware of the miraculous insight (*firāsa*) of the believer, for he sees by the light of God?'" Junayd said, "I hung my head down for a while, then I lifted it up and said, 'Embrace Islam, for the time for you to become a Muslim has arrived!'"

Imam Yāfi'ī says, "People think that there is one miracle by Junayd in this, but I say that there are two: firstly, his knowledge of the young man's infidelity; secondly, his knowledge that he would become a Muslim at that time."[34]

N4. Junayd also said, "People imagine that I am the disciple of Sarī Saqatī, but I am the disciple of Muhammad 'Alī Qassāb." I asked him, "What is Sufism?"

He answered, "I don't know other than noble qualities made manifest by the Noble One (*al-Karīm*) at a noble time through a noble man from among a group of noble men.'"

The Shaykh al-Islam [Ansārī] said, "These are subtle and lovely words, because he said at first, 'I don't know' but then said, 'noble qualities that the Noble One makes manifest through a noble man from among a group of noble men.' Only God knows what those characteristics are."[35]

N5. Someone said to Junayd, "I have found the masters of Khurasan to believe that there are three veils: first the veil of creation, second the lower world, and third the carnal soul." He answered, "These are the veils for the hearts of ordinary men. The elite are veiled by three different things: vision of one's own deeds, looking for the reward for them, and vision of God's bounty."

The Shaykh al-Islam (Ansārī) said, "The heart of whoever sees his own deed is veiled from God. Also veiled is the one who seeks a reward for it, and the one who turns from the Bestower of bounty to the bounty."[36]

NOTES

1. On the organizational framework of as-Sulamī's work, see J. Mojaddedi, *The Biographical Tradition in Sufism: The Tabaqāt Genre from al-Sulamī to Jāmī* (Richmond: Routledge-Curzon, 2001), ch. 1.

2. This material has been published in a bilingual edition, H. A. Abdel-

Kader, *The Life, Personality and Writings of Junayd* (London: Gibb Memorial Series, 1976).

3. See J. Mojaddedi, "Getting Drunk with Abu Yazid or Staying Sober with Junayd: The Creation of a Popular Typology of Sufism," *Bulletin of the School of Oriental and African Studies* 66, no. 1 (2003): 1–13.

4. The text used in this translation is Abū Nuʿaym al-Isfahānī, *Hilyat al-awliyāʾ*, 10 vols. (Cairo: Maktabat al-Khānjī: Matbaʿat as-Saʿāda, 1932–38). For further information about the history of the compilation of the *Hilya*, see J. Mojaddedi, *The Biographical Tradition in Sufism*, ch. 2; R.G. Khoury, "Importance et authenticité de texts de *Hilyat al-awliyāʾ*," *Studia Islamica* 46 (1977): 73–113.

5. For further information about the organizational framework of Jāmī's work, see J. Mojaddedi, *The Biographical Tradition in Sufism*, ch. 6.

6. The text used for this translation is ʿAbd ar-Rahmān Jāmī, *Nafahāt al-uns*, ed. Mahmūd ʿAbidī (Tehran: Intishārāt-i Ittilāʿāt, 1992).

7. *Hilya*, X, 255.5–9.

8. The transmitters listed in the *isnād* before al-Hāwandi are al-Jahdami and Muhammad ibn al-Hasan.

9. *Hilya*, X, 270.22–271.2.

10. *Hilya*, X, 274.9–15.

11. The transmitter listed in the *isnād* before Abū Bakr al-Khawwās is Abū ʾl-Hasan Ahmad ibn Muhammad ibn Miqsam.

12. *Hilya*, X, 255.18–256.3.

13. The transmitters listed in the *isnād* before ʿAbd al-Wāhid ibn ʿAlwān are a-Husayn ibn Mūsā and Abū Nasr al-Tūsī.

14. *Hilya*, X, 257.7–11.

15. *Hilya*, X, 278.4–10.

16. *Hilya*, X, 275.18–21.

17. The transmitter listed in the *isnād* before Ibn Muhammad is ʿUthmān ibn Muhammad al-ʿUthmānī.

18. *Hilya*, X, 271.6–9.

19. The transmitter listed in the *isnād* before Muhammad ibn Saʿīd is Abū ʾl-Hasan ibn Miqsam.

20. *Hilya*, X, 267.21–23.

21. *Hilya*, X, 267.4–7.

22. *Hilya*, X, 270.19–21.

23. *Hilya*, X, 274.24–275.1.

24. The transmitters listed in the *isnād* before Ibn ʿUthmān are ʿAbd al-Wāhid ibn Muhammad al-Istakhrī Abu al-Azhar and Abu Nasr Muhammad ibn Ahmad ibn Hārūn.

25. *Hilya*, X, 275.5–17.

26. *Hilya*, X, 268.16–20.

27. The transmitter listed in the *isnād* before Abū ʿAbd Allāh ad-Dārimī is Muhammad ibn al-Husayn (as-Sulamī).

28. *Hilya*, X, 264.1–3.

29. The transmitter listed in the *isnād* before Abū Saʿīd ibn al-Aʿrābī is ʿAbd al-Munʿim ibn ʿUmar.

30. *Hilya*, X, 281.11–18.

31. *Hilya*, X, 281.22–282.4

32. *Nafahāt*, 79.7–80.2.

33. *Nafahāt*, 80.3–7.

34. *Nafahāt*, 80.8–18. The scene described here is depicted in figure 7, as well as in color on the cover of the paperback edition of this anthology's companion monograph, *Friends of God* (Berkeley: University of California Press, 2008).

35. *Nafahāt*, 81.5–7.

36. *Nafahāt*, 82.2–5.

6 Saʻdī's Earthly Vision of Sainthood in the 'Bustān' and the 'Gulistān'

Fatemeh Keshavarz

Friends of God are often associated with the heavenly realm. They are extraordinary and can do extraordinary things. Persian popular and hagiographical literatures are peopled with such striking figures capable of miracles, intercession with the divine, and acts of boundless generosity. The seventh/thirteenth-century Persian poet and ethicist Saʻdī had a different vision of sainthood, however, one humorous, earthy, and personal enough for modern readers to relate to. What is more, Saʻdī's anecdotes about saints are encoded into vibrant and lyrical moments interspersed in his works. Regrettably, Saʻdī's reputation as a moralist has led modern critics to overlook the humor and lyricism in much of the poet's work including these anecdotes. The selection here offers a glimpse into this earthly heaven.

Muslih ad-Dīn Saʻdī of Shiraz (c. 692/1291) is the writer par excellence of the short lyric poem known as the *ghazal*, and one of the most colorful figures in premodern Persian poetry. His *Bustān* (*The Orchard*) and *Gulistān* (*The Rose Garden*) embody ethical/mystical anecdotes, typically brief, designed to prepare journeyers for progress on the spiritual path while honing their everyday practical skills. The down-to-earth humor in these anecdotes is an indication of Saʻdī's appreciation for the inseparability of the spiritual from practical wisdom. The wide popular

Figure 4 *(opposite).* "Saʻdī Visits an Indian Temple," by Shaykh Zāda. From manuscript of Saʻdī's *Bustān.* Overpainting attributed to Bishndas for Mughal Emperor Jahāngīr (r. 1605–27), c. 1531–32. Ink, opaque watercolor, and gold on paper, 23.1 × 13.6 cm (9⅛ × 5⅜ in.). Harvard University Art Museums, Arthur M. Sackler Museum, Gift of Philip Hofer in memory of Frances L. Hofer, 1979.20.C. Photo Imaging Department © President and Fellows of Harvard College.

reception of these works, in the literary tradition as well as in daily prov-
erbs and the like, point to Saʻdī's success in winning approval for this dual
purpose from his vast Persian-speaking readership. At the same time, the
poet's works are exquisite examples of pre-modern Persian poetry, and a
rich source of information about the environment in which he lived and
worked.

As colorful as Saʻdī himself are the Friends of God who appear frequently in the *Bustān* and the *Gulistān*. They are learned, witty, enter-
prising, practical, and at the same time, accessible. They provide flashes
of a vibrant pious subjectivity presented in these works as solutions to
the problem of life—social, individual, this-worldly, and otherwise. These
saints teach humility to many a smug ruler and commoner, show pity for
the rich and the destitute alike, and offer generosity as the most desired
mode of interaction with fellow humans. In many ways, they are ordinary, flawed, and susceptible to error. Their advantage is a corrective self-
awareness that helps them recognize—and remedy—personal shortcomings. If they appear larger than life, it is often due to our own inadequate
understanding of what they are all about. For their true greatness is in the
striking simplicity of the message they have to deliver. We are told, for
example, that "in times long gone, in the hands of saints, stone turned into
gold." Taking the testimony literally reduces the reported marvel to a plea
for suspending rational judgment and falling for superstition. The true
meaning, however, is remarkably simple: "If you do not want more than
what you need, to you a chunk of gold and a piece of stone are the same."[1]
The miracle is there to be sure; only, it is located not in the ability to
physically transform objects but rather in the equally complicated process
of altering one's perception of them.

Helping ordinary mortals to develop their version of this world-altering
subjectivity is the most prominent responsibility of God's Friends. Among
the various pedagogical tools they use are short and memorable anecdotes
sweetened with poetic charm. Another tool is gentle—or sharp—humor,
at times moving beyond surprise into the realm of shock. Take the example of the tyrannical ruler of Iraq Hajjāj ibn Yūsuf (no doubt a prototype
for many), who is given the chance to hear a Friend's opinion about his
governing style. The encounter occurs in the *Gulistān* where Saʻdī tells
us about the governor's desire for the blessings of a certain saint whose
every wish was believed to be granted by God. "Please say a prayer for
me!" requests Hajjāj. "O God! Please take his life!" the venerated saint
complies. "What kind of a prayer is that?" objects a startled Hajjāj. "This is
a prayer that would serve both you and everyone subjected to your rule,"

answers the saint. The two verses that follow the anecdote blend the voices of Saʿdī and of the saint. In a simple and clear tone, they serve the twofold purpose of restating the point and generalizing it beyond Hajjāj to include every despot:

> You who injure those serving under you
> How long will you be able to carry on with the charade?
> What good is ruling the world to someone like you?
> Death serves you better because it ends the hurtful deed.[2]

In the *Bustān* and the *Gulistān*, Friends of God enforce each other's thoughts and suggestions by providing variations on frequently evoked themes. The death wish articulated in the above story finds a more light-hearted variation in the anecdote that follows it. "Which of the ritual acts of worship is best to perform?" a tyrannical king inquires of a saint. "For you," responds the saint, "a daytime nap is the best act of worship, for it protects people from your tyranny!"[3]

The beauty and humor in these anecdotes notwithstanding, one might wonder if such speaking truth to power would yield any real results. Saʿdī is a man of this world, widely traveled and aware of social ills. He knows it is impractical to expect tyrants simply see the errors of their ways and correct them. He also knows that for every tyrant there are thousands of subjects who support the undesirable and unjust deeds. Saʿdī's saints, therefore, do more than appeal to the conscience of the powerful. They acknowledge the complexity of the social scene by addressing courtiers and even ordinary citizens who surround such figures and form the basis of their power. Here the teaching method is gentler. Instead of having the outspoken Friend issue a death sentence to Hajjāj, Saʿdī introduces the masses to an introspective holy personage. This one is not an unnamed figure but one whose iconic presence likely to resonate with many readers. And he is not there merely to criticize corrupt power but also to provide a new and personal perspective on the nature of the true sovereign. A vizier visits the celebrated Egyptian Sufi Dhū ʾn-Nūn and asks for his blessings. "I am busy serving the king day and night," he explains by way of intro-duction, "hoping for his favor and fearful of his punishments." Dhūʾn-Nūn says tearfully, "Would that I worshiped God Almighty in this way, for I would then be a true saint!"[4]

Despite their candid manner and, at times, admonishments, Saʿdī's saints often appreciate the limits of ordinary people and are compassionate toward them. Even wrongdoing is often viewed as a result of such short-comings and worthy of forgiveness. The holy man whose house is robbed is one example. The robber keeps looking, but there is little in the house to take. Feeling sorry for the frustrated intruder, the holy man quietly moves the mat on which he is sleeping to a spot where the thief will notice it and thus not leave the house empty-handed. In fact, one might describe this anecdote as an ontological exploration of the concept of sainthood. It is more concerned to awaken those convinced of their own holiness than poor men tempted to commit theft. Saʿdī's own voice is heard once more: do not see yourself "a man on God's path" unless you can have indiscriminate mercy even on your enemies.[5]

Through a moving anecdote that involves the celebrated Sufi saint of Baghdad Shiblī, Saʿdī tells us that this compassion is not really indiscriminate unless it extends to all life forms, even as small and seemingly insignificant as the ant. Compassion for ants is more powerful because it is expressed by Shiblī, a Sufi saint usually known for his strong and assertive personality:

> Hear now the true nature of good men
> If you are lucky, and follow their example.
> Shiblī bought some wheat from the wheat seller and
> Carried it on his back all the way to the village.
> There he looked and saw an ant among the grains
> Running restless in all directions.
> He pitied the ant so much he could not sleep that night
> And the next day returned it to its house.
> It is unkind, he thought, to let this injured creature
> Be displaced so far away from home.[6]

Once again, to conclude the anecdote, Saʿdī's voice enters the discourse and reinforces that of Shiblī: If you wish to live in peace, make sure you help others have the same experience.[7]

One of the most attractive traits in Saʿdī's saints and holy figures is their down-to-earth humanity. There is almost nothing extraordinary about them except an uncanny ability to recognize and value their own ordinariness. In other words, they know that stones can turn into gold if perceptions of wealth are altered. Like most skilled storytellers, Saʿdī understands that saintly qualities (including ordinariness) are best expressed in the saint's own words. In the *Bustān* and the *Gulistān*, these figures speak and confess to their shortcomings frequently. The confessions are compelling because they do not flow from exaggerated humility or self-flagellation in the hope of forgiveness. Rather, they are simple anecdotes illustrating concrete examples of inadequacy on the saint's part. Here is one from the prophet Jacob regarding his years-long lack of awareness of his son

Joseph's whereabouts. Note that the prophet is not named and is referred to instead as "the one who lost his child." In this way, Saʿdī underlines the ontological significance of this tremendous suffering and at the same time highlights the ordinariness of Jacob's helplessness:

> The one who lost his child was once asked:
> You are a bright-natured and wise old soul.
> How come you sensed the scent of his [your child's] shirt from Egypt,
> But did not see him in Canaan at the bottom of the well?
> [Jacob] answered: Our condition is that of a flash of lightening
> Appearing one moment and disappearing the next.
> Some days we mount our heavenly steed,
> Others, we do not see much beyond our footsteps.[8]

In this scheme of things, humility is the opposite of self-flagellation. It is an understanding of ups and downs, a kind of momentary awareness of one's shortcomings and strengths. Rope walkers, no matter how short the walk, must balance the euphoria of being in heaven and the fear of falling into the abyss. It is a much needed skill for being in the world.

Saʿdī displays this balance very well in a beautiful and moving piece about the medieval Khorasani Sufi master Bāyazīd of Bistam. First, a word about Bāyazīd. This is a figure resonant among Persian readers through ʿAttār's poetic and powerful telling of his life story in the *Tadhkirat al-awliyā'* and frequent allusions in other Persian sources to his unconventional behavior and utterances.[9] ʿAttār's Bāyazīd is observant of people and attentive to his surroundings. "I went into the open desert," he once observes. "Love had poured [down] and the earth was moist. As one's feet sink into snow, my feet sank into love."[10] The same Bāyazīd says to a young follower who wants a piece of his sheepskin coat for blessing, "It won't do you any good if you pull my own skin over yourself unless you do what I do."[11] That is, on this earth, which Bāyazīd views as showered with love, living a decent life is still a skill that one needs to learn and put into daily use. And yet this does not entail following the tradition blindly. Bāyazīd has a reputation for being thrown out of the city of Bistam more than once for offences such as eating in public during the month of fast and speaking in the manner in which only God can speak: "Glory to me! How great is my state!"[12]

Still, for ʿAttār, Bāyazīd is, for the most part, airborne. In the *Tadhkirat al-awliyā'*, the saint's prophetic nocturnal journey—the equivalent of what Jacob referred to as "riding the heavenly steed"—is described in great detail.[13] Saʿdī is well aware of Bāyazīd's lofty position, as well as his assertive character. Indeed, in the third of his five sermons, he alludes to

the saint's tendency to display spiritual triumph and glory during uplift-
ing moments of the journey by calling him *tāvūs-i 'ārifān*, "the peacock
among the knowers of God."[14] However, in the rare longer anecdotes, Sa'dī
chooses to bring the reader down to earth. In these, Bāyazīd is the quiet and
introspective master who suggests that one's ego is in a safer place when
facing an adversary than when subjected to the flattery of a disciple.[15]

This Bāyazīd misses no opportunity to teach his followers a lesson in
humility. One such occasion arises, in the *Bustān*, one morning when
the master steps out of the public bath. The opening line in this anecdote
tells us it is early morning. And since clarity and cleanliness are central
to understanding the point here, we have the brightness of a vivid dawn
(*sahargāh*) in the background. Not only that, it is the dawn of the '*īd*,
the new-year festival—perhaps *nowrūz*—when all Iranians, whether
Zoroastrian, Jew, or Muslim, clean their houses spotless. As if this is not
enough, our saintly figure Bāyazīd has just been bathing, which implies
that he is wearing clean clothes:

> I've heard that one day on an early morning during the time of 'Īd
> Bāyazīd stepped out of the public bath.
> Suddenly, without warning, a basinful of ashes
> Was dumped on his head from a certain building.
> The master wiped his face with his hands,
> His hair and turban were soiled and disheveled.
> "Only ashes?" Said the master, "How can I complain?
> I had thought I deserved fire all this time."

And Sa'dī's voice rings in the background, "Those who were really great
never saw themselves."[16]

NOTES

1. Sa'dī, *Kulliyāt*, ed. Muhammad Ali Forughi (Tehran: Amīr Kabīr, 1366/
1987), 339.
2. Ibid., 47.
3. Ibid.
4. Ibid., 63.
5. Ibid., 71.
6. 'Attār, *Tadhkirat al-awliyā'*, ed. Muhammad Isti'lami (Tehran: Zavvar,
1382/2003), 614.
7. Sa'dī, *Kulliyāt*, 264.
8. Ibid., 75.
9. For Bāyazīd's anecdote in the *Tadhkirat al-awliyā'*, see 'Attār, *Tadhkirat
al-awliyā'*, 160–210.
10. Ibid., 183.

11. Ibid., 187.
12. Ibid., 207.
13. Ibid., 202.
14. Saʿdī, *Kulliyāt,* 904.
15. Ibid., 331.
16. Ibid., 298.

7 Ostad Elahi and Hajjī Niʿmat

Master and Disciple, Father and Son

James W. Morris

> What I learned from my master Hajjī, in relation to what I learned and acquired through my own efforts after him, is like a single seed of wheat compared to a whole donkey-load of wheat. All the same, that single grain of wheat was very influential for me.[1]

In recent years, the spiritual figure of Ostad Elahi (Ustād Ilāhī, 1313/1895–1394/1974) has become more and more visible globally, thanks to the increasing availability both of recordings of his musical performances and of translations and other studies of his spiritual and philosophical writings and teachings.[2] In contrast, the remarkable spiritual personality and voluminous writings of his own father, Hajj Niʿmatullāh Jayhūnābādī (1288/1871–1339/1920)—or Hajjī Niʿmat, as he is more familiarly referred to in many of the sayings translated here—have generally remained unknown, outside his original cultural milieu, to all but a handful of scholarly specialists in the religious life and cultures of Iranian Kurdistan.[3] Ostad Elahi himself, in his mature reflections on his own spiritual development, placed a special emphasis on the wider significance of his own personal transition from the traditional, relatively closed and esoteric forms of spiritual training he received in his early years, to the more challenging and universal spiritual lessons he came to discover in the course of his subsequent years of active professional engagement as a respected jurist, and later as a writer and teacher communicating with ever-wider circles of students and seekers from many different cultures and backgrounds. Indeed his characteristic later focus on the richness and practical importance of a spiritual life rooted in and growing out of the constant ethical challenges and responsibilities of our everyday family and professional life—an approach that pointedly highlights the intrinsic universality and cross-cultural dimensions of the processes of spiritual growth—is already quite visible in his own parenthetical personal comments on several of the dramatic childhood incidents and stories included here.

Within the context of this anthology, the handful of sayings translated here have been selected to illustrate three broad dimensions of spiritual and religious life, perspectives that can facilitate our understanding of related phenomena throughout much of the Islamic world and beyond. First, on the most apparent and outward level, these stories provide an invaluable, compelling insider perspective on forms of traditional spiritual and devotional practice, with their distinctively ascetical and popular charismatic emphases, that we tend to encounter for many centuries throughout the global Islamic community.

Second, Ostad Elahi's own later mature judgments on many of his childhood experiences and traditional local practices immediately highlight the dramatic worldwide transition, throughout the twentieth century, from inherited religious and social forms—deeply rooted in centuries of agrarian life-structures and tribal cultures—to radically new, increasingly global conditions of social, economic, and cultural life. What we encounter here, in view of the larger context profusely elaborated in the rest of Ostad Elahi's voluminous personal teachings in his *Traces of the Truth (Āthār al-haqq)*, is not just an autobiographical "memoir." Instead, in the face of these radically new historical circumstances, we are asked to join in this personal reflection on the practical dilemmas posed by these historical transformations and on the opportunities for creative spiritual responses that Elahi himself went on to elaborate in his books and later oral teachings.

Third, when we ponder this handful of selected sayings, it provides us with a uniquely intimate and revealing account of the complex, lifelong inner relationship between an authentic spiritual guide and a student. The fifty or more years intervening between each of these sayings and the earlier childhood events they typically recount means that in most of these cases we are being offered a privileged insight into the most fundamental processes of spiritual growth: into the constant, lifelong active interplay between the workings of grace and inspiration on one hand and, on the other, significant experiences, ongoing reflection, derivation of underlying principles, and the practical testing and further elaboration of those principles in the unique crucible of each seeker's own life. Of course, in this case both the master and the disciple—and the opening saying below (*Āthār al-haqq* [AH], 1853) pointedly reminds us of the problematic nature of such distinctions—are themselves anything but typical. But the exceptional nature and vivid personalities of these two extraordinary teachers serves only to underscore the particular relevance and potential significance of the perennial lessons and potential insights these stories are intended to convey.

In conclusion, it is essential to point out a few of the distinctive qualities of Ostad Elahi's sayings collected in the two immense Persian volumes of

Āthār al-haqq, from which these selections are drawn. These qualities distinguish that recent work from most earlier hagiographies and *malfūzāt* collections that readers may encounter in this anthology or in other translations. To begin with, Ostad Elahi's sayings here (and throughout *Āthār al-haqq*) are marked by a directness, an intimate, familiar—indeed often highly colloquial—tone that reflects their original context within the flowing, informal give-and-take of oral instruction and personal questions and answers.[4] These English translations manage, I hope, to preserve at least some of that natural, relaxed, and colloquial style. Second, as students of Ostad Elahi's writings quickly discover, the apparent simplicity of many of these stories is indeed only apparent. For these sayings are meant to unfold their deeper meanings and complexities only upon repeated reflection, and the discovery of their depths normally depends on the right spiritual catalyst that can be provided, at the appropriate moment, only by similar experiences, inspirations, and testing situations within each reader's own individual experience.

Finally, there is an intentional and richly rewarding spiritual resonance among these different sayings, such that readers quickly discover that what is openly recounted or explained in one place tends to provoke further thought, questioning, and eventual insight through its relation to other, often originally scattered teachings. Bringing together a small number of sayings related to the limited themes of the master-disciple (and father-son) relationship thus intensifies and highlights that inherent thematic resonance, one far richer and more complex whenever we turn back to the vast range of sayings included in the original volumes of *Āthār al-haqq.* All this is beautifully summed up in one of Ostad Elahi's final reminders to his students, from the very end of his earthly life:

> I have not passed over any subject in silence: all that is needed is a grasp of the question and the aspiration [to understand]. And that aspiration comes from the angelic soul. In these things I say to you my purpose is not to recount stories, but to give you sound advice. I am not able to tell someone something until after I've put it into practice and tried it out for myself. . . . I have spoken with each person to the extent that he could understand. But I've still not told anyone all there is in my heart. [AH, 2074]

TRANSLATION

Selected Sayings from Chapters 23 and 24 of Āthār al-haqq (vol. 1)

When I was a little boy, between four and six, my father jokingly—or so it seemed—said to me: "Are you my daddy, or am I your daddy?" Then he said: "You're *my* daddy." I said: "No, you're my daddy," and we went on repeating that. [1853]

In my childhood I had a skinny, slender build. I was between six and seven when my father received his enlightenment. My father had twelve disciples, and during the first year they met in secret. From the age of six I took part in the gatherings of my father and those twelve persons, and I was the focus of their spiritual love. As soon as the *dhikr* began, I spun around like a top, and my long hair created a spectacle that filled them all with enthusiasm. Sometimes the *dhikr* would last for several hours, and I would spin around the whole time. At the age of nine I entered the training field of spiritual exercises. [1855]

During the first period, when [my father's disciples] were only twelve dervishes, what a wonderful world [of spiritual states] they all had! They would communicate with each other [spiritually] over great distances. But if I had been responsible for [guiding] them, I wouldn't have allowed them to be distracted and excited by such things: that is precisely why none of them reached perfection. . . . [1776]

. . . My father's dervishes were all completely dependent upon him, which is why only one or two of them reached the state of spiritual perfection. As for [the students of] my school, they must stand on their own feet and take responsibility for themselves, although we also watch out for them at a distance, because otherwise they wouldn't be able to reach perfection. In my opinion, there's no punishment worse than having to come back another time [on earth]: they come back dumb, and they have to learn everything all over again from the very beginning. . . . [1795]

During the time of my father, there were 1,145 men dervishes and five hundred women dervishes [among his followers]. . . . All of the men wore white robes, and the women likewise wore long white skirts, and they often sang this hymn: "O' you ones wearing white, you ones wearing white: drink from the [heavenly waters of] Kawthar, O' you ones wearing white!"

. . . While we were living in Sahneh, in the evenings they would gather to perform *dhikr* at the [beautiful park and stream of] Darband, outside Sahneh.[5] They would set out in procession from town, with the [traditional dervish] hatchet over their shoulders and their long hair flowing in the wind, singing the *dhikr* "God and Our Master ʿAlī" while they walked along. . . . All of them were handsome and attractive. It was through God's power that no one bothered them then—because that was during the Qajar period, when because of the assassination of the king, even if only four people were to gather together, the authorities would immediately come to break them up. Yet at that time no one ever came to disturb this immense assembly. [1800]

At the time when my father and I used to go to the shrine in the valley [of Darband] above Sahneh, it was customary for each of the four neighborhoods in that town to give a cow for an offering. We would perform the sacrifice, and then the poor people [of the town] would come and eat their fill before returning home. Even though it was others who actually collected the money to buy the cows, now I realize that the spiritual benefit I gained from that deed was greater than the rewards I've earned by some of my own acts of spiritual discipline. Because in this case I was the means through which a group of people who didn't have enough money to buy meat for themselves were able to eat some and to enjoy the feast. If my father and I hadn't gone there, no one would have made those offerings. As a result of our reputation these events could take place, and many people benefited from them. [2059]

I have a little notebook of about a hundred pages in which Hajjī [my father] wrote down all his intimate prayers (*munājāt*). When I was a child, every Thursday night I had to read them all through completely before I went to bed. I began reading every Thursday night after supper and continued until it was late. [1860]

What a tremendous effect these words of my father have on me, each time that I remember them! When he would wake up in the night for his personal prayers, he would always begin: "O Lord God, all the people are sleeping: only You are awake. . . . " Then he would continue with his personal prayers, which were always in Kurdish. [1819]

One day when I was little, my father told me: "Go on, get out of here!" An old woman who was there said to me: "What did you do, my dear, for your father [to get so upset with you]?" I answered her angrily, and she didn't say anything. Then Darvīsh Sāfī Khān brought me a message from my father, saying: "Even if I forgive your first misdeed, I won't forgive your second offense, which was to break the heart of that old lady, as long as you haven't become reconciled with her." [1865]

One day when I was around eight or nine, a man who seemed to be poor sat down on the ground next to me. I got up from there, found a better place, and asked them to bring a kilim for me to sit on. My father, who had seen me from his room, shouted to me and said: "Do you know what a great sin you have committed? Either you should have sat down next to that person, or you should have seated him next to you on the kilim." [1869]

One time, when I was eight, my father, my mother, and I were living in Sahneh in the house of Mr. Sayyid Habīb, together with Sāfī Khān, his wife Fakhrī, and Mīr Mazhar, who was the same age as me. We also had the use of a little room with a courtyard. During the day I went off to school with Mīr Mazhar. . . . Sometimes in the evening we would go out in the courtyard with my father and the others to do *dhikr*. And each time, once we had begun to perform the *dhikr*, something luminous and shining, like a white falcon, would come down and perch on one of the newly planted trees there; when the *dhikr* was over, it would go away. But there weren't any falconers in our region at all, so we didn't know where such a falcon could have come from.

. . . We used to perform *dhikr* inside the house, and the disciples would get together to do their *dhikr* outside. They had [as instruments] the *tanbūr, kamāncheh*, reed flute, Turkish *tanbūr*, and *tambourines. As long as he was alive, the late Sayyid Habīb kept that house just the way it was then; he wouldn't let anyone enter it. . . .* [1881]

I began fasting and spiritual exercises at the age of nine, and kept them up continuously for almost twelve years, taking only ten or twelve days between the forty-day periods of retreat.[6] Usually my evening meal to break the fast was only bread and vinegar, yet throughout that whole period I did not experience any sort of physical discomfort. I almost never went out of the retreat house, and I associated only with the seven or eight dervishes who were allowed to enter it. When I finally left the retreat house at the end of those twelve years and came into contact with other people, I couldn't imagine that it was even possible for human beings to tell lies. . . . [1873]

One day when I was a child, between the ages of nine and eleven, I was riding horseback and passed by a group of gypsies who had pitched their tents underneath the trees below our village of Jayhūnābād.[7] Suddenly I saw the reflected splendor of God's Essence in one of the little gypsy girls, and I was completely overwhelmed. I remembered Shaykh Samʿān,[8] and I fell into a spiritual state. Of course that girl herself wasn't aware of this; God had only made that theophany appear for me at that instant. For several years after that, whenever He wanted to come, He would appear in the form of that gypsy girl.

"The vision I want is that which knows God . . . ,"[9] in order to recognize God in every state. In the language of spirituality, such figures are called the people of the Unseen world (*rijāl al-ghayb*): they come for a few moments, manifest themselves in a particular form, and then disappear. [1874]

My mother was anxious about my worldly education, and she always used to ask my father: "So when is he going to do his studies?" My father replied: "As long as his domineering self (*nafs*) hasn't awakened, let him complete his spiritual training, so that his *nafs* won't be able to have an effect on him. After that he'll study."

Things turned out exactly as my father had predicted. I began my spiritual training when I was nine, and that course of spiritual discipline lasted for twelve years. After that I began to study, and desires and passions no longer had any effect on me. [1964]

Ordinarily during my childhood I was always involved in spiritual exercises. Only occasionally did we have a few days' break between two forty-day periods of spiritual retreat and fasting. During one of those periods of spiritual retreat, Sūfī Sultān, the guardian of Sultān Ishāq's shrine, brought me two strings of delicious dried figs. I set them aside specially for myself, and each night I broke my fast in a state of intense desire for those figs; after breaking the fast, I would take great pleasure in eating a few of them, until the forty days were over. On the last night of the retreat I had a dream in which I saw each person's spiritual exercises being recorded. I saw my own as a wall that I had built with beautiful bricks, except that a corner of each brick was broken off and incomplete. Someone said to me: "Because your mind was busy with those figs, your love of figs made those corners incomplete."

The next day my mother, as she usually did, asked my father's permission to prepare an offering meal [to mark the end of the retreat]. "No," my father replied, "because this person's spiritual exercise is imperfect, he'll have to perform another forty days of fasting and retreat, as a fine, so that his mind won't be filled with figs."

The point of this is that the essential condition for spiritual exercise and fasting is not just doing without food. Rather, the spiritual traveler must always have his attention on the Source and cut his attachments to everything else. Otherwise there are plenty of people who go without eating something. So the general condition for spiritual exercise is to have your attention continually on the divine Source. [1877]

During one of the fasts and spiritual exercises that lasted for three days and nights, I noticed during the second day that there was no longer anything holding me back, so that I was able to leave my body completely and ascend into the air. I saw my own body down on the ground below, but the power of gravity no longer had any influence on me at all. I went out through the roof of my room and kept on climbing higher and further away. I was busy looking around when suddenly there was a voice saying: "You're the loser!" That voice brought me back to myself, and I realized to what an extent I had forgotten God and turned my attention to traveling and looking around, how much I'd lost sight of the essential Goal. I immediately turned back to repentance and asking God's forgiveness. [1878]

. . . One day during my childhood (about ten or twelve), a pigeon had landed in our courtyard and mingled with our own pigeons. I really liked that particular pigeon, and since he was also rather tame, I was easily able to capture him. I imprisoned him in a cage in my own room, thinking that after a while he would get used to it and continue to stay with us. Now although my father apparently knew nothing at all about this matter and was ordinarily in the habit of taking a nap in the afternoon, suddenly I saw him burst into my room—despite the fact that he never entered it—and go directly to that cage; he took the pigeon outside and set it free. Then he scolded me, saying: "First of all, what was this animal's fault that you had to go and imprison it? And secondly, it didn't belong to you!" Afterwards he explained: "I was sleeping when this pigeon came to me complaining, 'What wrong have I done for this person to lock me up in a cage?'" [2041]

One night when I was young, I dreamed that I fell down into a ravine and was killed. When I woke up at dawn, in accordance with a precept I had from my father, I made offerings until my heart was calm and satisfied. That same morning I went out as usual to go riding on horseback. The horse I got on was one of our most docile and obedient horses. No sooner had I left the courtyard than I realized that this horse's state had completely changed and that he'd become crazy. I thought that if I let him gallop for a while he would calm down. But as soon as I let out the reins, he took off with me. I pulled on his bit with all my strength, but it broke in half, and he kept on galloping that way until he came to a ravine and fell right into it. I threw myself to one side so that I wouldn't fall under the horse, but all the same my arm was trapped under his body and I dislocated my shoulder. And the horse was unconscious for quite a while.

I was destined to break my neck and die. But since the danger was in my destiny, so was the removal of that danger. God warned me, and because of the precautions I took, breaking my neck was changed into dislocating my shoulder. [1879]

How beneficial a good master is! One day I came across a handwritten book about the esoteric science of numbers, and I took it to my father. "For the time being," he said, "these things aren't what you really need. Go on and complete your knowledge of spiritual things. When you've become perfect and can no longer be fooled, then these things will gradually become clear to you and there will no longer be any harm for you in studying them." Later on I did learn about hypnotism, the science of numbers, palmistry, and such, but I've never used them. [1900]

. . . Throughout the whole period of spiritual exercises during my youth, from when I was nine until I was twenty-one, I would take up the *tanbūr every night from evening until morning, and "They" would come and keep me occupied. My father would also come every night, very quietly, and listen outside the door. Sometimes I would throw the tanbūr up in the air and then catch it, but even in the air its sound didn't stop and it didn't go out of tune. [1887]*

I never really knew what hunger was until the time of the First World War, when that famine occurred. People were dying of hunger in great numbers, and yet I said to myself, "Can someone really die from hunger?"—until the day when I also became hungry. Whatever food I asked S. M. for . . . , she said, "We've given that to the poor," and there wasn't even a piece of bread to be found. I was so distressed by that hunger that I was sweating and fell down from the weakness—until finally I ate a piece of some kind of fruit that they found, and I recovered a little bit. Then I really understood for the first time what hunger is. My father said: "God has shown you what hunger is." . . . [1823]

When I was young, before they'd chosen a wife for me, I had decided to remain celibate for the rest of my life. One night in a dream I saw someone who brought a list and showed me that I would marry several times and would take care of orphans throughout my life. My way of raising orphans was difficult in that I obliged my *nafs* to love them truly from the heart, like my own children, and not out of pity. [1885]

My father didn't have any weak point, except for the tremendous attachment he felt for his children. I've never seen another soul so attached to his children as Hajjī [Ni'mat] was. [1830]

I've never seen any spiritually accomplished person (bātindār) who was as attached to their children as my father was. Even now he still intervenes in the smallest of matters concerning the members of his family. [1831]

During those last days, my dear father became exceptionally close and personal with my mother. He would ask her to come and would talk with her continuously—even though both of them already knew everything about every possible topic, because they had grown up in the same family and the same house. At that time, I even asked myself why my father was acting so close and personal with her. Now I understand that such intimacy is a good thing, that a human being ought to have someone he or she is really concerned about. [1843]

The last night of his life, [my father] had me come to him in the middle of the night; then he told me all the events of the rest of my life. Since he was speaking rapidly, I couldn't take notes, but I remembered it all. He even described my last son and said that he would look exactly like [my younger brother] Yār ʻAlī. [1835]

When my father was dying, my mother asked him: "What will become of the children?" My father answered: "I'm happy with Nūr ʻAlī. I entrust him to God, provided he doesn't leave the path I've traveled." Then he called me to him and put a drop of his saliva in my mouth. My state was completely changed, and I saw that I had become a different person. He died a quarter of an hour later, and from that moment on I alone had permission to give spiritual guidance, because that was a trust from God that my father had passed on to me, until I would hand it on later to whomever God should command me to do so.

If someone doesn't have the right to give spiritual guidance, but nonetheless offers such guidance without being aware of its Source, then he is considered guilty by God, even if that guidance is [outwardly] correct. As for myself, even now, whenever I tell someone something, I refer immediately to the authoritative sources. Of course the responses I give people are proportionate to the stage of development of their thinking. For example, J. asked me certain questions twenty years ago, and I answered them; now she repeats the same questions, but I give another answer. The essence of those answers is the same, but because the questioner's thinking has advanced, now I can answer her question in a different way that is appropriate to the current state of development of her thinking. . . . [1888]

. . . In my own case, despite the fact that I was entirely immersed in spiritual disciplines from the age of nine until the age of twenty-four, when my father passed away, God still didn't consider me worthy. It was only on the day my father left this world: at that moment He found me ready. My father placed a drop of his saliva in my mouth, and He gave me everything. My father was outwardly quite strict and stern, but inwardly he was very quick to forgive. On the contrary, I'm outwardly indulgent, but inwardly I'm extremely conscientious and exacting. [1978]

Even outwardly, everything about my father was extraordinary. Without having had any master, what spiritual power and strength he had, such feats of spiritual discipline and acts of devotion—and especially what faith he had, that faith of his! Whatever he wanted from God and set his will to, God would grant him that. How strong his will was, and what absolute confidence he had in himself with regard to God!

Of course his death also was not ordinary. For almost two months he was sick, but he showed no sign of pain, he never complained, and his appearance didn't change. At mealtimes he would eat his food, but he didn't speak to anyone, and no one was supposed to talk to him. He only seemed a bit weak. Before departing, he called for me and foretold all the events of my life, which I later wrote down. Around noon, my mother asked him: "How are you feeling?" He replied: "My heart is full of light, I'm very happy," and he drew the blanket up over his head. Then he didn't move for several minutes, and when my mother pulled the blanket aside, we realized that he had departed at that very instant when he said "I'm very happy."

. . . That man has seen and still sees things so [amazing] that each one of them is a divine Sign and Proof that could shake an entire world. . . . He predicted all of the events of my life, with their dates, right up to the birth of my last son. Those who would deny God, how could they deny such self-evident things? Of course one still needs the eye to see such things, and the heart to understand them. It is fifty-four years since he left this world, but right now he still intervenes in the details of my life. Whenever he has need of something, he comes to discuss it, to solve and decide the matter; then he says: "Such-and-such must be done in just this way." [1845]

My father always used to tell me: "I've raised you in a garden of purity. When you look outside the walls of that garden, there's nothing there but dirt and filth." After my father passed away, when I started out in life, I couldn't even imagine that it was possible for someone to lie or cheat or act in a way contrary to simple humanity. Because of that, I experienced many shocks. [1965]

There are two things to which I've always unsparingly given my time: one is the *tanbūr,* and the other is traveling the spiritual Path. Throughout my childhood I learned whatever my father taught me about spirituality and the Path. When I reached my youth and adolescence, I already knew the ways the *nafs* enters and attacks us; I blocked its way. But as for formal education in the affairs of this world, the time was limited. I began my advanced studies only at the age of thirty-two, and I worked very hard at them. [2034]

Two years had passed since the death of my father, and my heart was deeply yearning to see someone who resembled him. I was in Tehran then, and one day I noticed someone in the street who looked like him. I rushed ahead to catch up with that person—and there he was himself! He turned around and smiled at me, and said: "Since your heart wanted so much to see me, whenever you want, you'll always see me in this form." . . . [1841]

I'm always thinking of my master. In music, whenever I play a piece or a melody I've learned from someone, I say a prayer for that person if they're still alive; and if they're dead, I ask God to pardon them. [1950]

The rights of a master are something that we must never forget, that we must always honor and respect. My own master was my father, both outwardly and in the spiritual world. Whenever I am reminded of someone who has taught me something I speak and think well of that person. Mawlā [ʿAlī] said: "Whoever has taught me anything has made me his servant." A master deserves to be respected even if he receives money in return. So if a master takes nothing in return, we should respect him that much more. [2049]

After my father passed on, I decided to make the pilgrimage to [the shrine of] Sultān [Ishāq] walking barefoot. But of course I had been brought up in such an indulgent fashion that if I even walked a few minutes in the sun, I came down with a fever. In short, the first day, after endless pains, I was able to cover only about four miles; and by sunset my feet were so blistered and I was so exhausted that I couldn't even climb one step. The second day, with all my force, I was able to go only the same distance, and I had many more blisters. That night I dreamed that Sultān came to me and said: "You've really worn yourself out! Tomorrow morning I'll come myself to help you." The next morning, as soon as we started out, I no longer had any feeling of pain in my feet or any sense of fatigue. And that day we covered forty-five miles, so that my companions could barely stand up. Thus we completed the seven days' journey in only three, and from that day forward, walking has never made me tired. [1890]

My father always used to say: "O' God, whatever descendants You grant me, may they all have faith and Religion." Likewise I say: "O' God, whoever comes into being in this family, may they all have faith and Religion." [2048]

I've never seen anyone whose strength of faith could be compared to my father's: whatever he truly wanted, he obtained from God through that faith of his. Whatever he wanted would have to happen, and for him the "impossible" just didn't exist. I'm sorry that he spent all his time among that limited number of people and remained in [his small village of] Jayhūnābād. . . .

My father had such an intense spiritual presence that no one was ever able to look him in the eye, not even his own children. Different people conspired to come and argue with him. But whenever they were in his presence, their tongues were completely tied and they weren't able to utter a single word. Then once they'd gone away, they would ask each other: "Didn't we come to argue with him? So why didn't we say anything?"

. . . But I have come for another purpose. I would like to finish up my task as quickly as possible and go on to that place where I must go. Of course, if I had been given the order to perform miracles (may God spare me that), as others have been, then I would do so. But I have only the responsibility of guiding people: so if they listen, that's fine; and if they don't listen, then let them go. [1815]

Hajjī Ni'mat's assignment was spiritual struggle; my own assignment is spiritual guidance. [2075]

NOTES

1. Ostad Elahi (Nūr 'Alī Elāhī), *Āthār al-haqq* ("Traces/Influences of the Truth"), vol. 1, saying 1845. All the sayings of Ostad Elahi translated below are selected from the first volume of *Āthār al-haqq* (Tehran: Tāhūrī, 1357 AH/1957), identified here in each case by the particular number of each saying [in square brackets] as arranged in that collection. Short elided passages within a given saying are indicated by points of suspension [. . .]. To preserve the anonymity of certain interlocutors in the diary entries, only their initials are used.

2. Websites devoted to Ostad Elahi and his teaching include www.ostadelahi.com, www.nourfoundation.com, www.fondationostadelahi.org, and www.saintjani.org (the last for his younger sister Jānī, who was also an influential spiritual teacher). The most complete biographical study to date is included in Jean During's *The Spirit of Sounds: The Unique Art of Ostad Elahi* (Cranbury, NJ: Cornwall Books, 2003), and at least eight CDs of musical recordings from the later years of his life are now widely available. An English translation of Ostad Elahi's philosophical treatise on the soul and its destiny, *Ma'rifat ar-Rūh*, has just appeared: James Morris, trans., *Knowing the Spirit* (Albany: State University of New York Press, 2007), which includes an extensive bibliography. The most comprehensive outline of Ostad Elahi's teaching is to be found in B. Elahi, *The Path of Perfection*, rev. ed. (Bracey, VA: Paraview, 2005).

3. Most scholarly discussions of Hajjī Ni'mat have focused on his immense (20,000 verses) Persian poetic epic summary of Ahl-i Haqq tradition, *Shāh-nāmah-yi Haqīqat (The Book of Kings of Truth)*, edited with Ostad Elahi's own commentary: *Haqq al-Haqā'iq* (Tehran: Husseini, 1346/1967). A doctoral student, Mojane Membrado, is now completing an edition and translation of Elahi's earlier, autobiographical treatise *Furqān al-Akhbār*, including a broad study of his wider sociohistorical setting and background, which should provide a more comprehensive and revealing portrait of this fascinating spiritual figure.

4. The transcribed sayings in volume 1 of *Āthār al-haqq* have been divided and arranged in twenty-four chapters according to different topics; volume 2 (Tehran: Jayhūn, 1370/1963) also includes longer complete transcripts of teaching sessions (pp. 195–542), giving a more vivid picture of the actual variety of subjects often covered in a single conversation.

5. Sahneh is a good-sized town on the main road between Hamadan and Kermanshah.

6. *Chilleh* (Arabic *chilla*) refers to the spiritual practice of forty days of retreat and meditation (Ar. *khalwa*), often combined with daytime fasting, *riyāzat.*

7. Jayhunabad is a much smaller village roughly ten kilometers from Sahneh.

8. The respected elderly religious scholar who falls in love and renounces everything for a Christian maiden, in one of the most famous stories from ʿAttār's Persian mystical epic, *The Conference of the Birds.*

9. A famous verse from the lyric poetry of Rūmī.

8 A Miracle of an Afghan Friend of God, the Mulla of Hadda

David Edwards

Najm ad-Dīn Akhundzāda, who is usually referred to as the Mulla of Hadda or Hadda Sāhib, was one of the most important Muslim figures in Afghanistan in the latter half of the nineteenth century. A disciple of the Akhund of Swat, Najm ad-Dīn spent most of his adult life at the *khānaqāh* that he founded in Hadda, outside Jalālābād, but he also spent a number of years in residence with the Shinwari and Mohmand tribes. Most of Najm ad-Dīn's life was spent engaged in the practice of *tasawwuf*, or Sufism, and he is remembered as the most important Sufi figure on the Afghan side of the Afghan-Indian frontier during the late nineteenth century. But he also gained considerable renown as an opponent of the great Afghan king ʿAbd ar-Rahmān Khān, who ruled from 1880 to 1901.

While some documentary sources refer to Najm ad-Dīn, he is best remembered in Afghanistan through countless miracle stories about him and his disciple. The following story involves both Najm ad-Dīn and one of his chief disciples, Hazrat Sāhib of Butkhāk, who joined his *pīr* in his active opposition to the Afghan king. The story, which was told to the translator by a Pashtun descendant of Hazrat Sāhib of Butkhāk,[1] tells of the king's attempts to suppress Najm ad-Dīn and his followers and also indicates the different sources of temporal and sacred power and explains why, from the Sufi point of view, a king's authority ultimately has to give way to a saint's. The story begins as follows.

TRANSLATION

When Hadda Sāhib became popular as a saint, his influence grew, and people were coming to him all the time. One of the distinguishing characteristics for which ʿAbd ar-Rahmān was known was his suspicion of those who were becoming influential among the people. When someone was becoming popular among the people, he would feel threatened and worry that he would be challenged. Then he would find pretexts for arresting or expelling that person from the country.

['Abd ar-Rahmān] started opposing Hadda Sāhib and tried to destroy his reputation. Finally, he decided to arrest Hadda Sāhib, so Hadda Sāhib left his home during the night. He left his home in Kabul during the middle of the night, and he reached Mirān-i Zarbācha [in the Shinwar territory] before dawn. The people who lived there at that time were his followers. Since they were memorizers (*qārī;* lit., "reciters") of the Qur'ān, they were his sincere devotees. He spent the night there, and when the people of Shinwar were informed [of his arrival], all of them stood determined and expressed their readiness to fight 'Abd ar-Rahmān.

Hadda Sāhib told them, "Jihad against Muslims is forbidden because it will result in the shedding of Muslim blood. I don't want you to start fighting with him. I am going to the border so I will be beyond his authority. I want other Muslims to remain at peace and do not want to have their blood spilled."

Then the father of Feroz Khān (I can't remember his name) and some people of Mohmand Dārā took Hadda Sāhib to the ferry crossing. They crossed the river and took him themselves to Mohmand. When Hadda Sāhib arrived there, his fame increased.

At that time, Hazrat Sāhib was in Butkhāk, and 'Abd ar-Rahmān was saying things about Hadda Sāhib. At that time, some spies brought a report to 'Abd ar-Rahmān that "Hazrat Sāhib has called you an infidel (*kafir*). He has given his judgment (*hukm*) against you as an infidel."

So 'Abd ar-Rahmān summoned Hazrat Sāhib, and one of my uncles named 'Azīm Jān, who was a young boy at that time, says that he was with him. He says that, "I thought if they put him in prison, I'd like to be with him to serve him." He says that "when they took Hazrat Sāhib there, they told him to sit and wait."

('Abd ar-Rahmān was a very intimidating king. He was cruel and merciless.)

When 'Abd ar-Rahmān was face-to-face with Hazrat Sāhib, he asked him, "Is it true that you called me an infidel?" He told him, "I received reports that you have given a verdict of infidelity against me."

Hazrat Sāhib told him, "Our religious law doesn't permit a Muslim to call another Muslim an infidel."

(This is in accord with Sharia law. If any Muslim calls another Muslim an infidel, he himself will be the one who is an infidel.)

Then Hazrat Sāhib said to him, "I received some reports that you used bad words against Hadda Sāhib, who is the leader of the people. If you have called him these names, then you are an infidel. Do you understand?"

(In other words, "I may have given the judgment against you, but only if you have used these words. Then you are an infidel.")

Then 'Abd ar-Rahmān used bad words against Hadda Sāhib in front of Hazrat Sāhib. He even called him a *kāfir*. Hazrat Sāhib said, "Now I am sure that you have become an infidel."

Then 'Abd ar-Rahmān ordered that the beard of Mubārak [Hazrat Sāhib] be pulled out. He commanded them to tear it out by the roots, and he issued the order for his execution.

Hazrat Sāhib said, "You can't kill me because [the Qur'ān] says that 'God is the only one in the position [of life and death . . . God's is the only power.' You are something that can't even cure its own leg." ('Abd ar-Rahmān's leg was crippled. He had a problem with his leg that caused him to limp.) "Life and death are in God's hands. If you have the power to kill someone, then you should also have the power to bring them back as well. If you can do that, go to the graveyard and bring someone back to life."

When 'Abd ar-Rahmān ordered them to tear his beard out by the roots, Hazrat Sāhib said, "Thanks be to God. I have been ready to sacrifice my jugular vein, but so far I have suffered very little. I am thankful that this thing has happened in the path of Islam."

The order of execution was not carried out, but seven *ser* and one *charak* (approximately four pounds) of shackles and chain were placed on his feet, and five *charak* of handcuffs were placed on his wrists—in all, more than eight and a half *ser* [about 140 pounds]. But when they took Hazrat Sāhib to prison with those eight and a half *ser* of shackles and chains, they broke by themselves.

The jailer told him, "I know that the chains have broken of their own accord, but if 'Abd ar-Rahmān sees that the chain is not on your neck, he will kill me. If he finds out that you are not wearing your chains, he will accuse me of opening them." Then when Mubārak [Hazrat Sāhib] finished his ablution and prayers, he would put the nail [securing the chains] back in place.

He was in prison for two years and some months. Then one day, Tūr, the jailer, asked him, "Why don't you put these handcuffs back on?"

Hazrat Sāhib told him to come fix them himself. "I won't fix them anymore." When Tūr tried to fix them, they would just break again. Then Hazrat Sāhib said to him, "If you can't fix them, why should I?"

Then Tūr went to 'Abd ar-Rahmān and told him, "We are putting the chains on, but they are breaking by themselves," and 'Abd ar-Rahmān said, "If they won't remain secure on him, don't put them on."

Every night his bed would turn over, and ['Abd ar-Rahmān] would see in his dreams Hazrat Sāhib with his *shalgi* (an iron-tipped staff sometimes carried by *fuqarā'*). Hazrat Sahib would say to him, "Shall I stab you, tyrant?" and 'Abd ar-Rahmān would shout out in his sleep. Then he ordered that the shackles be removed.

During the two years [that Hazrat Sāhib was in prison], 'Abd ar-Rahmān's bed turned over many times, and he saw Hazrat Sāhib many times in his dreams. When 'Abd ar-Rahmān died, his son, Amīr Habīb Allāh Khān, came and kissed the beard of Hazrat Sāhib and asked him to excuse his father. Hazrat Sāhib said, "I have forgiven all Muslims."

NOTE

1. Originally published in David B. Edwards, *Heroes of the Age: Moral Faultlines on the Afghan Frontier* (Berkeley: University of California Press, 1996), 159–62. Reprinted with permission of the author and the University of California Press.

PART III

Turkey and Central Asia

. . . . .

Just to the north of Iran and Afghanistan lie the five former Soviet republics of Central Asia, the original homeland of the Turks. Stories from the important Central Asian Turkic language known as Chaghatay tell of the medieval Sufi Hakīm Atā and members of his family. Three figures from Turkish Anatolia appear here in two very different types of literature. Sarı Saltık was an early "missionary" and notorious trickster in early Ottoman Balkan lands, while Sarı İsmail was a disciple of the famed Hacı Bektaş Veli. Stories of both come from epiclike sources, as does an early account of the great eighth/fourteenth-century Mevlevi dervish and mystical poet Yūnus Emre. But a fourteenth/twentieth-century Turkish novel about Yūnus Emre adds a further dimension by demonstrating how a very recent author reinterprets the approach of classic medieval hagiography. Here again, the four selections represent an instructive sample of several significant prose hagiographical genres.

9 Three Tales from the Central Asian 'Book of Hakīm Ata'

Devin DeWeese

The Yasavī Sufi tradition,[1] linked with the legacy of Khwāja Ahmad Yasavī (c. 622/1225), is typically regarded as prominent among the Turkic peoples of Central Asia; this is largely true, but the literary legacy of the tradition is overwhelmingly in Persian. Apart from the collection of Turkic poetry known as the *Dīvān-i hikmat*, inaccurately ascribed to Ahmad Yasavī himself, and some little-known doctrinal works written in Turkic, the major Turkic work produced within the Yasavī tradition is a hagiographical work of a decidedly popular cast, known simply as the *Book of Hakīm Ata (Hakīm Atā kitābï)*. The work consists of narratives about Hakīm Ata, known also as Hakīm Sulaymān,[2] a saint usually portrayed as a direct disciple of Ahmad Yasavī and associated with the region of Khwārazm (to the south of the Aral Sea, in the delta of the Amū Daryā). The work reflects—in many cases more clearly than do the early Persian hagiographies—the broader reception of his saintly persona in a more public environment, shaped by but beyond the confines of the Sufi community that came to define itself in terms of Ahmad Yasavī and to trace its spiritual lineage (*silsila*) to him through Hakīm Ata. Focused on Hakīm Ata's spiritual training, his family, and especially his shrine, the narratives undoubtedly circulated in oral tradition, with a considerable infusion of folkloric elements, long before being recorded in literary form. In that literary form, the *Book of Hakīm Ata* was preserved in a number of manuscripts produced in Central Asia, and was published already more than a century ago in a scholarly edition prepared by the Russian orientalist Karl Germanovich Zaleman;[3] Zaleman's text is the basis for the excerpts translated here.

The *Book of Hakīm Ata* was written in Chaghatay Turkic, the literary language of the Turks of Central Asia from the ninth/fifteenth to the early fourteenth/twentieth century and the literary precursor of modern Uzbek.

Though the oldest known manuscript of the work dates only to the early twelfth/eighteenth century, it preserves a number of archaic linguistic features. The reflection of tales from the *Book of Hakīm Ata* in very early sources reminds us that although the work may have taken its final literary form fairly recently, the narratives it contains may indeed go back to the earliest phases of the Yasavī tradition. The three sections of the work presented below in translation mark important dramatic episodes in the hagiographical record about Hakīm Ata, but also convey a sense of the distinctive style and flavor of the *Book of Hakīm Ata*.

The first four narratives from the *Book of Hakīm Ata* follow Hakīm Ata from his childhood, when he is taken as a pupil by Ahmad Yasavī, down to his establishment as a shaykh in his own right in the Khwārazmian locality known as Bāqïrghān;[4] the fourth also notes his marriage to ʿAnbar Ana, a woman identified as the daughter of the ruler of Khwārazm and renowned as a saint herself. The fifth narrative mentions the three sons born to Hakīm Ata and ʿAnbar Ana and focuses on the improper behavior of the first two of them, Mahmūd Khwāja and Asghar Khwāja, while they were students in "the city of Khwārazm." The next three stories all deal with the youngest of his three sons, known as Hubbī Khwāja; the first of these excerpts is taken from the eighth narrative, which marks the culmination of Hakīm Atā's troubled relationship with Hubbī Khwāja.

The story of a father who grows jealous as his son surpasses him may well be universal, but in the context of the *Book of Hakīm Ata*, the tension between father and son is framed in terms of an ongoing issue in medieval Sufi communities regarding organization and succession: is the community to be led by the son of the shaykh who founded it or by one of the disciples of the shaykh without a blood relationship to him? The tension between hereditary succession and succession based purely on the master-disciple relationship was a recurrent focus of discussion in Sufi literature between the seventh/thirteenth and ninth/fifteenth centuries, and was often put to polemical use as different Sufi groups competed with one another. Groups that favored nonhereditary succession criticized their rivals as enshrining a purely formal brand of Sufism, without real merit, based only on the father-son relationship. It is thus not surprising that Hubbī Khwāja is contrasted with other, nonhereditary disciples of Hakīm Ata, or that he is an object first of disappointment and later of jealousy on the part of his father.

In the *Book of Hakīm Ata*, Hubbī Khwāja is far from the dutiful son and is hardly interested in the management of his father's Sufi community. Here he appears more interested in hunting, with his fine horse and dogs, than in heeding his father's summons or attending to the affairs of the community. Hubbī Khwāja exhibits a sanctity that is both innate and undomesticated, allowing him not only to surpass his father's disciples (with their labored efforts to achieve what Hubbī comes by naturally) but also to outdo Hakīm Ata himself. The father-son tension, as framed within the potential rivalry between a shaykh's offspring and his disciples, is thus further overlaid on the dichotomy of "natural" sanctity, effortless in its manifestation and cultivation, versus the hard work of Sufi disciples striving toward a spiritual goal.

The tension between Hakīm Ata and Hubbī Khwāja grows through the three episodes from the *Book of Hakīm Ata* that recount it. According to the first, Hubbī once irritated his father by tarrying, whereas one of Hakīm Ata's disciples responded promptly to his master's summons; it turned out that Hubbī had been detained by the need to save two ships on the verge of sinking into the sea. Hakīm Ata did not believe this story at first, but had to be convinced, first by seeing the marks left by the ships on his son's neck, and then by the 10,000 gold pieces brought by those he had rescued. The second story builds on a familiar motif in tales of saintly competition: Hakīm Ata, we are told, had the habit of miraculously traveling to the Kaʿba every day in order to perform the morning prayer, but Hubbī Khwāja, declaring that this was too much trouble, brought the Kaʿba itself to Bāqïrghān. Although Hakīm Ata was merely amazed by his son after the first episode, this bit of one-upmanship was more annoying; as the account concludes, "They say that arrogance appeared in Hakīm Khwāja's heart when he saw these wonders that day." The jealousy thus provoked in Hakīm Ata culminates in the final narrative of this series, which again commences with a hint of tension between the master's disciples and his son.[5]

TRANSLATION

They relate that one day, Hakīm Ata's disciples gathered together and slaughtered nine oxen [for a feast]; a *dhikr* session with music was arranged, and they invited the people [to attend]. Hubbī Khwāja was not present; he had gone off to hunt. They did not allot him a portion [of the feast].[6] [Then] Hubbī Khwāja came; he brought the gazelles he had shot and presented them as an offering to Hakīm Ata. He sat respectfully and addressed his father, saying, "Papa, your disciples have apparently come and slaughtered nine oxen; everyone, great and small, has received a portion. Evidently they did not leave a portion for me. What fault have you found in me?" When he said this, Hakīm Ata replied, "My son, the saints accomplished something and received a portion; if you too had accomplished something, you would have received a share." Hubbī Khwāja said, "If I had accomplished something, I would have made all the shares equal"; and with zeal he stood up and spoke loudly to his father's disciples, saying, "Bring the hides of the oxen you slaughtered!" The disciples went and placed the hides of the nine slaughtered oxen in front of Hubbī Khwāja. Hubbī Khwāja took a step in the direction of the *qibla* [i.e., toward Mecca], raised his hand for prayer (*munājāt*), and prayed; then he struck the hides of the oxen with his staff ('*asā*) and said, "Beasts, arise at once, by the decree of God most high!" When he thus made a sign toward the oxen, the nine oxen all bellowed and stood up. Hubbī Khwāja said, "There, Papa, I have accomplished something. Now let all the saints take an equal portion."

Seeing this marvel, all his father's disciples raised an uproar and fell weeping at Hubbī Khwāja's feet; they all repented and became his disciples. Seeing these events, Hakīm Ata was affected by jealousy and spoke irrevocable words:[7] "My son, two rams' heads cannot be boiled in the same cauldron; it will be either you or I." Hubbī Khwāja understood the secret meaning of these words; he said, "Papa, this is certainly a well-known saying, that two rams' heads cannot be boiled in one cauldron; they will not fit, but only if they are together with their horns. If one were to remove their horns, even three rams' heads would fit in a single cauldron. Nevertheless, you have uttered these words against me. Farewell; let me be the one to go, Papa."

So saying, he left weeping. He went to his mother, 'Anbar Ana; he asked his mother's leave. Now votive offerings and gifts used to come in huge amounts to Hubbī Khwāja; he used to spend all of it on the dervishes, for the sake of God.[8] And he said, "Mother, whenever something would happen to a young man, if he would make me his intercessor and ask for my help, with sincerity, I would appear to him and give assistance.[9] And when I was in your presence, I always fulfilled my obligations to you as my mother. Now I am traveling into the world of the unseen; Mother, convey a greeting to my father and let him remember me with a prayer."

When his mother heard these words, she embraced Hubbī Khwāja and with abject humility began to weep and lament: "Light of my eye, piece of my soul, slice of my insides, my dear son, what will I do without you? I do not want to let you go!" As she thus began to cry and lament, Hubbī Khwāja said, "Mother, let me go. Stand at the door." His mother let go of Hubbī Khwāja; [still] saying, "I will not let you go," she stood at the door. Hubbī Khwāja put on his shroud and came and sat in the middle of his room; he drew up the shroud and fastened it over his head. He said,

"Mother, do not cry much for me now; if my father has been angry with me, let him be happy. Be well. For you, let the land be blessed; for me, let the road be blessed." So saying, he disappeared from beneath the shroud; the shroud remained there on the ground. 'Anbar Ana lifted up his shroud and turned away her face; raising a cry, she went to Hakīm Ata weeping and told him what had happened. Hakīm Khwāja too began to cry; but however much they wept, it did no good. Hearing of the disappearance of Hubbī Khwāja, the entire people, great and small, raised an uproar and wept together. Hakīm Khwāja became greatly sorrowful; he went questioning and searching in many lands, but did not find [his son].

. . . . .

At this point the *Book of Hakīm Ata* includes several verses ascribed to the father that lament Hubbī Khwāja's disappearance and affirm the consequences of Hakīm Ata's careless dismissal of his youngest son: God commanded that, because Hakīm Ata's rash act had cut off the "sixty saints" who would have arisen from the lineage of Hubbī Khwāja, water would flow over Hakīm Ata for forty years, in order to cleanse him of his sin.

Before turning to the consequences of this episode, it is worth noting that both Hubbī Khwāja and his mother, 'Anbar Ana, remain the subjects of an extensive body of popular religious lore in many parts of Central Asia, above all in Khwārazm; folkloric versions of the tale of the disappearance of Hubbī (turned into an epic hero called Er Hubbī) are preserved in Central Asian manuscript collections, and versions continue to be recorded from oral tradition. Some of the popular lore about Hubbī Khwāja clearly reflects the content and structure, if not the style, of the version in the *Book of Hakīm Ata*, but much of it goes further, developing the image noted above of Hubbī rescuing ships on the Amū Daryā, and links both Hubbī and his mother with rivers and lakes, often casting one or both of them as protective spirits called upon for aid by those in danger on the water. Among the Qaraqalpaqs (who dwell in the region of Khwārazm), for instance, "Ubbi" was known as a protective spirit associated with water and as a patron-saint of fishermen, while among the Qazaqs, the figure of "Ubbe" or "Hubbe" was known both as a harmful spirit who lured men to death on water and as a protective spirit who rescued those in danger of drowning. Among the Uzbeks of Khwārazm, Hubbī is linked with the Amū Daryā and is the object of appeals by boatmen during storms; he is also pictured as a bird, the form in which he disappeared, according to some oral versions of the narrative known from the *Book of Hakīm Ata*.

What is remarkable about such adaptations is not the mere "survival" from pre-Islamic times of the protective functions assigned to these figures, or of the religious needs they address (which are, after all, universal), but the role of these figures from the Yasavī tradition in infusing such religious patterns with Muslim hagiographical form and content.[10]

To return to the *Book of Hakīm Ata*, the ninth narrative that immediately follows the dramatic story of Hubbī Khwāja's disappearance ignores that story's consequences altogether. It deals instead with Hakīm Ata's death, but does so primarily to recount how his widow, 'Anbar Ana, came to be married to another eminent saint, known as Zangī Ata. The story is of interest for entirely ignoring the master-disciple relationship between Hakīm Ata and Zangī Ata as portrayed in most early hagiographical sources. In the *Book of Hakīm Ata*, Zangī Ata is instead portrayed as one of forty *abdāl*s who come (as Hakīm Ata had predicted they would) to the memorial feast for Hakīm Ata held forty days after his death, during which Zangī Ata's marriage to 'Anbar Ana is arranged. Zangī Ata then takes her away, to Tashkent (where his shrine was a prominent pilgrimage site at least by the early ninth/fifteenth century).

It is the tenth narrative that resumes the story set in motion by Hubbī Khwāja's disappearance and the divine decree regarding Hakīm Ata's punishment.[11]

TRANSLATION

They relate that a short time after Hakīm Ata departed the world, the Amū Daryā began to flow past the land of the city of Kāt,[12] and flowed over Bāqïrghān, which remained under water and was destroyed. For forty years, water flowed over Hakīm Ata; then the river dried up. No one knew where Hakīm Ata's grave was.

One day, Hakīm Ata appeared to Khwāja Jalāl ad-Dīn of Manzil-khāna in a dream, saying, "My son Jalāl ad-Dīn, search for me and find me; build a structure atop me and take a portion from me." Khwāja Jalāl ad-Dīn did not make the dream known to anyone. One day, when Khwāja Jalāl ad-Dīn had gone off to Turkistan to trade, with a huge amount of livestock, and was returning with the good news of making a great profit, he stopped in the plain of Bāqïrghān to spend the night. During the night, clouds filled the air, the wind blew, adverse gusts arose, the sky thundered and lightning flashed, and the sun appeared as if the Day of Resurrection had come. All the merchants together with their cattle were scattered, and all of them were separated from one another, each in a different direction. When dawn broke and the sun rose, Khwāja Jalāl ad-Dīn of Manzil-khāna wandered about, separated from his livestock, wondering, "What kind of place is this?"

All at once, as he went up to the top of a hill and looked around, a nomad tent (*otagh*) appeared from a distance. He went to the tent and saw that a frail old man was sitting [there].[13] He greeted the old man; the old man returned the greeting. The old man said, "Young man, where have you come from, and where are you going?" Khwāja Jalāl ad-Dīn said, "Brother, do you know the shrine of Hakīm Ata?[14] If you know it, tell me about it; it is what I am looking for." The frail old man said, "Young man, I do not know. But I have an old mother who has lived a long time; if anyone would know, she will know." Khwāja Jalāl ad-Dīn asked, "Where is this aged mother of yours?" He set out on the road to the old man's frail mother; he saw that the old woman was performing sorrowful songs. Khwāja Jalāl ad-Dīn greeted her; the old woman returned the greeting and said, "Young man, who are you? Where do you come from, and where are you going?" When she said this, Khwāja Jalāl ad-Dīn begged her pardon, saying, "Mother, it doesn't matter where I'm coming from; I am searching for the grave of Hakīm Ata. You are a person of great age; if you know [where it is], tell me." The old woman said, "My son, how would I know? The country of Bāqïrghān was left beneath the water for forty years; now who would know where the grave of Hakīm Ata was? Even I do not know; but nearby there is a spindly tree, and when night falls, gazelles and wild asses come to its base and stay there until dawn breaks, performing *ziyārat*.[15] Listen carefully, for the sound of the *dhikr* comes from that place. If Hakīm Ata's grave is anywhere, it should be there!"

When she had said this, Khwāja Jalāl ad-Dīn, hearing these words, rose at once and went off toward that tree. As he came closer to it, he concealed himself at a certain place and waited. When he had waited until nightfall, he saw, by night, that gazelles and wild asses came to the base of that tree; they stood looking at that place and performed *ziyārat*. As he listened carefully, the sound of the *dhikr* came from that place. Khwāja Jalāl ad-Dīn went closer and lay down awhile on the ground. The previous night he had not slept at all; so he went to sleep. As he slept, Hakīm Ata came into his dream again and said, "My son Jalāl ad-Dīn, welcome! Now you have found me. Rise from this place where you have lain down and go seven paces forward; from there, dig into the ground. You will see a reed mat appear. If you lift up the mat and look beneath it, a handful of flowers will appear. You should go no farther: that will be my grave. And you should not worry about your livestock that went astray; your cattle have all gone to Manzil-khāna. You shall bring your livestock here; you shall construct a building above me; and you shall stay as *mujāvir* for me, and you shall take a portion (*ülüsh*) from me."[16]

Khwāja Jalāl ad-Dīn awoke and at once rose from his place. He went seven steps forward; then when he dug into the earth, he saw that a reed mat appeared from the ground. When he then raised up and lifted that reed mat, a bunch of flowers emerged from beneath the reed mat; he saw that they were fresh, just as if he had picked them from a garden at that very time. When Khwāja Jalāl ad-Dīn smelled the fine scent of those flowers, he lost consciousness and fell down; after a short time, when he came to himself, he saw the graves and the discipleship and the souls of all the shaykhs appear from the interior world.

After that, Khwāja Jalāl ad-Dīn placed a mark at that site, and, fastening the hem [of his cloak] to his waist, he set off toward Manzil-khāna. In the blink of an eye he reached Manzil-khāna; he saw all his livestock safe and sound. At once he assessed his property and goods and came to the city of Khwārazm, driving his livestock. He gathered all the master craftsmen [there] and went to Bāqïrghān with his property, amounting to 100,000 gold coins; he built a structure atop [the grave of] Hakīm Ata. Within a short time he had the structure completed, such that there was not a single brick less than [in] the former structure. The people came and offered congratulations. Khwāja Jalāl ad-Dīn stayed in Manzil-khāna as Hakīm Ata's *mujāvir*;[17] and people began to come from the surrounding regions with votive offerings and supplicatory gifts. They called Khwāja Jalāl ad-Dīn "Shaykh Jalāl", and the land of Bāqïrghān was put in good order.

.   .   .   .   .

The account thus sanctions specific "administrative" arrangements linked with the legacy of Hakīm Ata—Khwāja Jalāl ad-Dīn's status as the caretaker at Hakīm Ata's shrine and his share of the shrine's income. It also implies a genealogical connection between the newly appointed caretaker and Hakīm Ata, who in any case is shown as directly authorizing Jalāl ad-Dīn's custody of the site. Jalāl ad-Dīn is further said to have become known as Shaykh Jalāl, implying that the status of Sufi shaykh was conferred on him as well in this unconventional way. The eleventh narrative, however, poses a challenge to this arrangement and entails an interesting and multivalent confrontation that pits, in two stages, the hereditary caretaker against an apparent usurper (who is nevertheless typically shown as belonging to the Sufi lineage of Hakīm Ata), and more broadly, the local against the universal.

The identity of the usurper requires some preliminary comment. He is Sayyid Ata, a figure of enormous stature throughout Central Asia. His appellation signals his descent from the Prophet, but his reputation ranges from that of an Islamizer (he is credited with the conversion to Islam of Özbek Khān of the Golden Horde), to that of a saintly ancestor (his descendants are mentioned as a privileged group from the ninth/fifteenth century to the fourteenth/twentieth), to that of a prominent member of the Yasavī Sufi *silsila*. The earliest references to Sayyid Ata, indeed, show him as one of four disciples of Zangī Ata, who was portrayed, as noted, as a disciple of Hakīm Ata; but just as the *Book of Hakīm Ata* makes no mention of any master-disciple relationship between Hakīm Ata and Zangī Ata, it likewise says nothing about any such relationship between Zangī Ata and Sayyid Ata. Rather, in ignoring the *silsila* relationship, the eleventh narrative from the *Book of Hakīm Ata* serves in effect as an explanation of another, more tangible, relationship—not heredity in this case but simply the close proximity of the graves of Hakīm Ata and Sayyid Ata.[18] The eleventh narrative begins with the familiar motif of the Prophet's famous Ascent through the heavens, guided by Jibrā'īl, but ends with the Prophet's descendant Sayyid Ata firmly ensconced as a sacralizing presence in Khwārazm.[19]

TRANSLATION

They relate that when the Prophet ascended on the *mi'rāj*, he saw, in the realm of the Divine Throne (*'arsh*), that something like a black bird was flying past; the Prophet's gaze fell upon that bird, and the Prophet asked Jibrā'īl, "My comrade Jibrā'īl, what kind of bird is this?" Jibrā'īl said, "Prophet of God, this bird is the soul of a shaykh among your communities; that bird was flying in front of you in order to honor your holiness." The Prophet praised him [the bird] highly and made a promise, saying, "My comrade Jibrā'īl, if after our time he comes into the world, serves as a shaykh, and summons my communities to righteousness, let someone from my family serve as *mujāvir* for him." Now that bird, they say, was apparently the soul of Hakīm Ata.[20]

They relate that one day they were reading this treatise about Hakīm Ata in the assembly of Sayyid Ata. As they were discussing Hakīm Ata and speaking of his wonders and his sanctity, the Prophet's promise about someone from his family was recounted. When Sayyid Ata heard these words, he asked, "Has anyone from among the Prophet's descendants (*sayyids*) ever become the *mujāvir* for Hakīm Ata?" They looked at the treatise and said, "Down to this time, no one among the *sayyids* has become *mujāvir* [for him]." Sayyid Ata said, "If that is so, let me fulfill the promise of my ancestor, the Prophet, and let me become [Hakīm Ata's] *mujāvir*." He left the city of Khwārazm with the people of three house-holds and set out toward Bāqïrghān. They went and lodged some three leagues away from Bāqïrghān; [there] Sayyid Ata addressed the saints (*'azīzlïr*) and said, "You are in the real world; I am in the false world. We should share the good and the bad. For that reason, I will not presume to proceed." When he said that, they conferred a sign [upon Sayyid Ata], saying, "You are welcome; come forward."

After that, Sayyid Ata moved and settled close to Bāqïrghān. When Shaykh Jalāl ad-Dīn of Manzil-khāna heard [of it], his heart grew bit-ter toward Sayyid Ata. Sayyid Ata said, "Shaykh Jalāl ad-Dīn, will you allow us to assume the role of *mujāvir?*" Shaykh Jalāl ad-Dīn said, "When we came here, we came with Hakīm Ata's permission." Sayyid Ata said, "Shaykh Jalāl ad-Dīn, get up; let us go to the *khānaqāh* tonight and appeal at the threshold of the saints, and let the two of us tell our secrets as well. Upon whichever of us is conferred a sign, he will become *mujāvir*." When he said this, Shaykh Jalāl ad-Dīn accepted. That night, when the two of them together rose, entered the *khānaqāh*, appealed to the saints, and spoke their words, a sign was conferred upon Shaykh Jalāl ad-Dīn of Manzil-khāna, to this effect: "My son, Shaykh Jalāl ad-Dīn, know and be aware that when Sayyid Ata came here, he came according to the promise of the Prophet. Confer the status of *mujāvir* upon him, for now we have bestowed a portion [upon you] and given [you] permission: there is a place called Āq Tāsh ("White Stone"), beside the city of Khwārazm; you will go there and dwell there. Let whoever comes in order to perform the circum-ambulation (*tavāf*) to us first perform the circumambulation to you, and let him come to us after you. If he does not perform the circumambulation to you, or if he comes to us before [coming to] you, we will not accept that person's circumambulation." Thus he promised. When Shaykh Jalāl ad-Dīn heard this gracious good news, [he] became joyful; he rose and took his leave from the *khānaqāh*, exchanged farewells with Sayyid Ata, and moved from Bāqïrghān, heading for Āq Tāsh. He dwelled in Āq Tāsh, and his final resting place was also there. Now, because of the meaning [of what Hakīm Ata told him], [people] first go and perform the circum-ambulation to Shaykh Jalāl ad-Dīn and afterwards come to Bāqïrghān and perform the circumambulation to Hakīm Ata.

When Shaykh Jalāl ad-Dīn Ata left and moved from Bāqïrghān, Sayyid Ata became *mujāvir*, and for several years Sayyid Ata dwelled in Bāqïrghān. In the end, when the time arrived for him to depart from this useless, transitory world, his disciples asked him, "Descendant of the Prophet, shall we bury you here in Bāqïrghān, or should we take you to the Ka'ba and bury you among the saints (*erînlîr*) of the Ka'ba?" Sayyid Ata said, "Companions, this matter is not known even to me; but my testament is that you should wash me clean, put the clothes of the next world on me, place me in the coffin, load me upon a large wheeled cart ('*araba*), and send it off from Bāqïrghān toward the Ka'ba. And that night, tie up firmly your livestock and your [hunting] dogs and birds; and through the night sit, without making a sound, with the doors to your homes shut tight. If you hear a sound, do not go outside, for if you go outside when you hear a sound, you will be hurt. When dawn breaks, see where that cart has gone: the place where the cart stands will be my resting place. Bury me there." Thus he gave his testament.

When Sayyid Ata migrated from this world to the next, his disciples carried out Sayyid Ata's instructions. They loaded him on a cart and sent it off in the direction of the Ka'ba; then, tying up firmly their livestock and their [hunting] dogs and birds, they themselves went inside their homes, shut their doors tight, and sat. When it was the middle of the night, a tumult like a battle cry, with shrieks and shouts, arose such that the people, hearing this noise, sat still in their homes without making a sound and did not go outside. When it was time for dawn to break, the sound of those shouts subsided; [and] when dawn broke and the sun shone, all of them went outside their homes and saw that the cart was not where they had left it. They went in search of it and saw that the cart had come to rest next to the grave of Hakīm Ata. With honor and reverence, his disciples took Sayyid Ata down from the cart and buried him beside Hakīm Ata. Now the graves of Hakīm Ata and Sayyid Ata are next to each other.

And the situation with that tumult and shouting and uproar was that on that night, the spirits of Bāqïrghān had fought with the spirits of the shaykhs and saints of the Ka'ba.[21] The spirits who came from the Ka'ba were taking Sayyid Ata away, [but] the spirits of Bāqïrghān did not allow it. The spirits of Bāqïrghān pursued and drove off the spirits who came from the Ka'ba, brought [back] Sayyid Ata, and placed him at the side of Hakīm Ata. From that day down to this very time, people going to Bāqïrghān first perform the circumambulation to Hakīm Ata and then perform the circumambulation to Sayyid Ata.

·   ·   ·   ·   ·

The above narrative marks the end of the *Book of Hakīm Ata;* it is of considerable interest in a number of ways (not least of which is the self-referential comment on the treatise about Hakīm Ata), but the central point of the story is Sayyid Ata's displacement of the caretaker of Hakīm Ata's shrine, whereby the stage is set for Sayyid Ata to be buried next to Hakīm Ata. Neither of these narrative moments is uncontested, of course, but what is of special interest is the curious "polarity" of preeminence worked out in the narrative: the Prophet's promise regarding a descendant who would serve as the caretaker of Hakīm Ata's grave trumps the promise of the local saint, Hakīm Ata himself, whose own choice of *mujāvir*—his own descendant evidently, but one who in any case had gone to considerable trouble to rediscover the saint's grave following its forty-year inundation by the Amū Daryā—is quickly displaced by Sayyid Ata. (The latter is not, however, defeated or humiliated, but is rather "taken care of" and assigned a different area in which to continue serving as a shaykh and as a shrine caretaker). Upon Sayyid Ata's death, however, the local spirits prove stronger than those of the Kaʿba and ensure that the Prophet's descendant will lie in rest next to the local saint.

The graves of Sayyid Ata and Hakīm Ata are indeed found together; and the two are also linked in hagiographical lore in the *silsila* of the Yasavī Sufi tradition. Beyond this, they also share a pattern of genealogical connections in that just as Sayyid Ata was known as the saintly ancestor of distinct, self-conscious kinship groups prominent in Central Asia from the ninth/fifteenth to the fourteenth/twentieth centuries, Hakīm Ata too was regarded as the ancestor of a prominent family of Khwārazm, in a lineage traceable at least as late as the twelfth/eighteenth century. The two figures thus suggest the range of constituencies—spiritual descendants in Sufism, natural descendants in kinship groups, and the broader public of pilgrims to shrines—in which the legacies of saints were typically cultivated.

In the end, a work such as the *Book of Hakīm Ata* reminds us that we should not restrict our understanding of the Yasavī tradition's legacy to the Sufi order that emerged from it. Though clearly shaped by the worldview, ritual and devotional repertoire, and terminology proper to Sufism, the narratives of the *Book of Hakīm Ata* reflect the interests of a broader constituency, an audience less interested than Sufi adepts in the technical specifics of Sufi doctrine, issues of succession, or specific relationships among shaykhs, their disciples, and other communities. Yet the echoes of the narratives found in the *Book of Hakīm Ata* in hagiographies produced within those narrower Sufi communities may remind us that popular hagiographical lore was not merely a later and "degraded" version of tales told in Sufi circles, but arose and developed independently, as testimony to a saint's "public" charisma and prestige and to the continuing power and religious resonance of his shrine.

NOTES

1. For a discussion of scholarship on the Yasavī tradition, see my foreword to Mehmed Fuad Köprülü, *Early Mystics in Turkish Literature*, ed. and trans. Gary Leiser and Robert Dankoff (London: Routledge, 2006), viii–xxvii (the work is an English translation of Köprülü's *Türk edebiyatında ilk mutasav-vıflar* [Istanbul, 1918]); see also my "The *Mashā'ikh-i Turk* and the *Khojagān*: Rethinking the Links between the Yasavī and Naqshbandī Sufi Traditions," *Journal of Islamic Studies* 7, no. 2 (July 1996): 180–207.

2. See the discussion of issues relating to this figure in my brief article, "Hakīm Ata," in *Encyclopaedia Iranica* (New York), 11 (fasc. 6, 2003), 573-74.

3. K. G. Zaleman, "Legenda pro Khakim-Ata," *Izvestiia Akademii nauk,* 9, no. 2 (1898): 105–50. The passages presented here have now appeared in abbreviated form in English in Köprülü, *Early Mystics*, 91-92, 110–12, and are based on Köprülü's Turkish paraphrases, which were based in turn on one of the Kazan publications. A recent edition of the work prepared by Munevver Tekcan and published in Turkey has not yet been available to me.

4. This place-name is incorporated into the saint's alternative name "Sulaymān Bāqïrghānī," but the use of such a *nisba* [kinship name] is not found in pre-nineteenth-century sources; the verse ascribed to Hakīm Ata has occasionally been collected and published under the title *Bāqïrghān kitābï* (the *Book of Bāqïrghān*), but this appellation too is recent.

5. Zaleman, "Legenda," 114–15.

6. There is an interesting parallel between this element of the story of Hakīm Ata and Hubbī Khwāja and an account, preserved by the historian Rashīd ad-Dīn, about tensions between another father and son of the seventh/ thirteenth century—the Mongol conqueror Chingīz Khan and his eldest son, Jöchi (or Jochi). According to this account, Jöchi disobeyed his father several times and sent excuses when Chingīz Khan summoned him; he was indeed suffering from a real illness, but someone reported to Chingīz Khan that he had seen Jöchi out hunting in the mountains. (In fact, what the man had seen was a party sent out by Jöchi, too weak to go himself, to hunt in his place.) Chingīz Khan was angered by this report, declared his son a rebel, and set out against him with his army; then the father, upon learning that the son had died, was extremely distraught, having also learned that the informant's report was untrue. (Jöchi is even said to have sent a great deal of game to his father, paralleling the affirmation in the *Book of Hakīm Ata* that Hubbī Khwāja turned over all the game he shot to his father.) Rashīd ad-Dīn, *The Successors of Genghis Khan*, trans. John Andrew Boyle (New York: Columbia

University Press, 1971), 118-19. It is not clear that we should presume any direct modeling of one account on the other, even though both may have taken shape at approximately the same time; they no doubt reflect the use in different settings of a common stock of narrative themes, here focused on tensions between a father and son. In any case, the hagiographical lore of the Yasavī tradition is full of narrative parallels to stories and imagery known widely in Inner Asia in the aftermath of the Mongol conquest.

7. The phrase used here, *nafas tarttï,* "he drew a breath," can mean simply that he spoke or uttered these words, but the implication is that the words spoken by a saint, even in anger, have inevitable force and cannot be undone.

8. The text does not say so explicitly, but the implication seems to be that Hubbī handed over to his mother such offerings as he continued to receive.

9. Here again there is no specific statement to this effect, but the implication is that Hubbī continued to serve as an intercessor for any "young man" (*yigit*) who called upon him. Hubbī Khwāja's status as the patron of "young men" is noted by Navā'ī already in the late ninth/fifteenth century (the term *yigit,* moreover, often serves as the Turkic equivalent of the Arabic *fatā,* hence linking Hubbī Khwāja with the traditions of *futuwwa* organizations).

10. Our appreciation of these figures' religious roles has been skewed by the fact that we know of them chiefly through the works of Soviet ethnographers, whose ideological and academic training inclined them to interpret such stories and rites as "survivals" of pre-Islamic traditions (e.g., with discussions of "water-cults" or with 'Anbar Ana as the mother goddess and Hubbī Khoja as the "dying and rising deity").

11. Zaleman, "Legenda," 117-19.

12. I.e., Kāth, the chief city of Khwārazm in the early Islamic period.

13. For the most part the text uses a term identifying the person in the tent as an old man; occasionally, without comment, the text uses the corresponding term for an old woman.

14. The text places the word for brother, *qarïndash,* in such a way that it could be understood as referring to the old man he was addressing, or to Hakīm Ata; since it does not include the possessive suffix (i.e., *qarïndashïm,* "my kinsman"), the first reading appears preferable.

15. The animals are identified as *"kiyiklïr qulanlar,"* the first term referring to deer, gazelles, or wild animals in general, and the second referring more specifically to wild asses. Köprülü stressed that the deer's appearance in this story, as well as the tree mentioned in it, reflected "survivals" of pre-Islamic Turkic religious traditions (he did not mention the wild asses). A similar approach is found with regard to this story, again without reference to the wild asses, in Thierry Zarcone, "Le brame du saint: De la prouesse du chamane au miracle du soufi," *Miracle et karāma: Hagiographies médiévales comparées,* 2, ed. Denise Aigle, Bibliothèque de l'école des hautes études, sciences religieuses no. 109 (Turnhout, Belgium: Brepols, 2000), 413–33, esp. 416–17]. Although religious ideas, symbols, imagery, and rites undoubtedly "survive" across confessional boundaries, it should be clear that to pretend to reconstruct

pre-Islamic Turkic religious notions out of the imagery from these Muslim hagiographical tales is to misconstrue the sources and take them out of their proper context—especially when the imagery in question is simply that of animals of the steppe appearing at a holy man's grave in the steppe.

16. That is, the saint promises a portion of the votive offerings received at his shrine for Jalāl ad-Dīn's maintenance.

17. The text appears to read thus, although "Manzil-khāna" is not otherwise known (in this text or beyond it) as a name for the place where Hakīm Ata's grave was, and indeed the logic of the narrative requires that Manzil-khāna and Bāqïrghān be separate places; with the elimination of a locative suffix on "Manzil-khāna," however, the text would read simply, "Khwāja Jalāl ad-Dīn of Manzil-khāna stayed on as Hakīm Ata's *mujāvir.*" It is possible that this figure's name reflects that of a prominent Hanafī jurist of Khwārazm, Jalāl ad-Dīn Kurlānī (from the locality now known as Gurlen), who is ascribed links with saints of the Yasavī tradition in various (mostly late) sources.

18. A pilgrimage site called Bāghirghān Ata was mentioned as the burial place of Sayyid Ata, Hubbī Khwāja, and Hakīm Ata already in the late ninth/fifteenth century. It is discussed in unpublished hagiographies of the Kubrāvī saint Husayn Khwārazmī; see V. V. Bartol'd, "Otchet o komandirovke v Turkestan," *Sochineniia* 8 (1973): 147.

19. Zaleman, "Legenda," 119–21.

20. The most direct parallel to this motif, of a saint's soul being seen and blessed by the Prophet during the *mi'rāj*, appears in the legend of Islamization focused on Satūq Bughrā Khān, renowned as the first convert to Islam (in the mid-fourth/tenth century) from the Central Asian Turkic dynasty known as the Qarakhanids. In this account, Satūq's soul is seen by the Prophet, and is identified for him by Jibrā'īl; the parallel continues as an account of this witnessing is later read, in a book, by the saint who becomes the vehicle for Satūq's conversion.

21. The story of the nocturnal battle between the spirits of the Ka'ba and those of Bāqïrghān recalls a comment found in the fifth/eleventh-century lexicon of Mahmūd al-Kāshgharī (*Compendium of the Turkic Dialects*, trans. Robert Dankoff and James Kelly [Cambridge, MA: Harvard University Press, 1982], 2:267, 544–45): "The Turks maintain that when two groups do battle, the jinn who dwell in their respective lands fight each other beforehand, out of loyalty to the human rulers of their two lands. Whichever of them is victorious, victory comes to the ruler of that one's land on the morrow; but whichever of them is defeated during the night, defeat comes to the king in whose country that party of the jinn dwell. The armies of the Turks shield themselves on the eve of battle and keep to their tents, to protect themselves from the arrows of the jinn. This is a well-known belief among them."

10 Sarı Saltık Becomes a Friend of God

Ahmet T. Karamustafa

Sarı Saltık (or Saltuk) is the most famous "warrior-saint" associated with the Islamization and Turkification of Rumelia (the Ottoman Balkans). His historical personage is shrouded in obscurity, and the most that can be asserted about his historical life, though not with complete certainty, is that he was a holy figure who accompanied a large-scale migration of Turkish nomadic clans from northwestern Anatolia to the region of Dobruja in present-day Bulgaria and Rumania in the 660s/1260s.[1] His spiritual descendants may have included such famous Turkish Anatolian saints of the seventh/thirteenth century as Barak Baba, Taptuk [Tapduk] Emre, and the poet Yūnus Emre.[2] Over time, his saintly image became entangled with the image of the warrior hero popular among Turkish speakers in the form of epic romances about such figures as Ebū Muslim, Battāl Gāzī, and Melik Dānişmend.[3] This in any case was the image captured in the *Book of Saltuk (Saltuknāme)*, the only surviving "epic hagiography" about Sarı Saltık, which was compiled between 878/1473 and −885/1480 by a certain Ebu 'l-Hayr-i Rūmī for the Ottoman prince Cem (900/1495).[4]

In the *Book of Saltuk*, Sarı Saltık appears as the ultimate religious hero: he possesses superior physical strength and unmatched fighting skills, exceptional intelligence and cunning, unwavering faith, and profound scholarly knowledge, as well as all the supernatural powers of sainthood. He toils ceaselessly for the faith throughout Eurasia, West and South Asia, the Middle East, and North Africa, but he is especially attached to Rumelia and Crimea, and the brunt of his zealous struggles on behalf of Islam is more often than not directed toward Christians. He propagates Islam both by the sword on the battlefield and by a peculiar and highly colorful form of one-upmanship in religious expertise: he often disguises himself as a Christian monk or a priest, displays stunning skills in scholarly debate and ritual performance in foreign languages, and then reveals his true identity to his Christian audiences (typically clergy and aristocracy) and invites them to Islam.

The following selection from the beginning of the *Book of Saltuk* captures the story of Sarı Saltık's sanctification as an eighteen-year-old youth during his first foray into Christian Rumelia. At this early stage in the narrative, his heroic credentials have already been marshaled. He has been hailed as a descendant of the Prophet Muhammad both as a *seyyid* (Arabic *sayyid*, descendant of Muhammad through his grandson Husayn) and a *şerīf* (Ar. *sharīf*, descendant of Muhammad through his grandson Hasan), and indeed, both of these titles are used throughout the text to refer to him. His lineage has been linked also to Battāl Gāzī, who functioned as the premier Muslim warrior hero for all Turkish speakers of Anatolia. His proper name has been cited as Hızr, which associates him permanently with Khizr, the immortal prophet-saint of Islam at whose hand Saltık is initiated into sainthood in the episode translated below.[5] (See Figure 5.) The name *Saltık*—which, we are told in the text itself, means "mighty man"—is bestowed on him by a Christian opponent whom he defeats and converts to Islam. This "blond" Saltık (*sarı* literally means "yellow") is now venturing for the first time into Rumelia, which is Christian territory formerly unpenetrated by Muslims.

It would be foolhardy to attempt to place the events narrated in the *Book of Saltuk* in precise historical context. To judge by the presence of a Latin Christian ruler in the narrative, the epic seems to preserve some memory of the Latin Empire of Constantinople (1204–61), but the bulk of the historical activity of Sarı Saltık is supposed to have taken place during the rule of the Byzantine emperor Michael VIII Palaiologos (r. 1259–82), after the restoration of Constantinople to Byzantine control.

TRANSLATION

It is narrated that Şerīf parted from his companions and, adopting a new guise, headed by himself toward Rumelia. He reached a location by the sea whence infidel soldiers attempted to cross over [to Rumelia]. Some crossed [the sea] at Kilaşpol and others at the strait of Feranospol. Şerīf arrived at the strait of Kilaşpol and saw that no one could get across because of the high number of soldiers there. He was disguised as a priest. He asked for a boat from the infidels, but they did not give him one. Şerīf then walked up the shore for a while and came to a chapel crowded with infidels who were busy drinking. He sat in a corner. When night fell, he rose from his place and knocked down all the infidels. There was a ship next to the chapel. He

Figure 5. Moses and Joshua watch Khidr pray on a waterborne carpet. One of twelve paintings in manuscript of the *Qisas al-Anbiyā'* (*Tales of the Prophets*) of Ishāq ibn Ibrāhīm al-Nayshābūrī. Ink and opaque watercolor on paper; 34.5 × 20.7 × 5.5 cm (13 9/16 × 8 1/8 × 2 3/16 in.). The Edwin Binney, III, Collection of Turkish Art, Harvard University Art Museums, 1985.275_71656. Photograph by Katya Kallsen. © President and Fellows of Harvard College.

got in its fishing boat, headed out to the sea, and crossed over to Rumelia. He came ashore and sank the boat. Just then, he saw a group of infidels, who asked him, "Where are you coming from?" Şerīf replied, "I'm coming from Bosnia in Rumelia." The infidels said, "We're from Morina,[6] and we have relatives [there] but we don't know if they are alive and well." Şerīf said, "I'm going to that province, and I'll convey your news to them." They went their way.

Şerīf immediately headed into Rumelia.[7] He arrived at a place called Mıgalgara,[8] where there was a large church. He entered the church and greeted the clergy.[9] The monks asked him, "Where are you coming from?" He said, "I'm coming from the town of Kilaşpol." The priests said, "Did the patriarch Filyon of the Franks cross over?"[10] Şerīf replied, "I heard that they set sail to go back." Suddenly, a man appeared and informed the priests that the patriarch was about to arrive. The priests told Şerīf, "You were saying that he wasn't coming and yet here he is—you fooled us."

They welcomed the patriarch with gifts and presents and honored him. The patriarch came directly to the church. The lords arrived with wine and they sat down to eat and drink. Şerīf busied himself with serving them. As the infidels got totally drunk, the patriarch said, "Get up and close the church door so that no one can enter in on us." Şerīf rose from his place and closed the door. The patriarch offered the wine cup in his hand to Şerif. Şerīf took the cup but set it down and did not drink. The patriarch said, "Why don't you drink?" Şerīf replied, "I have some trouble with my stomach, and I was told not to drink wine. I'm being cautious and refraining from it." Filyon said, "So be it, young man."

When they all got drunk, they fell asleep. Şerīf took this opportunity, got up, and knocked them out. He carried the patriarch outside the church and tied him up to a tree by the stream. When morning came, the patriarch opened his eyes and saw Şerīf standing across from him with a bare sword in his hand like Mars. Filyon then gathered his wits and said, "Who are you to put me into this state?" Şerīf replied, "I'm Şerīf. Proclaim the [true] faith fast or I'll destroy you." The patriarch said, "O' Şerif, for the sake of the religion you follow, I'm not an infidel. I secretly hold [that] religion. I came here only because infidels in great numbers gathered around me. I pledge not to mobilize troops against Muslims from now on." Şerīf said, "No, proclaim faith in front of me so that I believe you." The patriarch said, "If I do as you say, I'll lose my country; instead let me give you a thousand gold coins annually as a tribute." Şerīf insisted, "Profess in front of me so that I hear you." The patriarch said, "I'll lose face." Şerīf said, "I won't mention it to anyone if you don't tell anyone that I was here." Filyon perforce came to the [true] faith. Şerīf said, "I'll leave you here and go inform your army."

He returned to the infidels and said, "Saltık arrived and tied up your ruler to a tree in such-an-such a place and he is torturing him. Hurry!" The lords rushed and found him tied up to the tree; they untied him and brought him to his post. In a while, some infidels arrived in an agitated state and announced, "Last night, Şerīf Saltık the Magician came and knocked out the priests of the church!" The patriarch immediately wrote a letter and sent it to the king in Istanbul, saying, "I saw with my own eyes that Saltık crossed the sea to this side and penetrated inland. Don't be heedless—he's after you. I [myself] escaped [from him] by a trick; you should take caution."

When the letter reached the king, he was terribly frightened. He left Istanbul and went directly to the fortress of Endriyye.[11] It is reported that close to Istanbul, in a distance of four days' travel, there was an old fortress built by Edrin son of Islam son of the prophet Adam.[12] His son Endriyye dug a moat around it. Surrounded by marshes with a river on one side and equipped with drawbridges, it was impenetrable. In it there was a mighty glass church built by the Roman emperor Cevher, which all infidels visited. Jesus had completed a forty-day retreat there. Infidels came to the church, made forty-day retreats, circumambulated the church, and gave alms. They called this town Endriyye. It was located at the heart of Rumelia. The king entered the town without delay, closed its gates, and began to reside there.

Then the patriarch, too, came to the fortress of Endriyye from Mığalgara with his Frankish Latin soldiers. The patriarch, accompanied by the Latin prince Mihal Miryanos, came to the fortress and joined the king. Together they walked to that church. Şerīf himself was among the Latin soldiers and arrived at the church dressed as a priest. He saw that the church was in the center of the town and infidels were rubbing their faces to its walls. Şerīf thought [of a stratagem]. There was a renowned priest in Latin lands, and the name of this accursed cleric was Cālūt.[13] He flew in the sky by magic, and all the infidels had faith in him. Şerīf had heard of his renown. He stepped forward, kissed the hand of the king, and saying, "My father Cālūt, Christ's blessings on him, sends you his greetings," he took out a letter from his head [cover] and presented it to the king. The king opened the letter and read it. Şerīf read and wrote in twelve languages. The patriarch, the Latin prince, and all the accursed infidels uncovered their heads. Şerīf ascended to the pulpit and recited from the Gospels in a full and beautiful voice. All the infidels wept and were beside themselves [with ecstasy].

When he descended form the pulpit, they brought delicious foods and wine at the king's orders. Şerīf did not eat the food, except for some olives, nor did he drink any wine.[14] He said, "These are harmful for one who's on a diet." The patriarch observed Şerīf and thought he looked familiar. He said to the military commanders, "I'm afraid that this man might be Şerīf." The king said, "This is a man of religion, do not think of him otherwise." Then one of the commanders rose from his place, sat down beside Şerīf, and said, "There are Latins here who know you, and they say that you are not the son of Cālūt." Şerīf got agitated by his words but remained silent. That Frankish commander got up from his place, came to the patriarch, the king, and the lords, and said, "I know for sure this person is Şerīf. He is an enemy of our religion." Then the patriarch said to the king, "Let's capture him by a trick." They prepared a sweet drink with a drug and placed it in front of Şerīf, who was seated by the pulpit. Şerīf took that drugged potion from their hands and drank it. After a while he lost consciousness. They immediately tied him up, took him to a jail, and imprisoned him.

When he came to his senses in the morning and saw himself in chains, he sighed but he did not object to his fate. Just then, executioners arrived and took Şerīf to the king's court. The king said, "O Şerīf Saltık the Magician, see how my fortune brought you to my feet! What kind of a ruse will you perform [now,] when I'll do such a thing to you that will be a lesson to the whole world?" Then he ordered firewood to be piled up in front of the town and Şerīf to be burnt. They were in the habit of burning those with whom they were incensed. They kept Seyyid Saltık Şerīf imprisoned for ten days while they built a mangonel [catapult] with which to throw him into the fire.[15] They started such a fire with the pile of wood that no one could go near it. Then they brought out Şerif, placed him into the mangonel and threw him into the fire.

Now, it is said that across from that town was a hill that Hızr [Khidr] visited, and some Sunni jinns also frequented that place. It so happened that Hızr was seated on the hill [that day] and the jinn Minuçihr, one of the Sunni jinns, was on his way to pay a visit to Hızr. As he was making his way with his soldiers, he suddenly saw a human youth, all tied up, flying into a fire. He immediately swooped down, snatched him, and brought him to Hızr's presence. He placed Şerīf down in front of Hızr. When Hızr saw Şerīf, he got up from his place, untied his hands, and said, "Don't worry, O' Şerīf, death is not decreed for you just yet. There will be no death for you so long as water doesn't appear as fire to your eyes. This will be the sign [of your impending death], so don't be startled [when you see it]." Şerif, Hızr and Minuçihr the Jinn all sat down. They watched the fire burn in front of the town.

Suddenly, the prophet Ilyās also arrived.[16] They stepped forward, greeted him, and sat back down. Ilyās asked Şerīf how he was. Then Şerīf said, "What are you [all] doing among these infidels?" Hızr said, "This location is the place of Şerīf in Rumelia. This is Eden on earth. It will become the hearth of the warriors for the faith. From now on for forty years, we will pray the morning prayer in this place. Whoever prays and fasts for forty days and prays the morning prayers here will become righteous; we will appear to them and they will benefit from us." Nowadays, they call this location the station of Hızr-Ilyās. Hızr and Ilyās got up to leave. Hızr bade farewell to Şerīf and said to him, "From now on, have no fear. Open your mouth." Şerīf opened his mouth, and Hızr placed some of his own saliva in it and said, "From now on have no fear, and march on!" Şerīf gained as much additional strength as he already had, and he entered into [the realm of] sainthood and saintly marvels (Arabic *karāmāt*). Veils were lifted from his eyes and his heart; all secrets became apparent. Afterwards, the prophet Ilyās taught Şerīf the prayer of spirits—which is the greatest name of God—and Hızr taught him the prayer of the angels. Then Hızr and Ilyās departed. Minuçihr the Jinn told Şerif, "O' Şerif, do not omit me from your prayers." Seyyid replied, "Be my sibling in this world and the next." Minuçihr the Jinn also taught Şerīf a prayer and said, "Whenever you say this prayer, I will come to your presence with my soldiers." Minuçihr the Jinn then asked permission to leave and departed.

Şerīf rose from his place and went down to the town. Just before the town, he came to a bridge where an infidel looked at Şerīf and said, "This youth really looks like Saltık, whom they threw into the fire today." One of his companions said, "These Turks know magic, and they don't burn in fire. Didn't you hear [told] in books how many times they burnt Seyyid Battāl and he came back to life and how they threw him down a well and he came back up? Since this Saltık is his son, it is not strange [that he didn't burn]." Şerīf stepped forward and said, "Young men, tell me what your conversation is about because I too would like to know." Those infidels said, "Where are you coming from?" Şerīf said, "I'm coming from Serbia; I'm traveling." They replied, "Young man, we were talking about how a Turkish youth named Şerīf appeared around here and made much trouble for us. He spilled the blood of many Christians. It was the king's fortune that he was captured when he came with his own feet, and today they burnt him, so he was destroyed. That's what we were talking about." Şerīf said, "May the fortune of the king increase—he eliminated the enemies of religion."

Then he headed toward town and directly entered the fortress. On the ramparts right above the gate they were playing drums and feasting. The news of Şerif's burning spread everywhere. Muslims heard [the news] and grew dismayed. As Şerif entered the fort, on that side [of town] there was a church close to the gate of the fortress. In addition to the main church, this was a second important church, and infidel travelers alighted there. Şerif went straight to the church and settled down. They asked him, "Where are you coming from?" He said, "I'm Şem'ūn son of the priest Rahval. I came here to debate with the priests of this place, who, they say, are unmatched in knowledge, so that it will be known who is truly qualified, and [thus] I will be honored and respected by the king, the patriarch, and the princes and will acquire some property and a few coins. The lords too might give me something." Those priests were pleased—they went to the king and conveyed his words. The king went to the patriarch and said, "O Filyon, what's happening is that the son of a priest has arrived in the lower church, and he is engaged in debating." The patriarch, the king, and the lords rode down to the church and sat down.

Şerif stood up, honored the lords, and said, "O community of Christ, whoever among you is superior in knowledge should come forward so that we [may] debate and converse." Three hundred monks and priests stepped forward and debated. Şerif bested them all. Afterwards, he climbed the pulpit and started to preach and interpret the Gospels. All the infidels wept and were beside themselves [in ecstasy]. The king turned to the patriarch and said, "That Turk we burnt should have been alive now. He would have answered this [man] if he had debated him." The patriarch replied, "This young man too is perfect [in knowledge]."

$\cdot \quad \cdot \quad \cdot \quad \cdot \quad \cdot$

After he establishes his scholarly credentials, Sarı Saltık performs a few miracles and soon achieves legendary status among Christians of Rumelia as a wonder-working holy man. After traveling through a few more towns and amassing great wealth through donations from his Christian audiences, he returns to Anatolia to continue his exploits.

NOTES

1. The most comprehensive, most recent scholarly study on him is Ahmet Yaşar Ocak, *Sarı Saltık: Popüler İslâm'ın Balkanlar'daki Destanî Öncüsü* (Ankara: Türk Tarih Kurumu, 2002) (in Turkish). For concise accounts in Eng-

lish, see *Encyclopaedia of Islam,* new ed., s.v. "Sarı Saltūk Dede" (G. Leiser); and Ahmet T. Karamustafa, "Early Sufism in Eastern Anatolia," in *Persian Sufism: From Its Origins to Rumi,* ed. Leonard Lewisohn (London: Khaniqahi Nimatullahi, 1994), 190–93.

2. *Encyclopaedia Iranica,* s.v. "Barāq Bābā" (H. Algar), and *Encyclopaedia of Islam,* new ed., s.v. "Yūnus Emre" (E. Ambrose). For a recent historiographical essay on early Anatolian Sufism, see Ahmet T. Karamustafa, "Origins of Anatolian Sufism," in *Sufism and Sufis in Ottoman Society: Sources, Doctrine, Rituals, Turuq, Architecture, Literature and Fine Arts, Modernism,* ed. Ahmet Yaşar Ocak (Ankara: Turkish Historical Society, 2005), 67–95.

3. *Encyclopaedia Iranica,* s.v. "Abū Moslem Korāsānī" (G.H. Yūsofī) and s.v. "Dānešmand" (T. Yazıcı). On Battāl, see Georgios S. Dede, "The 'Battalname,' an Ottoman Turkish Frontier Epic Wondertale" (PhD dissertation, Harvard University, Department of Near Eastern Languages and Civilizations, 1996).

4. *Saltuk-nāme,* ed. Şükrü Halûk Akalın, 3 vols. (Ankara: Kültür ve Turizm Bakanlığı Yayınları, 1988–90). This edition is based on all the available manuscripts, with an apparatus of variant readings at the end. There is also a facsimile edition, based on one manuscript copy: *Saltuk-nāme,* ed. Fahir İz, 7 pts. (Cambridge, MA: Sources of Oriental Languages and Literatures, 1974–84). The section translated here is from pp. 29–36 in the Akalın edition.

5. *Encyclopaedia of Islam,* new ed., s.v. "Khadir" (A. J. Wensinck).

6. Possibly present-day Morina in the Czech Republic.

7. The original text has no paragraphs; all paragraph breaks have been inserted by the translator.

8. Present-day Malkara in Turkey.

9. Throughout the text, the words for clergy, priest, and monk are used interchangeably.

10. Although he is referred to as the patriarch (*pap*) in the text, this "Filyon" appears to be a Frankish king.

11. Present-day Edirne in Turkey.

12. The town was heavily patronized by the Roman emperor Hadrian and named Hadrianapolis (or Adrianople) after him.

13. The biblical Goliath appears as "Cālūt" (Jālūt) in the Qur'ān.

14. Olives are mentioned in the Qur'ān.

15. This may be an allusion to the story of Abraham, whom Nimrod launched into a bonfire with a catapult.

16. He and Khadir functioned as the ultimate powers of saintly initiation in the popular imagination. *Encyclopaedia of Islam,* new ed., s.v. "Ilyās" (A. J. Wensinck and G. Vajda).

11 Sarı İsmail

The Beloved Disciple of Hacı Bektaş Veli

Vernon James Schubel and Nurten Kilic-Schubel

The following narrative comes from the *Vilâyet-Nâme* (Arabic/Persian, *Wilāyatnāma*) of Hacı Bektaş Veli (Hajjī Bektash Walī), one of the central texts associated with the Bektaşi and Alevi ('Alawī) traditions. Originally composed in Ottoman Turkish, the earliest manuscript dates from the eleventh/seventeenth century; it has been continuously rewritten over the centuries and exists in a variety of manuscript versions. It is also available in numerous modern Turkish versions. The *Vilâyet-Nâme* tells the life story of Hacı Bektaş Veli—popularly known as Hünkâr (the Monarch)—who is believed to have came from Central Asia to Anatolia in the seventh/thirteenth century. Hacı Bektaş (pronounced Hajjī Bekātsh) is perhaps the most famous of all the Turkish Sufis. His tomb in the Central Anatolian town now named Hacı Bektaş in his honor is a major center of pilgrimage especially for followers of the Alevi and Bektaşi traditions.

The *Vilâyet-Nâme* describes how Hacı Bektaş, who comes from the lineage of the Eighth Shī'ī Imam 'Alī Rizā, begins his spiritual education in Central Asia where he studies with both the great *pīr*s Lokman Perende and Ahmet Yesevi (Ahmad Yasawī), is personally initiated by Muhammad and 'Alī, and finally comes to Central Anatolia in the form of a dove, settling in the area around Göreme, where he converts the people to Islam. Hacı Bektaş is presented as a great worker of miracles, and the sites of his miraculous actions, like his tomb, remain places of visitation by pilgrims. The story that follows is the narrative of one of Hacı Bektaş's greatest disciples—his second *halife* (*khalīfa*, spiritual assistant), Sarı İsmail or "Yellow İsmail." According to the *Vilâyet-Nâme*, following the death of Hacı Bektaş, Sarı İsmail traveled to the town of Tavaz, near the modern city of Denizli in western Anatolia, where, like his spiritual master, he converted the people to Islam and created numerous *murīd*s (disciples). His tomb is located in a small Bektaşi village on the modern road between Denizli and Tavaz. The village is unmarked from the road and the tomb is not located on any map, but it is still visited with some regularity by faithful pilgrims from the Alevi and Bektaşi traditions. The story that follows is remarkable in the way it affirms the major concepts of both Bektaşi Sufism and the larger Sufi tradition. The text presents Sarı İsmail as one of the Friends of God, who are referred to in Turkish most often by the term *erenler*, which means "those who have attained." As such he is worker of marvels (*keramet*, Ar. *karāmāt*) and a possessor of authority (*velayet*, Ar. *wilāya*). He knows things from the hidden, or *bātınī*, realm. He demonstrates the importance of disciples' love for their master in the Sufi tradition both through his love and obedient devotion to Hacı Bektaş and through the loving devotion of his followers to him. The text also points out the importance of permission (*icazet*, Ar. *ijāza*) from one's *pīr* to become a teacher in the Sufi path. Despite its relative brevity this narrative, taken from an eleventh/seventeenth manuscript of the *Vilâyet-Nâme*,[1] is in many ways a short course in the essentials of the Sufi worldview.

TRANSLATION

The Second Halife of Hacı Bektaş Sarı İsmail (Yellow İsmail)

Now, his second great *halife* was İsmail Padişah. Hazret Hünkâr's (the noble Monarch's) relationship with him was more special than his relationship with his other great *halifes* or even his special relationship with the other Friends of God (*erenler*). The love between him and Hazret Hünkâr was a mystical symbol. No one else from among his *halifes* attained to that rank. He was the keeper of Hazret Hünkâr's ablution ewer. If [Hazret Hünkâr] needed to travel somewhere from his home in Karahüyük, he usually took [İsmail Padişah] along as his companion. He was recognized as one of the *erenler* who held authority and could work miracles. He was someone dear to [Hazret Hünkâr] who was fully initiated.

One day while in the presence of Hacı Bektaş a thought passed through Sarı İsmail's mind. He thought: "I wonder what Hacı Bektaş will grant this poor *fakir* [Ar. *faqīr*] as a territory. What place will he show me as a homeland and a place of residence where I can live out my life in peace?"

This thought became known to Hacı Bektaş. Immediately Hazret Hünkâr Hacı Bektaş—may God protect his secret—said, "My İsmail, remain here until I pass to the other world. After that you should go out and throw the staff that is in your hand. We give you the place where it decides to land as a homeland."

Then he said, "My İsmail, take this green decree (*ferman*) and keep it with you. We entrust it to you. There will come a time after this when people will come to you seeking it. Deliver it to them."

When the time came, Hacı Bektaş died. His disciples covered their beloved in his prayer rug. Sarı İsmail Padişah took permission from Hacı Bektaş and decided to go. He set out on the road. He threw his staff. Being a man of knowledge, he looked into the secret realm and saw that his staff had gone straight to a town called Tavaz in the province of Menteş and had hit the dome of a church. It had pierced the dome and fallen inside.

As it happened, there was a priest sitting in the church. He was reading the Gospels. The true staff appeared to him in the form of a dragon.[2] Meanwhile, while all this was happening, night fell. The priest went out and met Sarı İsmail. He kissed his hand and touched his face to his feet. Traveling in front of him, he took him and brought him to the church. He tore the church down and built a splendid dervish lodge. Sarı İsmail Padişah converted the priest to Islam. İsmail Padişah said to the priest, "I shall take up residence in Tavaz. You should also remain here. Let us be neighbors."

After this, Sarı İsmail Padişah assumed the form of a yellow falcon. Then he came and landed in a place in Tavaz. He had a ring around his neck and a bell on his talons. In those days there was an infidel ruler (*bey*) named Zupun. Some people told Zupun that at such and such a place a yellow falcon had come and landed. They said, "There is a ring around his neck and a bell on his talons. We have never seen such a falcon."

Zupun said, "That falcon that you have described has either escaped from an infidel ruler or a Turkish ruler. Having left there, he has come here. We must try to catch him now. We will need two people for this. One dressed in the clothing of a Muslim and the other in the clothing of a *kāfir* (unbeliever). If he has escaped from a *kāfir*, he will be drawn to the [one who is dressed as a] *kāfir*."

Then he arranged two people for this purpose. One dressed in the clothing of a Muslim and the other in the clothing of an infidel, they rode out to catch the falcon. While they were coming, Sarı İsmail Padişah again assumed the form of a human being. He sat under the place where he had landed. They rode out and came to the place where the falcon had landed, and they saw seated beneath that place a blond, beautiful-faced, and hardy holy man. However, there was no longer any falcon. They came forward and kissed the noble Sarı İsmail Padişah's hands and feet. Then they came back to Zupun *bey* and said, "That thing that appeared in the form of a falcon was not a falcon. It was Jesus Christ. He has come to protect you. He has taken the form of a man and is sitting under the place where he landed in the form of a falcon."

When Zupun heard these words, he rejoiced. Love overwhelmed him. His reason left him. He soiled himself. He brought together the nobles of the tribe, and he made a gesture of supplication (*niyaz*) and rode out to that place. He saw Sarı İsmail Padişah sitting there. He went forward and kissed his hands and touched his face to his feet. He said, "Welcome. Your coming is a blessing. May you be blessed."

And then, Sarı İsmail invited them to accept the religion of Islam. Zupun *bey*, his tribe, and the tribes of his land all became Muslims. Sarı Isma'il gave them regards from Hünkâr Hacı Bektaş. Then he said, "He has granted me a homeland (*yurt*) here."

They said, "Welcome. Any place that you desire in the city of Tavaz is yours. I will make a place for you there according to your wishes."

Sarı İsmail Padişah said, "A place of dervishes should be a humble low-lying place."

At the lower end of the city, there was a place between two gathering places that were two miles apart from each other. He agreed to that place and he made it a place of residence for himself. They also wanted to make a place for him adjacent to that place. But there was no water there. He would have to bring water to the garden and orchard himself. They said, "You will need to water them." He cast his glance at a place overlooking that place, and suddenly a pleasant stream came out. It was sufficient for the garden and orchard. That water which came from his power (*vilayet*) and miracle (*keramet*) is famous. Many more miracles were demonstrated in that place. Many people from that locality came and became his dervishes.

Then one day when he was wandering there with his community, he dropped by and visited a farmer. One of [the farmer's] two oxen began to speak. He said, "O' king of the Friends of God (*erenler*), Sarı İsmail Padişah."

Sarı İsmail Padişah rode alongside them and said, "What's up? What's wrong, black ox?"

The ox said, "It has been twenty years that I have been pulling my master's plow. I have gotten old. I have no strength or power left. This time he will send me away and they will slaughter me. Please, for the love of God, rescue me from this! Save me!"

So Sarı İsmail Padişah bought this ox from his owner and freed him. For that reason in that territory (*velayet*) they gave him the nickname "Sarı İsmail Who Made the Ox Speak."

Sarı İsmail Padişah demonstrated numerous miracles and wonders in that land. Our tongues are not able to tell about all of them. He made lovers of the people of that place. Many of them became his disciples (*murīd*) as a result of his miracles and the will of the Friends of God. For some time he lived out the rest of his life there.

At the time when he passed to the next world, they buried with him the green decree that Hacı Bektaş had written. And it stayed with him until one of Hacı Bektaş's sons discussed issues of succession (*icazet*, Ar. *'ijāza*) and information about the path with the sons of Seyyid Ahmet who lived to the east of Sivrihisar. Remembering the writing of Hacı Bektaş, they came to the tomb (*mezar*, Ar. *mazār*) of Sarı İsmail Padişah in Tavaz in the land of Menteş. They said, "Oh Sarı İsmail Padişah, that green *ferman* entrusted to you is needed. Give it to us."

Suddenly, the grave of Sarı İsmail Padişah opened up. His blessed hand came out, and he presented the green *ferman*, and the sign of Hacı Bektaş again appeared. They took it with them and carried out its instruction. Whatever his intentions [as written on the *ferman*], they carried them out completely.

NOTES

1. This account is translated from an Ottoman manuscript of the *Vilâyet-Nâme* dated 1624 and preserved in the National Library in Ankara, Turkey.

2. An allusion to the story of Moses in which his staff becomes a dragon as he confronts Pharaoh's magicians.

12 Yūnus Emre Seeks His Share

Traditional and Modern Accounts

Mark Soileau

Yūnus Emre (c. 720/1320–21) was the first great Anatolian Turkish poet, and his mystical verses of divine love have for centuries inspired Sufis and influenced mystical poets in the Turkish-speaking world. Yūnus's lyrical poems were collected in a *dīvān* (anthology of poetry), and many of them have continued to be sung as *ilāhīs* (hymns) by Sufis in Turkey, even since the official closure of the *tekkes* (dervish residences) in 1925.[1] Until the twentieth century, no individual hagiographical work had been written about Yūnus Emre's life, but brief stories about events in his life were included in the hagiographies of other saints and in other literary works, mostly emphasizing Yūnus's faithful service to his master, Tapduk Emre.

The earliest and most extensive premodern written narrative about Yūnus Emre is an episode from the *Vilâyet-Nâme* ("Book of Sainthood") of Hacı Bektaş Veli, the seventh/thirteenth-century eponym of the Bektashi dervish order. Probably first set down in writing in the late ninth/fifteenth century, the work incorporates Yūnus, whose fame as a poet and mystic had no doubt spread widely by that time, into Bektashi tradition by portraying Yūnus as seeking his spiritual inspiration and initiation from Hacı Bektaş. In the narrative excerpted here,[2] Yūnus is a young man from a village called Sarıköy who comes to the great saint's convent at Suluca Karahöyük seeking material sustenance, but soon realizes that what he really needs is spiritual blessing or inspiration, signified by the breath of the saint.

TRANSLATION

Hazret-i Hünkâr Hacı Bektaş Veli Sends Yūnus Emre to Tapduk Emre

They relate that Hazret-i Hünkâr Hacı Bektaş Veli's sainthood, his miracles, and his exquisite exploits had become known all over the world. From every direction, seekers and lovers began to come, and there was eating and drinking, *samāʿ* [spiritual audition], and exalted gatherings. Everyone of poor state would, under the eye of the saint, find his share and go. And those who came would surely take a share.[3]

Yet, north of Sivrihisar, in a place called Sarıköy, was one called Yūnus. He was a very poor farmer who grew grain. Once, there was a drought, and nothing came of his crop. He heard of the saint's (*eren's*) praiseworthy qualities, and because everyone would have his desires satisfied and not leave disappointed, he resolved to reach the dust under the noble feet of the saint and request enough to subsist. He loaded a load of medlar fruit onto an ox and took it to the presence of Hazret-i Hünkâr in Suluca Kara[hö] yük. He said, "I am someone of poor state, and nothing came of my crop. Accept this fruit and give something in return, so that we can subsist, in your honor." Hünkâr made a sign, and the *abdāl* took the medlars and ate them.

Yūnus stayed one or two days, then wanted to leave. They [townspeople or members of Hazret's entourage] informed the Hünkâr. He instructed them to ask him, "Shall we give wheat, or else shall we give breath?" They asked. He replied, "What would I do with breath? I need wheat." Again, they informed the Hünkâr. He instructed, "If he needs wheat, let's give it. If he needs breath, let's give two breaths for every medlar seed." Again, they told Yūnus. Again, he said, "I need wheat. What need do I have for breath?" Again, they informed the Hünkâr. Again, he instructed, "If he needs wheat, let's give it. But if he needs breath, let's give ten breaths for every medlar seed." They told Yūnus. He said, "What would I do with breath? I have a family. I need wheat. Let him give it, so I can go and subsist and get by with my family." Yūnus did not understand signs like this and did not accept this much fortune. Hazret-i Hünkâr gave an order, and they loaded as much wheat as his ox had brought. He took it and set off.

He came to the lower end of the village. He went up the slope next to the baths. Now he thought, "I reached the saint. He offered me this much advice, and he was going to give ten breaths for every medlar seed. I didn't accept it. What an inept thing I've done! The wheat will be gone in a few days. Why didn't I accept that breath? It wouldn't run out even at death. I'll turn around and go back again. Perhaps he'll still bestow that gift he so generously offered."

He returned, came to the *tekke*, unloaded the wheat, and said, "Let the saint give me the share he offered. I don't need wheat." The *khalīfa*s informed the Hünkâr of this situation. He commanded, "That matter can no longer be. It had to be before. We have presented the key to that lock to

Tapduk Emre. Let him go and take his share from him." They told these words of the Hünkâr to Yūnus.

Then, upon that speech, Yūnus set off and came to Tapduk Emre.

.   .   .   .   .

The account in the *Vilâyet-Nâme* goes on to describe briefly Yūnus's arrival at Tapduk Emre's *tekke*, his faithful service to his master for forty years carrying firewood (during which he never once brought in green or crooked wood), and the "opening of his lock," during which, at Tapduk Emre's command, he began to give voice to the songs that would form a great *dīvān*. It is at this moment that Yūnus is said to have received his share.

This thirteenth/nineteenth-century account of Yūnus Emre's meeting with Hacı Bektaş Veli is essentially the same as that found in the oldest extant copies of the *Vilâyet-Nâme*, dating from the early eleventh/seventeenth century, so the story seems to have been repeated virtually unaltered for several centuries. In this unembellished form, the narrative reads like a story told orally, as by a Sufi master illustrating to his disciples the need to avoid heedlessness, which is likely the context in which it was told at the time the *Vilâyet-Nâme* was first set down in writing in the ninth/fifteenth century.

By the second half of the twentieth century, however, new literary genres had fully developed in Turkish literature, and the expectations of a growing readership had changed in accordance with them, so authors began to develop and expand the few written and oral legends about Yūnus Emre into longer, fuller narratives of his life, particularly as novels and plays. Soon after the *Vilâyet-Nâme* was first published by Abdülbâki Gölpınarlı in 1958, the writer Nezihe Araz (b. 1922) published in 1961 what is perhaps the first full-length fictional treatment of Yūnus's life, the hagiographical novel *Dertli Dolap* (*Woeful Waterwheel*). Tracing her life of Yūnus from his youth in Sarıköy, through his meeting with Hacı Bektaş Veli and his service under Tapduk Emre, to his founding of his own *tekke* and his death, Araz incorporates the various traditional legends, tying them together in a continuous narrative sequence with additional scenes to fill in the gaps. She creates secondary characters and fills in the skeletal depiction of events with the dialogue she imagines would have accompanied them. She further incorporates many of Yūnus's poems, portraying the contexts in which she imagines he might have composed them. Her Yūnus is an introspective, often tormented spiritual seeker, but also a man with a mother and with a beloved. The author gives voice to Yūnus's thoughts, through both third-person narration and Yūnus's interior monologue. This is particularly evident in the critical scene outside Suluca Karahöyük in which Yūnus, having rejected Hacı Bektaş's offer of spiritual inspiration in favor of material wheat, comes to the realization that ultimately what he really needs is the spiritual inspiration. In Araz's modern telling,[4] the distraught Yūnus's entire life has collapsed, and all of the indecisiveness, the inner turmoil he has been experiencing is given dramatic expression as he comes to realize that what he has just so heedlessly passed up is actually the remedy he had been so ardently seeking.

TRANSLATION

A Guest for Three Days

> He sent me forth on the far-off road
> These eyes of mine welling
> What would he know of the woeful state?—
> The one of sound heart

On the way from Inn of the Strangers to Suluca Karahöyük, which took a full day, Yūnus lost his resolve. Where was that peace he had felt the whole way? Where was that settledness? It was as if he had lost all of it at Inn of the Strangers!

He became Yūnus, the old Yūnus of Sarıköy, woeful Yūnus! He came to the point of crying out, "If only I hadn't set off on these roads, if only I hadn't crossed those mountains! If only I had stayed in Sarıköy and fought with myself!"

God's countryside, God's mountains. There's no one but himself to hear his voice. He shouts as much as he can shout. He shouts out:

> A fear has fallen on my soul
> I wonder what will become of me?

Eventually, he entered Suluca Karahöyük. What a bright, pleasant, auspicious place it was.

There were other guests inside. The man who had met him was walking over to the guests. Yūnus took him by the arm.

"Excuse me," he said. "I'm not going to stay here long. They say you have a blessed man, called Hacı Bektaş. I have something to ask of him. I'd like to see him at once, submit my request, get my answer, and go. Can't you take me to him?"

The man laughed. He stopped, then laughed again. "How were you able to wait nine months and ten days in your mother's belly?" he said.

"Everybody who comes wants first to see him. Everybody who comes has pressing business. Is that proper, dervish? Well, let's chat, let's get to know each other. Let's separate the sticks and stems. After that . . . "

"But I really have to go back right away."

"Have you come to get fire?"

"Something like that!"

Yūnus was so insistent that the man left in order to ask. A little while later he came back, laughing. He shrugged, as if to say "What can we do?" "I asked," he said.

"What did he say?"

"You're a guest for three days!" Then, [you can see] the Sultan [i.e., Hacı Bektaş]. "Come, this place is your home, your village for three days. It'll pass quickly."

The Eye That Sees Faults

> Love for the homeland has fallen before me
> Let me go, calling O' Friend!
> He who arrives there right away stays
> Let me stay, calling O' Friend!

Yūnus, as a guest, had no choice; he gave in. And what an orderly, regulated place this is, he thought. In other places where one stops, there are no restrictions like being a guest for three days. But here there was wheat, bulgur. He needed to wait for that.

While thinking in this way, he asked the person next to him, "Friend, may I know your name?"

"My name is Ali, but they call me the Guide.[5] Because of my job! I look after those who come and those who go—I show them the way."

"All right."

"Come now, let's go to the guesthouse. I'll show you your place. Wash up, get clean. There's a mosque across from the Pīr's home; if you want, go there. It's almost dinnertime; if you want, rest until then, then come to dinner. No one's a stranger here. Since the Sultan said you were a guest for three days, you're his guest, not ours. As a matter of fact, at lunchtime he set aside a morsel for you."

"He set aside a morsel for me? How is that?"

"It's a custom at our table. The Sultan 'sets aside a morsel' from some of the food that's put in front of him. He separates it on a dish 'for the hidden saints' share' and puts it in a corner. It's the guest's share!"

"At every meal?"

"At every meal! This lunchtime, the Presence [Hazret, i.e., Hacı Bektaş], as he set aside the morsel, said, 'There should be someone coming from the direction of Mihalıççık. God knows, but this morsel is his lot!' Aren't you coming from that direction?"

"Yes, but . . . that's so. How would your Presence know this? I didn't send word with anybody."

The Guide laughed. "What need does he have for news? That's Hacı Bektaş's eye—it sees everything. Except for human faults. He has blinded his eyes from seeing the faults of humans. There's nothing that isn't known to him. . . . Come on, I'll show you your place!"

He takes his head between his hands and falls on the bed. There's only one thing he wants now: to hear the sound of the waterwheel, his waterwheel. Its creaking, creaking sound . . . its voice . . . And to ask it:

Waterwheel, why do you moan?

And to get the answer:

I have woes—that's why I moan!

"I hear the woeful voice of the waterwheel, so why don't they hear the voice of my woes?" Then he asks, astonished: "Who is this I'm calling 'I'? Who is this I'm calling 'they'? Who, my God, who?"

I Lay Down—God, Raise Me

O friends, take no notice of me
What I've again become, I don't know
Don't ask me about theory and practice
I've become mad, I don't know

Into the cell walked a tall, swarthy man with a thick black beard and hair falling down the back of his neck. His age seemed to be around fifty, but perhaps he was younger. The twilight made him look older than he was.

"Welcome, son!" he greeted Yūnus, and then sat on the bed. "Is your journey from far away?"

"I've been on the road for thirteen days . . . "

"Before that?"

"Before that . . . I was in the village?"

"Before that you were on the road as well, but you didn't know it then. Because you were stopped, and the road was going. Now the road is stopped, and you're [still] going."

"I didn't understand a bit of that."

The man laughed. "It doesn't matter. I didn't say it so that you'd understand; I just said it for the sake of conversation. My name is Secret Baba [Gizlice Baba]. The youths around here call me that. As if everything I say has some secret meaning! As for the name my father whispered into my ear along with the *ezan* [call to prayer]—even I've forgotten it. What have you come here for?"

"I have some business to discuss with Bektaş Veli."

Yūnus had said this in such a way that his statement implied that he wouldn't speak this to anyone but him. In order to change the subject, and also to soften a little his previously harsh expression, he said, "I've seen many things here I didn't know about. I don't understand anything of what I've seen; I can't grasp anything."

"You're right. For one thing, you're ignorant. Ignorant of the Truth, that is—don't misunderstand. You don't know this road, this custom. This place is a 'hearth.' Here, something is being cooked—a new thing! It comes all the way from Khorasan, from our real home. I studied at Ardabil. Do you know where Ardabil is? Forty days' journey from here—maybe farther. Whatever there was to read, I read it. When I came here, I understood that all I had read was in vain. Whatever there is, is here. A little later, a lamp will awaken in the Pīr's home.[6] It's an oil lamp with three branches and three wicks! Don't look at this with everyone's eye—look at it with the eye of the soul! Then you will see: this lamp is not any lamp; it is the lamp of Khorasan. It is the illumination coming from there, the light! Before all lamps, this one was awakened. Here, before the lamp of the Pīr's home awakens, nobody touches light. This is a way, a rule. What does this mean? Whatever there is, is in the lamp of Khorasan. That lamp was awakened in Anatolia in the Pīr's home. It means that whoever wants to awaken and be enlightened, to redeem his ancestral legacy, should waken his lamp here and take his lot from the food cooking in this hearth. Isn't that so? Are you sleeping, young man?"

"No . . . No! You're saying beautiful things, very beautiful things. But, forgive me, I'm having difficulty understanding. It's hard. I've never heard such things."

"You're right. But when I began, I told you these are new things and this hearth is a new hearth."

"All right . . . Secret Baba, if everybody has to come one by one to the hearth to learn these new things and to understand, wouldn't the whole country have to move here? How is that possible?"

"Those who take their share from here and go are likewise charged with wakening new hearths in the places they go."

"All right. So why have you stayed and not gone on?"

"Don't look to me, young man. I need him. And he needs me and people like me."

"People like you? What kind of people are you, Secret Baba?"

Secret Baba laughed. He liked Yūnus. He explained: "On my head is the crown of state, on my forehead the prostration of obedience, in my blood the victory of power, in my eye the light of sainthood, in my ear the prayer of Muhammad, in my nose the fragrance of love, in my mouth the faith of testimony, in my breast the Qur'ān of wisdom, in my hand the hand of sainthood, at my waist the belt of guidance, at my knee the point of service, at my foot the rules of the way, behind me the appointed time, before me destiny!"

"Wow!" Yūnus let out such a burning *wow* from the heart and soul, it was as if a handful of flame had spewed out of his mouth.

"'Wow' is right," said Secret Baba.

"I want to memorize this. When I get back to the village, I want to say it to Merdan Koca. Tell me that again."

Secret Baba repeated it again and again. Yūnus engraved it, carving each word into his memory. He was worried he would forget it.

Much time had passed; nobody was around anymore. Secret Baba stretched out on his bed.

"We need men like that," he said, as if whispering. "Men like that with their love intact and their faith intact."

"What will you do with men like that?"

"A new building is being set up for you, I'm saying—in order to work there."

"I saw the great buildings at Seyid Battal Gazi. How big they were!"

"Not like that. A building embracing all of Anatolia."

"Explain this a little more to me. Speak a little more."

"It's late. Tomorrow I'm going to wake up before the sun rises and go out to plow the fields. Tomorrow there's a lot of work. Come on, may God give you comfort."

Does He Want Wheat, or the Inspiration of the Saints?

A strange state has come
Upon the state in me
It's made my heart a throne
It's sat upon my soul

Yūnus said to the Guide: "Brother Guide, go tell your master: today I want to leave from this place. May you never be lacking; I've eaten, drunk, washed, and bathed. I've seen a lot and learned a lot. But I had a request. I wanted to present it to him. I wasn't able to. At least let me tell it to you and you can take word to him. If he says yes, great, but if he says no, fine . . . I'm wondering if your master would give a meager amount from his wheat, from his bulgur for Sarıköy. Go, ask him. If he says yes, let him give it and I'll go. If he says no, may he forgive what I've eaten and drunk while here. Still, I need to go. The village is waiting, the village is hungry!

The Guide left. Yūnus waited and waited, feeling as if his heart were being squeezed inside a hand of fire. It seemed to him that he waited a long, unbearable time. When the Guide appeared, he was surprised. He felt tired, old, wearied. However, the Guide was young and vigorous as if he had just left. He was laughing. He took Yūnus's arm, walked him toward the door of the guesthouse, and when they had gotten well away from the crowd, he let go of Yūnus's arm. Now he wasn't laughing, but he was smiling. He looked into Yūnus's eyes and said with the sweetest expression in the world, "Brother Yūnus, I presented the matter to Bektaş Sultan. He listened to me without making a sound. He thought for a long while. Then he said, 'Ask him if he wants just wheat, or the inspiration of the saints.'"[7]

He hadn't understood! And what is the inspiration of the saints supposed to be? Fine, but the starving people in the village? Let's suppose he was polite and said he wanted the inspiration of the saints. Would this inspiration fill Sarıköy's belly? What a strange thing! And these people are strange people! They must not know what hunger is. Or they don't have wheat to give Yūnus, or they don't want to give him any, and that's why they send that message.

The young man, trying not to express what was going through his mind, and doing his best to smile, said, "Your great Bektaş must be a joker. Is Sarıköy's belly going to be filled with the inspiration of the saints? If he'll give it, I want wheat. If he won't give it, I want permission to leave."

The Guide again left Yūnus and went to convey the message. The poor boy sat on a nearby horse block. He put his chin in his hands and began to think. He now regretted a thousand times over that he had come. This was how charitable people could be to each other. It's clear God favored people like that. He was smiling on them.

Yūnus was scratching his chin and did not even notice the Guide, who was standing in front of him, waiting. This time he wasn't smiling, but looked at Yūnus skeptically and said, "Friend, there's a matter within this matter. This matter is not like other matters. Poise yourself, think it over well, then give your answer. The Presence is asking, 'If he wants it, one breath, one inspiration, for every seed of the medlars he brought!' What do you say?"

Do the medlars he brought have a name? And each seed! What hard tests they put him to! Surely nothing like this had ever befallen anyone; Yūnus had never heard of this kind of thing before. He shook his head resentfully.

"I told you, the whole village is starving. While the Presence is prolonging the bargaining, I'm worried that when I get back to the village, there won't be anybody left to eat the wheat I bring. Beyond that, it's up to him. His inspiration for those who are full, his wheat for those who are hungry! That's all I have to say."

When the Guide came from the Presence for the third time, he was neither laughing nor skeptical. He was absolutely afraid. His hands, his feet were shaking. He took his friend's arm tightly and said, "Yūnus, this is the last time. Think it over well. Yūnus, think well! He said, 'If he wants, ten breaths, ten inspirations for every medlar seed!' What do you say?"

"I have nothing left to say. Let's untie the oxen and harness them to the cart. I need to set out before it gets late!"

"Wait, Yūnus. He said, 'If he still wants the wheat and not the inspiration of the saints, load wheat onto his cart and let him go in peace.'"

One sack, three sacks, five sacks. They loaded a full twenty-six sacks of wheat. There was no more room.

The young man said his farewells to everyone individually. He kissed the hands of the elders, and embraced the younger ones. He thanked them all. He drove the cart along Flow Spring Road toward the meadow.

What was he going to say back in Sarıköy to those who should ask him if he saw Bektaş Veli? The Presence had not shown his face to him. But hardly anyone had come all this way and not seen him. Yūnus resented this. He had been thinking about all the things he was going to tell when he got back to the village. Now it was as if there was nothing left to say. It was as if he hadn't seen anything. Though there was an emptiness inside him, a vast emptiness, he was returning to Sarıköy.

Awakening

> That goblet is full
> Those who drink from it go crazy
> That teacher's students
> Have girded their loins for his way

The meadow has gone mad, and within it crazy winds are blowing. There is something constantly on his tongue, something he keeps repeating: the inspiration of the saints! The inspiration of the saints! What is this inspiration of the saints? What kind of thing? Is it something to be bought and sold?

By the medlar seed. By the seed within each medlar, ten inspirations of the saints for every medlar seed? So that's how it's measured!

So the Presence, too jealous to show his face, was going to offer him as much inspiration of the saints as medlar seeds—not as much, but ten times?

But what was this inspiration of the saints?

He knew what wheat was, what it was good for, how it was used. He also knew what hunger was, and how it was to be eliminated. But he didn't know what the inspiration of the saints was, or how it was used, or what it was good for.

Maybe it was a good thing, an important thing. If only he had asked for a little wheat and a little inspiration. See, he hadn't thought of that. If only he had told his friend the Guide, "I want the wheat, but let's have your master give a handful of that saintly inspiration too. Let him give some, and we'll see what kind of thing it is. We'll have a taste."

When he had asked for the wheat and not the inspiration, why had the Guide's face looked so confused, I wonder; why had he gone pale?

His heart is tightening, tightening, tightening. He himself is shrinking, shrinking, shrinking. He becomes a tiny weevil. Then they put this weevil in a huge grain bin. Before him are mountains of wheat! Then they tell that weevil, "Let's see you eat all this wheat. Eat every grain! Eat until it's all gone! Don't eat the inspiration of the Friends of God, but eat the wheat!"

The weevil is intimidated by this much wheat; his head spins, his stomach turns. The weevil vomits. It's a watery, sticky thing. And Yūnus, walking avidly across the green-crazed meadow with his hand on the yellow ox's rump, is talking to himself: "No," he says, "I don't want to be such a weevil. Such a filthy, soft, tiny thing! Nobody can make me like that. I want to live like a human."

What had he wanted? Wheat! What had the giver said?—"Forget the wheat, you need the inspiration of the saints." The inspiration of the saints? But who was it who was going to present this inspiration? One who didn't show his face! Good God! There were two persons inside Yūnus: one was asking, one was speaking. It was as if a knot had come undone, as if a precipice had collapsed. It was as if there were water inside, gurgling as it flows.

I'm Fed Up with Duality

> I'm fed up with duality
> I'm filled with the food of unity
> I've drunk the wine of woe
> Let my remedy be plundered

The water was flowing, gurgling. It was flowing so much, Porsuk River would have been a handful of water beside it. Mountains were toppling over inside Yūnus. It was as if there was an earthquake and the ground was roaring, sliding under his feet.

Oh! The waters were coming, the waters—waters that would crack Yūnus, beat him and split him open, tear him down.

From inside Yūnus a light was being born. An indescribable, undeniable, never-before-seen light. A brilliant thing. Was this what they call the Light (*nūr*)?

And what about what they call the Fire (*nār*)? There was light within Yūnus, and also fire! Yūnus was roasting. What was happening, my God, what was happening? Such cries were coming from inside him that even the yellow ox was turning around and looking at him.

"A road," he said. A road appeared to me—it was revealed! This was a road that would solve my problems, would make flow the fire within me. They offered that to me and I didn't want it!

Maybe what they called the inspiration of the saints was the auspicious hand of the Lord being extended to me. Hadn't I cried out to the firmament, hadn't I yelled to God: "See me too! See me too!"? Maybe He saw me and wanted to take me by the hand.

That's how it is. How does God see man? With the eye of a beloved. Didn't everyone call him—this one who wouldn't show his face—the Friend of God, the Beloved of God?

Surely there was meaning in his holding the light of inspiration into his face again and again. But he had not wanted that light; wheat had been loaded up in sackfuls.

On his forehead were beads of sweat. He was walking as if he was fleeing, as if he was flying.

Then he started to weep, to cry out loud, to sob, and he said,

> I know my crimes, my sins are many
> It is God that I implore
> I've no request of anyone
> I ask my wish of God alone

Yes, but . . . When God presented to you your wish, what did you say? You said wheat! You didn't want the inspiration of the saints!

Yūnus could hold out no longer. A sigh like a fire erupting from his breast scorched all the green of the meadow. The yellow ox stopped and was looking at the poor man. Yūnus had thrown himself face down on the ground, had become one with the soil, had melted into the soil and disappeared. He passed out of himself.

The birds in the air, the crops turning green, the blossoming trees—in short, all of lively nature—petrified. Something was happening. Not between slave and slave, but between God and slave! Something incomprehensible, strange, big!

They wouldn't grasp this. Even humans wouldn't grasp this. Not even the angels! This was such a mysterious moment between slave and Lord that there was no place in it for even Gabriel. This was the Lord showing His beautiful face to a dear slave, in a way that those who do not see it, do not know it, cannot fathom.

When Yūnus came to himself, it was afternoon. He was collapsed in a heap. He straightened up. First he saw his hands. He turned them over and looked long at them. They hadn't changed. So they were like they had been before. Maybe his face too had not changed. He couldn't see his face. Who knows? Maybe it had changed a lot. He couldn't know about his face and his eyes. But he himself had changed a lot. Something had happened. Something like a flash of lightning!

Slowly he got up. He held onto the yellow ox's horns. "What happened to me?" he asked. The ox didn't make a sound. Yūnus repeated, "What happened to me?" What would this animal know? Even he himself didn't know. He just wept. But how was he weeping? In torrents. He had never cried like that in his life. A while ago, there were swelling floods within him. Now, those floods had turned to rain. Oh! It was as if cool mercy was raining, washing his inside.

Yūnus turned the yellow ox's head toward the road it had come on. Then, stroking its horns, he said:

> I'm not here to stay
> Without reaching the presence of the Friend
> From grief, my heart won't open
> Without seeing the face of the Friend

Then he asked, "Do you understand? We're going back. Without seeing him, my heart won't open, from grief, from sorrow. It'll be a fatigue on you—there's a heavy burden on your shoulders. But what about what's on my shoulders? Believe me, my burden is heavier—like the weight of the world. And your burden we're going to put down in Suluca Karahöyük and go. Come on."

Take Your Wheat, Give Your Inspiration

> My eye to see you
> My hand to reach you

Today I put my life on the road
Tomorrow to find you

Nobody in Suluca Karahöyük was surprised to see young Yūnus returning with sacks full of wheat so late in the evening.

The Guide again received him in front of the gate and brought him
toward the guesthouses.

It was as if Yūnus had come down with a fever. His lips were covered
with cracks. His eyes were burning brightly.

When he saw Secret Baba in front of the guesthouse, the young boy
leapt into his arms like a wounded falcon.

"Hold me," he moaned. "Hold me. The ground is slipping from beneath
me, it's as though I'm going to fall. What have you done to me? Something's
happened to me. Hold me!"

Secret Baba embraced Yūnus with his strong arms and pressed him
close.

The other, as if raving, was shaking as he spoke: "Take me to him right
away—that one who wouldn't show his face to me, that one who turned
me away from his door—right away! For God's sake. I can't stay here like
this any longer. What did he do to me? I have to ask, I have to know. Take
me to him—right away!"

Secret Baba sat Yūnus on the bed he had left him on that morning. He
brought cold water in a beautiful tin-coated cup. "Drink this. Drink it and
wait! What's happened to you has happened!"

He doesn't know how long he waited. He doesn't know what he did
while he waited. From within him, words are welling up in waves:

I've passed out of my selfhood
I've opened the veil of my eye
I've reached union with the Friend
Let my doubt be plundered

Finally, Secret Baba came out. He extended his hand to Yūnus and
called, "Come!"

What happened next Yūnus did not forget for his entire life. Nor what
he now saw. . .

They entered the Pīr's home. In the courtyard, a sparkling fountain with
three channels. Just like the lamp of Khorasan with the three branches.
One is burning sparklingly, the other is flowing sparklingly.

Two spiral staircases, leading up from each side of the fountain to a hall
above. The stairs covered with felt rugs. All of the rooms on the upper
floor open onto the hall. Right in the center, a niche in the shape of a

mihrab. The lamp of Khorasan is there. On one of the doors, a green covering, embroidered in yellow metal, its edges stitched with leather.

Secret Baba stood in front of the door with the green covering. He closed his eyes, brought his right hand over his heart, and, with that sweet, rich, strong voice, called out slowly, "*Destuuur* [by your leave]—my master, my Pīr!"

This was not a call, it was really an entreaty, a supplication.

At that moment, it seemed to Yūnus that time had stopped. From within, no response would come. For none of these events had in reality happened; it was either a dream or an illusion.

But from within a voice did come. If you ask Yūnus, it was not a human voice. This had to have been the voice of the Lord inviting His slaves to the realm of existence in order to make Himself manifest—the voice of the Lord issuing from a human. Yūnus said:

> I've passed out of my selfhood
> I've opened the veil of my eye
> I've reached union with the Friend
> Let my doubt be plundered

Yūnus entered, slipping behind the door covering that Secret Baba had pulled back.

Into the world, into the hereafter—he can't say anything about that. That world within the world that he had mentioned—into there!

A large window, reaching down to the floor. Looking out of that window, one could see the mulberry tree and the meadows behind the mulberry tree.

In front of the window, a divan. On the divan, a mattress covered with a red sheepskin. On the mattress, a man whose face Yūnus could see less than half of.

He's turning his head slowly toward the guest. He's smiling. Even in the twilight of evening he is so beautiful that the darkness cannot conceal this beauty. It seems as if there is such a long distance between Yūnus and the hand being extended for him to kiss that in crossing this way Yūnus wants to shout:

> I've found the soul of souls
> Let this soul of mine be plundered
> I've given up profit and loss
> Let this shop of mine be plundered

When he held that hand, the young man's matter was settled. He says just one thing—he doesn't know anything else—"Take your wheat, give your inspiration!"

Some time later, when he opened his eyes, Yūnus was on the floor, curled up on his knees.

The other, with moist eyes, with the sweetest look in the world, is looking attentively at the young man. "Yūnus," he says, "you have acted foolishly. You did not want our hand of inspiration . . . Take Sarıköy's portion. Listen to us: we have entrusted your lock to Tapduk Emre. He's not a stranger to us. Go, find him. After me, it's him you need."

NOTES

1. For a critical edition of Yūnus Emre's *dīvān*, see Mustafa Tatçı, ed., *Yūnus Emre Divânı*, 3 vols. (Ankara: Kültür Bakanlığı Yayınları, 1990). For a comprehensive study of Yūnus and his poetry, see Abdülbâki Gölpınarlı, *Yūnus Emre ve Tasavvuf* (Istanbul: İnkılâp, 1961). For studies in English of various aspects of his poetry, see Talat Halman, ed., *Yūnus Emre and His Mystical Poetry* (Bloomington: Indiana University Turkish Studies, 1981). Many of Yūnus's poems have been translated into English in Grace Martin Smith, *The Poetry of Yūnus Emre: A Turkish Sufi Poet* (Berkeley: University of California Press, 1993).

2. The following excerpt, translated from a manuscript of the complete prose version of the *Vilâyet-Nâme* copied in 1226/1811, is included in facsimile in Abdülbâki Gölpınarlı, ed., *Vilâyet-Nâme: Manâkıb-ı Hünkâr Hacı Bektâş-ı Velî* (1958; repr., Istanbul: İnkılâp Kitabevi, 1995), 117b–119a.

3. *Nasib*, meaning "a share, lot, portion." "To take a share" (*nasib almak*) also refers to initiation into a dervish order.

4. Excerpts translated from Nezihe Araz, *Dertli Dolap: Yūnus Emre'nin Hayat Hikâyesi ve Şiirleri* (Istanbul: Atlas Kitabevi, 1984 [first printing, 1961]), 91–114. The translator made every attempt to contact relatives of the author, and though he received an enthusiastic response, he was unable to secure a formal statement of permission.

5. *Delil* (Arabic *dalīl*), meaning "a sign, indication, proof, or guide." In the context of Bektashi ritual, the *delil* is the first candle lit during the ceremony, from which the other candles are lit.

6. In Bektashi parlance, lamps or candles (*çerağ*) are not lit; they "awaken" (*uyanmak*).

7. *Erenler himmeti.* The *Vilâyet-Nâme* version has "breath" (*nefes*), and Araz below uses both *nefes* and *himmet* for the alternative to wheat.

PART IV

Africa: West and East

. . . . .

Muslim communities have long constituted major populations in many African nations, in addition to those of North Africa. From the far western edge of the continent comes a poem in Wolof, the principal language of Senegal, in praise of major figures in the Tījānīya Sufi order. Nigeria, the most populous nation in Africa, was home to the highly influential thirteenth/nineteenth-century Fodiyo family, an engine of revolution in early modern West Africa. Nana Asma'u, daughter of the family's leading figure Usman, composed several remarkable hagiographical panegyric poems in honor of her father as well as his most important successors. Not least among her works is a poem dedicated to Sufi women throughout Muslim history. Her poems represent both the Hausa and Fulfulde languages. Moving farther east, a Swahili source represents another distinct literary form, with a selection from an epic poem about the prophet Job that features his wife, Rehema. Finally, from Somalia, in the Horn of Africa, comes an early-fourteenth/twentieth-century Arabic account about the death of a major East African Sufi leader of the Qādirīya order.

13 Shaykh al-Hajj Abbass Sall: In Praise of the Tījānīya Order

Souleymane Bachir Diagne

THE POEM

Devoted to the praise of the Tījānī Sufi path, this poem in Wolof by the Tījānī shaykh Abbass Sall celebrates the many scholars who distinguished themselves in the Tarīqa (Path). Shaykh Abū 'l-Hasan ash-Shādhilī (656/1258), the founder of the Shādhilī Sufi order famously answered, when asked about the fact that he did not write books, "My disciples are my books." Shaykh Abū 'l-'Abbās Ahmad at-Tījānī (1230/1815) could have declared the same thing. The sourcebooks of the Tījānīya order are those written by his disciples, presenting his biography, sayings, teachings, and so forth. Who he was is manifest not through treatises but through the spiritual achievements of his disciples. That is the message of this poem: many great scholars and men of high spirituality have been produced by the Tījānīya, and they manifest the continuous flood generated by the founder of the order, whom Tījānīs consider the Seal of sainthood. To sing the merits of the Tījānīya is therefore to sing the merits of those men who bore the "color" of Ahmad at-Tījānī.

The metaphor of coloring is central here. Seriñ Abbass Sall (*seriñ* in Wolof means "master") uses the West African traditional method of dying clothes in indigo as a metaphor for those who have received the spiritual guidance from the Shaykh of the Order. As a result, they have been (spiritually) dyed by him, the metaphor goes, and they are in turn dyeing others in an endless chain that spreads the indigo color of the Tījānīya. The poem is, then, an enumeration of prominent disciples that evokes their writings or "miracles" or sometimes just their names. It starts with the very first disciples initiated by Shaykh at-Tījānī even before he founded his own order: he used to initiate his disciples into the Khalwatī order before he

received the "illumination," during which the Prophet Muhammad himself appeared to him and revealed to him the *wird* (litany or office) by
which the new order was founded. The poem ends with El Hajj Malik
Sy (1272/1855–1341/1922), who can be credited for spreading widely the
Tījānīya in Senegal, where it is the largest Sufi order.

A chapter (12) in a longer poem titled *The Book That Recommends the
Truth and Guides on the Path toward the Truth* (*Téeré buy tektalé dëgg
ak di womate jëmé ci yoonu dëgg*),[1] the text excerpted here was written in
1386/1966 in Abidjan, Ivory Coast, during the author's particularly propi-
tious journey in that city.

THE AUTHOR

Shaykh Abbass Sall is one of the leading figures of Tījānīya in Senegal.
He was born in 1327/1909, under the sign of number 7, as he once told one
of his sons, Abdallah Sall. "I was born on Saturday, the seventh day of the
week, the seventh child of my mother," he said, "and I came to have a home
in seven places of our country: Saint-Louis, Ross-Bethio, Louga, Nguick,
Taba, and Caïra, in addition to Dakar." He died in the seventh month of
the year 1411/1990, on July 2. He was the son of Mayoro Sall, a renowned
Muslim scholar and guide, and Sokhna Fatou Wade, a woman known for
her piety. After his father died in 1342/1923, he went to pursue his Islamic
studies in Saint-Louis, where he followed the teachings of a famous scholar,
Birahim Diop. Later, he was to study with Muhammad al-Lida, a prominent Mauritanian figure. Both Birahim Diop and Muhammad al-Lida are
said to have been impressed by their disciple and to have predicted his
brilliant future as a scholar and spiritual leader. In fact, the many poems
(more than 10,000 verses) he wrote in Arabic and in Wolof—some to teach
the basics of Islam and Islamic ethics, others to explain different aspects
and dimensions of the Tījānīya Sufi path, still others as panegyrics to the
Prophet or to the Shaykh at-Tījānī—all manifest what his masters had
predicted. He created an important Islamic institute in his hometown of
Louga. Every year during the month of Muharram, he used to organize
a spiritual retreat. For three days during that month his disciples would
gather in the village of Nguick for collective readings of the Qur'ān and
collective recitations of the Names and Attributes of God (*dhikr*). This
retreat, which he called the feast of souls, continues to be organized by his
successor, Mansur Sall and his other children. The year 2008 marked the
fiftieth anniversary of the first celebration of "the feast of souls."

WOLOF SUFI POETRY

One of the most famous poets in the Wolof language, Musa Ka, a disciple of Shaykh Ahmadu Bamba, founder of the Murīdīya order, wrote the following verses:

> Let me tell this to those who say that writing in Wolof is not
> appropriate:
> Rhyming in Wolof or in the noble Arabic language or in any other is
> the same
> Any language you use to praise the Prophet of God will then reveal its
> innermost value

"Those who say Wolof is not appropriate," to whom Musa Ka is responding, are those who think that only Arabic, the language of the Qur'ān, should be used for any matter religious or spiritual. Historically, with the Islamization of many parts of the world, Arabic has been adopted as a scholarly language and as a literary medium, in particular to write praise poetry. But people in those regions have also widely used their own indigenous tongues, thus making virtually all human languages "reveal their innermost value" as the voices of Islamic scholarship and literature. One needs only to consider the contribution of Sufi poetry in Persian to Islamic and world literature to be convinced that the languages of Islam are many and that there is no such thing as a tongue nobler than any other when it comes to praising the Prophet or the Friends of God.

Islamic literatures in non-Arabic languages have often used Arabic script. Such literature is known as *'ajamī* (non-Arab). But of course "non-Arab" is not a definition, or at best, is a negative ethnocentric definition. Islamic literature in Wolof is called Wolofal (literally: "to put in Wolof"), and the following poem by Shaykh Abbass Sall presents the usual features of Wolofal literature. Phrases in Arabic are often intertwined with the Wolof, and in one instance, even a French word is playfully used.[2]

Shaykh Abbass wrote the poem using an Arabic script. His son and successor at the head of the Sall branch of Tījānīya in Senegal, Hajj Mansur Sall,[3] has decided to publish his father's poem in the Latin alphabet, as well, as Wolof is officially written today in Senegal in that script. Dr. Mansur Sall's decision corresponds to his will to reach out to people schooled in French who are more at ease reading and writing in Wolof expressed in Latin script. Such a move corresponds to the modernizing spirit so characteristic of Shaykh Abbass Sall.

TRANSLATION

Praise be to God and to Him we give praise[4]
Asking that He shower the ocean of His generosity and bounties
Drowning in it our Shaykh[5] so that drowning he drowns us with him
And that we partake in all the great gifts he receives.
The judgment is for the one followed not the follower.[6]
He is the reason for all that we witness *high above* our reason;
He is the philosopher's stone that transmutes a vile mineral
And in a blink changes its substance into that of a diamond.
By the grace of God, when he says to a thing *be, that thing is.*[7]
For whom has it been said, *you did not throw when you threw?*[8]
God filled him with the substance of his grandfather's light;[9]
He made him an ocean of light from His light.
He has created a jar of light and anyone who gets dyed
From this jar shines with utmost beauty, so let's get immersed in it.
How good this jar is and what brilliant colors it creates! Look out for
    those who got soaked in it, who got soaked, then got others soaked;
    who are those?
Start your enumeration with *his friend* Damrāwī,[10]
Who was his envoy *from his grandfather and was his messenger.*
He used to see the Prophet, *peace be upon him,*
Up to twenty-four times every day, no doubt about it.
Now who could be compared to that man,
Let alone be his like in what he achieved?
Don't bother after that asking about the miracles
They performed: this is bigger than anything one could ask for.
After him comes the author of *Jawāhir,*[11]
The one who did not learn *from books,*
The successor, the shaykh Ali Harazim.[12]
His like among the Men you will not see, this Ali
Who stood in our Shaykh at-Tijānī's stead in all aspects
From life to *death,* up and down in everything.
Whatever one receives from our Shaykh
Through him passes before it goes to its destination.
Then comes the great one who did great actions, Ali,[13]
The spiritual axis of these times, the man from Tamasin.
Never will you see, never hear about somebody like him,
Not among those who came before and not among those who came after.
He is the one who wrapped up a snake ready to hit;

More than a thousand kilometers did he cross in just one step:
The call for the afternoon prayer found him in Tamasin
But he still led that prayer for the *people of Fez*.
He threw a bunch of dates from Tamasin
That fell in Fez for everybody to witness.
This man you see with all his knowledge and power
Drank from our Shaykh's blood out of faith in him.[14]
Now tell me about the shaykh Ghali the great.[15]
It suffices to say about him that he educated Shaykh Umar
Al-Futīyu,[16] the pole who united in him everything pure,
The champion who did great deeds and authored *Rimah*.
He is the one who made us proclaim Tījānīya Ahmadīya;
When all are gathered *his great merit is be beyond question*.
And now our Shaykh al-Hāfiz,[17] the best among the Alawi,
In these times the first who brought the *wird*
To these well-known areas, he is the one who surpassed everybody,
And those who said so are his peers who knew him well.
It is about him that the story is told when our Shaykh asked him
Not to reveal himself as his disciple before a sign occurs. Be as before, he
    commanded;
So he came back and, just as before, resumed his teaching.
He showed no sign that he kept a spiritual treasure
Until the day when someone came to him, a man renowned for his
    spiritual encounters.
Every Thursday night, for sure, he would meet
With *the best of all creatures,* the best of what God has brought into
    existence,[18]
Whose noble being is the origin of all those who are *sharīf,*
Our Master Muhammad, upon him
Be the peace of God and His blessings.
That man's arm, the one that would salute the Prophet,
Could be seen, for sure, to be longer than the other.
After he greeted al-Hāfiz, he said, "O' you master,
Give me from what you have earned in your journey."
"All I have," Hāfiz said, "is books.
If you want any of these just take it, you are welcome to it."
The man replied, "I did not come for that.
This Tījānī *wird* that you have is what I am sent for."
The master then knew the time was up, so he came out and he spoke out
About all the aspects of this Path and he gave advice.

The men of Dawālī[19] and the women all rushed
Toward him and pressed him to give them the *wird.*
Add to those cited our Shaykh Riyāhi,[20]
The man from Tunis whose light filled *the horizons.*
The poem *"Saa irkabil"*[21] is a good enough mirror for all of them.
Nobody ever mentioned his like among those who came before,
Nobody was like him then or there, unique as he is.
He is the one who transmitted esoteric and exoteric knowledge.
He is known as the author of the book *Jāmiʿ.*[22]
He was for a long time the imam of our Shaykh;[23]
For thirty years this is sufficient to show how great his *merit,*
Muhammad ibn Mushrī, the great scholar.
Knowledge of the fear of God *is what distinguished him.*
Let this be sufficient for you, and about those who have not been
    mentioned,
Know that not one-tenth of a *tenth* have been spoken about *here.*
All of the Shaykh's disciples, wherever they are, have dyed with his
    colors
Others who have in turn dyed others, starting all over again.
Consider now Sīdī Arabī ar-Ribātī:
To look at him is like watching a deep ocean from the *shore.*
His book *Bughya al-mustafīd*[24]
Is sufficient as a summary of all different chapters of spiritual
    knowledge.
Now look at our theologian Kansūsī:[25]
It suffices to know him through his *Thābit al-usūs;*[26]
He got dyed from Sīdī Arabī.
He knew that good dyeing is from the purest indigo.
And to those who got dyed beyond any imaginable brilliance,
From our Shaykh came the coloration that set them apart,
Starting with the *singer* of the Path al-Baddi,[27]
The successor of Shaykh Hāfiz al-Mujīd.
Let me just mention what Shaykh al-Walī said
To him: *"You are indeed* [another] *Bakri;*[28] O have you heard that?"
Let me just mention that nobody ever heard the word *Baddi*
Before the angels from heaven said it as their name.
Let me just mention the one who was born *from these perfect men,*
The offspring whose *grace* surpassed everybody's.
Look at the son Ahmad ibn al-Baddi:
You may want to say *that nobody is like him*

Until you consider the son of master Shaykh
Ahmad and then think of them as twins.
But then you may want to forget about all of them
As soon as is mentioned their son Muhammad al-Amīn.
Nobody has ever seen his like; you may *glorify him*.
He stood apart in his times, which he dominated.
Are you forgetting Sīdī Mawlūd?[29]
After the master he *was known* as
A man of commitment and engagement, the first to travel to Fez,
To find there those great men with whom he drank the best of drinks.
Among them he found the scholar of Daymānī,
Mahandu Bāba[30] who led the Daymānī
As well as other non-Daymānī people bearing the flag
Of the knowledge *that comes from learning and from inspiration.*
Count among those the *scholar and teacher*
Who educates on the Path to God all who so desire,
Who drank from the light of Ahmad ibn Baddī
Before he was showered by Sīdī
Al-'Arabī Sā'ih, who filled him with knowledge
And he came back with great secrets and new bounties.
He is known as Abba Muhammad Fal,[31]
The son of Baba, the best among the Fal.
Mention next Ubayd ibn Mūja:[32]
Never in Tichitt has lived his like.
His older brother, the author of *Jayshul Kafīl*,[33]
He was distinguished by his *knowledge* of God;
His book *Mīzāb* gives the measure of his high merits
And manifests his greatness without doubt.
Let me close the list of *those men*
Who stand tall and have no consideration for *Farā'id al-la'ālī*
With the Shaykh of Shaykhs, the master of the elite.
His fame rests on his commitment to the Sunna and he is a model;
He is the one who enlightened Senegal, no one will deny it,
Filling the country with knowledge and also with men of faith
So that wherever you go in Senegal, you find
His disciples standing firm for the religion, leading everybody—
The son of Uthmān the famous Mālik.[34]
When he went on pilgrimage, he gathered all sorts of graces and brought
    them back.
It suffices to say about him that anyone you see bearing the scent

Of Sunna comes from him as he leads everybody.
If you want to know him *beyond that,*
Meditate on his *"Khilas"* and his *"Ifhām"* and his *"Kifāya."*
May God shower again upon our Shaykh at-Tījānī
And upon his companions the rain coming *from the clouds of His
    satisfaction;*
In the face of a troubled ocean, to try to keep count of its waves
Only leads to exhaustion, so what about trying to walk into it?
And one wave from our Shaykh, *the ocean,*
Is like all[35] the oceans together; you will not see another,
By God I swear, and I know what it is to swear,
That nobody can know our Shaykh; God will not allow it
Only two know him: God and the Prophet.
That's all; let's end here until another time.

NOTES

1. Shaykh Abbass Sall, *Téeré buy tektalé dëgg ak di womate jëmé ci yoonu
dëgg* (Dakar: NIS Impressions, 1999), ch. 12. The translator's work has the
blessing of the family owning the copyright to the work.

2. Amar Samb thoroughly studies these features, and others present in
Islamic poetry written in Wolof, in his work, *Essai sur la contribution du
Sénégal à la littérature d'expression arabe*, Memoir 87 (Dakar: IFAN, 1972).

3. I thank Dr. Mansur Sall and his brother Abdallah Sall for their help
with the translation of this poem.

4. The Arabic *Al-hamdu li 'llāhi*, meaning "Praise be to God," is followed
by a Wolof phrase meaning the same thing. The poem thus juxtaposes an
Arabic phrase with its Wolof translation from time to time. In this line and in
the rest of the poem, the translator uses italics for the phrases in Arabic.

5. That is, Shaykh Abū 'l-'Abbās Ahmad at-Tījānī. For further studies of the
Shaykh and his path, see Jamil Abun-Nasr, *A Sufi Order in the Modern World*
(London: Oxford University Press, 1965); El Hajj Rawane Mbaye, *Le grand
savant El Hadj Malick Sy. Pensée et Action*, 3 vols. (Paris: Dar Albouraq, 2004);
Jean-Louis Triaud and David Robinson David, *La Tijaniyya. Une confrérie
musulmane à la conquête de l'Afrique* (Paris: Karthala, 2003); and Zachary
Valentine Wright, *On the Path of the Prophet: Shaykh Ahmad Tījānī and the
Tariqa Muhammadiya* (Atlanta: African American Islamic Institute, 2005). I
thank Zachary V. Wright and Andrea Brigaglia for all the insights they generously offered me, on many occasions, on the Tījānīya and Tījānī scholars.

6. This saying has become a proverb. Shaykh Abbass used it to insist on the
heavy responsibility anybody has who claims to be a guide for others.

7. Qur'ān 36:82: "Surely, when He wants anything, His command to it is,
'Be,' and it is."

8. Qur'ān 8:17: "You did not throw when you threw but God threw."

9. Shaykh at-Tījānī is considered a *sharīf,* or descendant of Prophet Muhammad.

10. Sīdī Muhammad ibn al-'Arabī ad-Damrāwī at-Tāzī (1204/1789) is one of the early disciples of Shaykh at-Tījānī. His ability to experience the waking vision of the Prophet is emphasized in the Tarīqa Tījānīya.

11. The *Jawāhir al-Ma'ānī wa bulūgh al-amānī fī fayd Sīdī Abi 'l-'Abbās at-Tījānī (The Jewels of the Meanings and the Attainment of Hope in the Flood of Sīdī Abū 'l-'Abbās at-Tījānī),* completed in 1214/1799 by one of the early disciples of the shaykh, 'Alī Harāzim al-Barada, is the primary source for the Tījānī path. It is a report of the founder's life and teachings.

12. Referred to as Harāzim 'Alī for the sake of rhyme.

13. This other companion is Sīdī al-Hajj 'Alī 'Īssa al-Tamāsinī. He led the *zāwiya* of the path in Tamāsin (Algeria) and was designated by the shaykh as his successor.

14. The story goes that once, after the shaykh underwent a bloodletting, Tamāsinī could not find a spot he judged appropriate to receive the blood and decided to drink it.

15. Muhammad al-Ghālī, another companion of Shaykh Ahmad at-Tījānī.

16. *Kitab ar-Rimah (The Book of the Spears),* Shaykh 'Umar al-Futīyu's commentary on *Jawāhir al-Mānī,* is a treatise on Sufism in general and the Tījānīya in particular.

17. Muhammad al-Hāfiz at-Tījānī ash-Shinqītī spread the Tījānīya in Mauritania.

18. Here again the Wolof phrase translates exactly the Arabic expression.

19. The Idaw 'Alī (Dawālī) are a Mauritanian tribe believed to be 'Alawī *sharīfs.*

20. Ibrāhīm ar-Riyāhī (1267/1850) is credited with having introduced the Tījānīya to Tunisia. His poems have been collected into a *dīwān,* and each is known by its first words.

21. The title of the poem is its beginning phrase, "Take for your companion. . . . "

22. The *Kitāb al-Jāmi' li 'l-'ulūm al-fā'ida min bihār al-Qutb al-Maktūm (The Comprehensive Book for the Bountiful Sciences from the Seas of the Hidden Pole),* completed in 1223/1808 by Muhammad ibn al-Mushrī, is, like the *Jawāhir,* a major book of the Tījānīya.

23. The shaykh, who did not like to lead the prayer at the mosque, had appointed Ibn al-Mushrī as imam; thus the latter is often referred to as "the Imam of his Master."

24. The book *Bughya al-mustafīd li sharh munya al-murīd,* a major source for Tījānī Sufism, is a commentary on the Sufi poem *Munya al-Murīd,* by Mauritanian scholar Ahmad al-Tījānī ibn Sīdī Bāba al-'Alawī ash-Shinqītī.

25. Muhammad ibn Ahmad Kansūs (or Kansūsī or Akansus) (1211/1796–1294/1877) was a disciple of Muhammad al-Ghālī and the head of the Tījānī

zāwiya in Marrakesh. He is famous for his writings in defense of the Tījānī order against its detractors.

26. *Establishing the Foundations.*

27. Muhammad ibn Shaykh al-'Alawī (1265/1848), nicknamed "Baddī," was initiated into the Tījānīya by Muhammad al-Hāfiz who called him the Singer of the Path. He succeeded Muhammad al-Hāfiz. His son Ahmad ibn al-Baddī was also a famous Tījānī scholar.

28. Muhammad al-Bakrī (1262/1845) spiritually "received" the *Salāt al-Fātih*, a prayer on the Prophet highly praised by the Tījānīya that was an important part of their *wird*.

29. Shaykh Mawlūd Fal.

30. Mahand Bāba ibn 'Ubayd ad-Daymānī was a scholar from Shinqīt who defended the Tījānīya.

31. Muhammad Fal ibn Bāba al-Alawī.

32. 'Ubayda ibn Muhammad as-Saghīr ibn Anbūja is a Mauritanian scholar, author of *Mizab al-rahma al-rabbaniyya*.

33. The poem *"Al-Jaysh al-Kafīl,"* by Muhammad bin Muhammad as-Saghīr, was written in the margins of the *Bughya al-mustafīd*.

34. El Hadj Malik Sy (1272/1855–1341/1922) founded Tivaouane, the main center of the Tījānīya in Senegal.

35. The author here uses for the word *all* the French *tout*.

14 Imitating the Life of the Prophet

Nana Asma'u and Shehu Usman dan Fodiyo

Beverly B. Mack

Nana Asma'u bint Shehu Usman dan Fodiyo (1208/1793–1281/1864) was born into a Fulfulde-speaking Fulani family of Qādirīya Sufi intellectuals in the region now known as northern Nigeria. Her father, the Shehu, or Shaykh (1168/1754–1233/1817), is renowned as leader of the Sokoto Jihad (1218/1803–1246/1830), a reformation movement that changed the face of Islam in West Africa. Her active involvement as a teacher, scholar, and poet testify to her role as a principal player in the orchestration of the jihad and its aftermath, the resocialization of its refugees. She accomplished this in part by crafting poetic works in the *sīra* mode in which she described the Shehu's life as a clear imitation of the life of the Prophet Muhammad. In addition, she elevated women's roles in their thirteenth/nineteenth-century West African community to the status of Sufi women revered throughout history. It is difficult to appreciate the effect of Asma'u's work without an understanding of the cultural history of the period. Asma'u's poems incorporate allusions to other works by her contemporaries and to commonly known circumstances of her time. Asma'u's known poetic works number approximately sixty, and they in turn complement other poems and treatises written by her father, the Shehu; her uncle Abdullahi; and her brother Bello. Thus, attention to three of her works only hints at the impact of these biographical works on a Muslim community and the extent to which they promoted the authority and credibility of her father's and family's mission to reform Islam.

Asma'u's *Yearning for the Prophet* (YP)[1] presents an authentic tradition of the life of the Prophet while drawing clear parallels with the life of the Shehu.[2] Her poem *The Journey* (J) details the events of the Sokoto Jihad, selecting events with clear parallels to first/seventh-century events. Exploring the Shehu's own life and jihad endeavors, *The Journey* clarifies that despite being separated from the Prophet by twelve centuries, the Shehu sought to engage in Sunna of the most active kind, imitating the Prophet in both personal and political matters. Thus, each work complements the other, as each presents an image of the Shehu imitating the life of the Prophet.[3] Finally, *Sufi Women* draws women from Asma'u's community into the picture, comparing them with Sufi women of renown as far back as the third/ninth century and with exemplary women as far back as the Prophet's time.

'YEARNING FOR THE PROPHET' AND 'THE JOURNEY'

Links between the Shehu's life and that of the Prophet can be made only in a society in which the Qur'an, and hence the life of the Prophet, is known by heart, as was the case for Asma'u, the Shehu, and other principal leaders in the Sokoto Caliphate.[4] Asma'u's audience would not have missed the intended parallels. *Yearning for the Prophet* follows the classic pattern for poems of its genre. It opens with accounts of miracles associated with the Prophet's birth but also uniquely established within the Hausa cultural context. It refers to the thirteenth/nineteenth-century Shehu (*YP* 70), and its mention of Asmā, daughter of Abū Bakr, the Prophet's Companion (*YP* 216), surely brought to mind for its thirteenth/nineteenth-century audience the image of, Asma'u, their contemporary. That divine revelation is first bestowed on the Prophet and the Shehu in the middle of the third decade of his life (*YP* 82) would have been evident to Asma'u's audience, familiar as they were with the Shehu's life story.[5] Preaching began shortly thereafter for each of these men. The Prophet's age at the onset of his preaching (*YP* 84) was comparable to that of the Shehu, and just after the birth of a daughter for each—Fātima and Asma'u, respectively (*YP* 83).[6] The parallel implied between the daughters would have been clear. Shortly thereafter, God's message was confirmed for each man: for the Prophet when he was just beyond forty (*YP* 85–86), and at the same age for the Shehu.

Both the Prophet and the Shehu embarked on comparable jihads to actively promote Islam (*YP* 112; *J* 26).[7] That the Prophet's life was a model for the Shehu is evident even in the names of people surrounding the Shehu. The Prophet chose as one of his commanders a man called 'Abd Allāh, who seems also to have been his commander at the Battle of Badr (*YP* 121); the Shehu's commander at the Battle of Tabkin Kwato was Abdullahi, his brother. Just as the Prophet encountered formidable numbers at the Battle of Badr (*YP* 123), so too the Shehu's defeat of the Gobir forces at

Kwato was comparably impressive.[8] The Prophet faced great numbers of the enemy at Battle of Uhud (*YP* 135), and although nothing in this poem suggests that men fled the field, evidence exists in the Qur'ān that they did (Qur'ān 3:121). Thus, Asma'u's reference to soldiers fleeing is an evident parallel for "those who know" (*J* 77, 79).[9] Sokoto Caliphate forces, like the Prophet's defeated soldiers, spent the night cauterizing their wounds (*YP* 151).[10] Just as the Prophet "fought the unbelievers" at the famous Battle of the Trench (*YP* 166), the Shehu made use of a comparable tactical aid at the fortress of Alkalawa.[11] Another description of battle action is comparable: at the height of a battle the Prophet sought to disarm the enemy by drawing attention to himself, which must have drawn the fire of enemy archers (*YP* 241–44; *J* 78). Asma'u's audience knew that at the Battle of Alwasa the Shehu's son Bello drew attention to himself, defiantly drawing fire when surrounded by the enemy. Further, the importance of names again is evident in the fact that the Prophet's war camp was called Sala, and Bello's war camp, before his forces set out for Alkalawa, was also at a place named Salah.

The Shehu was involved in other episodes of warfare that can be viewed as directly parallel to those recounted in stories of the Prophet (also referred to as Muhammada and Ahmada): the refusal of many young men and their leaders to convert to Islam led to their being slaughtered (*YP* 179);[12] both the Prophet and the Shehu rejected their enemies' attempts to compromise with the leaders (*YP* 190–91; *J* 51); both the Prophet and the Shehu sent messengers seeking a peace agreement (*YP* 192; *J* 64). These tactics helped to win converts in both cases. (*YP* 251–53; *J* 90–95, 100). Even at the ends of their lives the Prophet and the Shehu continued to preach (*YP* 303; *J* 107). When the Prophet died on June 8, 632 A.D., and the Shehu on April 20, 1817, both were aged sixty-three.

Translation from Yearning for the Prophet

70. He said the Shehu would be the leader[13]
And told them that he would promote Muhammada.
82. He was thirty-five years old
When the Holy Spirits were made known to Ahmada.
83. Next came the birth of his daughter Fātima.
The death of Zaidu[14] was keenly felt by Muhammada.
84. He was thirty-eight
When he started to preach and see the light of Ahmada.
85. When he was forty
Plus a day; God sent to Ahmada

86. The Archangel Gabriel;
God sent the Qur'ān to Ahmada.
112. In the fourteenth year he made his Hijra to Medina
And his enemies came to destroy Muhammada.
121. The commander Abdullahi, son of Jahashu [Rajab 2/November 623]
Led the army against the enemies of Muhammada.
123. There were nine hundred
And fifty of the enemy at Badr when they met Ahmada.
135. They came in a great horde
Of three thousand men to fight Muhammada.
151. They spent the night cauterizing their wounds.
The following day they pursued the unbelievers, the enemies of
    Ahmada.
179. Their refusal meant death to all the young men and their leaders.
They were executed in front of Ahmada.
190. He was enraged and they cowered with fear,
So they sought to reach agreement with Ahmada.
191. They wanted to settle matters between them
And he agreed, peace be upon them, Ahmada. . . .
204. Do not leave me alone, it's not fair my friends;
Come, join me as I long for Muhammada.
205. Stop finding difficulties where there are none
And listen to the exploits of Muhammada.
216. Asma'a stored all these acts in her memory
So that all would know of the miracles of Ahmada.
240. Do not leave me by myself, I am serious;
Please go on helping me as I long for Muhammada.
241. The Hawazilu and Sa'kifu were excellent archers,
But for all their fire, they had no chance against Ahmada.
244. When he was on the promontory-mount, he called attention to
    himself,
Saying, "You should know I am the Prophet Muhammada."
250. When they reached him, he gave them all the booty.
Who has the patience of Muhammada? [9/630]
251. Then the whole populace began to come;
Town by town they entered the religion of Ahmada.
252. Among them were the people of Jibu,
The tribes of Asadin and Kilabu; all followed Ahmada.
253. And also the tribes of Baliyya, Dayyu, and Da'iffai,
They came at the same time to follow Muhammada.

303. He preached to them and of his wisdom,
Explaining the whole truth to them, Muhammada.

TRANSLATION FROM 'THE JOURNEY'

Chapter I. Doxology: The Shehu's Preaching Life

1. Let us thank God, the Almighty, for His generosity.
It suffices us, brethren, let us praise him.
2. Let us invoke His blessing and God's peace upon our Prophet,
His Family, Companions, and all his Followers.
3. Now I am going to explain the practice of the Shehu
For you to hear what was done in his time.
4. Usman dan Fodiyo, Shehu—the Almighty God
Gave him to us here in Hausaland through His mercy.
5. He brought the True Believers out of ignorance, dispelled the
   darkness, and made
Everything clear for us with His light.
6. You should know that he called people to Islam in Degel
And also at Dauran and there at Faru, through his zeal.
7. He turned northward, proselytizing
Until all the people answered his call.
8. He returned home to Degel and then went
On to the Niger, always giving his sermons.
9. The Muslim community accepted his call everywhere,
Those of the East and West, because of his high standing.
10. He overthrew non-Islamic customs and
Established the Muslim Law. Let us follow his path.

Chapter II. Preparation for War (1800–1804)

11. He said men should take up their bows and quivers
As well as swords: you hear his command.
12. He said, "Make ready the horses, and firm up your intention
To prepare for the jihad."
13. He sent messages to all the major towns,
Calling everybody who would listen to him.
14. He said, "Show by your dress who you are and what you intend.
Make up your minds what to do, and be prepared."

Chapter III. The Shehu's Move to Gudu—Tabkin Kwatto

15. Aliyu Jedo went there to Gudu with
Mahmud Gurdam, where they prepared a camp for the Shehu.

16. Then Agali came;
He carried the Shehu's things and his books.
17. On the twelfth day of the month of Zulkida [1. Dhū 'l-Qaʻda
    1218/2. February 1804]
Our Shehu made his Hijra; . . .
26. The Shehu fought five battles
At Gudu, all victories due to his blessedness.
27. Yunfa gathered men from everywhere;
To Gudu they came, where he attacked in anger.
28. There Yunfa was driven away, and all his army
His horses, and their armor were captured when he ran away.
29. As well as the royal drums, umbrella, and other paraphernalia,
They were all taken to the Shehu as spoils of victory.
30. Together with his [Yunfa's] personal effects, his boots and sword,
Even his kola nuts were found and seized.
31. At the battle of Kwato, the Habe were in disarray [2. June 1804].
They never returned again to attack him at his open encampment. . . .

Chapter V. The Journey into Gobir and the Battles There

36. He left there and he camped at Sokoto [7 October 1804].
First he conquered Rabah,
37. Then Dangda as well as Gudawa.
The people of Rima were dispersed because of his warning.
38. He started out and traveled via Gududu and
Maitaguwa and Huci.
39. He camped at Makada and Kirare.
He fought wars because of his determination
40. In Gobir, and returned in good order.
There Moʼi died, his man.
41. Mane was attacked, and there Mammadi
Found martyrdom as soon as he went there.
42. Mamman Tukur and Agali made their own Hijra to join
The Shehu; a time of joy.
43. The countryside was pacified,
and Birnin Konni feared him.
44. He left there and set out for the East,
To the towns of Gobir; they deferred to him.
45. The king of Adar and Yunfa, the king of Gobir,
Allied together to fight him.
46. There they met Shehu at Tsuntsuwa,

Where God showed the people His might.

47. The imam Muhammad Sambo, Sa'ada, and Riskuwa
Obtained martyrdom while helping him.

48. So also Zaidu and the son of Farouk,
Ladan as well as Nadumama, his teachers.

49. Many of the reciters of the Qur'ān were killed,
And also the students among his community.

50. Then he camped at Baura,
And raids were carried out with utmost zeal.

Chapter VI. Retreat to Safety in Zamfara

51. Then Shehu traveled toward Zamfara [February 1805].
They made peace with him because they feared him.

52. The places that resisted the jihad were all destroyed;
While he was in Remuwa, he was victorious.

53. He left there and settled at Sabon Gari,
The Muslim community increased in love for him.

54. There Namoda came;
He too helped the Shehu because he loved him.

55. From there the Shehu's younger brother, Abdullahi Bayero, led
A campaign against Kebbi and he obtained victory [1. April 1805].

56. Among the towns, he even captured Birnin Kebbi,
And Hodi, chief of Kebbi, ran away.

57. Booty was obtained, even gold
And much silver, when he ran away.

58. Well done Bayero; he helped
The Shehu greatly in spreading his word.

59. Teaching and composing songs: all of this
He did. Everyone knew how much he helped the Shehu.

60. As Aaron helped his brother Musa [Moses],
So Abdullahi helped his brother the Shehu.

61. The envious ones did not get the least chance of
Opposing the Shehu, because Bayero guarded him.

62. May God redeem Bayero, O Lord of
The Day of Resurrection, so that we may see him.

63. May God give him happiness because of the help
He gave to the Shehu, who was his senior brother.

64. Then Umar of Dallaji was given
The flag to go to Katsina with the Shehu's word.

65. Dan Alhaji he also met; they all accepted

The message when they heard it; they knew it would lead to victory.
66. The people of the East all arose with firm intention
Of helping the religious fight; Alwali ran off, defeated.
67. Then they came to the city, and the chief of Kano fled;
Destruction came upon Burumburum.
68. Mallam Jamo, Dan Zabuwa, and Dahiru
Mallam Jabir, all helped for his sake.
69. With Mallam Bakatsine they came in great numbers,
They helped, and they accepted his message.

Chapter VII. Advance on Gwandu—Battle of Alwasa

70. The Shehu left Sabon Gari, and he slept at Bukkuyum,
Bunasau, Sadawa, and Falam on his way.
71. And also Gazura Margai; he slept at Bagida,
Then on to Gwandu and the river Samu, that was his route.
72. It was there that his friend that he loved died;
When he was at Zauma. they came with the news.
73. He was merciful, so the people knew him.
He was completely trusted by the Shehu, his man.
74. Umaru of Alkammu was the Shehu's friend;
The Muslim community knew it.
75. The grief at his death became so great that the Shehu
Preached a sermon to his people about his death.
76. At the end of the month of Sha'aban the Shehu entered Gwandu;
He remained there through the month of Ramadān until the time of the 'Id.
77. Then the Tuaregs gathered under Agunbulu;
He offered battle and he was defeated at Alwasa.
78. The community gave battle, and Hammadi
Obtained martyrdom shortly after his arrival there.
79. So the men fled;
He alone remained: everybody knows of his valor. . . .
84. A testing time befell the Muslims.
It was a fever; the community begged the Shehu
85. To pray to God to give them health
So that they might escape from it, by His mercy.
86. Even the Shehu became ill, and the people
Became frightened because they loved him.

Chapter VIII. Victory of Alkalawa, Names of Emirs (1806–1807)

87. Then God restored good health
To the Shehu, the father of Muslims.

88. The army he sent to Gobir
Was joined by every man of note. . . .

Chapter IX. Sifawa, Sokoto, Death of the Shehu (1810–1817)

99. The Shehu left there [Gwandu] and settled at Sifawa.
Opportunity and prosperity increased.
100. Nupe, Songhai, Yorubaland, and Borgu, all
There in the West, were in awe of him.
101. Victory was obtained in every quarter;
The chief of Gwari was confronted at Illo.
102. When people heard the Shehu's call to religion, they all came
From north, west, east, and south, for his sake.
103. He composed *Tabban Hakika* and
"Sitirajo" in order to praise God's blessing to him.
104. Then he made preparation for his arrival in his town Sokoto.
He set out and came; his house was made ready.
105. One Monday he came to Sokoto,
And he spent two years there [1815].
106. Then he passed on to the next world, in the month of Jimada.
It was on the third of the month [3 Jumāda 1232/2. April 1817].
107. From the beginning of that year he was preaching;
All people knew what he meant.
108. May God forgive him and reunite us
With him in paradise, we pray.

Chapter X. About Bello's Reign

109. Then things became very difficult.
The community selected Bello, his son to succeed him.
110. At the house of Dan Ashafa, people went
To pledge allegiance to Bello.
111. He organized a campaign in which Shehu Nuri
Obtained martyrdom in battle.
112. Revolts became numerous; even Abdulsalam
At Kware rebelled, together with his people.
113. Dan Jada as well as Namoda
Were martyred.
114. He fought the wars of Gobir and Zamfara
And Kebbi, and all other regions before him.
115. He was just and fair:
He brought about order through exhortation.
116. He shouldered the burdens of the peasantry,

Likewise those of his kinsmen and the whole community.

117. He built cities and he fought battles;
So too he built mosques in his city.

118. He protected all the frontier posts.
The community was organized through his efforts.

119. He established law and preached, so that
The people should do as he admonished them.

120. He taught religion and Islamic law, as well as medicine,
And he introduced the reading of Hadith in the council chamber.

121. He bought horses for the jihad, as well as
Shields and swords, dividing them among his kinsfolk.

122. Representatives were appointed to all places;
In his own city he ruled with justice.

123. He sent men to the frontiers
To live there—O' listen to his foresight.

124. Some were stationed at Gandi and some were sent
To Burmi; Fodiyo, his son, went to Gobir.

125. Bello was ill for seven months;
There in Wurno he died, in Rajab, on a Thursday [2. Rajab 1253].

126. May God forgive him, and may He reunite us with him
In Paradise; we pray to him for His mercy.

127. People gathered and made up their minds:
Atiku succeeded Bello.

128. May God forgive the Shehu and also Bello
And Atiku, his children who were Caliphs.

129. May the Peace and blessings of God be forever
Upon our Prophet and his Followers.

130. I thank God and I have completed one hundred verses,
And you have heard this story.

131. I also add some thirty to praise My Lord, the Almighty,
for His mercy.

132. Asma composed them in Fulfulde,
And Isa translated them into Hausa.

133. Rewards come from Allāh, my kinsmen,
And He is All Powerful and fulfills desires.

134. The chronogram of the Hijra of our Prophet Muhammad,
Shurafāʾu [1282/1865]; let us always thank Him for His generosity.

'SUFI WOMEN'

Asma'u's poem *Sufi Women* is one in a long line of comparable works on the topic. Caliph Muhammadu Bello wrote *The Book of Women* (*Kitab an-Nasīha* [sic]), which he modeled either on the twelfth-century work *Sufi Women* (*Sifāt as-safwā*) by Ibn al-Jawzī (597/1200) or on as-Sulamī's eleventh-century work, *Remembrance of Early Sufi Women* (*Dhikr an-niswa al-muta'abbidāt as-sūfīyāt*).[15] In this as in her other works, Asma'u's aim was to draw her own community into history. Her father, the Shehu, had written the poem *The Qādirīya Order* (*al-Qādirīya*). This work explained the origins of the Sufi brotherhood to which the clan belonged; it was written in Fulfulde, the language of the Fodiyos, for the benefit of those in the inner circles, not for the masses, who were Hausa speakers. Although Bello's and Asma'u's poems on Sufi women focus on Sufi women saints, Asma'u's is uniquely honed to omit Bello's admonitions concerning behavior and to include her own contemporaries among the ranks of saintly Sufi women in history. Asma'u herself is by implication included in this listing because she is the work's author and was legendary in her time as a teacher of women. That she wrote this work both in Hausa and in Fulfulde indicates that she intended it to instruct Hausa-speaking refugees as well as the educated elite. It was clearly intended to be used as a teaching device among those who were engaged in resocializing the Hausa majority following the Sokoto Jihad, as well as to clarify for the intelligentsia saintly women's roles in history and their own times.

Following the introductory section, Asma'u's list moves to the brief citation of luminaries of Islamic history, Muhammad's wives 'Ā'isha (11–12) and Zaynab (13), and his daughter Fātima (16). Asma'u's structure in this work appears to be chronological, beginning with the names of women closest to the Prophet Muhammad and moving to thirteenth/nineteenth-century women in the Sokoto Caliphate. But her description indicates that the work circles around the thirteenth/nineteenth-century Caliphate community like a pilgrim on the Hajj. Anyone listening to Asma'u's poem in 1837 would immediately compare the father-daughter team of 'Ā'isha and Abū Bakr with the contemporary father-daughter team of the Shehu and Asma'u (11–12). Another allusion to her own role is evident in a verse (13) about Zaynab, who was divinely supported in her work and held in esteem in her community, qualities that also apply to Asma'u. She implies in this verse that as poet she plays the role of the reporter 'Ā'isha, whom she describes. The next verses raise the image of the Prophet's wives, "Mothers of the Believers," and his daughter Fātima (15–17). Asma'u's reputation was widely known as an illustrious daughter of the Shehu, so the parallel with Fātima would have been clear to her audience. The significant role of mothers as teachers in the Fodiyo clan was easily paralleled with Asma'u's mention of mothers in the Prophet's home, beginning with the Prophet's own mother, who is described as "pious, / A reformer, and upright" (20). An unnamed wife of the Prophet (21–25) exhibits the timeless qualities of a Sufi: asceticism, generosity, weeping, silent meditation. But no earlier historical version of *Sufi Women* mentions the buying of horses, which were of central importance to the success of the Sokoto Jihad. With this image, Asma'u binds her present time to the Islamic past, imbuing her work (25) with contemporary reference and confirming that the nineteenth-century Fodiyo family is following the "Way of the Prophet of God."

Keeping to the pattern of the historical listing of women in earlier versions of *Sufi Women*, Asma'u's work moves on to cite women in later periods and regions of Islamic history (18–19, 31, 34, 36, 39–41). The list of names well known in Islamic history and attached to exotic and far-flung places important to the Muslim world must have impressed her audience in Sokoto, new to both Islamic history and knowledge of these historic sites. Having established for her unlettered audience that saintly women are to be found in the origins of Islam and then extensively throughout the Muslim world, Asma'u pauses to describe at length a few select individuals important to Sufism (27–30, 43–57), draw implicit parallels between Fātima's bold action as a teacher and her own role (51–53), and contrast the role of a Sufi woman who retreats from the world (54–55). One set of verses describes a woman who actively teaches—just as Asma'u did—and another who retreats from the world, as was the case for many Sufis—sending a message that allows for a wide range of expression of devotion in Sufism, including both activism and the meditative life.

Departing from the classical version of this work, the final twenty-one verses of Asma'u's poem catalogs contemporary women who deserve to be included among the revered Sufi women in history. In a clear allusion to Islamic historic figures, Asma'u describes Iyya Garka (66) as pious and generous: she was Aisha, the second wife of the Shehu, who bore the same name as the Prophet's second wife. Other wives of the Shehu are described in relation to the pursuit of knowledge, Asma'u's primary focus (65), and Sufi attributes (68–71). Asma'u notes that "as many as a hundred" (75) women in the Sokoto Caliphate community are noteworthy and pious, some of whom are *hāfiza*s (women who know Qur'ān by heart) but remain unnamed in this work.[16]

TRANSLATION OF 'SUFI WOMEN'

1. Alhamdulillahi, we thank God,
We invoke blessings on God's Messenger.
2. We invoke blessings on his Family and Companions
And those who followed them; thus we gain self respect.
3. We invoke blessings on the Companions of the Prophet,
Who are now sanctified.
4. My aim in this poem is to tell you about Sufis;
To the great ones I bow in reverence.
5. I am mindful of them while I am still alive
So that they will remember me on the Day of Resurrection.
6. The ascetic women are all sanctified;
For their piety they have been exalted.
7. They prayed ceaselessly to be delivered from the Fires of Hell.
Take this to heart my friends.
8. I have written this poem to assuage my heart:
I remind you how they yearn for God.
9. I swear by God that I love them all
In the name of the Prophet, the Messenger of God.
10. The scent of their yearning engulfs me;
Its intensity exceeds the perfume of musk.
11. To the Prophet's disciples who draw close to God
I bring all Muslims to 'A'isha.
12. Aisha, the noble daughter of [Abū Bakr] As-Siddīq
The believer, an honest man, Abubakar the esteemed.
13. To Muslim women I speak of Zaynab Jahshi;
I cherish them, Lord of the World.
14. You made her to exceed, according to 'A'isha;
She was held in esteem by the Prophet.
15. I speak of all the mothers
Who were the wives of the Prophet.
16. And Fātima Zahrā', or Batulu ["cut off" from worldly interests],
Gracious lady, close follower of the Prophet.
17. She was peerless, she who shunned the world,
The Prophet's daughter, who was better than any other child.
18. I speak of Āmina Ramlīya,
And Umm Hassan of Kufa.
19. As was Umm Sufyān of Suriyyi [i.e., ath-Thawrī]
And the relative of Fudayl [ibn 'Iyād], a most kind person.

20. The mother of the Prophet was pious,
A reformer, and upright.

21. I speak of the wives of the Prophet,
For his wives were ascetics.

22. She was very generous and kind;
Daily she gave away gifts: she never ceased.

23. She gave alms most generously.
Undoubtedly she wept day and night.

24. She used to say, "I have no tongue";
She had no wish to speak.

25. She bought horses for the Jihad of the Lord
And to follow the Way of the Prophet of God.

26. I speak of Al-'umatus Salliyatu
For her asceticism and also Umayya.

27. Umm Hārūn had radiance
and Habība al-'Adawīya recited the Divine Names.

28. I speak of Rābi'a al-'Adawīya,
Who was more pious than anyone else.

29. 'Adawīya Kaisiya of Basra,
Exalted, able to see the unseen, radiant.

30. She had a mastery over learning and exceeded all women.
She was the outstanding pious person of her time.

31. And so to Umm Ayyūb of Lansariyyatu [i.e., al-Ansārī]
And Umm Darḍā'u and Mu'ādha.

32. Her prayer was a thousand prostrations.
Rābi'a was cognizant by day and by night

33. In order to please the Prophet's heart.
On the Day of Judgment you will understand her zeal.

34. Rābi'a, the daughter of Ismail [also known as al-'Adawīya],
Zealously praying to God.

35. She could see male and female jinns
Because of her sainthood and praying to God.

36. And Ru'qayya of Mosul,
And Rayhāna al-Majnūna the Pious,

37. And Sha'wāna, also pious,
And 'Atīka Unawīyatu [Ghanūya?] Hidatu,

38. 'Ā'isha, the daughter of Ja'far, 'Ubayda,
Daughter of Abū Kulab, and Ahhiratu.

39. Umratu ['Amra?] was an ascetic, and so was Mu'ādha
Of Mosul, and so too Mājida.

40. And Maryam of Basra and Muʿadha
Maymūna Majnuʾatul Akilatu.

41. I speak of Maymūna Saudāʾ,
All pious, and Zahrāʾ [the intoxicated],

42. Whose intense piety made her appear transformed;
For when they reached this stage of Sufism, they gained much.

43. I speak of Fātima of Nisabur,
Who was zealous even to those who understand enthusiasm.

44. And so too the daughter of Hasan, Nafīsa,
Who prostrated herself on account of her piety.

45. She recited the Qurʾān six thousand times in the grave,
Prayed, and fasted: note well her devotion.

46. Born at Mecca, she was a descendant of the Prophet;
She grew up in Medina, where she was honored.

47. Anyone visiting her grave
And praying there would receive blessings.

48. The blessings and compassion of God
Fell upon Egypt on account of Nafīsa.

49. I speak of Fātima, daughter of ʿAbbas Sayha,
Who taught and was a preacher.

50. She used to mount the steps outside the mosque and preach to
    women;
Her sermons caused them to fear and repent.

51. She made an attempt to stop using the steps
But realized that the Prophet had heard of this decision.

52. "She is a truly noble person on account of her work,"
He the Prophet told Tarinu in a dream.

53. She set aside considerations of family and possessions,
Choosing instead God and his religion.

54. I speak of the ascetic who withdrew from the world
Fakhrīya of Basra, mother of Yūsuf.

55. She entered into a Sufi state of holiness
In which she stayed for forty years.

56. At the end of her life she went to Mecca,
Where she died and was buried near Khadīja.

57. I pray, O' God, for their blessings.
Give me the grace to repent my sins.

58. Out of respect for their greatness I dedicate myself,
Believing that I will receive what I request,

59. For their majesty will wipe away my sins,

And because of them I will escape the burden of my wrongdoings.
60. In this world and the next, where souls await judgment,
I will rely on them for my salvation.
61. I know full well that I have committed many sins,
Yet I hope for escape on the Day of Retribution.
62. The rest is about the women members of the community of
Shehu Dan Fodiyo, for whom I pray.
63. I speak of those who are still alive
And those who have died.
64. I mention first of all Shehu Degel, our father;
Dan Fodiyo, he is our leader.
65. And Inna Garka, who was exceedingly pious;
Giving alms, she completely ignored worldly things.
66. Then Iyya Garka who was very pious,
Good natured, and generous to her kinfolk.
67. I speak of the other wives of the Shehu,
For they were all pious.
68. The teacher of women, Habiba:
She was most revered and had great presence.
69. I speak of Aisha, a saint
On account of her asceticism and determination;
70. And Joda Kowuuri, a Qur'ānic scholar
Who used her scholarship everywhere.
71. I speak also of Biada, who was diligent,
For her attribute was in reclusion.
72. And 'Yar Hindu, daughter of the imam,
Who was diligent at solving disputes.
73. There were others who were upright
In the community of the Shehu; I have not listed them.
74. Very many of them had learned the Qur'ān by heart
And were exceedingly pious and zealous.
75. They never tired of preaching the righteous Faith.
Those of the Shehu reached as many as a hundred.
76. The song that has listed them is now finished
And you now know of their fine reputations.
77. May God reunite us with them in the Next World,
And through them may we achieve salvation.
78. Together with my mother and father and all Muslims
May we be delivered, Oh Lord of Gifts.
79. For the sake of the glory of he who was exalted

Above all other mortals. My song is finished.
80. I thank God Almighty,
To whom all prayers are addressed.
81. May He bless Ahmadu and all his Family
And all those who followed them,
82. And his Companions, all of whom were exalted,
And the faithful who are enshrined in light.
83. The chronogram of the year of the Prophet's Hijra is Nabshiru.
It is ended; let us say Nabshiru.

NOTES

1. Comparison of Asma'u's *Yearning for the Prophet* and *The Journey* was the focus of a paper Jean Boyd and I presented at the 1997 African Studies Association program; it remains unpublished. This version is my own work, based on concepts conveyed in that study. I appreciate Jean's reading this version; I remain responsible for any errors. All translations included here and any references to Asma'u's other works come from *The Collected Works of Nana Asma'u, Daughter of Shehu Usman dan Fodio (1793–1864)*, ed. Jean Boyd and Beverly Mack (East Lansing: Michigan State University Press, 1997), and are reprinted here with permission. Numbers in parentheses with abbreviations of either of the two works refer to verse numbers.

2. Asma'u's *Yearning for the Prophet* is typical of *sīra*, biographies of the Prophet Muhammad. It is by itself 316 couplets long and therefore beyond the limits of this publication to reproduce in its entirety, so only the relevant excerpts are included below in translation. *The Journey* and *Sufi Women* are included in translation in full. Jean Boyd and I are responsible for all translations of Asma'u's works included here.

3. Asma'u's audience would have been familiar with corroborating works, such as her poem "The Battle of Gawakuke," contemporary poet Muhammad Tukur's works on the topics, the Shehu's own works about his life experience, and the Qur'ān. The context of this volume does not allow for a thorough description of all these sources.

4. At Tsuntsuwa (northern Nigeria) in 1804 A.D., two hundred people were killed who had learned the Qur'ān by heart. Twentieth-century scholars can only faintly reconstruct the context for these works, painstakingly piecing together connections that would have been clear to Asma'u and her audience.

5. The Shehu writes of himself, "When I reached 36 years of age God removed the veil from my eyes" (quoted in Mervyn Hiskett, *Sword of Truth* [New York: Oxford University Press, 1973], 64–65). This fact would have been common knowledge to Asma'u's audience and can be assumed to be understood by readers of *The Journey* during her lifetime.

6. The Shehu's age and the birth of his daughter Asma'u were well known to Asma'u's audience and need not be explained. Theses facts are cited in His-

kett, *Sword of Truth*, as is reference to the confirmation of God's message for each.

7. Asma'u relates in *The Story of the Shehu* (v. 16): "he made his hijra setting out for Gudu, Yunfa attacked him there and was routed." See also the Shehu's poem *Munasaba* (vv. 8 & 14); Hiskett, *Sword of Truth*, 87–88.

8. "And there was nothing, except that I saw their waterless cloud / Had cleared away from the sun of Islam which was shining / By the help of Him who helped the Prophet against the foe at Badr." (Abdullahi, *Tazyīn al-waraqāt* [*Decoration of the Pages*], 115). Such reference to Badr in a work on the Sokoto jihad indicates a clearly intended comparison of the two.

9. Abdullahi's *Tazyīn*, familiar to Asma'u's audience, recounts how the "rabble of young hooligans deserted the field" (pp. 118–19).

10. A comparable scene is described in *Tazyīn*: "You saw naught but angry and enraged men / Cauterizing other's wounds when drawing out the arrows" (p. 116).

11. At Alkalawa, "by God, were it not for a deep ditch," (*Tazyīn*, 64) disaster would have ensued. The Arabic word used in each is *khandaku* (i.e., *khandaq*, "ditch"). Asma'u's use of the exact word and the phenomenon made so famous by the Battle of the Trench invites direct comparison.

12. Asma'u's poem "The Battle of Gawakuke" echoes this passage: "After resting two days the army advanced to Zana, / Where many thousands of the enemy were caught and slaughtered. The rest were executed" (vv. 57–58). This parallel served to reinforce the validity of Bello's action.

13. This is not so much an anachronism as a prediction that reinforces the idea that the Shehu was meant to be the leader. Nana Asma'u would not have written this by mistake, but more likely intended it as a direct connection between the story of the Prophet and the Shehu's history.

14. Zayd ibn al-Hārith was the Prophet's adopted son and freed slave.

15. One of these works must have been in the library holdings of the Fodiyo clan. In the late twentieth century, Javad Nurbaksh produced his own *Sufi Women* (London: Khaniqahi Nimatullahi Publications, 2004). Recent scholarly translations by Rkia Cornell (Abd ar-Rahman as-Sulamī, *Early Sufi Women*, trans. Rkia Elaroui Cornell [Louisville, KY: Fons Vitae, 1999) indicate that the twelfth-century work by Ibn al-Jawzī was itself patterned on the eleventh-century version by as-Sulamī, which several early scholars mention as a source of inspiration for their works (Cornell 43). As Cornell notes, prior to the invention of the printing press, it was common for manuscripts to be hand-copied and for one poem to constitute a revised form of the work of another author; but she also notes that this particular work on Sufi women has in fact been rarely cited through the centuries since its origin. It is indicative of the Fodiyo clan's concern for women's participation in their Sufi community that this work was prominent among the works in the Shehu's library, and an inspiration for Bello's work and subsequently for Asma'u's.

16. The editor has striven to use fuller Arabic transliterations for names of historical figures, but retains the "vernacularized" forms for figures closer in time to Nana Asma'a.

15 Job's Wife in the Swahili 'Epic of Job'

J. W. T. Allen

A Swahili *Epic of Job* (*Utendi wa Ayubu*) was composed in the early thir-
teenth/nineteenth century by an unknown author, using the traditional
tendi stanza form.[1] The poetic genre's stanza comprises four lines of eight-
syllables each, the first three end-rhyming and the fourth end-rhyming
with the fourth line in every other stanza. This intriguing work, brimming
with arrestingly earthy and vivid imagery, provides a marvelous insight
into an East African Islamic reading of an originally biblical tale. In this
version of the narrative, Satan's conflict with Job begins with the tempter's
frustration in his unsuccessful attempts to lure the faithful prophet away
from his prayer mat, which becomes a powerful symbol of Job's servanthood. Satan (Iblis) first assails Job's goats, then the rest of his livestock, and
when Job remains unflinching in his devotion, the devil kills his children.
Job refuses to budge from his prayer rug, and it is at this juncture that
our excerpt takes up the story. When Job remains dedicated to his ritual
prayer, Satan devises a ruse by which to undermine the prophet's physical health. As Job is performing his ritual prayer, Satan enters the earth
before him, and when the prophet prostrates himself, Satan inflicts him
with disease by blowing into his nose. The latter part of the story repro-
duced here showcases the role of Job's devoted wife, Rehema, featuring her
in a much more important role than the wife has in the biblical account.

Rehema's dedication is matched by her steadfast refusal to succumb to
the wiles of Satan, who repeatedly appears in the guise of a wealthy man
and attempts to turn her against Job. Indeed, Rehema suffers psychologi-
cally at the hands of the Tempter every bit as severely as her husband does
physically. At the same time, this vibrant, vivid text raises other questions
about gender roles, prophetic authority, and the treatment of women in
the society that produced the text. Note the author's occasional comments

about how his own experience in procuring, translating, and recounting the ancient story. (Ed.)

TRANSLATION

The breath that [Satan] sent caught Job like a blast of Hell. It entered his head and spread over his body. There on his mat the plague took him. His blood was scattered and poured away, and sores were opened and spread over his body. And at the time that the sickness took hold of Job, maggots appeared like termites in the rains, and the pus that flowed from him was like water pouring from the eaves in the time of rain. And his smell—he stank so that a man would avoid him by two hundred paces.

Iblis did not loiter, he did not cease plotting, flitting hither and thither, stirring up trouble for him. He said, "This man's sickness is leprosy; cast him out, all of you; it is dangerous to harbor him. Come together, gentlemen, cast him out of the town; send him to the forest to unfrequented paths."

The people came together and accepted what he said. They all cast him out; not one objected. They rejected him and there was none to take his part, save Lady Rehema, his noble wife. The Lady Rehema was born of good stock, daughter of Ephraim, son of Joseph, and this lady, I must tell you, the Creator had made her in the likeness of her grandfather, Joseph. This good, well-born lady was filled with sorrow when her husband was expelled because of his sickness. She stayed with her husband, not heeding the leprosy, and they lay down together and together they awoke. Job was tormented by the disease that afflicted him, and Rehema was sad and wept continually. She left her rest to go to work to obtain bread to give to her husband. She did not disdain to go to every house, saying, "I am ready to work for you. Give me your work that is in your houses, whether to grind corn, give it to me and I will bring it back; or I will polish your rings; I will rub you down and plait your hair. But give me the bread that is left over when you eat. No, do not prevent me if I pick up a piece when I see it fall on the ground. You need not worry if I pick up what falls, for if a cat eats it, it is of no use to you; but for me it is my food to eat with my husband. May God grant that this much may come to us."

She worked all day for two handfuls of flour, and when evening came, she took her way home to her husband, the prophet Job, and she took his body and turned him over. Job was unable to turn himself over as he lay. His body was so wasted that somebody had to help him. Rehema took him and the maggots fell down, and Job spoke and said to his wife, "Do not lose the maggots; pick them up and put them back. If there is any food left for them, it is a sin to take them away."

The noble Lady Rehema did as she was told. She stooped down in pity and gathered up the maggots. She picked them up and arranged them on his bones, until all were collected on his body, and there they stayed. After tending his body, my friends, she spoke and said, "Sir, take the food that I have been given by the Creator. Do not give way to distress; He who brings affliction brings relief. I have a bit of bread; take it and swallow it; it is food. We creatures must be brave and not be dismayed by sickness."

Job answered his wife, "My throat is parched; bread is a trouble to me. The bread will not go down; it is hard to swallow it. Forgive me, I do not want it. Do not say that this is ill temper." His wife replied, shedding tears, "This comes of disliking it, when you should be given what you like; but today I have some millet bread. Do not refuse it. Eat, sir, and then I can eat. Do not starve yourself." She went on, "My Lord, take a crumb of food; it will do you good if you get it down." He said, "Bring it," and he finished the bread, sucking it to draw some saliva and spitting out the hard bits.

Next morning Lady Rehema went out to go the rounds of the houses and serve the people. At every house that she visited, they drove her away, saying, "We have heard all about you. You are actually a woman who has taken a man who is a leper and you live with him. Do not come into our houses, do not stand at the door; you are forbidden even to enter our town." She went back sadly, grieving in her heart because she had lost her work and her livelihood.

She went back sorrowing and weeping, and on the way she saw a man coming clearly before her, wearing a splendid turban, and he said, "Greetings, good lady. Tell me your name and your parents. I should like to talk to you." In answer she said, "I am Rehema, daughter of Ephraim, son of Joseph." Iblis said, "Why are you so changed? The beauty that the Mighty gave to you is lost. Where are the charms given you by the Lord God? Your face is so shrunk that I did not recognize you. What has happened to you? Tell me, hide nothing, keep from me nothing that is in your heart." The good woman said, "I am sad because my husband is ill and has been sick for years. It is now seven years since this sickness attacked him and the Lord God Almighty does not grant him health; but do not hinder me. I want to go quickly. I have neither time nor desire to tarry."

Satan replied to the woman, "Since man was created, he has never been perfect. Rightly is man praised for his wisdom; but he is not complete so as to understand everything. You are outstanding and of great intelligence, and for such a one to be your husband is disgraceful to hear. That a beautiful woman, with a lovely smile, should be married to a leper is disgraceful hearing. My good woman, do not serve Job. Do you not think it a disgrace? The soul is not to be bought."

When Rehema heard what he said, she did not wait. She avoided him and went on her way. "All this time I have been standing here, waiting while you talk; but you are not at all a person that I want to speak with." So Rehema the well-born went away in a rage and came to Job and greeted him. When she came in, her face was changed and Job asked her why she was angry. Rehema said, "Listen, my Lord. The people have agreed to expel me from the town. At the houses where I always go to help them now, they say, 'Go away,' and they abuse me. All are agreed to tell me not to come back, and if I do, I shall be thrown out. Then, as I was coming home in sorrow, I met God's enemy. He met me on the way. He talked nonsensical folly to me—"Your husband is sick; do not go near him."

When she had spoken, Job understood, "This is no man; it is a devil." And Job said to Rehema, "If he comes again, repel him, I tell you. He is bad, I say he is bad. Do you hear what I say, Rehema? He is the enemy." She told him her story and Job exhorted her; and she asked his permission to go and search for bread. And he said, "Go, and I will await you here, and if a lion does not come upon me, you will find me here when you return. And if the Gracious Lord has refused my plaint, he will let hyenas and dogs take me." Rehema said, "God grant I find you. Health will return; the Lord will send deliverance."

She combed her hair and plaited her locks and went to the women to show them her wealth. The shining locks of her hair were so long that they came down to her feet when they were unbraided, and when the women saw them, they wanted them, and she said, "Buy them and I will cut them off for you." They asked, "What is your price, for we have nothing to buy them with?" Rehema answered, "To sell hair is disgraceful; but I have a compelling reason. I am ready to sell my hair because of my earthly needs and the trouble that is come on me and my husband. If you want it, you shall have it cut off; twenty hairs for a loaf I will accept and will not refuse." The women said, "Cut off fifty and we will pay a loaf, not one less." Rehema the prophet's wife agreed, "But I want them separately, not all on one day." She cut her long hair and counted out fifty and gave to them, and they took them and light shone from them. And the women said, "Come, let us buy all the hair on her head. It will be fun to take it all. Let us cut it so that she has not a hair left; for among us women, there is none to compare with her. When she combs her hair and plaits her locks, her hair outshines everyone of us here." So they did their very best, and their real purpose was to spoil her looks. They came together and said to Rehema, "Come tomorrow early. Do not wait for sunrise."

Rehema said, "Farewell, Ladies, it shall be as we have agreed"; and she went. On her way she saw a man coming along her road. He had a sword ornamented with silver and gold, and he was girt with an embroidered baldric. The appearance of the man was outstanding and he was clad in splendid clothes. When he came near to the gentle lady, he spoke and said to her, "Why do you not fear the sun? At midday the sun is fierce and the eyes cannot bear it. Will you not come and rest in the shade? And if you are busy, tell me. I am at your service. Give your body a rest and let me support you."

Rehema said, "I have need of nothing. Out of my way, I want to pass. Go away at once so that I may go to my husband and rest my dear prophet. Too long have I tarried."

The man asked, "Who is your husband? I am amazed and I want to know. Tell me that I may know his tribe, his father and mother, and all his lineage." Rehema answered him, "His name is Job, the messenger of the Lord, the gifted prophet." Iblis said, "Listen, Rehema, man needs rest to avoid anxiety. Take me for your husband. I have real authority, kingship and wealth, and women to obey me. And the woman that I marry will have all she wants; and she who rejects me is bad and unfortunate. What man is Job that you should wait on him? Have me for your Lord and know real power."

When he spoke of Job in his answer, Rehema made no reply. She was silent and went on without turning back. She stood before Job and greeted him, and said, "I have sold my hair for a barley loaf and then I saw a most extraordinary thing. On the way home I met a man. From the way he talked, he must have been drunk. He said, 'Your husband has no wealth or position. You have gone too far; the prophet will kill you.'" Job said to her, "Now I ordered you to repel Satan and to spit at him if he again appeared to you. You did not listen, and now today he has appeared. Do not say that you forgot; listen to my charge. When I recover from my misery, have no doubt that I shall beat you, when God gives me strength. If you repeat this offence, I will beat you when I recover. There is no escape, I tell you."

Lady Rehema said, "Very good, sir; if I do it again, you shall give me a hundred strokes. But, sir, do not take it to heart and grieve; let us eat the bread that I have bought." Job became calm and recovered his temper when he heard the soothing words of her answer. They ate their bread that she had brought. They made their bed and laid themselves down.

Next morning they awoke and Rehema went out to pray to the Almighty.

She thought over the terms of the agreement, wondering if it were true or false. When Rehema arrived, those with whom she had agreed were all ready and waiting. They said, "Ha! We have brought the bread. Cut us our hair; we want to go off with it. Cut your hair quickly—we want it—and take your bread." Rehema took it. She counted out fifty [locks] and cut carefully and gave to them and they took them. She returned without trouble, carrying her food.

Then on the way she looked up and saw light shining as far as the eye could reach, and Rehema gave praise and thanks to God. When she looked, she saw rays of light and she was puzzled and disturbed. As they continued to spread, she saw a man coming down from Heaven and standing before her. He said, "Rehema, I am sent by the Generous, the Almighty with a message for you. The Lord has sent me to tell you that he is very angry with you and extremely vexed. He is wroth with you, in truth and not in jest; but the best is clear to him, so he spoke to me, saying, 'Go down to Rehema and speak with her lest I be so vexed with her as to remove her from mercy. Among the angels you have great compassion, so I send you to lead her aright.' The Lord God Almighty gave the order to me myself, and he told these lights to accompany me. These lights that you see, say not that they have come for nothing. They are a curtain to hinder you. I am sent by God to take Satan from your heart, lest you be lost. Let not Iblis catch you and come where you are. Heed what I say and am sent to tell you. I have come to implore you, Rehema, to submit to God, who saves those who pray to him. I cannot detail to you the grace of God nor his love that he bears you for the sake of the prophet Joseph, your grandfather, great though we know it to be. But if it happens that Satan has led you astray, do not vex the Lord until he begins to hate you. Restrain yourself, Rehema; follow the Generous. Satan deserves to be stoned; do not follow his path. Do not oppose the love of God. Come, grant my request so that I may return and go to my worship, the worship of God; for I have been here too long and I am awaited. For in Heaven I have authority, and what I say commands attention. Among the angels all heed me. Receive the word of the love of the Lord that he speaks and give me an answer, and I will go to the Almighty. Thus he says: Job was a prophet and I gave him wealth and health; but after receiving these, he changed his heart and I took away my gifts; all left him. I robbed him of his wealth, I slew his children, and from his body I took away his health.

"Listen, Rehema, forget your passion for him. I have taken from him his message; be in no doubt that he is no longer a prophet. I have taken grace from him; I will not grant his wishes, and I have given him leprosy.

Follow him not; go not where he is; let hyenas and other scavengers take him. I have warned you; stop; do not go back, Rehema. Job is not a good man, or I would not hinder you. If you do go back and I find you with Job, I will not admit you to Paradise, but will send you to Hell."

Patient Rehema listened to all this. She pondered deeply. Then she saw the deceit and recovered herself. As she pondered, she was much amazed; but the darkness was lifted and Rehema saw clearly. She racked her brain—"How can this be, that I am selected for an angel to be sent to me? I have never heard that an angel ever came down to speak to anyone but a prophet. I am very doubtful whether this is an angel at all. I will say to him, 'Go, let me pass on my way.'" Lady Rehema said, "Go, do not take me from my work, you have greatly disturbed me. I quite understand all that the Lord of his generosity has said to you." Lady Rehema went on, dragging her feet, and when she came to Job, she fell at his feet. "Today, as I came, I saw an angel with light shining round him. He came down from Heaven and stood before me in the way and he said, 'My friend, I am sent by the Almighty.' Then he said to me things that were clearly not true, until I was no longer able to listen. I was distressed and I left him and came home. Forgive me, my Lord; I did not do this intentionally."

Job said, "I have heard, and when I recover I will certainly flog you. You have made a habit of idling about, and I will pay you for it when God gives me health. When the love of God cures me and my strength returns, I shall beat you thoroughly. Have no doubt about it." All this time Rehema was at his feet, and she said, "I am your servant, your bought slave. When the Lord cures you and restores your health, I will pay the penalty. You shall demand it and I will consent. I pray to God for you, be not angry, sir. I shall not repine if you beat me when you recover. Do not imagine that I shall be angry. I have made a vow that you are to give me a hundred lashes when you stand up in health. And if you do not beat me, I will ask somebody else, so as to perform my vow. Forgive me, sir, forgive me. I will obey you in everything to obtain your forgiveness; but, sir, take bread. Do not starve yourself."

Job answered and said to Rehema, "You are of good stock, the grand-daughter of a prophet. You have borne trouble; you have sold your hair; you have not been afraid of the scorn of your companions when they laugh at you. Come, let us give ourselves food and drink, and when the sun goes down, let us lay ourselves down and give praise to the Almighty."

The good woman was glad. She broke the bread and that day they ate it with relish. They ate, and when they had eaten, they lay down to sleep. They awoke and Job declared, "There is no praise nor glory—none can afflict, none can kill but the Lord himself, the Alone the Almighty." Then Job said, "Lord, you are my creator; here I pray to you, save me from this plague. God, who give release by your power and might, save me from the disease that is upon me."

The Lord God replied, saying to Job, "The time is near to send deliverance down to you." God, the Almighty and most merciful Lord, said, "Your sufferings are over. Today is deliverance. Come, leave your sufferings. This, Job, is the end. Ask for water; wash your face and the whole of your body. The water of which I speak to you is here at your feet. It is this that will cure you, and you will be well. This is your remedy. Stretch out your legs and without trouble water will come here. Push out your leg, set it in the sand, press with it firmly, and water will appear. Extend your leg, bury it in the sand and move it about gently, my apostle, my prophet. When you push in your leg, good water will appear, not of wells nor of the sea nor of lakes. And there will come perfume not of the forest, and water unsullied, pure to be drunk, sweet to the mouth, cool to the body, with the power of healing, and the sick will be well."

When he heard this, he put forth his leg and buried it in the sand, and the earth boiled. With a roar there came out water in torrents and covered his limbs as Job watched. Job bathed in it and the water covered him, and when he came out, he gleamed. When he emerged, Job was cured and more beautiful than he had ever been. Gabriel came down and dressed him in clothes of Paradise brought for him. Job accepted the clothes that he was brought, and he put on carefully the garments that were provided. Gabriel was there, and [Job] purified himself and he said his prayers. There on the mat he thanked the Almighty. When he stood up, he praised the Lord and cursed Satan and his brood.

I have read in the book and counted the days of the sufferings of Job, and I will tell you the number of them. This was indeed the seventh year of his suffering since the plague took him, not one less. And in addition seven months, I tell you, in this same tale, and seven days more; the eighth was not completed, as I understand. On the eighth day at noon he was cured by the power of the Mighty and he was well. And as soon as he was well, he went to his worship and he worshipped the Lord as was his custom.

While he was reciting the prayers, Lady Rehema came and stood turning about and weeping. She turned and turned, searching and wondering, shedding tears and weeping and wailing. She turned about in wonder, saying, "Where is Job, the apostle of the Lord, the prophet?" Job asked her, "Tell me, Rehema, you shed tears and go round weeping. Tell me what distresses you. Let me hear from you what is causing you distress, so that I may know. I want to hear your explanation, so that you may lessen your grief and stop crying." Job went on, "Listen, Rehema, why are you changed and full of dismay?" She said, "In this place I was with my husband, Job, the apostle and prophet of the Almighty. While he lay here, I eagerly sought, and when I found a bone, I would bring it to him. We ate, we praised God, and to pray to him was always our way, and I was not vexed. I waited on him gladly and prayed for strength for him, that the Lord, the healer of wounds, would give him his health. Today I am just come from seeking for scraps, and when I arrive, I do not see him. I do not know what has happened."

Then the prophet spoke to his wife and said, "Be calm, do not be sad; this is I, your husband; be at peace. I am indeed your husband. Do not be troubled, stop your grief, and put away regret. Believe what I say; do not be sad. Almighty God has taken away the evil. Deliverance has come down, have no doubt. I am your husband; listen, do not be afraid to come near me. If you want to know what has happened, listen and I will tell you from beginning to end the whole story. This is it, my dear: Gabriel came and greeted me from the most High. 'The most High, the most Mighty is pleased to be merciful to you. Your portion is complete and you may escape from your sufferings. Stretch out your leg, thus says the Lord, and this shall be the end of your troubles. The water is at hand, under your own feet, Job; drink and take your fill. This is the remedy.'"

"When he told me this, I pushed forward my leg, and before my eyes I saw it recover. As the water poured out, frothing and bubbling, I bathed in the water and became as I used to be. I looked at my body, my dear, and I found that it was as of old or even better. When I was whole, I moved away and sat down, and I saw Gabriel bringing me clothes. He said, 'Take them, Job; I have brought you garments given to me by the Giver and raiment to wear.' I received the clothes, Rehema, and I put them on. Be not amazed; it is I; come to me. Sit, let us give thanks, let us praise the Lord. What is past is past and is better forgotten."

Rehema spoke with joy and laughter, "This is what I desired, that my husband should be cured. I praise God, who spreads the heavens. He has taken every bit of sorrow from my heart. Now I want one thing. Of your kindness do it for me. There are the hundred strokes to perform my vow. Do not refuse me, my Lord. Sir, give me at once a hundred strokes. Job, prophet, apostle, it is right to beat me. Do not take it to heart, but let me cleanse my own heart. If I die, I shall go to Paradise; if I recover, I shall live well, because I have performed my Lord's word. Here am I, your wife, here before you. Fulfill your oath, Job, which you spoke, and be not sad. Put sorrow from your heart. Almighty God himself has ordained this."

She went on speaking, and when she stopped, Job embraced his wife in amazement. Job was sad; but before he said a word, he looked and saw Gabriel coming down. Gabriel said, "Job, listen carefully. Almighty God sends you his greeting. The Lord tells you to perform the oath that your wife may be free of her vow. Do not go back on your word. Listen and I will teach you. Take a leaf of a date palm with a hundred fronds. Cut it, Job, and count the points. Be sure that there is not one too few. The Lord commands you to count the hundred and to perform your promise in full."

When the prophet heard Gabriel's words, he went at once to look for it. He went to take the leaf for which he was looking; he searched for one that would suit his purpose. He went in among the palm leaves, and he found one with exactly one hundred fronds. He brought it and went in to Rehema and told her that he was required to flog her with it. "The Lord told me to beat you with this to ease your heart and to take all doubt from you."

Rehema smiled and said, "Of course I accept the order of the Generous." He arose and smote her one hundred strokes at once. So was fulfilled the vow of the prophet Job. God returned to him as before all and more also, and his herdsmen too by divine command. His folds returned, camels, cattle, and small stock, and the Mighty blessed them more than ever. His children returned, the boys and the girls, and they flourished and blessings abounded; his houses increased, his children flourished; they were like lions in beauty and strength. When you saw them, they were like lions, and their years were completed and they lived in health. They lived happily and in plenty and God gave them help. They were assisted to prosperity by the Lord God himself, and they rejoiced at what the Lord did for them.

As before, Job worshipped the Almighty and continued earnestly in prayer to him. I have finished writing the story of the prophet Job, with the help of the love of God, who has made it easy for me. He has made it simple, God, the Lord Almighty, to turn it from Arabic into Swahili. We found it in books and in the Qur'ān; observe that I have left out nothing.

When God ordered the end of his sufferings, he was at peace and all his wealth returned. His fortune came back and he was cured of his sickness, and immediately he was better than ever before. One thing never changes. He says *fiat* and it is. It is the Lord that gives the order. There is no god but HIM. What the Lord wills must be, and what the Lord does no man can do.

Lord God, of your favor give us your help, both the faithful reader and the hearer. This is the story of Job. Read it, gentlemen. You will be amazed by the story if you understand it. I have finished and have no more to write, with the help of the Generous, in health and safety. I have finished; read it when you are at ease in your houses. We found in the books all that happened. Lord, give us health, protect us from sickness, and forgive us our sins, you Almighty. Forgive us our sins, Lord our God. Bless us with goods to wear and to use. Bless us, most High, and give us gifts for our use in this world.

If you are afflicted by the will of God, be patient. Patience is a virtue, I assure you. He that is patient receives; of that there is no doubt. He will be perfected and his hopes will be fulfilled. The most High has said, "Have patience," and often we see that patience brings good fortune. Everyone who is patient obtains his desire. His heart is pure, whatever his trials. Be patient and God will help you. What is the use of fretting? It brings nothing but error. If a man restrains himself from saying that God has forsaken him, in the end he receives good. But if you fret, your end is trouble; it does no good and is foolishness.

Blessing and peace. That is the final end.

NOTES

1. Excerpted from J. W. T. Allen, trans., *Tendi: Six Examples of a Swahili Classical Verse Form* (New York: Africana Publishing/Heinemann Educational, 1971), 391–425 (English text on odd-numbered pages only). After numerous unsuccessful attempts to ascertain the copyright holder of the text, the editor and Press decided to reproduce the text under the rubric of Fair Use. Every effort was made to contact the original publisher, its successors, and relatives of Professor Allen (1904–79), who contributed so much to scholarship on East African Islamic literatures. Should the copyright holder come forward, the editor and Press will be pleased to rectify the situation to his or her satisfaction. I have taken the liberty of deleting the stanza numbering in the original publication and of recasting certain archaic usages, replacing, for example, "thou" and "ye" with "you." I hope the inclusion of the text here will serve as a small memorial to the important contribution of J. W. T. Allen in broadening the scope of Islamic studies by making accessible such treasures of the Swahili language. (Ed.)

16 The Death of Shaykh Uways of Somalia

Scott Reese

Unlike most hagiographies, this story begins with a violent murder. Shortly after dawn on April 14, 1909, a raiding party loyal to the religious reformer Sayyid Muhammad 'Abd Allāh Hasan entered the Somali village of Biyoole. The horsemen were searching for the Qādirīya Sufi shaykh Uways ibn Muhammad, who maintained a compound within the village and who was rumored to be there with his wives and children and a handful of followers. Shaykh Uways had spent the previous two years preaching against the teachings of the Sayyid and refused to leave, swearing that he would remain in the village until death rather than flee in the face of the enemy. As the *manqaba* (account of marvels) below recounts, when the riders entered the village, they were met with a spirited resistance from the shaykh and his followers. The battle raged throughout the morning, with Uways's followers valiantly defending the village and their shaykh. By midafternoon, however, outnumbered and outgunned, the shaykh and all but one of his followers lay dead or dying.[1]

The murder of Uways and his students at the hands of a rival religious group was, in Somalia at least, a rare violent manifestation of a long-simmering conflict over differing views of the proper path to religious reform. The thirteenth/nineteenth century was host to numerous reform-minded thinkers all searching for ways to arrest the political, economic, and moral decay that plagued Islamic society. In East Africa this debate was shaped by the leaders of the various local mystical orders. Sayyid Muhammad, the so-called Mad Mullah, was head of the Sālihīya order and was influenced by many of the most conservative reformist voices, including the teachings of the puritanical Arabian scholar Muhammad ibn 'Abd al-Wahhāb (1202/1787). In accordance with this doctrine, Sayyid Muhammad and his followers argued that reform could occur only through a strict reliance on the Qur'ān and Hadith as the only sources of inspiration and the individual believer's relationship with God. Popular practices that sought the deceased, such as the Prophet or the saints, as intermediaries with the divine were viewed as *shirk* (idolatry).[2] As the case of Shaykh Uways illustrates, however, other reformers opposed the message of Sayyid Muhammad and were more than willing to die for their beliefs.

SOMALI SUFISM

Organized Sufism was a relative latecomer to the Horn of Africa, emerging only in the late 1200s/1800s. While known in Somalia before that time, mysticism was largely the preserve of a few ascetics and appeared as a prominent social movement under the guidance of a number of charismatic preachers only after 1298/1880. The efforts of these clerics were so successful by the beginning of the Second World War that virtually all Somali males identified, at least nominally, with one of the local schools of Sufism, either the Qādirīya, Ahmadīya, or Sālihīya.[3]

At the beginning of the fourteenth/twentieth century, the Qādirīya was by far the largest *tarīqa* in Somalia and East Africa. Founded by the Hanbalite theologian 'Abd al-Qādir al-Jīlānī (562/1166), the Qādirīya is believed to be the first organized Sufi order to arrive in Northeast Africa. According to the order's written traditions, knowledge of "the Path" was first brought to Harār, in what is now southeastern Ethiopia, by the Hadramī sharif Abū Bakr ibn 'Abd Allāh al-'Aydrūs (909/1503), also regarded as the order's main popularizer in Aden. Sources of information about Qādirīya activities in East Africa from this point until its expansion in the late thirteenth/nineteenth century are sparse. The little information that exists indicates that the order became a small but active component of town life, especially in Harār and to a somewhat lesser extent in the towns of the Somali coast.[4]

This limited sphere of influence may have been due to the order's traditional emphasis on the study of *'ilm*, the "religious sciences," in addition to mystical training as a prerequisite to progress along the Path to enlightenment and union with God. The founder of the order, al-Jīlānī, was a noted scholar of *fiqh* (jurisprudence) and Hadith who argued that in order to gain entry into the esoteric (*al-bātin*, lit. "the interior") realms of the soul necessary for enlightenment, one had to first master the exoteric (*az-zāhir*) duties of religious observance and learning.[5] Given the centrality of this dictum to Qādirīya teachings, it is likely that the virtual absence of literacy beyond the boundaries of urban centers before the late thirteenth/

nineteenth century prevented the order from gaining popularity amongst the rural populations. For whatever reason, the Qādirīya order did not gain widespread currency in East Africa until the last two decades of the nineteenth century.

The emergence of the Qādirīya as a popular movement was tied directly to the appearance of a number of charismatic shaykhs who embodied the Qādirīya ideal of esoteric ability and formal learning. Among these was the order's first popularizer, Shaykh ʿAbd al-Rahmān ibn Ahmad az-Zaylāʿī (c. 1236/1820–1298/1880), credited with the foundation of a new branch known as the Zaylāʿīya. He succeeded largely because of his ability to propagate a notion of Sufism based on spirituality and religious learning that attracted members from both the general population and the learned classes. Zaylāʿī's influence, however, was limited primarily to the rural areas of the upper Shebeelle River. Credit for the widespread propagation of the order in Somalia and throughout East Africa is given to the slightly later Shaykh Uways ibn Muhammad al-Barawī (1264/1847–1327/1909). Countless oral and written traditions exist that extol the learning and spiritual prowess of Uways, placing him among the greatest Qādirīya shaykhs, second in holiness, in East African circles at least, only to the order's founder, ʿAbd al-Qādir al-Jīlānī.

Born in the southernmost Benādir town of Barawe to a family of modest means, Uways belonged to a servile client lineage of the Tunni clan known as the Goigal. There is some indication that his father may have been a minor religious figure. Many accounts, however, contend that as a child, the future leader of the Qādirīya learned the weaver's trade. Muslim religious practitioners of secondary importance frequently practiced other trades in order to earn their livelihood. Thus, it is certainly plausible that Uways was descended from a line of fairly well educated but poor *'ulamā'* (religious scholars). Uways, however, proved something of a prodigy and eventually rose to study with members of Barawe's religious elite. He traveled ultimately to Baghdad, where, after a period of further study, he received the mantle of the Qādirīya from the order's head, Shaykh Mustafā ibn Salmān.[6]

Between the time of his return to Somalia in 1300/1882 and his death in 1327/1909, what became known as the Uwaysīya branch of the Qādirīya spread rapidly. Expanding throughout southern Somalia and over the entire East African littoral as far south as Tanganyika, the order became arguably the largest in East Africa.[7] Uways's significance, however, derives also from the his movement's permeation of every level of East African Muslim society. As Qādirīya oral and written traditions are quick to point out, the shaykh attracted followers from every walk of life and social class. His adherents were drawn from both rural and urban segments of East African society as well as elites and non-elites. The Qādirīya viewed their order as pan-Muslim and aimed at all believers, attracting followers from both "town and countryside," both "free and slave."[8]

The sudden popularity of the Qādirīya, and other orders, appears to stem directly from the massive social, political, and economic disruptions of the late thirteenth/nineteenth century. As was the case across most of Africa, the profound disruptions of that century provoked a period of great hardship and uncertainty throughout the Horn of Africa. Disease, commercial competition, and encroaching colonialism spelled economic disaster for both rural and urban Somalis. For many, the causes of these maladies lay not with external factors such as the vagaries of international economics or epidemiology—which they viewed as mere symptoms—but in their own moral failings. While certainly devoted to propagating the teachings of ʿAbd al-Qādir Jīlānī, Uways and his followers promoted with equal verve their version of orthodox belief as a remedy for the social ills of the age. Preaching from bases in towns as well as the countryside, Uways and his followers are generally portrayed as open-minded and nondogmatic when reconciling perceived Islamic orthodoxy with local practice. They turned a blind eye to custom as long as it did not violate the spirit of the Islamic law too egregiously.[9]

However, the Qādirīya were not the only reform-minded thinkers who sought to influence the beliefs of Somali Muslims at this time. In the interior, at least, their greatest rival came in the shape of the Sālihīya order led by Sayyid ʿAbd Allāh Hasan (1273/1856–1339/1920). From the late 1310s/1890s until his death in 1339/1920, the sayyid led an armed movement in the Somali interior aimed in part at European and Ethiopian imperialism but also, as the following story demonstrates, at his theological rivals. Sayyid ʿAbd Allāh and his followers have generally been portrayed (from a religious perspective) as a group of neo-Wahhābī reformers and religious demagogues determined to root out what they perceived as heretical local practices to be replaced by a puritanical theocratic regime.[10] The charges of "Wahhābism" leveled at the sayyid by his detractors do not hold up under close scrutiny. However, as the following episode demonstrates, violence against religious opponents was an option that, if not encouraged outright, was at least tacitly condoned. Despite their "victory" over Uways, Sayyid Muhammad's disciples were not the winners in the long-term struggle for reform in East Africa. By the early twentieth century the Qādirīya of Uways far outstripped Sayyid Muhammad's Sālihīya in both membership and territorial scope. In spite of the shaykh's murder, the order continued to flourish, while the Sālihīya declined into obscurity following the sayyid's death in 1339/1920.

The following account was first recorded in the *Majmūʿa al-karāmāt* (*Gathering of Marvels*), compiled by Uways's disciple Qāsim al-Barawī sometime around 1336/1917, which constitutes the earliest hagiographic work about Uways. This collection, which exists only in manuscript form, was edited and published as part of the *manāqib* collection *Jalāʾ al-ʿaynayn* by Shaykh ʿAbd ar-Rahmān bin ʿUmar in 1374/1954, from which this translation is taken. The story of Uways's murder carries many messages. It reifies the sanctity of the *walī*, his dedication to God, and the punishment that awaits those who harm a Friend of God (cannibalism and eternal damnation, in this case.) More important, it emphasizes the qualities inherent in the followers of the true Friends of God—loyalty, bravery, commitment, and above all, sacrifice.

TRANSLATION

I have been informed by the transmitter ʿAbd al-Qādir, known as Mamzaylī, about the death of the Friend of God. He said he was with the Shaykh when [he] entered the village of Biyooley and approached the Sarman Ashrāf. The enemy heard of his whereabouts and sent people to inform them [the villagers] that they were heading for their town. And the Ashrāf said to the Shaykh, "The enemy has us in their sights and we are frightened, as they are heavily armed. We cannot stay here; its better to go to another place until the enemy has left, and then return." The Shaykh said to them, "As for you, if you leave, that is your reward. As for me, I will not leave from here until I die. If I leave here, I will be erased from the *dīwān* [register] of the Friends of God." The Ashrāf left with the people of the town and went to another place. So there remained the Shaykh with his disciples. And the disciples said to the Shaykh, "The town's people have left, and we are poor and we should leave with them so that there may be peace and preservation of our spirits." The Shaykh replied, "You all placed yourselves in my service to receive *baraka* from me and from Shaykh ʿAbd al-Qādir Jīlānī. But truly, if I leave this place, I will be erased from the *dīwān* of the Friends of God." They then agreed to remain with the Shaykh and [secure] his victory over the enemy.

After several days the Shaykh sent his nephew [sister's son] Shaykh Muhammad Kawawa to Baidhabo [Baidoa] to gather news of the enemy's progress, because God showed him the fear in his nephew's heart. . . . On the morning of the fourth day, the enemy arrived in the town. The followers heard their voices calling, "Sh' Allāh yā Muhammad Sālih." And the Shaykh said to two of his followers, "Go out to them with the learning of the Qādirīya and with the memory of peace as was his custom." So the two went out to meet them with the knowledge of his saying: "Our lord God, master of glory; our lord God, master of perfection."

When the enemy saw the learning of the Shaykh, they shouted with their voices, "Sh' Allāh yā Muhammad Sālih," as I said in my[11] *qasīda* (ode) titled "With the Sharpness of Swords on the Necks of the Sinners," whose first line is "O' God, protect us from evil with the Family [of the Prophet] and the Friend of God 'Abd al-Qādir," and which continues:

> They are cast to the fire, the reciters of "Muhammad Sālih,"
>> Averting their gaze and running.
> The image of my Shaykh, my [spiritual] father, my teacher,
>> My protector, Uways is like that of 'Abd al-Qādir.

They killed the students who fell before the door of the Shaykh's house. The Shaykh dragged the two into the house, and the twenty-four remaining students stood before the Shaykh, took up their rifles, and asked his permission to engage [the marauders]. The Shaykh gave his permission with the proviso that he remain in his house because it was from that spot that he would enter Paradise. They said, "We hear and obey." They went out and excelled against them. The Shaykh sat in his chair and took up pen and ink to copy down [the verses] he had composed the night before. The disciples continued to fight the enemy, and Mamzaylī sat with the Shaykh in the house trembling, scared and awed.

They battled the enemy until they defeated them, and God supported them in his victory with what he had said to them and the blessing of the Shaykh . . . despite their few numbers.

Then they said to the Shaykh, "Our Shaykh! The enemy is defeated, all of them." But the Shaykh did not speak, so they said to him, "Our Shaykh, let us move from here to another place." But he would not go. Then the enemy returned a second time, and they were five hundred and more. They fought with the students, and as each one was struck with a bullet, he withdrew into the Shaykh's room. Those who fell in the front part of the house the Shaykh would drag inside until they all died in his room and the blood flowed and ran like water before him. And all the while he continued writing what he had composed in praise of the Prophet. "There remained only the Shaykh and I," said Mamzaylī. "The enemy surrounded the house and looked in. They saw two men, but believed there were many people inside. They fired, and I was wounded in my right arm and fell in the Shaykh's room. Then they started to move [toward us]. I [Mamzaylī] said to the Shaykh, 'Let's move from this place to another because they are going to fire upon the house. . . . '" He would not speak of leaving. He [Uways] said to me, 'As for you, you will not die in this place, *in shā'a Allāh*; you will die in your home of Barawe. Go from this place.' He [Uways] then spit on my arm [i.e., on the wound] and said to me, 'My son, you are healed, with the permission of God Most High.'" The transmitter [Mamzaylī] said, "I left and went under a shade tree near the Shaykh's house. I sat under it, and blood continued to flow from me like rainwater. There was opposite the tree a house and in it were his wives and children, and they were crying and asking me how the Shaykh had died. But I had no reason (*'aql*) and no voice (*hass*); I was in an enfeebled state within sight of death, and I said to them 'I don't know.'"

After an hour the enemy returned a third time and surrounded the house, and they looked in and found the Shaykh sitting, writing. They thought there were a lot of people inside, and this was the reason for the attack, jealousy of him. Because the Qādirī *tarīqa* was gaining ground in all the land and they cry [about this,] as is their custom. After surrounding the house and seeing the Shaykh in it, they said in unison, "Sh' Allāh Shaykh Muhammad Sālih," and opened fire, all of them, until the house caught fire. The fire raged, with the Shaykh inside along with the wrongly martyred, until [the house] was razed and fell. Then we heard a call, like the call to prayer, inside the house, and when the enemy heard the Shaykh's call, they fled, all of them trembling and fearful, and they backed off from their intentions. Terror and hostility entered their hearts amongst themselves, and they died, all of them, from that terror after some time. This was told to me by a son-in-law of the Shaykh [Uways], Shaykh 'Umar. He said that if one of them died, the others ate him.

Mamzaylī told me, after the call to prayer the fire went out and was reduced to ashes. The women and children were crying and bewildered at what had happened to the Shaykh, and I was beneath the tree until the time of *'asr* [the midafternoon prayer]. Then the sky became overcast and it began to rain. The rain divided the ashes into two raised piles, each resembling a burial mound. We sat there three days with hunger and sadness. On the third day the Ashrāf returned and with them [the Shaykh's] brother-in-law Shaykh 'Amār, and this was Saturday. And then after them arrived the Shaykh's nephew Shaykh Muhammad Kawawa from Baidhabo, and he asked them what had befallen the Shaykh and his followers.

They cried, all of them, asking us how he had died, and we told them what we had witnessed. [Here the compiler repeats the death scene at length.] And they were amazed by what they heard. They sat and inspected the site and searched through the ashes carefully. They found much that was burned, but found the Shaykh in another spot as if he were asleep, his face radiant with light, with his clothing [intact] as if he were alive. And with him were a knife and a gold *hirz* [a Qur'ānic amulet] wrapped in cloth tied around his waist; and that amulet had been with him for a very long time, and when they saw it, they were amazed and thought that he was alive. It was only when they moved him that they discovered he was truly dead. The fire had affected neither his body nor his clothes except for his sandal, and the fire had burned all that was in the house along with the house itself. They then performed the rituals that are performed for the dead and buried the Shaykh in one place and his students in another, near him. And the date was the 23rd of Rabī' al-Awwal, Wednesday, 1327 [1909].

. . . And the tomb that was built for him became a place of blessings. And during the days of its *ziyāra* the most prominent shaykhs of the Qādirīya would come, flooding the place with divine blessings, making sacrifices and reciting the Qur'ān and other things related to the remembrance of God, bringing gifts of clothing, and distributing the slaughtered meat to those present as charity. It became famous as a *ziyāra* at which numerous miracles (*karāmāt*) occurred and were witnessed by countless pilgrims.

And it says in one poem that is his elegy:

> The *ziyāra* to his tomb is like the Hajj.
>   His path is the best one to God;
> Happy is the one who walks it,
>   As the Messenger of God said.
> May Calamity befall the Somalis
>   Who killed a Friend of God.

NOTES

1. Abd al-Rahman ibn Umar, *Jalā' al-'Aynayn fī manāqib ash-shaykayn ash-shaykh al-walī hajj Uways al-Qādirī wa al-shaykh 'Abd al-Rahmān al-Zaylā'ī* (Cairo: Matba'at al-Mashhad al-Husaynī, 1954), *manqaba* 70, 52–57. The translator's attempts to contact the publisher to obtain permission were unavailing.

2. For a more complete discussion of the ideology and activities of Sayyid Muhammad, see Said Samatar, *Oral Poetry and Somali Nationalism: The Case of Sayyid Mohamed Abdille Hasan* (Cambridge: Cambridge University Press, 1983). Also see B.G. Martin, *Muslim Brotherhoods in Nineteenth-Century Africa* (Cambridge: Cambridge University Press, 1976).

3. A fourth *tarīqa*, the *Rifāʿīya*, was also present in the towns of the Benādir during this period. However, its membership was limited largely to Arabs from the Hadramaut region of southern Yemen. See J. S. Trimingham, *Islam in Ethiopia* (London: Frank Cass, 1965).

4. J. S. Trimingham, *The Sufi Orders in Islam* (London: Oxford University Press, 1965), 240; the main source for the Qādirīya during this early period appears to be the *Futūh al-habasha*.

5. See "'Abd al-Kādir al-Djīlānī," in *Encyclopaedia of Islam*, new ed., 1:69–70.

6. Ibn 'Umar, *Jawhar an-nafīs* (Delhi: Maktabat Ashāt al-Islām, 1964), 1–10.

7. See "The Qādirī and Shādhilī Brotherhoods in East Africa, 1880–1910," in Martin, *Muslim Brotherhoods*.

8. Ibn 'Umar, *Jawhar*, 11–12.

9. See Scott S. Reese, "Urban Woes and Pious Remedies: Sufism in Nineteenth Century Benādir (Somalia)," *Africa Today* 43, nos. 3–4 (1999): 169–94. Other important treatments of Somali Qādirīya ideology include I. M. Lewis, "Sufism in Somaliland: A Study in Tribal Islam," *Bulletin of the School of Oriental and African Studies* 17 (1955): 581–602, and 18 (1956): 146–60; Trimingham, *Islam in Ethiopia*.

10. See Samatar, *Oral Poetry and Somali Nationalism*; B. G. Martin and Abdi Sheikh Abdi, *Divine Madness: Mohamed Abdulle Hassan (1856–1920)* (London: Zed Books, 1993).

11. The compiler, Qāsim al-Barawī.

PART V

South Asia

. . . . .

South Asia is home to nearly half a billion Muslims today. Following are samples of hagiographical literature from all three of the modern nation-states that once constituted greater India: Pakistan, India, and Bangladesh. Eight texts are presented here in roughly geographical order from west to east. Three selections represent the northwestern portion of the subcontinent. Stories in a contemporary Urdu work tell of the tenth/sixteenth-century Panjabi figure Sadr ad-Dīn Sadr-i Jahān; texts of various genres and languages (Persian, Urdu, and Arabic) portray the expansive spiritual role of a major early modern figure, Ahmad Sirhindī; and a relatively recent panegyric in an important language of the region of Sindh called Siraiki fits the broad category of hagiographical text in several unusual ways. From the center of the region, present-day India, we have Persian, Gujarati, and Urdu texts of very different genres: one offers guidance to pilgrims as they make ritual visitation to shrines of Friends of God; the second provides a sample of panegyric devotional poetry; and the third presents autobiographical reflections of a contemporary Sufi leader. Finally, from Bangladesh to the northeast come the wondrous tales of two "mythic" Friends of God, Bonbībī and Mānik Pīr, both translated from the Bengali tongue. A prominent subtheme in these selections is the striking interrelationship among elements of other major South Asian religious traditions, leading Muslim figures interacting especially with Sikhs and Hindus. Some readers might find it instructive to begin with the "pilgrim guide" since it describes a variety of ritual activities and related matters of practice associated with countless shrines in South Asia and beyond.

17 A 'Tazkira' for the Times

Saving Islam in Post-Partition Punjab

Anna Bigelow

In the Urdu *tazkira* (Arabic *tadhkira*), or biographical dictionary, *Bāgh Anbiyā' Punjāb* (*Garden of the Saints of Punjab*),[1] Sufi Muhammad Ismail describes the rich landscape of Punjab through the tales of many Sufi saints who have lived and died in the region. Yet unlike most *tazkira*s, the chief concern of the author of *Bāgh Anbiyā'* is as much the political realities of post-Independence India as it is the holy Muslims. Typical biographical dictionaries of Friends of God from the classical and medieval periods recount each saint's many miracles, give examples of pious behavior and poetic compositions, and describe the saint's encounters with renowned figures of the times.[2] Their miraculous powers are rooted in their piety, and the chief concern of such hagiographies is to establish the individual's reputation as a Friend of God. If political and worldly leaders appear in these accounts, the encounters often seem intended to demonstrate the superiority of spiritual authority. Even saintly figures possessing temporal powers tend to be esteemed for their conformity to models of piety rather than of royalty. However, in much of *Bāgh Anbiyā'* Ismail appears to be primarily interested in the political and demographic context in which he himself is situated as a Muslim in Hindu India.

Ismail gives brief biographical and historical details about thirty-two saints representing all the major Sufi orders represented in South Asia, including Naqshbandīs, Suhrawardīs, and Chishtīs. He attends especially to Shaykh Sadr ad-Dīn Sadri Jahān (921/1515), a Suhrawardī Friend of God credited with founding the town and bringing Islam to the region in which Ismail lived. Malerkotla was the only Muslim-majority town remaining in Indian Punjab after the 1947 Partition and Independence of India and Pakistan. Almost painfully aware of the minority status of Punjab's Muslims, Ismail focuses his entry overwhelmingly on the Friend's role in preserving Islam in a region that is overwhelmingly Sikh, in a country that is overwhelmingly Hindu. Ismail himself is an imam at a local mosque and a Sufi guide in the lineage of celebrated Naqshbandī Friend Shaykh Ahmad Sirhindī (971/1564–1033/1624).[3] A sober and serious man, he is the author of a number of books on Islamic belief and practice.[4]

SHAYKH SADR AD-DĪN SADRI JAHĀN: LIFE AND LEGEND

Shaykh Sadr ad-Dīn Sadri Jahān, often referred to as Hazrat Shaykh, was a tenth/sixteenth-century saint born in the central Pashtun region of what is now Afghanistan.[5] According to Ismail and other sources, the Shaykh displayed great spiritual prowess as a child. He went to Multan, where he trained in the Suhrawardī *tarīqa*, which was centered there. *Bāgh Anbiyā'* and the other available accounts are silent concerning the type of training he received and whether he was schooled in any of the legal traditions of Islam or other specialized subjects. Most frequently mentioned in regard to his religious education is his Sufi guide, variously identified as Bahā' ad-Dīn Zakarīya (661/1262) or his grandson Rukn ad-Dīn Abū 'l-Fath (736/1335).[6] At the behest of his spiritual mentor (*murshid*, whoever he may have been), Hazrat Shaykh went east, eventually settling in Punjab on the banks of a river that then ran through Malerkotla. There, on a stormy night, the Afghan warlord Bahlol Lodhi encountered him. Impressed with his piety, the emperor married his daughter to the shaykh and gave a substantial land grant as dowry. The Friend died on 14 Ramadan 922/1515. His eldest son, Hassān, was denied the inheritance of the *jagir* (land grant), having fallen out of favor with his father. Thus, after Hazrat Shaykh's death, the second son, 'Īsā, inherited the *jagir*. A third son, Mūsā, became a dervish and did not marry, and the descendants of the disowned Hassān became the caretakers, or *khalīfas*, of the saint's *dargāh* (tomb shrine).

Ismail briefly recounts the Shaykh's meeting with Bahlol Lodhi. This encounter is central in most available renditions of Shaykh Sadr ad-Dīn Sadri Jahān's life, both oral and written.[7] The essence of the meeting between Lodhi and the shaykh is that the saint's piety and miracles impressed the Afghan warlord and, being from the same elite Pathan Afghan lineage, he married his daughter to the shaykh, giving a number of villages in dowry. Eventually this land grant became the princely state of Malerkotla. In other hagiographies of Hazrat Shaykh, this story is elaborated more fully and is said to exemplify the pious power of the saint. In those accounts, the Afghan warlord comes upon the shaykh in a storm after the tents of his army have been blown away in the tumult. Only

Hazrat Shaykh's hut remains undisturbed and the candle by which he is reading the Qur'ān does not waver—attesting to his spiritual prowess. In all renditions, the Friend prays for Lodhi's victory in battle, and after winning, the emperor gives him his daughter in marriage. Often the saint's lack of concern for worldly things is further attested with a story in which Lodhi offers the saint a fabulous horse. The shaykh protests that he is a dervish and has no need of such luxuries. Bahlol Lodhi insists and leaves the horse with the saint. Soon he hears a report that Hazrat Shaykh has ordered the horse killed in order to feed the dervishes who have gathered around him. Angry at the treatment of his gift, he demands that the saint return the horse, knowing that the horse is dead and the shaykh will have to admit to his disrespectful actions. Hazrat Shaykh then produces myriad identical horses and instructs Lodhi to take back his horse. Unable to identify the horse, the saint calls it forth, establishing himself as a higher authority than the emperor, who wields only temporal power.

Tradition attributes numerous other miracles to the saint, but none of these popular legends appears in Ismail's account. For example, a story in the oral lore of the saint involves the wall of his tomb shrine, said to have been built overnight by jinn after the saint's death. Another tale reports that once, when he was performing his ablutions before prayer, his shoe fell into the river that ran through Malerkotla in those days. He asked for it back, and the entire river moved north and east, where it now flows near the city of Ludhiana. Hazrat Shaykh's piety and orthodoxy are further attested by an account in which he threw money offered to him by a solider into a bucket of water, declaring that it was not *halāl* (ritually acceptable). A few seconds later, the coins bubbled to the surface as spots of blood, confirming the saint's judgment on their impure state.

POLITICS OF MEMORY: PARTITION AND INDIAN MUSLIMS

The miraculous tales that fascinate the local population and the devotional community around Hazrat Shaykh's tomb shrine are of little concern to Ismail. He writes as a minority Muslim in Sikh Punjab in Hindu India, and this is the situation of greatest interest to him. Although before the Partition in 1947 Punjab was majority Muslim (53 percent, Census of India, 1941), today Muslims number less than 2 percent of the total population (1.6 percent, Census of India, 2001). When Punjab was divided in 1947, most Punjabi Muslims migrated to the new Islamic republic. For those who stayed in India the challenge was how to remain Muslim in a culture that was, and in many sectors still is, deeply suspicious of Muslims—their loyalties, motives, and ways.[8] In Indian Punjab, Malerkotla was the only substantial population center that stayed overwhelmingly Muslim, and it remains so to this day. Furthermore, at Partition no one was killed in Malerkotla due to the interreligious violence that ravaged the rest of the region.[9] Accounting for these two unique features of the town—the peace at Partition and the Muslim-majority population—is a kind of cottage industry in Malerkotla, with everyone offering his or her own viewpoint. Among the most common explanations for the town's unusual demography and history is that the many saints buried in the territory, especially Hazrat Shaykh, protected the residents and preserved the integrity of the population. Sufi Ismail's account also offers this explanation, but gives the greatest credit to God. In his view, God saved Malerkotla through the agency of the founding saint, Shaykh Sadr ad-Dīn Sadri Jahān, to preserve the town as a bastion of Islam in post-Partition Punjab.

After living through Partition himself and witnessing numerous subsequent periods of heightened tension between Hindus, Muslims, and Sikhs, Ismail is acutely aware of communal politics and conflicts. Yet the tone of his writing suggests that he believes that other Punjabi Muslims are in grave need of reminding that they have an enormous responsibility to defend their faith from the various forces that threaten it—in particular, deculturation and assimilation, since Muslims are so vastly outnumbered. Furthermore, they are targets of repeated, direct assaults by Sikh and Hindu nationalist politics in Punjab and India. In the 1980s and early 1990s, Punjab experienced prolonged violent conflict, this time between the Indian government and Sikh separatists. In 1984 Prime Minister Indira Gandhi (Congress Party) authorized an Indian Army assault on the Golden Temple in Amritsar, where a militant Sikh leader and his loyalists were ensconced. The conflagration was profoundly damaging, killing hundreds of people and destroying ancient manuscripts and buildings. The greatest casualty was Sikh trust in the central government. These tensions were exacerbated when Gandhi herself was killed by her Sikh bodyguards and when thousands of Sikhs were later killed in riots across Delhi. This fed a militant Sikh separatist movement, and so the Sikh-majority state of Punjab was wracked by violence for almost ten years, resulting in tens of thousands of deaths. In the aftermath of this violent period, a government came to power in Punjab dominated by the Sikh nationalist party the Shiromani Akali Dal (SAD). The SAD then forged an alliance with the Hindu nationalist Bharatiya Janata Party (BJP), which controlled the central government in India.[10]

Some alienated Punjabi Muslims regarded the alliance between Sikh and Hindu nationalist parties with suspicion. Muslim antipathy for the BJP is rooted in one of the party's core tenets that promote *hindutva*, or Hindu-ness—the notion, which all native Indians must accept, that they are inherently Hindu and embrace Hindu culture as their national culture.[11] According to this ideology, rejecting the Hindu-ness of the nation meant rejecting the nation itself. The BJP has long advocated policies to "Hindu-ize" school curricula, abolish any special status granted to minorities (such as Muslims), and "reclaim" properties identified as originally Hindu that may have been "converted" during the nearly 1,000 years of Muslim rule. One such site was the Babrī Masjid, a mosque built in the northern Indian city of Ayodhya in the sixteenth century under the direction of the first Mughal emperor, Babur. A movement to "liberate" the site, claimed by some to be the birthplace of the Hindu god Rama, accelerated in the late 1980s and early 1990s, culminating in the mosque's demolition by over 200,000 Hindu extremists. Many BJP leaders were implicated in these events that led to the destruction of the Babrī Masjid and triggered riots across India that resulted in at least 3,000 deaths.[12]

Writing in the polarized context of Ayodhya's aftermath, Ismail is acutely aware of the broader condition of India's Muslims, who are on average poorer, less educated, underemployed, excluded from coveted government jobs, and more vulnerable than other religious or ethnic groups during periods of communal conflict.[13] His awareness manifests in his portrayal of Malerkotla as a stronghold of Islam in a Punjab whose formerly plural society had changed radically since 1947 due to migration and the subsequent division of the state into three parts (Punjab, Haryana, and Himachal Pradesh). The demographic shifts and the ascendancy of religious nationalist politics provide the subtext to Ismail's concerns about the fate of the Muslim minority. Thus it is perhaps understandable that Ismail's entry on Hazrat Shaykh should contain pointed references to the indignities suffered by Muslims during and since Partition. The text is also full of nostalgia for a time when Muslims dominated the region. Indeed, stories of the saint's life are few here in comparison to details of the history of Malerkotla. This is not as irrelevant as it may at first appear, as Hazrat Shaykh's descendents were also the rulers of the kingdom of Malerkotla. Ismail gives brief details on several of these Nawābs, mentioning their achievements and locating their gravesites in town. Regarding the saint himself, Ismail is less interested in his spiritual accomplishments or miracles than in his encounter with Bahlol Lodhi, the founder of the brief Lodhi dynasty

(855/1451–933/1526), which led to the establishment of the territory that would become Malerkotla.

Ismail does not discuss the miracles of the candle or the horse, which feature so prominently in other accounts of Hazrat Shaykh. Instead, after recounting Lodhi's giving of his daughter in marriage, Ismail digresses from Malerkotla history to give a brief account of the Lodhis, ending with their defeat by Mughal emperor Babur. Ismail closes this section by remarking on Babur's establishment of a mosque in Ayodhya in 933/1526. Of course any reader of this Urdu *tazkira* would know that Hindu militants destroyed that mosque in 1992. Evidently, evoking this event was Ismail's sole purpose in referencing Babur: having established a connection to this moment in history, he gives no further information about Babur or the other Mughal rulers. Instead, his attention turns to the descendents of Hazrat Shaykh and their impact on local history. Rhetorically, this reference positions Ismail in opposition to Hindu nationalist politics, highlights the travails and injustice the Muslim minority in India must endure, and generates a link with the lineage of Hazrat Shaykh.

Although passages in which Ismail describes Hazrat Shaykh's descendents are terse, his choice of Nawābs to reference is revealing. He singles out rulers for whom extant villages were named and gives special attention to several Nawābs whose legacies have been most significant for Malerkotla. He elaborates at length on the most famous Nawāb, Sher Muhammad Khān, well known in Punjab for his role in Sikh sacred history. In 1705, when the tenth Sikh guru Gobind Singh was fighting against the Mughals and their allies (including Malerkotla), his two youngest sons were taken captive at Sirhind. Pressured to convert, they refused and were sentenced to death. Only Sher Muhammad Khān spoke up, saying that young boys should not be killed for the sins of their fathers. His plea was ignored and the children were executed, but upon hearing of these events, Guru Gobind Singh blessed the Nawāb and his lineage, saying that their lineage would endure. Many people believe that this blessing has preserved Malerkotla from attack by the Sikhs ever since.[14]

Ismail focuses in greatest depth on the rule of Ahmad Alī Khān, the second-to-last ruler, under whose governance Partition occurred. From his detailed treatment of this period, it is evident that Ismail's primary concern with the entire biographical entry is to make sense of Partition and its impact on Malerkotla, Punjab, and Islam in India. As Ismail himself is old enough to recall Partition, his writing becomes particularly vivid as he recounts scenes of death and destruction. He describes a vivid, if clichéd, image of Holi (the Hindu festival in which a mixture of colored powder and water is sprinkled liberally), comparing the Hindu shedding of Muslim blood to the religious carnival. Yet Malerkotla was one of very few places in Punjab that were not devastated by the killings in 1367/1947. Instead, the urban center of the kingdom became a safe haven for migrating Muslims from other regions. Although violence surrounded Malerkotla, within its borders no one died because of interreligious conflict. In Ismail's view, Malerkotla's survival and retention of its Muslim identity is the miracle most in need of publication and explanation. Although he does mention the role of Shaykh Sadr ad-Dīn Sadri Jahān in this regard, he effusively gives the credit to God alone. Ismail indicates that God saved Malerkotla so that His religion might be preserved to continue to guide the people of the region. Only after crediting Malerkotla's preservation to God does Ismail remark upon Hazrat Shaykh's role in this miracle. After all, it was Hazrat Shaykh's power that brought Islam to the region, providing God with the reason for saving the people who had accepted his faith. Thus, because Hazrat Shaykh established the religion there, the town itself and all its Muslim residents are now responsible for maintaining the faith as a beacon of Islam in the overwhelmingly Sikh and Hindu state.

TRANSLATION

Hazrat Shaykh Sadr ad-Dīn Sadri Jahān Khān, Maleri, Malerkotla

Then there is Hazrat Shaykh. His father's name was Ahmad Shāh . . . [and he] was renowned by the name Zinda Pīr. [Zinda Pīr's] revered tomb is in Banur [near Patiala]. He was Afghānī.

Hazrat Shaykh's Arrival in Multan He came from Kabul, Afghanistan, by way of Daraban [in the Northwest Frontier Province of Pakistan] and arrived at Multan. At that time Multan was a great center of *pīrs*. There he took initiation (*bay'at*) from Shaykh Bahā' al-Haq Sāhib [Bahā' ad-Dīn Zakarīya, a Suhrawardī saint of Multan, 578/1182–661/1262], who was in that time a saint of revelations and miracles and giver of victory. Having stayed there for a year to serve his spiritual guide (*pīr-o-murshid*), in 872/1468 he chose to settle in the town of Maler by way of Jalandhar. Afterward, [this place] became known as the kingdom of Malerkotla.

At that time Maler was a Hindu Rajput settlement. Settling in this place, he spread the religion of Islam and called people to the path of righteousness. Through his spiritual gifts they were enriched.

A Page from History It is well known that through the illuminating light of many histories, readers and listeners can obtain proper knowledge.

At that time in Hindustan the Lodhi clan ruled and had also founded Ludhiana [a town near Malerkotla]. When the authority of the Tughluq and Sadat—meaning the Sayyid—clans had ended, the Lodhi clan's rule began. [Among the Lodhis] there were three famous rulers: first, Sultan Bahlol Shāh Lodhi; second, Sikandar Shāh Lodhi; third, Ibrāhīm Shāh Lodhi. All were Afghans. Ibrāhīm Lodhi had a very severe and strict temperament. The populace was not happy with him. For this reason they called Zāhir al-Dīn Babur, the Mughal from Kabul in the Farghana kingdom. They revolted against Ibrāhīm. They helped Zāhir al-Dīn and turned against Ibrāhīm. When the news reached Ibrāhīm Shāh, he came bringing 12,000 soldiers and elephants and cannons, and the two armies confronted each other on the field of Panipat. There was a very bloody battle in which Ibrāhīm Shāh was killed, some of his soldiers kept fighting, and the rest dispersed. The crown fell into Zāhir al-Dīn Babur's hands, and the Mughal clan's founder and the king of kings Zāhir al-Dīn Babur's name became famous.

Shortly thereafter he had his minister, Mīr Bāqī, built the Babri Masjid in Ayodhya, District Faizabad, in Uttar Pradesh, in his name.

[Hazrat Shaykh's] Fame and Bahlol Lodhi   Sultān Bahlol Shāh Lodhi had a very pious heart. He greatly revered the Friends of God, the pious elders, the noble '*ulamā*', and pious people, and he was constantly desirous of their prayers. The commander at Sirhind who was in the service of Sultān Bahlol Shāh Lodhi wrote about the particulars of the perfected Friend (*walī kāmil*) and worker of miracles. Reading and hearing of his genius, excellence, and miracles, the Bādshāh desired greatly to meet him. Bādshāh Bahlol Shāh Lodhi went on a pilgrimage to meet him and arrived in the town of Maler in 870/1470 to serve him. And he sought [the saint's] prayer for his victory in a battle. [Hazrat Shaykh] gave the order that he should be victorious. He issued a prayer that was accepted by Allah Most High. His desire was fulfilled and the Bādshāh was successful. Following this the B&dshāh believed from his heart.

His Wedding   Because of this, Sultan Bahlol Lodhi became a disciple and believer, and so he arranged the marriage of his daughter Tāj Murassa Begum with [Hazrat Shaykh]. And he gave fifty-six villages and plenty of other resources in dowry. In this way he established a strong bond of friendship with the perfect dervish.

From his first wife [the daughter of Bādshāh Bahlol Shāh Lodhi] was born a daughter whose name was Bibi Mango. She was married to a ruler of Tohana [in District Hissar in the state of Haryana]. She also performed the Hajj on foot.

After this, in 878/1474, a son was born whose name was Shaykh Hasan Muhammad and whose descendents are the *khalīfas* of his holy grave. And the current *khalīfas* are his descendants. His garments and shoes are still in the possession of these *khalīfas* today.

His Second Marriage   His second marriage was with the Rajput ruler of Kapurthala's daughter Murtazā Begum in 875/1471. From her were born two sons: first, Shaykh Muhammad 'Īsā and, second, Shaykh Muhammad Mūsā Hazrat Shaykh Muhammad 'Īsā[, who] was born in 879/1475. Shaykh Muhammad Mūsā was born in 882/1478 and remained childless.

[Hazrat Shaykh's] Death   He died in 921/1515 and his blessed tomb is in Maler. In Malerkotla there are special and regular pilgrimages. From all over Punjab people come on pilgrimage. They make wishes and entreaties and give every kind of offering.

Concise History of Malerkotla

Some information about Malerkotla should be given a few lines, so that there will be a memorial for the future generations and researchers. [Hazrat Shaykh's] *pīr-o-murshid*, Bahā' al-Haqq, was a victory-giving saint of mysteries and miracles and a clairvoyant. He sent [Hazrat Shaykh] far away from Multan to the town of Maler so that the people here could be called to Allah's way and receive the blessings of his power and essence.

Thus from his having lived in this place of Maler, the whole region today has been unified. And he called the forgetful and lost people back to the path of righteousness. In this way it is clear that the people here accepted Islam at his hands. From his service and example, Islam spread in the region, and the kingdom of Islam arrived within these boundaries, and Allah knows everything.

As the Qur'ān declares: "Whoever is with Allāh, Allāh is also with him." Because Hazrat Shaykh was one of the elect saintly and pious elders, a perfected dervish and beloved of Allah, therefore Bādshāh Bahlol Shāh Lodhi believed in him unreservedly from the heart. When through his prayer he was victorious in battle, he believed even more greatly. Because of this faith, he united his beloved daughter to [Hazrat Shaykh], and he gave to her in marriage portion the whole area of Maler, which afterward was known as the kingdom of Malerkotla. Kotla was settled later, but the town of Maler was there from the beginning. Kotla was eventually joined with Maler, making Malerkotla. Between them is a bazaar. All the surrounding villages were part of the kingdom. The nearby villages are all known by two names. For example, Dugani is also known as Mahmūdpūr, and likewise Maharpūr's second name is Mahmūdpūr. Almost all the villages are like this.

Shaykh Muhammad Īsā's Descendants

Hazrat Shaykh Sadr ad-Dīn Sadri Jahān's two wives had three sons, of whom two are mentioned above. The third son was Shaykh Muhammad Īsā, who was the second leader and landowner of this Malerkotla and from whom are descended the Nawābs of Malerkotla. In this lineage came Nawāb Sikandar Ali Khān Sāhib,[15] Nawāb Sher Ali Khān Sāhib,[16] Nawāb Sube Khān Sāhib, Bhikan Khān Sāhib,[17] Nawāb Wazīr Ali Khān,[18] Nawāb Rehmat Ali Khān Sāhib, Nawāb Ahmad Ali Khān Sāhib, and the last, Nawāb Iftikhār Alī Khān Sāhib. His descendants were the rulers and land grant holders such as Jamāl Khān Sāhib, Ināyat Alā Khān Sāhib, Isar Alī Khān Sāhib, Zulfiqār Alī Khān Sāhib, Muhammad Alī Khān Sāhib, Ghulām Muhammad Khān Sāhib, and so on.

In the time of Ahmad Alī Khān the railway station was built and the trains came. He ruled Malerkotla for forty-one years. In 1367/1947 Pakistan came into being. In that terrifying time when the refugees fled the murder and destruction that was going on in other kingdoms and cities, they fled to Malerkotla. In that time, outside Malerkotla's borders the murder of Muslims became a normal thing. They were robbed. Their women and young girls were disrespected and were stripped naked. They played *holi* with their blood and rolled their children's heads like balls and burned their houses. So the looted and ravaged refugees came in caravan-loads, filling Malerkotla. There was not a single unoccupied space. The Nawāb's great garden and palace were also filled with refugees, food, clothes, and the like. People kept arriving in the camps. The first camp was in front of the Rehmatgarh Fort on Nabha Road. And then the water began to flow. This took place during the rains. For two months the sun did not show itself; thus there was water above and below. So much slaughter and destruction took place that in this way the rainwater and the canal water became [red] like the sun, and the corpses kept falling in the water.

Then the Nawāb Sāhib had the dead brought behind the 'Īd Gāh, near the railway line on the Imamgarh Road. In the end, he could not endure through this great misfortune. On 30 September 1367/1947, he departed this world.

Qur'ān: Verily we belong to Allāh and to Allāh we return.

Allāh Most High ordered our salvation, and from His mercy He orders our descent, Amen.

In all of Punjab, only in Malerkotla did peace and security remain, since the whole of Punjab is empty of Muslims today. All of Haryana and Himachal were once part of Punjab. This is entirely thanks to Allah Most High and His special desire that this portion of Muslims [be left to] save the rest. In His mercy, this great Master commanded our protection and that of our beloved city. From His doing everything becomes easy. He is victorious, He is the Lord, the Protector, the Helper.

Qur'ān: Verily Allāh has power over everything.

Allāh is one and there is nothing like Him; He has power over all things. He is the King of Kings. There is no doubt that, as He likes, He makes the rich and the poor. Just so, if the Merciful Allāh did not desire or cause it, today Malerkotla also would be empty of Muslims. It was His desire that the Malerkotlans protect the others, since through His sovereign power He desired that some work continue to be done for His religion. Therefore here [in Malerkotla] all of us Muslims need to work to expand the religion of Islam. And to our other brothers we must bring forth the message of Allāh and His Prophet. In this way we Muslims must uplift this world and the next. The other [factor in the preservation of Malerkotla] is Hazrat Sadr ad-Dīn Sadri Jahān's power and miracles—he whose original throne this is. It is because of him that Islam has come to this whole place and from this town of Maler the (kingdom) city of Malerkotla was made.

Qur'ān: Such is the pleasure of Allāh, he guides whom He wills.

If it were not the case that Allāh saved us, when on all sides fire burned, then and also now, then in the middle of this how were we saved? Yes, Allāh saved us from this and Allāh preserves us from this still. And by Him they are punished.

It is so that for Allāh the Pure, all things are easy. When He wants things a certain way, He is able to make it so easily.

Nawāb Iftikhār Alī Khān Sāhib assumed the throne after the sorrow of his father's death. He was crowned, but just a little while after that the [independent] kingdoms came to an end and the Indian government took the reins into their hands. All the rajas and maharajas were without power and were given pensions from the Indian government. From this dying world some were left in this condition. Nawāb Sāhib had five marriages, but the Lord decreed that from none were there any children. And for eternity, this kingdom's light has gone out.

> It was a high, high place that is now a small grave
> Allāh is everything, the rest is false love.

During Jamāl Khān's rule his base was at Jamalpura. Everything about his rule was different, even the villages and so on were different. Near his settlement at Badhla he fought with the English, who were victorious. He took the cannon from there and put it at the gate of Jamalpura, where it is still found today. Jamāl Khān's grave is on the Dhurri road.

Ināyat Alī Khān was Ahmad Alī Khān's uncle who was very generous. Every day he made a great deal of offerings and improvements. Masjid Kalsanwali was his mosque, and his palace was at the side of this mosque.

Īsār Alī Khān's palace was on the left side of Kalsanwali mosque where the girl's school is now.

Baqr Alī Khān was on the left side of the Jāmiʿ Masjid where today there is a pilgrims' hostel. Baqr Alī's famous garden is near the Ludhiana Bypass Road. Today his name—Baqr Alī Khān—is still found written over the gate. Previously this garden was very beautiful. It was thickly settled by all kinds of fruit trees. Now it is all deserted. The fruit trees have died and crops have been planted. This blooming place is blooming no more. This garden is a religious endowment property in the possession of the Shīʿas. They take the income from it and take out a horse in the taʾzīya procession [at Muharram].

Ihsān Alī Khān's palace was across from and to the right of the Dīwān Khāna where now there is a Sindhi [Sikh] gurdwara [Sikh sacred place]. These [structures] are all connected. They were built by the father, children, and grandchildren who were all from one house. Zulfiqār Alī Khān Sāhib's palace was just across from Purani Kacheri Gate where now all the Sindhis have built a large and completely new gurdwara. Muhammad Alī Khān's home was also in Purani Kacheri. It has gone, to build the Sherwani Kot (Kelon) neighborhood. Now everywhere you look, these [great] houses are disappearing. Now there are only a few names and memorials. Ghulam Muhammad Khān was another of those [from the Nawāb's lineage]. He joined Mirzā Ghulām Ahmad Qādiānī, about whom God knows the truth. In this way [Ghulām Muhammad Khān] became worthless (and God is all-knowing).

Most of the graves of the Nawābs and rulers are in the graveyard (maqbara) neighborhood near Sirhindī Gate in Malerkotla; now these too are disappearing. Allāh Most High assures us that all—even the greatest—must die.

NOTES

1. Sufi Muhammad Ismail, Bāgh Anbiyāʾ Punjab (Garden of the Prophets) (Malerkotla, India: Janab Doctor Muhammad Nizamuddin Sahib,

1995). Attempts to contact the author and the publisher by mail received no response.

2. See, for example, Mir Khurd, *Siyar al-awliyā'* (Delhi; Muhibb-e Hind Press, 1885); Farīd ad-Dīn 'Attār, *Tadhkirat al-awliyā'* (*Muslim Saints and Mystics*) partially trans. A. J. Arberry (London: Arkana, 1966).

3. For more information on Sirhindi, see Yohanan Friedmann, *Shaykh Ahmad Sirhindi: An Outline of His Thought and a Study of His Image in the Eyes of Posterity* (New York: Oxford University Press, 2001).

4. Ismail, *Bāgh Anbiyā' Punjab; Kabr Ki Pahali Rat* (Malerkotla, India: Kutub Khāna Ibrāhīmīya, 1996); *Kabr Kya Kahti Hai* (Malerkotla, India: Maktaba Rahimiyan, 1971); *Na'atun Ka Bagh* (Malerkotla, India: Kutub Khāna Ibrāhīmīya, 1965).

5. In Malerkotla, Shaykh Sadr ad-Dīn Sadri Jahān is more frequently referred to as Hazrat Shaykh by his devotees, but as Ismail has chosen to refer to him as Hazrat, I do so as well.

6. Bahā'ad-Dīn Zakarīya and Rukn ad-Dīn Abū 'l-Fath were grandfather and grandson and among the most famous saints of the Suhrawardī lineage in the subcontinent. However, their dates are clearly inconsistent with those of Hazrat Shaykh, who died in 921/1515. Still, it is certainly not uncommon to link later Sufis to the most renowned, popular, and powerful saints in their lineages. Furthermore, although the shaykh's death date is typically given as 921/1515, the Hijrī date actually converts to 11 October 1516.

7. Available accounts of the life of Shaykh Sadr ad-Dīn Sadri Jahān include Isrār Afghānī, *Hayat Lodhi* (Pakistan: Tarikh Jamiat, 1325 AH); Iftikhār Alī Khān, *History of the Ruling Family of Shaykh Sadruddin Sadar-I-Jahan of Malerkotla (1449 A.D. to 1948 A.D.)*, ed. R. K. Ghai (1948; repr., Patiala: Punjabi University Press, 2000); Ināyat Alī Khān, *A Description of the Principal Kotla Afghans* (Lahore: Civil and Military Gazette Press, 1882); Khalīfah Anwār Ahmad Khān, *Hazrat Sadr Udin Sadare Jahan (Rehmat) Urf Baba Hazrat Shekh Ji Malerkotla Di Puri Jivani* (Malerkotla, India: Jivan Glass House, n.d.); Mohammad Khālid Zubairy, *Malerkotla: Itihas Ke Darpan Me* (Malerkotla, India: Tarkash, 2000).

8. This conundrum is well articulated by Gyanendra Pandey in "Can a Muslim Be an Indian?" *Comparative Studies in Society and History* 41, no. 4 (1999): 608–29.

9. The death toll during Partition is notoriously difficult to determine, with numbers ranging from 200,000 to a million lives lost. Approximately 15 million people shifted from one side of the new border to the other.

10. This alliance was clearly a matter of convenience and was not undisputed among Sikh nationalists, several of whom left the SAD over the union with the BJP, founding their own branches of the party.

11. BJP party platforms have typically emphasized three issues of particular relevance to the Muslim population in India: Kashmir, Ayodhya, and the Uniform Civil Code. The ongoing militancy in Kashmir between Kashmiri separatists, Islamist militants, and the Indian Army has fed fears of Islamic extremism and forced the emigration of most Hindu residents of the region.

The Babrī Masjid in Ayodhya was torn down in 1992 by Hindu militants who believed it to be the Ramjanmabhumi (birthplace of Lord Rama). The push to build a temple rather than a mosque on the site has been a BJP priority since the party's inception. The Uniform Civil Code seeks to end the application of Muslim personal law in matters of marriage, divorce, and inheritance. All three of these positions target and threaten Muslims, identifying them as an internal enemy of Indian unity.

12. Although few indictments have emerged from these events, it is clear Lal Krishna Advani, Murli Manohar Joshi, Uma Bharati (who has since left the party), and other BJP leaders were instrumental in fomenting the movement to destroy the mosque and build a temple. The destruction of the mosque on December 6, 1992, by unarmed, unequipped *karsevaks* (volunteers) is regarded as nothing short of a miracle by those who supported the action.

13. The low status of Muslims in India is well documented. See Zoya Hasan, *Unequal Citizens: A Study of Muslim Women in India* (New York: Oxford University Press, 2004), and Mushirul Hasan, *Legacy of a Divided Nation: India's Muslims since Independence* (Boulder, CO: Westview Press, 1997). See also the website of Ali Asghar Engineer, http://ecumene.org/IIS/csss.htm

14. This is a patently false, though strongly and widely held belief. Malerkotla was attacked by a Sikh group in 1289/1872, the kingdom's forces battled against the Sikhs in numerous campaigns, and Malerkotla often fought with neighboring Sikh kingdoms.

15. [Ismail's note] Sikandar Alī Khān's wife was Abū Fātima Begum, who built the Shāhi Masjid in the Dīwān Khāna. [She] put up a golden spire, which from October 1959 stood outside and in front of the Dīwān Khāna and in which this humble servant, writer of this book, for forty years was imam, and for this reason has special knowledge of this mosque.

16. [Ismail's note] The town of Sherpur was founded in the name of Nawāb Sher Alī Khān Sāhib, who in Sirhind at the court of Wazīr Sube Khān, had sympathy upon the children of Guru Gobind Singh and called for their release. Because of this, the Sikh people believe strongly in him and remember him. His grave is in the Malerkotla Dhabi Gate, Barahdari [a neighborhood] graveyard, but now no one goes there at all. Now all the care of the graves has been given to the Islāmīya School Branch.

17. [Ismail's note] There is a town called Bhikam in Bhikam Khān Sāhib's name in District Sangrur near Dhanula. In the time of Ahmad Shāh Abdāli, the Sikhs attacked Malerkotla. The Sikhs fought outside Bhikam Khān's city, and due to bad luck, Bhikam Khān was defeated and the Sikhs completely looted Malerkotla. By the time the news reached Ahmad Shāh, the Sikhs had completely escaped.

18. [Ismail's note] Nawāb Wazīr Alī Khān built Malerkotla's fortress and built gates on all sides: Mandi Gate, Sirhindi Gate, Delhi Gate, Sunami Gate, Sherwāni Gate, Dhabi Gate, Pa'ilya Gate, etc. Inside Dhabi Gate in the Barahdari, under a neem tree and inside four walls is the grave of Wazīr Alī Khān

Sāhib. He was an extremely wise and brave ruler. It was he who unified all the villages and rulers and created the permanent kingdom. In the first place, he fixed all the different divisions, and so Malerkotla took its form. He built the bazaars. All the bazaars were different as he determined in his plan. The biggest bazaar and best is Moti Bazaar. Then there are Lal Bazaar, Bans Bazaar, Loha Bazaar, Dana Mandi Bazaar, Sata Bazaar, etc.

18 Tales of Renewal

Ahmad Sirhindī, Reformer of the Second Millennium

Arthur Buehler

Ahmad Sirhindī (1034/1624) is the best-known Indo-Pakistani Sufi in the Islamic world. His major literary legacy is the *Collected Letters*, which contains 536 letters intricately detailing Sufi practice and philosophy. No other collection of Sufi letters and few Sufi treatises have had such a lasting impact on Muslims in the eastern Islamic world as have the *Letters*, translated into at least half a dozen languages. Through networks of *'ulamā'*, these letters facilitated the spread of the Naqshbandī-Mujaddidī lineage from India to Central Asia, the Ottoman Empire, and China. For a variety of reasons, including the timely message of Sirhindī's letters and the zeal of his followers, almost all Naqshbandī worldwide had become Mujaddidī—that is, followers of Ahmad Sirhindī's practices and ideas—by the beginning of the eighteenth century.

The first part of the story in this chapter relates how Sirhindī came to be given the title "the renewer of the second millennium" (*mujaddid-i alf-i thānī*), making him a cofounder figure (along with Bahā' ad-Dīn Naqshband, who died in 791/1389 in Bukhara) of the Naqshbandī-Mujaddidī lineage. The story begins with Sirhindī, like other Sufis before him, having visions and realizations that indicate his preeminent spiritual status in the world. For example, Rūzbihān Baqlī (606/1209 in Shiraz) had an experience of God, who declared him to be His vice-regent on earth and all other worlds. Ibn 'Arabī (638/1240 in Damascus) had multiple visions that identified him as the Seal of God's Friends, the eternal source of being a Friend of God (*walāya*). In a like manner, Sirhindī declared himself to be the unique one (*fard*) with absolute authority from the empyrean to earth.[1] In the story related here, Sirhindī introduces the concept and rationale of a millennial renewer in his letters. This was an unprecedented move. There had been the notion in Sunni Islam of a centennial renewer, but no one before Sirhindī had considered the idea of a millennial renewer of religion. Although Sirhindī never explicitly stated in his letters that he was this very renewer, it is very strongly implied. Such is the autobiographical aspect of the story presented here.

The second and third parts of the story in this chapter involve the hagiographical and polemical strands of Sufi literature as the tale of millennial renewer unfolds over the next two centuries. The hagiographical strand progressively inflates his status, while the polemical sources simply present him as the centennial renewer of the eleventh/seventeenth century.

AHMAD SIRHINDĪ BEGINS THE SAGA

Sirhindī details his experiences in spiritual travel leading to his becoming the unique one.

TRANSLATION

When this dervish [Ahmad Sirhindī] began aspiring to the Sufi path, God's favor bestowed upon me a successor of the great Naqshbandī Masters (*khwājagān*). Choosing the path of these notables, I entered into intimate spiritual conversation (*suhbat*) with Bāqībillāh (1012/1603 in Delhi). With the blessing of the spiritual concentration (*tawajjuh*) of Bāqībillāh and the spiritual attraction of the Masters, I achieved complete annihilation of the ego in the attributes of supporting the cosmos (*qayyūmīyat*). Then I proceeded on the path that includes "the end in the beginning" [i.e., the Naqshbandī path]. When that attraction became well established through the guidance of the spirit of God's victorious lion [i.e., 'Alī ibn Abī Tālib (40/661), the Prophet's cousin and son-in-law], I arrived at the end of the Path. That is, I ascended as far as 'Alī had. From there I ascended to the first degree of capability (*qābilīyat*), which is the bridge to the Muhammadan Reality. With the help of the disembodied presence of the Master of Naqshband (Bahā' ad-Dīn Naqshband), I kept ascending with the assistance of the disembodied presence of Fārūq ['Umar ibn al-Khattāb al-Fārūq (24/644), the second caliph]. I traveled even higher, beyond the first degree of capability to the attributes of God. Then I ascended to an even higher station, the station of the Muhammadan Poles, which manifested as God's Essence.

With the guidance of the disembodied presence of the last messenger—greetings and peace be upon him—further spiritual development took place. At that station I received assistance from the spirit of 'Alā' ad-Dīn 'Attār (803/1400), who is the successor of the Master Naqshband, the axial guide (*qutb-i irshād*). There I arrived at the end of the ascent of the Poles to this station where the circle of shadows ends. After that it is either the pure origin or the origin mixed with shadows.

The group of unique ones (*afrād*) is distinguished by their favor from God. Thus it occurs that some Poles ascend to the place of origin mixed with shadows (*asl-i zill*) by means of the unique ones. In other words, those who see the origin mixed with shadows will return to the shadows. When, however, they arrive at the pure origin or go beyond it and witness it, they are distinguished by a special degree of attainment. Thus they are called the unique ones. This happens by the grace of God "who gives to whom He desires" ([Qur'ān] 3:73)—and "God is the Source of all favor" (3:74). This dervish (Ahmad Sirhindī) received the robe of axial guide after arriving at the station of the Poles. I was graced by that sovereign of religion and the world (Muhammad). In that way I was bestowed this exalted rank.

Again, I received God's favor, and from there I was directed upward. One time I was taken to the origin mixed with shadows and experienced an annihilation (*fanā'*) and a remaining (*baqā'*) there as in the previous stations. Then, ascending by God's grace, I went to the stations of the origin to the origin of origins. In this last ascent [i.e., the ascent through the stations of the origin] the spirit of the Supreme Helper (*ghawth*) and preserver of religion, Shaykh 'Abd al-Qādir Jīlānī, assisted me. By the strength of his spiritual power I passed through those stations, finally arriving at the origin of origins. With each station I returned to the physical world. This dervish [Ahmad Sirhindī] had received the essential connection of being a unique one, which is especially like the last ascent described by his own noble father ['Abd al-Ahad, 1007/1598]. He ['Abd al-Ahad] in turn received his teaching from an honored one [Shāh Kamāl Qādirī, 981/1573]. The latter had a very strong attraction to God and was famous for facilitating miraculous events (*khawāriq*).[2]

[In his *Return to the Source* (1019/1610) Sirhindī discusses the events of the second millennium for the first time.]

There will come a time after the passage of a thousand-some-odd years after the death of the death of Muhammad, when the reality of Muhammad ascends from its station and unites with the station of the reality of the Ka'ba. At this time the reality of Muhammad takes the name of the reality of Ahmad and becomes the manifestation of the unique essence of God. Both blessed names [Muhammad and Ahmad] are established [as the aggregate of the reality of Muhammad and the reality of the Ka'ba]. The station that used to be the reality of Muhammad becomes vacant until

Jesus descends and acts in accordance with the Sharia of Muhammad. At this time the reality of Jesus rises to its own station and rests in the station of the reality of Muhammad, which had previously been vacant.[3]

[Explaining this passage to Mīr Muhammad Nuʿmān Badakhshānī (1058/1648), the first disciple whom Sirhindī authorized to teach, Sirhindī says in his *Collected Letters*:]

When a thousand years have passed since the death of Muhammad, which is a very long time, his spiritual aspect will predominate completely over his bodily aspect to the point that this spiritual aspect will imbue his being in the material world with that of the world of command. By necessity, Muhammad's reality in the material world will return to its reality, that is, the reality of Ahmad. The reality of Muhammad will ascend and unite with the reality of Ahmad. . . .

When Jesus descends, he will follow the Sharia of Muhammad, ascending from his [Jesus'] station and arrive at the reality of Muhammad as a follower [of Muhammad's Sharia], thereby strengthening his [Muhammad's] religion. From this it is related from previous Sharias that a thousand years after a great prophet (*payghambar-i ūlī al-ʿazm*) died, blessed noble prophets and great messengers were sent out to enact the Sharia of that great prophet and exalt his words. When the time of this great prophet's propagation of religion and Sharia was over, another great prophet was sent to renew his own Sharia. Since the Sharia of the Seal of the Prophets is protected from abrogation and change, the *ʿulamā* of the community have been given the authority to strengthen the Sharia and support the community. Therefore, a great prophet [Jesus is meant here] becomes the follower of Muhammad and enacts [Muhammad's] Sharia. God said, "We have sent down the remembrance and we safeguard it" (15:9).

Know that a thousand years after the death of the Seal of the Prophets, the friends of God in his community who will appear [then], although few in number, will be perfected so that they can completely strengthen this Sharia in every aspect. The Seal of the Prophets has already spoken of the blessed coming and good news of the Mahdī who would come after one thousand years. Jesus also will descend after one thousand years. In short, the perfections of the friends of God of this time [one thousand years after the death of Muhammad] resemble the perfections of the noble Companions, even though after the prophets the Companions have precedence. Because of the perfect resemblance [between the Companions and the aforementioned Friends of God], one cannot give preference to one group over another. From this the Prophet was able to say, "[My community is like the rain]; I do not know who is better, the first or last among them."[4]

[In a letter to his eldest son, Muhammad Sādiq (who received permission to teach in 1021/1612, d. 1025/1616), Sirhindī further explicates the nature of the millennial renewer:]

It became evident to this poor one [Ahmad Sirhindī] that after the passage of one thousand years the particularities of Muhammad are also readily available, since Muhammad's request has been granted. May God be praised for that and for all His favors. The perfections of that high station [the reality of the Kaʿba] are above the perfections of intimacy with God, the perfections of prophethood, and the perfections of messengership. Why shouldn't this station [the reality of the Kaʿba] be higher than the noble prophets and great angels who prostrate to it? In the treatise *Return to the Source*, written by this poor one [Ahmad Sirhindī], it is discussed how I ascended from my station to the reality of Muhammad and from there to the station of the reality of the Kaʿba. [When I arrived] above the reality of the Kaʿba, everything became one [in unitary awareness]. The reality of Muhammad became designated the reality of Ahmad [as I realized that] the reality of the Kaʿba was a shadow of the reality of Ahmad. When the reality of Ahmad disappeared, there was nothing but the reality of the Kaʿba.[5]

O son! A person who perfectly imitates the Prophet becomes complete when that imitation is based upon the perfections of the station of prophethood. If that person is among the dignitaries [in imitating the Prophet], he will be elevated to leadership in that station. After completing the perfections of greater intimacy with God [intimacy of prophethood] and becoming worthy of high office, he will be honored by being the Prophet's successor. The person presiding over the stations of shadowy perfections corresponding to the imam has the office of axial guide, while the office corresponding to the successor is called the central axial authority (*qutb-i madār*). They say that these two lower stations [the axial guide and the station of shadowy perfections] are the shadows of the upper two stations [central axial authority and successor to Muhammad].[6]

[The renewer of the second millennium is also tied in with the axial guide. Sirhindī not only seems to claim this role but also equates it with the rank of uniqueness (*fardīyat*), connecting the millennial renewer with the unique one.]

Consider how extraordinary the axial guide really is—he has the total perfections of uniqueness. After many centuries and the innumerable passage of time, this kind of jewel appears! The dark world becomes filled with light from the light of his appearance. His light of guidance encompasses the whole world—from the ocean of the heavenly throne to the center of the earth. Any guidance, belief, and inner knowledge that a person receives and benefits from, comes from his path. No one can get these benefits except by his mediation.[7]

[Toward the end of his life, Sirhindī wrote to Hāshim Kishmī (1054/1644), the author of *The Quintessence of Stations:*]

After the passage of a thousand years there will be an effect from the great changes [that have occurred], namely, the Muhammadan intimacy with God (*wilāyat-i muhammadī*) will end up becoming Ahmadī intimacy with God. This involves two rings of serving God [represented in the two round letters *m* in Muhammad's name] becoming one ring. Instead of the first "m" there will be the letter "a," which is the symbolic sustainer (*rabb*) of Muhammad, so that Muhammad becomes Ahmad. This is explained by the two rings of serving God being represented by the two ring-shaped "m"s in Muhammad's blessed name. It is possible that these two rings refer to two of Muhammad's spiritual entifications [sing. *ta'ayyun*]. One of these is bodily-human and the other is spiritual-angelic. While the bodily-human aspect of Muhammad diminished after his death, the spiritual-angelic aspect became stronger. The bodily-human aspect still continued to have an effect for a thousand years as it diminished, until no signs of the bodily-human aspect remain by the end of this thousand years [i.e., now]. So one of these two rings of serving God [represented by the two letters "m" in Muhammad's name] broke and disappeared to remain with God as the "d" [lit. "u" for *ulūhiyat*] of Divinity. One can say that Muhammad necessarily became Ahmad as Muhammadan intimacy with God shifted to become Ahmadī intimacy. Muhammad [the two *m*'s] means two aspects and Ahmad involves one aspect, period. The name Ahmad is closer to God and further from the world.[8]

[About the same time, Sirhindī wrote to his son and eventual successor, Muhammad Ma'sūm (1079/1668). He discusses an individual—or common believer, as it is usually translated—but as we have seen above, *fard* as "unique one" is also a very high spiritual rank of uniqueness. To be spiritually polite, Sirhindī uses the ambiguous term *fard*, whose technical meaning would be known only by well-read Sufis:]

The source of intimacy with God is a unique one from among the unique ones (*afrād*) of Muhammad's community who has realized Muhammadan intimacy, a center corresponding with a circle whose circumference [is belovedness] and the perfections thereof. It is known that the unique one's good fortune [being in the circle of belovedness] is that he has also realized the intimacy of Moses. By means of these two great intimacies [of Muhammad and Moses] the unique one realizes the totality of perfections of both the center [Muhammadan intimacy] and its circumference [intimacy of Moses]. It is established that each perfection of the unique one [*ummat;* lit., "follower"] will come easily to him and the prophet of that community will also realize that perfection. This is according to the dictum, "Whoever puts a worthwhile Sunna into practice." The Prophet, through the mediating of this unique one, will also benefit from the perfections of the circumference of this circle. He will also become perfected in the intimacy of friendship (*wilāyat-i khillat*). The supplication "May God bless Muhammad as He has blessed Abraham" after a thousand years will be accepted and answered. After perfecting the intimacy of friendship, the secret of Muhammad's situation is that the center of the circle [mentioned above] has been entrusted to him. One finds elegance in explaining this. The unique one returns to the world from that station in order to protect and preserve the Muslim community, while the Prophet regains his place in the retreat of Divine Mystery.[9]

[In this fashion, Ahmad Sirhindī experienced himself as the preeminent Sufi in the world and the millennial renewer. The authors of the subsequent hagiographical tradition use Sirhindī's autobiographical references in his *Collected Letters* to continue their tales of Sirhindī's rank as the millennial renewer.]

THE HAGIOGRAPHICAL TRADITION: PORTRAYING SIRHINDĪ AS THE MILLENNIAL RENEWER

Four years after Sirhindī's death in 1038/1628, Hāshim Kishmī completed the first hagiographical treatise honoring Sirhindī, *The Quintessence of Stations*. It includes many long excerpts from Sirhindī's *Collected Letters*.

The first formal written notice of Ahmad Sirhindī as the "renewer of the second millennium" appears here.

TRANSLATION

As I [Hāshim Kishmī] was writing, it occurred in my heart that, of the great religious scholars of the time, God had made [Ahmad Sirhindī] the renewer of the second millennium. I did not think any more of it until one day when in the presence of my shaykh [Ahmad Sirhindī] the thought came to mind again. He [Sirhindī] said, "Mawlānā 'Abd al-Hakīm Sīalkōtī [1067/1656], who is known throughout India as a great religious scholar with many books, wrote me a letter." Smiling, he continued speaking. "One of his epistles of praise was [my being the] 'renewer of the second millennium' should not be kept a secret but actually declared." I looked at my shaykh as he recited a Qur'anic verse. After all this happened I went back to serving my shaykh.[10]

[Ahmad Sirhindī wrote to his eldest son, Muhammad Sādiq, alluding to a renewer of the new millennium (instead of the customary renewer every hundred years):]

O Son, this is a time of darkness. In the past a great prophet would be sent to the community to enliven the new Sharia. In this [Muslim] community, the best of communities whose prophet is the Seal of the Prophets, the *'ulamā* have been given the rank of the prophets of Israel. In the place of prophets, the *'ulamā* have sufficed. Therefore at the beginning of each century there is a renewer (*mujaddid*) designated from the *'ulamā* of the community who enlivens the Sharia. Especially [at this time,] after the passing of one thousand years, there would have been a great prophet sent to the community—but it is not possible now to send a great prophet [because Muhammad is the Seal of the Prophets and so no prophets come after him]. In a time like this a religious scholar having deep experience of God (*'ālimī 'ārifī tam al-ma'rūf*) is necessary—someone with the stature to succeed the preceding great prophets.[11]

[Twelve years later, in 1050/1640, Badr ad-Dīn Sirhindī (1038/1628) finished his *Holy Presences*, which includes many sections from *The Quintessence of Stations*. Instead of waiting until halfway through the book to discuss Sirhindī as the millennial renewer, the author gives Sirhindī many titles, including that of Supreme Helper, on the first page of the main text, with the next page entitled "Sirhindī's Station." The following excerpt details the highlights of this station.]

His affair is beyond rational understanding—there is no way to step into that place. A thousand years after the beloved Prophet's death, [Sirhindī] perfectly follows him with the perfections of the Prophet's inheritance; a renewer comes after a thousand years. As Muhammad said, "My community is like the rain. I do not know who is better, the first or last among them." One can say that this points to the blessed presence [Sirhindī] who, after a thousand years, is at the end [times] of the Muslim community. The Prophet said that after each century a renewer would come and refresh anew my firm religion. From a renewer of a century to a renewer of a thousand years—there is a difference between one hundred and one thousand! More importantly, it took a thousand years for such a jewel to come into existence.[12]

[Later in *Holy Presences*, excerpts from the *Collected Letters* are included to "verify" Sirhindī's rank of renewer of the second millennium. The following is addressed to Mīr Muhammad Nu'mān.]

Know that at the beginning of each century there is a renewer, but the renewer of a thousand years is not like the renewer of a century because there is a difference between a hundred and a thousand in terms of power and rank. This is so much the case that the renewer [of a thousand years] knows that even though divine effulgence reaches his contemporaries, the friends of God, it does so only by his mediation. This occurs in spite of the central leaders [*aqtāb;* lit., "axes"], fixed supports (*awtād*), appointed ones (*budalā'*), and nobles (*nujabā'*) of the time.[13]

[The third principal hagiography, a greatly exaggerated version of its predecessors, *The Self-Abiding Garden* by Muhammad Ihsān Sirhindī, was finished in 1201/1783. The first volume focuses on Ahmad Sirhindī, the first "support of the universe" (*qayyūm*), followed by his next three lineal descendants, who are also declared *qayyūm*s: Muhammad Ma'sūm (1068/1668), Muhammad Hujjatullāh Naqshband (1114/1702), and Muhammad Zubayr (1152/1740). Sirhindī's status rises considerably.]

Ahmad Sirhindī [lit., "the presence of the renewer of the second millennium"] in his *Collected Letters* has written that all the friends of God over the first thousand years [since Muhammad's death] have achieved only lesser intimacy (*walāyat-i sughrā*) with God—including those having the rank of Pole (*qutb*), Supreme Helper, or others. Except for the noble Companions no one has reached greater intimacy (*walāyat-i kubrā*) or highest intimacy (*walāyat-i 'ulyā*) with God. Only after a thousand years have passed have these [higher] stations been realized by Ahmad Sirhindī.[14]

After the Prophet no one else is the *qayyūm* except Ahmad Sirhindī, because to serve as the *qayyūm*, it is necessary to have the nature of Muhammad. He [Sirhindī] has realized [this nature] from the blessed body of Muhammad's earthly nature. By definition, the stations of Friends of God, the Pole, and the Supreme Helper are all subordinate to the *qayyūm*.[15]

One day Ahmad Sirhindī was sitting in contemplation after the noon prayer in the presence of a person reciting the Qur'an when Sirhindī saw an incredibly shining robe on himself. He realized that this was the robe of being a *qayyūm* [having sovereignty] over all the possibilities [of creation] that God Almighty had bestowed on all the great prophets. A hundred of these robes were given to him with a glance by the Seal of the Prophets [confirming Sirhindī] as his follower and inheritor. From that day the support of all of creation was connected to Sirhindī from His essence (*dhāt*).[16]

AHMAD SIRHINDĪ AS THE CENTENNIAL RENEWER

Hagiography was not the only means of communicating Sirhindī's greatness as a millennial renewer. What some found to be admirable in Sirhindī's ideas and practices others found quite controversial. On average, another tract defending Sirhindī was written every decade in the four centuries following Sirhindī's death. In on example of this polemical literature defending Sirhindī, Shāh Walīullāh (1176/1762) reiterates eleven signs of renewal that prove Sirhindī to be the renewer of the eleventh/seventeenth century.[17]

TRANSLATION

In the eleventh century (*hijrī*) God caused to appear a great light and radiating full moon—that is, the perfect and perfection-bestowing Shaykh Ahmad Sirhindī who has been bestowed the robe of *qayyūm* and uniqueness (*fardīyat*) and all the corresponding intimacies with God. He was honored with the perfections of the Prophetic inheritance. . . . The signs [lit., "witnesses"] of renewal are (1) He spread many branches of religious knowledge, clear injunctions, and inner knowledge [lit., "secrets"] to people both East and West. (2) He performed countless miracles, a testimony to his stations. (3) A very recognized sign [of pre-eminence] is being acknowledged by the religious scholars of his time as a renewer. 'Abd al-Hakīm Sīalkōtī [did this] when he declared Ahmad Sirhindī to be the renewer of the second millennium. 4) He explained the stations on the Naqshbandi path in an unprecedented amount of detail. (5) God chose thousands of religious scholars and mystics (*'urafā'*) who entered the high [Naqshbandi] path. From the blessings of their light the entire world has become illuminated. These perfected shaykhs perform miracles and as representatives they honor Sufism by bringing people to follow the sharia.[18] (6) He was blessed by being able to read the mysterious letters at the beginning of some Qur'anic verses and understand ambiguous verses. (7) He was able to withstand the cruelty of the Sultan [Jahāngīr] and bear the damage of opponents while still standing up for God and declaring the truth. (8) God opened up the doors of inner knowledge to him as no one before him had experienced, such that people who would not have ordinarily entered the path did so. . . . (9) Many infidels accepted Islam at his hand. Thousands of Muslims repented of their sins, entering the Naqshbandī path and, becoming friends of God, blessed countless people both East and West, Arab and non-Arab. (10) The greatest proof of Sirhindī's being a renewer is that the Messenger gave good news of his birth, just as past shaykhs informed us of his birth. The details concerning this can be found in the epistle entitled *The Eight Paradises.*[19] (11) God gave him knowledge concerning the hierarchy of being close to God, prophethood, messengership, the perfections of the great prophets, the stages of friendship (*khillat*), love (*mahabbat*), and the special aspects of the Prophet. By the grace of God it is proven that he is the renewer of the eleventh century.[20]

[In 1112/1701 'Abd al-Ghanī Nābulusī (1143/1731 in Damascus), a well-known Sufi adherent of Ibn 'Arabī's ideas, wrote a detailed treatise defending Sirhindī, *The Spiritual Consequence of Knowledge*, which outlined many aspects of Sirhindī's spiritual situation. In the first excerpt below, Nābulusī comments on the meaning of "a unique one from among the unique ones" (*fard min afrād*), a clear allusion to Sirhindī:]

All of creation is derived from God Almighty by the mediation of Muhammad, similar to what has been said before concerning the unique one from among the unique ones of the community. Likewise, the sole unique one is a manifestation of the divine name "unique one," which is the Muhammadan reality from which God Almighty brought about creation.[21]

[Sirhindī writes in his *Collected Letters,* "It is hoped that [the perfections of prophethood] will be renewed afresh and generally practiced after a thousand years have passed [from the time of Muhammad's Hijra to Medina]. May the original perfections appear." Commenting on this statement, Nābulusī writes:]

The goal of renewal of religion is clear in the Hadith, "God sends a person to renew the religion for this community at the beginning of every century." It was he [Ahmad Sirhindī] before a thousand years passed after the Hijra at the beginning of the eleventh century [referring to his birth in 971/1564 and subsequent life to 1034/1624]. This is the renewal mentioned in the Hadith.[22]

[Note here that Nābulusī, like Shāh Walīullāh, perceives Sirhindī to be the renewer of the fifth/eleventh century, not the second millennium.[23] In the thirteenth/nineteenth century, the famed Mujaddidī shaykh Ghulām ʿAlī Shāh (1220/1824 in Delhi) discussed his view of Sirhindī as a renewer:]

Every hundred years there appears a renewer like Junayd Baghdādī (297/910), ʿAbd al-Qādir Jīlānī, and others. Each one has renewed religion— the meaning of renewer is one who has enlivened religion (*muhyī ad-dīn*). In this regard, God sent Imam Rabbānī (Ahmad Sirhindī) to renew religion in the eleventh century. The renewer of the second millennium, according to Sirhindī and his followers, is him [Sirhindī]. The mediation of God's divine effulgence in the second millennium is due to Sirhindī's blessed existence. Sirhindī himself has related how it was revealed to him that ʿAlī [Muhammad's cousin] and his wife, Fātima [Muhammad's daughter], were the mediators of divine effulgence and intimacy with God even though there have been numerous Friends of God in former religious communities. After them the Shīʿī imams had the same [mediating] rank. Then Muhyī ad-Dīn (ʿAbd al-Qādir) Jīlānī was distinguished with this great fortune (taking over from his predecessors). At the beginning of the second millennium God has given me [Ghulām ʿAlī is repeating Sirhindī's words] the same rank as ʿAbd al-Qādir and has bestowed upon me (Sirhindī) a robe making me ʿAbd al-Qādir's deputy. Therefore in the second millennium anyone realizing any closeness with God does so through the divine effulgence that I mediate through ʿAbd al-Qādir. Without our combined mediation no one can realize intimacy with God.[24]

AFTERWORD

In the fourteenth/twentieth century a plethora of biographical/hagiographical treatises have been written about Ahmad Sirhindī. Some have ignored the issue of millennial renewal altogether, focusing on Sirhindī as a social reformer, while others have kept a thread of his millennial renewal still active.[25] This is not surprising when one notes that the term *mujaddid-i alf-i thānī* is in the title of most of his twentieth-century hagiographies—which simply assumes Ahmad Sirhindī to be the millennial renewer. After four centuries *mujaddid-i alf-i thānī* is not only typically included in book titles but has become Ahmad Sirhindī's own unique personal title.

But the story of a millennial renewer recounted briefly here is just one of many Sirhindī tales beginning in the eleventh/seventeenth century.

Muhammad Masʿūd Ahmad, who has just finished editing a mammoth eleven-volume encyclopedia on Ahmad Sirhindī,[26] writes with quiet authority:

> ʿAbd al-Hakīm Sīalkōtī, in a letter, was the first person to commemorate the Renewer as "*mujaddid-i alf-i thānī*." . . . And as time passes, from this very letter Ahmad Sirhindī is remembered. The chronicles of renewal, along with his zeal and greatness, are recognized.[27]

Indeed, rivulets of stories get collected into what becomes a book-length river of stories, ending in an encyclopedic ocean four centuries later.

NOTES

1. Muhammad Dhawqī, *Sirr-i dilbarān*, 4th ed. (Karachi: Mashhūr Offset Press, 1985), 176–77. This definition of *fard*, outlining one's development from central axial authority (*qutb-i madār*) to the status of the unique one is confirmed by Sirhindī's experience further on in this chapter (Ahmad Sirhindī, *Maktūbāt-i Imām-i Rabbānī*, 3 vols., ed. Nūr Ahmad [Karachi: Educational Press, 1972], vol. 1, letter 260, page 91 [hereafter expressed as volume. letter:pages]), and in Sirhindī's experience advancing from axial guide (*qutb-i irshād*) to the unique one (Ahmad Sirhindī, *Mabda' wa-maʿād*, translated into Urdu (with original Persian text) by Zawwār Husayn [Karachi: Ahmad Brothers Printers, 1984], 9–11).

2. Ahmad Sirhindī, *Mabda' wa-maʿād*, 9–11. This passage continues with Sirhindī receiving blessings from the leading figures of the rest of the major Sufi lineages.

3. Ibid., 79.

4. Ahmad Sirhindī, *Maktūbāt*, 1.209:105–6. This letter goes into a very technical explanation of the previous quote from *Mabda' wa maʿād*, 9–11.

5. Ibid., 1.260:85–86.

6. Ibid., 1.260:91.

7. Ibid., 1.260:95.

8. Ibid., 3.96:58. Note the conflation of the prophetic name of Ahmad (i.e., Muhammad) and the *Ahmad* of Ahmad Sirhindī.

9. Ibid., 3.94:52–53.

10. Muhammad Hāshim Kishmī, *Zubdat al-Maqāmāt* (Istanbul: Isik Kitabevi, 1997), 176. This passage is preceded by a verbatim recitation of the account of Sirhindī's spiritual experience found in *Mabda' wa maʿād*, 79, and in *Maktūbāt*, 1.209:105–6, both cited above. The next three sections (16 pages) are predominantly excerpts from the *Maktūbāt* that emphasize Sirhindī's special rank. Often these latter passages are described with the vocabulary typically reserved for the Qur'an, namely, the "holy verses of the *Maktūbāt*" (*Maktūbāt-i qudsī ayāt*). Kishmī, *Zubdat al-Maqāmāt*, 217, 240, 251.

11. Ibid., 175. The letter is from Ahmad Sirhindī, *Maktūbāt*, 1.234:33.

12. Badruddīn Sirhindī, *Hadarāt al-Quds* (Lahore: Maqama-yi Auqāf, 1971), 26.

13. Ibid., 68, transcribed from Ahmad Sirhindī, *Maktūbāt*, 2.4:20–21. Badruddīn Sirhindī quotes from *Mabda' wa-ma'ād*, 9–11 (translated above), to demonstrate Sirhindī's rank, and follows this with another of Sirhindī's accounts of his spiritual rank in *Collected Letters* 3.87—the latter having become controversial by Badruddīn's time.

14. Muhammad Ihsan Sirhindī, *Rawdat al-Qayyūmiyya*, 4 vols., trans. Iqbāl Ahmad Fārūqī (Lahore: Maktaba-yi Nabawiyya, 1989), 1:61.

15. Ibid., 1:62.

16. Ibid., 1:171.

17. The numerous treatises defending Ahmad Sirhindī began to appear shortly after his death with a treatise attributed to 'Abd al-Hakīm Sīalkōtī, *Dalā'il al-tajdīd*. Iqbāl Mujaddidī (in "Hadarat Mujaddid-i Alf-i Thānī kê dafā' men likhī jānī wālī kitābê," *Nūr al-Islām* 33, no. 1 [Jan.–Feb. 1988]: 47) incorrectly attributes Sīalkōtī's *Dalā'il al-tajdīd* to a treatise by Shāh Walīullāh, *Shawāhid al-tajdīd*, found in the first eight pages of 'Abd al-Ahād Wahdat Sirhindī, *Sabīl al-rashād*, ed. with Urdu trans. by Ghulām Mustafā Khān (Hyderabad, Sind: n.p., 1979). Khān mentions that these eight pages are not 'Abd al-Ahād's but does not correctly identify the text. In addition, these eight pages match the description and summary of Shāh Walīullāh's *Shawāhid al-tajdīd* found in Yohanan Friedmann, *Shaykh Ahmad Sirhindī: An Outline of His Thoughts and a Study of His Image in the Eyes of Posterity* (Montreal: McGill-Queen's University Press, 1971), 103–4. Iqbāl Mujaddidī identifies forty-one polemical texts defending Sirhindī, not all extant.

18. The Arabic is difficult to read in point 5, and I have relied on the Urdu translation.

19. Sirhindī's father's shaykh, Shāh Kamāl Qādirī, sensed Sirhindī's greatness as a small child. See Kishmī, *Zubdat al-Maqāmāt*, 127, 134. The stories mentioned here that foreshadow Sirhindī's birth involve Muhammad, Ahmad Jām (536/1141), and Ahmad Jām's sons, Zahīruddīn, Khalīlullāh Badakhshānī, and Bāqībillāh. See Badruddīn Sirhindī, *Hadarāt al-Quds*, 42–44. These stories are further embellished, and other shaykhs foreshadow Sirhindī's birth, including 'Abd al-Qādir Jīlānī, 'Abd al-Quddūs Gangōhī (944/1537), and Salīm Chishtī (979/1572). See Muhammad Ihsān Sirhindī, *Rawdat al-Qayyūmiya*, 1:101–10.

20. 'Abd al-Ahād Wahdat Sirhindī, *Sabīl al-rashād*, 4–8.

21. 'Abd al-Ghanī Nābulusī, "Natījat al-'ulūm," in Samuela Pagani, *Il Rinovamento Mistico Dell'Islam: Un commento di 'Abd al-Ghani al-Nābulusī a Ahmad Sirhindī* (Naples: Il Torcoliere, 2003), 244. Pagani has done a masterful job of editing this manuscript in addition to providing insightful commentary and contextualization. This passage is a commentary on one of Sirhindī's *Collected Letters* (3.88) but is also applicable to the translated portion of letter 3:94 above.

22. Pagani, *Il Rinovamento Mistico*, 254, referring to a passage in Sirhindī, *Collected Letters*, 1.260.

23. Also reiterated in Nābulusī, *Natījat al-'ulūm*, 267.

24. Ghulām 'Alī Dihlawī, *Sharh-i durr al-ma'ārif: Minhāj al-rāghibayn illā makūbāt imām al-muttaqīn imām rabbānī mujaddid-i alf-i thānī*, ed. Ayyūb Ganjī, (Sanandaj, Iran: Intishārāt-i Kurdistān, 1997), 245. Ghulām 'Alī follows Sirhindī's *Collected Letters*, 3.123:144–46, but deviates from the text. Technically Sirhindī never admitted to being the renewer of the second millennium in his texts. It is possible that Ghulām 'Alī prefers not to distance himself from certain controversial aspects of Sirhindī's teachings; hence he does not directly declare Sirhindī to be a millennial renewer.

25. In the former case, there is Muhammad Mansūr Nu'mānī, *Tadhkira-yi Imām-i Rabbānī Mujaddid-i Alf-i Thānī* (Lucknow, India: Skyline Printers, 1992). In the latter, the modern Urdu translator of Sirhindī's *Collected Letters*, Zawwār Husayn, has written a monumental 830-page monograph, *Hadrat-i Mujaddid-i Alf-i Thānī* (Karachi: Ahmad Brothers Printers, 1983), which contains more discussion of what religious notables have said on the subject of renewal than the use of Sirhindī's autobiographical spiritual memoirs provides to justify his rank as a millennial renewer. Another strand in this story—and beyond the genre of hagiography per se—is the twentieth-century appropriation of Sirhindī to buttress the ideology for what was to become the separate nation of Pakistan.

26. Muhammad Mas'sūd Ahmad, ed., *Jahān Imām- Rabbānī: Mujaddid- Alf- Thānī Shaykh Ahmad Sirhindī*, 11 vols. (Karachi: Imam Rabbani Foundation, 2005–7).

27. Muhammad Mas'sūd Ahmad, *Sīrat-i Mujaddid-i Alf-i Thānī* (Karachi: Madina, 1976), 11.

19 Sufi Poetry of the Indus Valley

Khwāja Ghulām Farīd

Jamal J. Elias

INTRODUCTION

Khwāja Ghulām Farīd (1262/1845–1319/1901) is the most celebrated Sufi poet of the Siraiki language spoken in the Indus Valley in the border region of Punjab and Sindh in Pakistan. Born at Mithankot (sometimes called Kot Mithan) into a Muslim family that claimed Arab descent, he received a traditional religious education centered around Qurʾānic memorization as well as Sufi training under his elder brother, Khwāja Fakhr ad-Dīn. Following his master's death, Farīd retired to the desert wilderness that surrounds Mithankot. Following his death, he was buried in his hometown, where his shrine remains a popular place of pilgrimage. Mithankot is located where the four main tributaries of the Punjab join the Indus, a largely arid area that borders the high desert of northeastern Baluchistan and that traditionally has formed the southwestern boundary of the states ruling the Punjab.

Khwāja Ghulām Farīd is of particular importance as a South Asian Sufi poet because he provides the early modern period's best example of the tradition of vernacular Sufi poetry that goes back to the pre-Mughal period. One hallmark of this style is the consciously ecumenical message that includes Hindus along with Muslims in the intended audience. Farīd accomplishes this overtly by referring to Hindu scriptures such as the Vedas and by his frequent references to a variety of Hindu religious figures, from yogis and other ascetics referred to very commonly in Sufi poetry from the Indus Valley, to less well known types such as ritual specialists and reciters of scripture.

One of the hallmarks of Farīd's style, reminiscent of earlier poets from the Punjab and Sindh, is his frequent use of place-names. Some of these references are literary or mythic, such as when he evokes the birthplace of Sassi, the heroine of a well-known romance. Others are specific to his own experience, such as repeated references to the deserts of Ruhi and Cholistan, which lie near Mithankot.

Another noteworthy aspect of the poetry of Khwāja Ghulām Farīd is his use of the feminine voice. A characteristic of vernacular Sufi poetry in South Asia, with no real precedents in Muslim literature, this practice shares many elements with Hindu writing, in particular the *virāhinī* tradition of northern India, in which the poet addresses God in the voice of a young woman.

Farīd's poetry is not overtly hagiographic, in that the subject is not a prophet or specific holy person. However, his poetry (and that of other vernacular Sufi poets from the Indus valley) functions hagiographically at several levels, both textually and performatively. Poems such as the ones translated below are routinely performed by professional musicians at festivals held at saints' shrines and on other religious occasions. Both performers and audience are aware of the identity of the poet whose verses are being sung, especially when the performance is held at the tomb of the Sufi poet himself. As such, both performers and audience participate in a hagiographic process when they recite or listen to the works of Farīd, celebrating him not just as a fine poet who wrote on religious themes but also as a Sufi saint.

In a more complex way, Farīd's poetry is hagiographic (or perhaps panegyric) at a textual level. In almost all the poems the beloved, or subject of the poem, is not identified clearly. This object of love is normally assumed to be God, but this assumption is based not on the text of the poems themselves but rather on our common presuppositions concerning the nature of Sufi poetry. In fact, a close reading of Farīd's work makes clear that the author is intentionally ambiguous about the beloved's identity and points not only toward a divine beloved but also toward Muhammad and Farīd's own Sufi master (all this in addition to the obvious possibility of a more ordinary human object of desire, the very possibility of which makes the genre what it is). Through his praise of this ambiguous beloved, the poet evokes in the audience's memory love for Muhammad as well as a wide group of dead Sufi saints—the latter because he does not evoke his own master as a specific individual but rather as the generic model of a Sufi master.[1]

TRANSLATION

You are my love, you are my beloved,
You are my religion, you are my faith.
You are my body, you are my spirit,

You are my heart, you are my soul.
  My Ka'ba, my Qibla, my mosque, and my minbar,
  Your are my scripture and my Qur'ān,
  My ritual duties, pilgrimage, and charity,
  You are my fasting and my prayers.
  My worship, obedience, asceticism, and piety—
  You are my science and my learning;
  You are my meditation, you are my thought;
  You are my experience and my ecstasy.
You are my lover
In the sweet dark night,
My spiritual guide on the mystical path;
You are my master who knows all truths.
  My hopes and aspirations, my earnings of a lifetime,
  You are my sustenance and my pride.
  You are my law, you are my doctrine;
  You are my honor and my glory.
You are my sadness and happiness, tears and laughter;
You are my pain, you are my remedy;
You are the cause of all my joys.
You are the subject of my words of love.
You are my beauty, adornment, and my good fortune;
You are my luck, my name and identity.
You are my understanding, you are my learning,
You are my perceiving, my comprehending.
  You are my soft sighs and my grief;
  You are the raging flood of my tears.
  My nose and earrings, and my bracelets,
  You are my adornment and my jewels.
You are my henna and my kohl;
You are my rouge and my lipstick.
You are my wildness, my passion, my obsession—
You are my beseeching, my crying, my sighing.
  You are my verse, rhyme, and meter,
  You are my poetry and my prose.
  You are my first and last, inner and outer,
  You are my visible and my hidden.
You are my tomorrow and my yesterday;
You are my here, you are my now.
You are my dark cloud, my lightning and thunder;

You are my rain and my snow;
You are my town of Malir and desert of Thar;
You are my wilderness of Rohi and Cholistan.
    If you, my Beloved, accept Farīd—
    You are my lord and my king.
    No one is lower or more wretched than me;
    You are transcendent, without place, without kind.

.   .   .   .   .

Who can I tell the state of my heart—
I find no one to share my secret.
Dirt on my face, dust on my head,
    Naked and disgraced—
No one even bothered to ask about my state;
    Quite the contrary, they all laughed.
The burden of love is crushing—
Wandering the alleys in grief,
I spent my whole life crying—
Never found my way home.
    My heart cries out for the beloved;
    It convulses and trembles in sadness;
    It tries to bear its burden of grief—
    See how your heartbroken lover goes on!
Many a physician has gotten rich
Feeding me pills and potions;
Yet none has learned what ails my heart—
Not a grain's difference has come to it.
    My friend left without seeing me;
    He took the road, leaving me alone.
    My beautiful one intentionally made me cry
    And I played along by feigning sleep.
Listen, Laylā! Listen to the cries!
Your Majnūn is wailing in grief![2]
Your lover is so sad without you—
Lift the curtain on your carriage just this once.
    The heart is being drawn to the City of Love;
    The travails of the road are torturous;
    There is no path to it nor river—
    It truly is a hard journey!

· · · · ·

The Beloved appeared in the shape of the world,
Showing himself clearly in all forms:
Somewhere as Adam, somewhere as Seth,
Somewhere he came as Noah with his flood,
Somewhere as Abraham, the Friend of God,
Somewhere he came as Joseph in Canaan.
Somewhere as Jesus and the prophet Elijah,
Somewhere he came as the god Krishna,
Somewhere as Zakaria, somewhere he was John,
Somewhere he came as Moses, son of Imran.
    Somewhere as Abū Bakr, ʿUmar, and ʿUthmān,
    Somewhere as the glorious "Lion of God,"[3]
    Somewhere Hasan and Husayn were martyred,
    Somewhere as the guide, Fakhr-i Jahan ["Pride of the World"].
Somewhere as Ahmad, King of the Prophets,
Beloved of all those who are pious,
Teacher of all pure intellects—
Somewhere he came as the sultan of sultans.
    Somewhere as the Qurʾān, somewhere as Gabriel,
    Somewhere as the Torah, the Psalms, or the Gospel,
    Somewhere as verses, somewhere as chanting—
    He came as the line between truth and falsehood.
All is apparent in all visible things;
The Beautiful One is apparent in his own reflection.
Somewhere he came as the picture of elegance and grace,
Somewhere as pain, somewhere as solace.
    Somewhere he dresses for a wedding,
    Somewhere he wanders like a jilted lover,
    Somewhere he spreads his ensnaring locks down his shoulders,
    Somewhere he comes as a beggar with matted hair.
    Somewhere a Hindu priest, an astrologer, or a yogi,
    Somewhere a swami or a beggar,
    Somewhere a saint, somewhere a sinner,
    Somewhere a scholar reciting the Vedas.
Quiet, Farīd! Stop talking of secrets!
Stop saying such absurd things.
But never forget your Beloved—
Remembering is the one divine command.

·　·　·　·　·

Prince Ranjha of the River Bank—[4]
the mendicant is a sorcerer—
He played his flute so well,
I forgot my house and husband.
　　Ranjha played his intoxicating song
　　With such skill and beauty.
　　His song of union stole my heart;
　　Now I wander the forests alone.
His town is so beautiful,
With rings in its ears and garlands on its neck.
Ranjha came from Takht Hazara
To the home of Heer, the unfortunate.
　　I'll become an ascetic, rub ashes on my body;
　　I'll wander the towns and fields.
　　I've left my parents and taken your hand,
　　So look out for me just a little.
I want for nothing apart from my lover,
Not for gold and not for jewels.
　　So much cruelty is unjust—
　　Fear God just a little!
Ranjha is an ascetic, I a beggar woman—
Such is what love commands.
Farīd! I'll die of grief and longing
But I won't stop thinking of him—
　　Not even for a moment.

·　·　·　·　·

I am that drunken mystic
Who is sometimes in a mosque and sometimes in a temple.
　　Sometimes I am a thief, sometimes a sinner,
　　Sometimes I am regretful and repentant,
　　Sometimes I am an ascetic in worship,
　　Sometimes I wallow in sins of the flesh.
Sometimes I am pain, sometimes solace,
Sometimes I am Egypt, sometimes Canaan,
Sometimes I am Katch, Bhanbur, or Kashan,
Sometimes I am the heart of Jalandhar city.

Sometimes the mosque, temple, or church,
Sometimes hell, sometimes the garden of paradise,
Sometimes a wayward sinner, sometimes a pious believer,
Sometimes I am lost, sometimes I am saved.
I am that drunken sot
Before whom all India bows down;
Surely I am that rare knower [of God]
Before whom all pages of mystery and truth lie open.
Sometimes nothing but beauty and grace,
Sometimes grief and sadness all around;
Sometimes among friends, sometimes left abandoned,
Sometimes at the door, sometimes inside.
Farīd! Watch your mouth in what you say!
Never recite such verses again!
Your posture tells your inner state—
So what if you're in a state of trouble?

．　．　．　．　．

I know for sure, I know for sure,
The beautiful one is proud.
My face and head are caked in dust,
I wear a garland of tears—
My beloved is home and home is far.
My beloved strikes up new friendships—
Why does he burn me and make me suffer?
My heart is fragile like glass. . . .
By day I devour my flesh and bones;
My nights I fill with wrenching sighs;
Each dawn I suffer a burning death.
I'll recite the Bismillāh ["In the name of God"] and bear my pain;
I'll fill my arms with happiness
If this is what will please You.
My heart's desire lives far away;
Death comes without my meeting him;
Day and night are nothing but torment.
Sitting or standing, I weep and wail;
I lament and cry in my sad song,
Each vein of my body the string of a lute.
Ever since the long wait struck

an arrow through my heart,
My rouge has run, my henna has washed away,
My bangles are broken and lost.
The Beloved gave Farīd nothing but sorrow;
Qamru really did speak the truth—[5]
It's folly to love a heartless person.

.   .   .   .   .

My old wounds made me weak—
My Beloved didn't take me with him.
   They deceived my dear friend—
   They took him away by force,
   May God strike them down!
I search for footprints but find nothing;
I cry and wear a garland of thorns;
My eyes have gone blind with searching.
   I'll dress as a traveler and leave for Thar;
   I'll wander through Landhi and Lasbela—
   The desert and wilderness is now my home.
There is no water, sweet or bracken,
There is no food, nor any support,
There is no horse nor rider to be seen.
Green and colorful places are all forgotten—
Orchards, gardens, the cool shade of a tree.
My tiara, necklaces, earrings, and bracelets—lost.
O', my mercurial, proud, and delicate one!
After vowing love, you became a stranger—
Where did all your promises go?
   The sorrows of this wretch don't end;
   He never cast one sweet glance toward me.
   I'm still alive, but I've lost at the game of life.
As long as I live, I'll labor to reach his home;
May I be damned as a disbeliever,
   Should I think of giving up!
On my neck I wear a string vowing fidelity.
   Difficult paths, strewn with rocks,
   Ups and downs, narrow passages,
   Cliffs and canyons on every side.
To hell with Bhitta Vahan's festival!

Bhambhor town is no use either—
The only place is my lover's home.[6]
    Farīd, my Beloved didn't take me as his maidservant;
    Now my lipstick feels like the bullet from a gun,
    And a line of kohl like the blade of a sword.

.   .   .   .   .

Day and night, the *qalandars*
Are drunk within themselves.
    No need for prayer or fasting,
    No desire for pilgrimage and alms-giving,
    No wish for essence or attribute,
    Only the longing for the glory of divine union.
No search for wealth and riches,
No goal of title or station.
Drunk in contemplating God,
They need never look to humankind.
    Even though they have drunk an entire river
    Full of surging currents, they are quiet;
    They are treasure chests full of mysteries;
    They remain silent, not prattling at all.
They are lovers as well as the beloved,
They are what was before [*sābiq*] and what after [*masbūq*].
They are the treasure and the treasure chest,
Content with whatever befalls them.
    They are wretched on top of tortured;
    They are sad on top of mournful,
    At all times, as if nonexistent—
    Not a wish or a hope in their hearts.
Whatever is visible in the physical world—
How can one see it as other than Him?
My guide drilled the important lesson
    into me:
All is Him.
This is the only thought, the only word,
The only ecstatic state, the only trance,[7]
The only experience in every breath,
    The only truth—all else a lie.
Get rid of all suspicion and doubt—

There is no other god at all.
The same cry inside and out:
"God is present! God is present!"[8]
    There is no one other than You;
    In fact, there isn't even the hint of another.
    There is always One, never a second;
    Be with the One, leave the other.
Search for your own reality;
Stop searching for another.
Remember these words of mine;
Do not doubt that this is the only truth.
    Drink from the goblet of singularity;[9]
    Become a lover, ever-drunk;
    Keep stepping forward, day after day—
    All of creation will be amazed.

·   ·   ·   ·   ·

Love is a strange sickness:
One is filled with words of sorrow,
Eyes flood with tears,
The heart's wounds never heal.
    The problems of love are strange:
    Friends and strangers pick fights with you;
    Your mother, father, and brothers torment you;
    Your neighbors become your enemies.
A strange form of waiting, like a stray lance—
My spirit burns, my heart breaks;
An arrow strikes my body and soul,
Shot by my lover, that gifted archer.
His glances bewitching, his posture of an enemy—
Eyes magic, sight a thief.
His hair painful shackles
With torturous blades and nails.
Lovers' passions are for an instant,
Hot, like the sands of the deadly Thar;
He heaps grief upon me
And does as he pleases.
A soft pillow scares like a demon witch—
I've forgotten the ways of comfort and ease;

A million cuts in every vein,
Struck by the sword blade of separation.
Farīd! Your beloved never looked this way
And pain made its home in my heart.
My mind and body were burned—
And I will bear the scars to my grave.

. . . . .

Even if all of creation obeys you,
What does it matter?
The real purpose is to lose yourself.
   No doubt, your wishes and you commands
   Reach as far as Persia and Arabia—
   What does it matter?
You can read the scriptures, the Vedas and Puranas,
You can learn your literature and your science—
What does it matter?
   You can rule the whole world,
   Realize your royal station—
   What does it matter?
You've made a habit of prayer and fasting;
You've attained enlightenment through untiring effort—
What does it matter?
   You've won honor in this life;
   You're facing death with a light heart—
   What does it matter?
You're a pious Sunni of the Hanafī school;
You've adopted the ways of the Sufis—
What does it matter?
   In His effects, His acts, and His attributes,
   You've realized your Beloved—
   What does it matter?
You've attained the status of the spiritual Pole;[10]
You've gained the title Master of Masters—
What does it matter?
   Farīd, your verses have gained fame
   All over India and in Europe—
   What does it matter?

NOTES

1. All poems are translated from *Diwān-i Khwāja Farīd,* critical edition and Urdu translation by Khwāja Tāhir Mahmūd Korija (Lahore: Al-Fayʿal, 2002).

2. Majnūn (lit., "possessed by a jinn") fell madly in love with the beguiling but unattainable Laylā in a story of desperate but unrequited love.

3. A reference to ʿAlī, Muhammad's cousin and son-in-law, considered the first imam by the Shīʿa, and the fourth caliph and a major religious champion by the Sunnis. Farīd's verses list ʿAlī together with the first three caliphs on the one hand and with his sons Hasan and Husayn, the second and third imam, on the other. Such conscious attempts at reconciling or transcending sectarian differences are characteristic of much of vernacular Sufi poetry in South Asia. The final line of the stanza refers to Farīd's own Sufi master.

4. The romance of Heer and Ranjha is the most famous epic in the Punjabi language.

5. Qamru was a poet and a devotee of Farīd.

6. These three lines refer to the romance of Sassi Pannu (sometimes Punhu), widely known in Sindh and Punjab. Bhitta Vahan is the birthplace of the female protagonist Sassi, and Bhambhor is the town in which she grew up.

7. Farīd uses the Sufi technical terms *wajd* and *hāl.* The latter refers to a temporary state of consciousness or emotional awareness that results from meditational practices. *Wajd,* translated here as "ecstasy," also carries the sense of discovery or invention. As such, it refers to a state of ecstatic realization either of some form of mystical knowledge or of the state of union with the divine beloved.

8. The word translated as "God" is *haqq,* which also means "truth" or "reality."

9. Farīd plays on the meaning of his own name, using the word *farīdī* to mean "singularity" and, at the same time, inserting his name into the second-to-last couplet.

10. Farīd uses the term *Ghawth-i qutbī* to refer to the supreme spiritual Pole (*qutb*), believed to be the Sufi individual who serves as the axis around which the spiritual universe orbits and through whom it is sustained.

20 The Ismāʿīlī Pīr Sadr ad-Dīn

Ali S. Asani

Among the world's Muslim communities, the Nizārī Ismāʿīlī constitute a distinctive minority. As Shīʿī Muslims, they affirm that after the Prophet Muhammad, religious and political authority was inherited by imams, his direct descendants through his daughter Fātima and son-in-law ʿAlī ibn Abī Tālib (41/661). According to their beliefs, the imams possess special knowledge to interpret the inner and esoteric (bātin) meaning of the Qurʾān, by virtue of which they alone can correctly guide the faithful. Currently, they acknowledge Shāh Karīm al-Husseinī, Aga Khan IV, as their forty-ninth imam, or spiritual leader.

During the course of their history, the Ismāʿīlī have been ruthlessly persecuted. Various Sunni rulers viewed the Ismāʿīlī imams and their followers as a threat to their authority, while Sunni religious scholars (ʿulamā) found Ismāʿīlī veneration of the Prophet's descendants and their strong emphasis on esotericism to be antithetical to their vision of Islam. Despite this persecution, Ismāʿīlī were able to disseminate their doctrines in several regions of the Middle East and South Asia through the daʿwa, an organized system of propagating the faith. The work of daʿwa was executed by a hierarchically organized group of knowledgeable and skilled individuals called dāʿīs who, under the guidance of the imam of the time, were sent on missions to different geographic regions. Since propagating Ismāʿīlī teachings in Sunni-dominated parts of the world was dangerous, these dāʿīs often adopted taqīya, a strategy traditionally used by Shīʿī groups to hide or camouflage religious beliefs in order to escape possible persecution.

Traditional Ismāʿīlī histories recount that from the fifth/eleventh century onward, Ismāʿīlī imams residing in Iran entrusted the responsibility of propagating the faith in the Indian Subcontinent to a series of dāʿīs.

Locally, these *dāʿīs* were known as *pīrs*, the term *pīr* commonly used among mystically inclined Muslim groups to indicate a spiritual preceptor and guide. In an effort to indigenize their teachings to the local Indian context, Ismāʿīlī *pīrs* referred to their teachings as Satpanth, the "True Path." Hence, their followers identified themselves as Satpanthī rather than Ismāʿīlī. As a way of providing mass instruction on a variety of doctrinal, ethical, and mystical topics, the *pīrs* are believed to have composed hymnlike songs in various indigenous languages. Eventually, these songs crystallized into the corpus known as *ginān*s, still recited by Nizārī Ismāʿīlīs today.

In the *ginān*s the *pīrs* employed terms and ideas from a variety of Indic religious and philosophical currents in order to articulate core Ismāʿīlī concepts so that local populations could best understand them. For example, some *ginān*s created an ostensible equivalence between the Vaishnava Hindu concept of *avatāra* (Sanskrit, "passing over downward") and the Ismāʿīlī concept of imam. Kalki, the messianic tenth incarnation (*dasa avatāra*) of Vishnu, renamed in the Satpanth tradition as Nakalanki, "the Stainless One," was identified with ʿAlī, the first Shīʿī imam. In this way, the *pīrs* represented themselves as guides who knew the whereabouts of the long-awaited tenth *avatāra* of Vishnu, meaning the Ismāʿīlī imam who, they proclaimed, was living in the west (Iran). Other *ginān*s formulated their teachings within a Sufi framework, reiterating a long-standing relationship between Sufism and Ismāʿīlī thought and also acknowledging the significant presence of Sufi orders in the areas where the *pīrs* were most active, namely, Punjab and Sind. In such *ginān*s, the goal of *Satpanth* was to foster the spiritual development of a disciple (*murīd*) through control over the *nafs*, or ego self, a task best accomplished under the guidance and supervision of a spiritual preceptor, the *pīr*. Through regular repetition/remembrance (*sumiran/zikr*) of the Divine Name (*nām/shabd*), one realizes the ultimate experience for Muslim mystics—the "face-to-face meeting with God," or *dīdār*. The Divine Name is given to those who follow the True Path with the help of the Satguru, the True Guide, ambiguously identified in most *ginān*s as either the *pīr* or the imam.

The most important of the Satpanthī *pīrs* was Pīr Sadr ad-Dīn, believed to have flourished in the late fourteenth and early fifteenth century. He appears to have played a key role in organizing and consolidating the Satpanth tradition. To him are attributed the greatest number of *ginān*s, the establishment of the first *jamāʿat khānah* (house of congregational worship), and the invention of Khojki (a secret alphabet for recording religious texts). His disciples are said to have belonged originally to trading castes of Sind and Gujarat, principally the Lohānas and Bhātias. Upon their joining Satpanth, Pīr Sadr ad-Dīn is said to have given his new disciples the title Khwāja to replace the original Lohana *thākkur,* both meaning "lord" or "master." This title was later distorted to "Khoja." The intent behind the new title was to bestow a castelike status on his followers, a concession to their social milieu in which caste was fundamental in defining status and societal relationships. Pīr Sadr ad-Dīn is believed to have died around 819/1416 in Ucch, currently in Pakistan, where his mausoleum has become a pilgrimage site for those who revere him as a great teacher and Sufi master.

The account of Pīr Sadr ad-Dīn translated here is from a 180-page work in the Gujarati language titled the *Nūram Mubīn,* the first history of the Ismā'īlī imams and *dā'īs* in an Indian vernacular. It was first published in 1355/1936 under the auspices of the Ismā'īlī Association for India, an institution responsible for promoting religious education in the community. The *Nūram Mubīn* was written within the sociopolitical context of colonial British India, in which religious identity and the categories "Hindu" and "Muslim" were being rigidly and narrowly demarcated. Doctrinal formulations such as those of Satpanth that drew on multiple traditions were perceived as syncretistic and became difficult to sustain in a climate of rising religious communalism and nationalism. The Khojas were pressured to reshape their identity to better conform to narrowly defined religious categories. As a result, they splintered along religious (Hindu/Muslim) as well as sectarian (Sunni/Shī'ī) lines. Only a few came to specifically identity themselves as Ismā'īlī.

In this regard, the work's Arabic-based title, *Nūram Mubīn (The Manifest Light),* is significant in that it alludes to a Qur'anic expression (4:174) that has been interpreted by Ismā'īlīs as a reference to the light of the Imamate, which is eternally manifest in the world as a divinely ordained form of guidance for humanity. The work's Gujarati subtitle, *Allāhnī Pavitra Rasī (God's Sacred Rope),* echoes another Qur'ānic phrase, *habl Allāh,* "God's Rope" (3:103), which is commonly interpreted in Shī'ī sources as a reference to the continuous guidance of the institution of the Imamate. The use of these two phrases in the title thus underscores the Qur'ānic bases for newly emerging understandings of the Imamate among the Khojas.

In the preface to the book, the author, 'Alī Muhammad Chunārā (1386/1966), writes that this book was intended to combat widespread ignorance among Khojas about matters related to their faith, so that they would not fall prey to misinformation and be swayed by propaganda spread by unscrupulous persons intent on leading them away from their faith. He expressed the hope that, armed with the knowledge acquired from the *Nūram Mubīn*, Ismāʿīlī Khojas, would be able "to stand on their two feet."[1] These remarks clarify a broader objective for the publication of the *Nūram Mubīn*: it was a means through which Ismāʿīlī Khojas could acquire sufficient knowledge with which to articulate and defend their faith against an anti-Ismāʿīlī polemic, particularly powerful in the first half of the twentieth century, intended to "convert" Khoja Ismāʿīlī to either Sunni or Ithnā ʿAsharī forms of Islam or to Hinduism.

The first edition of the *Nūram Mubīn* sold briskly and was reprinted several times. It was also translated into Urdu. In 1370/1950, a second revised edition was published, to be followed by two further editions: the third edition appeared in 1371/1951, the fourth in 1381/1961.[2] In the last decades of the twentieth century, further publication of the *Nūram Mubīn* ceased.

TRANSLATION

The Renowned Pīr Sadrūdīn [Sadr ad-Dīn]

Pīr Sadrūdīn was the chief preacher of the *dāwat* [*daʿwā*] during the imamate of Imam Islāmshāh. This renowned Pīr was born on Monday the 2nd of Rabīʿ al-Awwal, 700 AH in the city of Sabzwār in Iran. His mother was Nur [Nūr] Fātimā bint Sayyid Ibrāhīm Sabzwārī. The ancestry of this famous Pīr, as recorded in the *Gulzār-e Shams*, is as follows: [the text here provides a detailed genealogy tracing Pīr Sadrūdīn's paternal ancestry to the Shīʿī imam Jāʿfar as-Sādiq (148/765 CE)].

The Study of [Hindu] Scriptures in Order to Carry Out the Work of Dāwat [Daʿwa]

The renowned Pīr Sadrūdīn came to Hindustan from Khurasan. He learned Ismāīlī [Ismāʿīlī] doctrines (*tālim*) [*taʿlīm*] while traveling with Pīr Shams to Sind, Punjab, and Kashmir. Before embarking on his "mission" (*dāwat*), he thoroughly studied Hindu religious scriptures. From these, he distilled the principles related to *mārifat* [*maʿrifa*] deep knowledge of the self (*ātmā gyān*), and wisely began his "mission" after matching them to the principles of Islamic philosophy and God's Word [the Qurʾān]. He explained that after the ninth *avatāra* [of Vishnu], the tenth Nishkalanki Avatāra, meaning the blemishless one (*māsum*), was Mawlā Murtazā ʿAlī, whose genealogy extends to the beginning of creation. He also clarified that after the three great teachers (*gurus*) of the three ages (*yugs*), Prophet Muhammad, the Chosen One, was the universal preceptor (*jagat guru*) of the present age (*kaliyug*), a fact to which the Vedas and Puranas bear testimony. With this evidence and true guidance, he established Satpanth religion (*dharma*), that is, the "True Path," composing hundreds of *ginān*s in which he introduced the concepts of God, Prophet, and Imam.

The Dāwat of Pīr Sadrūdīn [Sadr ad-Dīn] and the Emergence of the Khoja Community

On account of the renowned Pīr Sadrūdīn's erudite guidance, great numbers of enthusiastic and curious people as well as many castes began accepting the Ismā'īlī faith without any sort of force or obligation. He bestowed the title Khojā on the community of those who became Muslim in this way. The word *Khojā* was originally *Khwājah*, which was later distorted to *Khojā*, whose meaning is "merchant, trader," "honorable," or "householder; one worthy of trust." Currently, this community is universally known by the name Khojā. Within the Khojā caste (*jāti*), the majority are Lohānas and Bhātias who today live together as one *jamāt* [*jamā'at*] (community) without any discrimination. The Khojās recite *duaa* [*du'ā*] (prayers) in the evening, at night, the early hours of the morning, and at dawn, a tradition that, historically, was established by Pīr Sadrūdīn, the twenty-sixth Pīr of the Ismailīs. According to *Āsāre Muhammadī*, a historical compendium, after Imam Shamsudīn [Shams ad-Dīn] Muhammad [c. 710/1310], Imam Islāmshāh succeeded to the seat of the Imamate. It was during the period of this Imam that Sayyid Sadrūdīn was appointed to the Office of [religious] Guidance and sent to Sind in Hindustan to engage in *dāwā* [propagation of the faith]. Sayyid Sadrūdīn was also known by the epithet *Wasī Muhammad*.

Obstacles in the Path of Preaching of Religion

In his book *The Preaching of Islam*, T. W. Arnold describes the manner in which Pīr Sadrūdīn matched the principles of the Hindu religion with Islamic philosophy and wisely began the work of *dāwā*. According to [Arnold], Pīr Sadrūdīn first began the work of *dāwā* in the villages of Sind; later he spread these ideas in Kutch, then Gujarat, and eventually toward Mumbai. At present, this community known as Khojā can be found in western India and in villages along the shores of the Indian Ocean. Pīr Sadrūdīn was not the first Ismaili "missionary" sent to India; rather, the Ismaili rulers of Alamut (Iran) had previously sent Hazrat Nurudīn [Nūr ad-Dīn], who adopted the "Hindu" name Nur Satāgur (Satguru Nūr), the name by which he is generally known. He came to Gujarat during the reign of the Hindu King Siddraj and initiated people from the Kanbi, Kharwa, and Koli castes into the Islamic religion (*dharma*).

During Pīr Sadrūdīn's time, the work of *dāwā* was intensely difficult because he had to face countless obstacles in the work of propagating religion. Traveling on foot, through deserts and jungles, mountains and plains, he journeyed continuously. Wherever he saw a group of people, he began to preach. In order not to inconvenience anyone with the need to feed and host him, he used to tie wooden *rotlis* [bread] around his stomach so that people would not force him to stay with them more than was necessary. During his travels, he was unhindered by heat, cold, or rain. Many times his feet would swell from extreme fatigue, but he never took a respite from the work of *dāwā*.

Journey to Iran for the Imam's Dīdār [Vision]—
An Iron Wall Obstructs

While preaching the Ismailī faith in Sind, Pīr Sadrūdīn longed for the Imam's *dīdār*, and since he also had to submit tributes, he set out on a journey toward Iran. At that time, his son, Pīr Hasan Kabīradīn [Kabīr ad-Dīn], was very young. Yet he earnestly pleaded with his father that he should accompany him to the holy presence of the Imam. Pīr Sadrūdīn, mindful of his son's tender age, and fearful of the dangerous man-eating animals along the way, did not think it appropriate to take him on an arduous journey through difficult jungles. Pīr Hasan Kabīradīn was heartbroken. According to his [Pīr Sadrūdīn's] *ginān*s, [once he had embarked on the journey,] an "iron wall" obstructed his path [because he had refused to take along his son,] and he could not proceed any further. The Pīr performed *zikr* [meditation on divine names] and prayed and pleaded earnestly for six months and six days, after which the wall collapsed and he could continue his journey.

A [Chance] Meeting with the Imam in a Mountainous Region

Finally, after months of slow and tedious journeying, Pīr Sadrūdīn reached the environs of the city of Isfahan. There, near a mountain called Bābā Kuhī, he met a group of dervishes. They asked him where he came from and what he was searching for. The Pīr replied that he was from India and wanted to meet the Imam of the time, Imam Islāmshāh. But the dervishes refused to reveal this information. Nevertheless, the Pīr did not give up and persisted in his inquiries. One of the dervishes set out to see the Imam, accompanied by some of his disciples. Impressed by the Pīr's persistent devotion, the dervishes had come to trust him. Therefore, the chief dervish sent his nephew, Shaykh Muhammad, along with the Pīr. After journeying three days through extremely dangerous jungles, they stopped to rest and began to prepare a meal. It happened that Imam Islāmshāh was hunting in this mountainous region. Suddenly, the Pīr met the Imam, who blessed him with *dīdār* and also [the opportunity of performing] *dastboshī* [kissing the hand as an expression of loyalty]. After that the Imam, Pīr Sadrūdīn, and Shaykh Muhammad sat down to eat the meal, during which the Imam inquired about the well-being of his disciples in India and commanded the Pīr to establish official *jamāt khānās* and appoint Mukhīs [Heads/Chiefs] and Kamadias [Assistants]. The Pīr then returned to India, where he began to openly preach the Ismāīlī faith with great vigor and implemented the Imam's commands. According to the *Gulzār-e Shams*, it took the Pīr one year and five months to journey to Iran for the Imam's *dīdār* and return to India.

The Establishment of Jamāt Khānās [Jamāʿat Khānahs]

The Pīr established the very first *jamāt khānā* in the village of Kotda in Sind and appointed Mukhi Trikam as the Mukhī [Chief] of that *jamāt* [congregation]. He also appointed Seth Shāmdās Lāhorī as the Mukhī of the Punjab *jamāt* and Seth Tulsīdās as the Mukhī of the *jamāt* of Kashmir. In this way, he established three *jamāts* in the three provinces. He then received the tributes that were due to the Imam [from these *jamāts*] and once again set out for Iran to submit these in the Imam's presence. At that time the Imam's residence was in the Iranian towns Bābak and Kekht. Historically speaking, it is evident that he met Imam Islāmshāh in person only twice during his lifetime.

Pīr Sadrūdīn's Immediate and Extended Family

Pīr Sadrūdīn worked tirelessly to nurture the Islamic seed that Pīr Nurudīn, also known as Pīr Satgur Nur [fifth/eleventh century], and Pīr Shamsudīn Sabzwārī [mid-eighth/mid-fourteenth century] planted during their religious preaching. It is due to his efforts that a living community of Ismāīlī emerged. Pīr Sadrūdīn had five sons: (1) Sayyid Zaherdīn, whose tomb-shrine is in Jaunpur; (2) Sayyid Salāhdīn, whose tomb-shrine is in Ghizni; (3) Pīr Tājdīn, whose tomb-shrine is in the district of Lad in Sind in a place called Shāh Turel by Sindhī Khojās; (4) Sayyid Jamāludīn, whose tomb-shrine is in Delhi; (5) Pīr Hasan Kabīrdīn [c. 875/1470], whose tomb-shrine is in Ucch.

Pīr Sadrūdīn had six brothers in all: (1) Sayyid Ruknudīn, (2) Sayyid BadrudŬCn, (3) Sayyid Shamsudīn (the Second), (4) Sayyid Nasīrudīn, (5) Sayyid Giyāsudīn, [and] (6) Sayyid Nāsirudīn Qalandarshāh. The sixth one moved in 665/1266 from Sabzwār to Multan to serve Pīr Shams. Pīr

Shams sent him to the regions of the Himalayas to propagate the Ismailī
religion; he settled in the frontier region and undertook the task of preaching. Pīr Nāsirudīn's son, Pīr Kamāludīn Sabzawārī, settled at the city of
Thatta in Sind. Along with his five sons, he was involved in preaching
there and in surrounding areas. After his death, Pīr Kamāludīn was buried
in Devalpur, where his tomb-shrine is located.

Pīr Shahābudīn, who is also known as Pīr Sāhebdīn, had seven sons.
Among these, Pīr Sadrūdīn became the most important Pīr of the Ismailī,
while the other sons were involved in preaching (*dāwat*) under the supervision of Pīr Shams, as we have discussed previously. Pīr Sāhebdīn had
two wives, of whom Nur Fātimā was the mother of Pīr Sadrūdīn; the other
wife was Khadījā bint Sayyid Kāsam.

Titles of Pīr Sadrūdīn and His Death

Among the *awliyā* (Friends of God) of India, Pīr Sadrūdīn is known as
Sayyid Sadrūdīn al-Husseinī. Since he explained religion and brought
awareness of the Imam to twelve *crore* [120 million] souls, he is called the
Bār Gur [Teacher of the Twelve]. Since he was well versed in the Hindu
Vedas, Puranas, and other scriptures, he was also called Harischandra,
meaning "divine moonlight," or Sohdev, meaning the "great dervish."

In addition to Sind, Pīr Sadrūdīn preached in Multan, Punjab, Kashmir,
Gujarat, Kutch, and Kathiawad. He traveled with the most intelligent and
knowledgeable disciples from among those who had accepted the Ismailī
faith, so that they could assist him in his work. Pīr Sadrūdīn established
the city of Kotda in Sind as the main center of his *dāwā*. After years of
continuous service to the Imam, he died on the 12th Rajab, 819 AH [1416
CE] in the town of Ucch, in the Bahawalpur region of the Punjab. The
Ismailīs of Sind constructed a marvelous mausoleum over his tomb.

NOTES

1. ʿAlī Muhammad Chunārā, Preface to First Edition, in *Nūram Mubīn*,
2nd ed. (Bombay: N.p., 1950), 7.
2. The source for the following translation is *Nūram Mubīn*, 334–38.

21 An Indo-Persian Guide to Sufi Shrine Visitation

Carl W. Ernst

While the Hajj pilgrimage to Mecca is of paramount importance in the Islamic tradition, other local forms of pilgrimage are also practiced. Throughout Muslim societies, from Morocco to Chinese Turkestan, the tombs of the Friends of God are the resort of Muslims of many varying backgrounds. Reformers from Ibn Taymīya (729/1328) down to the Wahhābīs of Saudi Arabia have tended to denounce the veneration of the Friends of God as the idolatrous worship of fallible human beings. In the Indian Subcontinent, where "visitation" (Arabic *ziyāra*, Persian *ziyārat*) of Sufi shrines is particularly common, Protestant British civil servants and modern Muslim reformers alike have often seen in this ritual the insidious influence of Indian paganism. From the frequent denunciations of *ziyārat* as "*pīr* worship" (worship of the master), one might suppose that it was a transparent case of the corruption of Islam by Hindu polytheism, but a closer look reveals that the case is not so simple. Sufi masters found *ziyārat* to be an authentic expression of Islamic piety, Qur'ānic in spirit and firmly based on the model of the Prophet Muhammad. The text translated here illustrates the Sufi interpretation of pilgrimage to the tombs of the Friends of God according to the traditions of the Chishtī Sufi order.

The treatise in question is a guide to observance of Sufi festivals known as *'urs* (pl. *a'rās*), written as a preface to the *Treasury of Death Anniversaries* (*Makhzan-i a'rās*) in 1155–56/1742–43 by Muhammad Najīb Qādirī Nāgawrī Ajmerī, a Sufi of the Chishtī order who lived in the city of Awrangabad.[1] The main body of the book is a calendar of Friends of God, which lists for each day of the year the Sufi Friends of God whose festivals are to be celebrated according to the Islamic lunar calendar. Like Catholic calendars of saints, this Muslim calendar lists festivals of the Friends of God by the death anniversary or *'urs* (lit. "wedding") which records the

Figure 6.   Devotees at the shrine of Nizām ad-Dīn Awliyā' in Delhi. Photograph by
Marcia Hermansen.

date when the soul was "wedded," that is, united with God. This name
for death anniversaries of the Friends of God seems to be peculiar to the
Islamic East, since in Mediterranean countries, celebrations are referred
to as the birthday (*mawlid*) of the Friend of God. To make a pilgrimage or
ziyārat to the tomb of a Friend of God is considered beneficial at any time,
but at the time of the '*urs*, special blessings are available, since Paradise
rejoices at the return of that supremely happy moment when a human soul
was united with God. [See Figure 6.]

The *Treasury of Death Anniversaries* was not a novelty, but was based
on an earlier calendar of Friends of God and a number of other literary
sources. While the introduction to the *Treasury of Death Anniversaries*
cites by name or quotes from more than two dozen Persian and Arabic Sufi
texts, it quotes most extensively from two texts: the *Ashrafian Subtleties*
(*Lata'if-i ashrafī*), the discourses of Sayyid Ashraf Jahāngīr Simnānī
(829/1425); and *Rules for Aspirants* (*Adab at-tālibīn*), by Muhammad
Chishtī Ahmadābādī (1040/1630). The intended audience of the *Treasury
of Death Anniversaries* was the elite group of Sufi disciples educated
in Persian and dedicated to the practices and piety of the Chishtī order,
established by Mu'īn ad-Dīn Chishtī (634/1236) late in the sixth/twelfth
century, and the text itself was written at the order of a contemporary

Chishtī master, Nizam ad-Dīn Awrangābādī (1142/1729), as a summary of centuries of Chishtī practice.

Among the most important rituals mentioned in this text are determining the exact hour and day of death, and distributing food, drink, and other gifts. Muhammad Najīb lists the superior nights and days of the year for prayer, according to the encyclopedic *Revival of Religious Sciences* of Muhammad al-Ghazālī (505/1111), and he gives instructions for prayers of intercession on behalf of deceased sinners undergoing pre-resurrection torments in the grave. He places particular emphasis on the suras of the Qur'ān that are to be recited during pilgrimage, especially the first sura, the Opening (Fātiha). He describes circumambulation of tombs and reminds the reader to observe proper manners (*adab*) and reverentially correct behavior. The pilgrim is also instructed to perform a deep psychological self-examination while visiting tombs, for receptivity to supernatural communications is then greatly increased and one may hope for spiritual guidance by this means. Muhammad Najīb concedes that there is controversy over honoring the dead, but he maintains that those souls who received honors while living are still worthy of honor after their death. Muhammad Najīb's introduction to the *Treasury of Death Anniversaries* shows a learned Sufi's understanding of *ziyārat* pilgrimage to Sufi shrines as a religious practice comparable to the Hajj pilgrimage and generally permissible according to Islamic law.

TRANSLATION

Introduction to the Treasury of Death Anniversaries

1. Praise be to God, Lord of Creation, and blessings and peace on the chief of Messengers and Seal of the Prophets, Muhammad the Chosen, and on his family, and all his Companions. Now, this special treatise is [taken] from the collection of death anniversaries of the prophets, Companions, imams of guidance, and noble shaykhs that was assembled previously by Shaykh Sharaf ad-Dīn ibn Qādī Shaykh Muhammad Nahrawālī. Since the names of the Friends of God who were joined to the mercy of God after the compilation of the aforesaid treatise were lacking, as well as some names of the ancients, therefore a selection was made from biographical works in the year 1155 [1741–42] by this slave of dervishes, Muhammad Najīb Qādirī Nāgawrī Ajmerī, who is one of the intimates and disciples of the threshold of all creation and the resort and exemplar of those united with God, the revered Shaykh Nizām ad-Dīn Chishtī Awrangābādī [1142/1729] (the disciple of the exemplar of the Friends of God), Shaykh Kalīm Allāh Chishtī Shāhjahānābādī [1142/1729], who was the disciple of the axis

(*qutb*) of those united with God, Shaykh Muhammad Yahyā Chishtī al-Gūjārātī al-Madanī [1101/1689], grandson and disciple of the axis of axes, Shaykh Muhammad Chishtī al-Gūjārātī [1040/1630]). These works include *Breezes of Intimacy* (*Nafaḥāt al-uns*); *The Mirror of the Heart* (*Mir'āt al-janān*); the history of Imam Yāfi'ī, *Tricklings* (*Rashaḥāt*); *Desire of the Seekers* (*Matlūb at-tālibīn*); *Lives of the Friends of God* (*Siyar al-awliyā'*); *Lives of the Knowers of God* (*Siyar al-'ārifīn*); *News of the Pious* (*Akhbār al-akhyār*); *The Jalalian Treasury* (*Khizānat al-jalālī*); *Excellences of the Friends of God* (*Fadā'il al-awliyā'*); *Miracles* (*Khawāriqāt*); *The Nasirean Generations* (*Tabaqāt-i nāsirī*); *Garden of the Martyrs* (*Rawdat ash-shuhadā'*); *Rose Garden of the Pious* (*Gulzār-i abrār*); *The Ship of the Friends of God* (*Safīnat al-awliyā'*); *The Reporter of Those Who Are United* (*Mukhbir al-wāsilīn*); *The Generations of Shahjahan* (*Tabaqāt-i Shāhjahānī*); and other authentic texts.

He found that for some [Friends of God], the year and date and tomb and Sufi order were in books, and the dates of others, both ancient and modern, were not to be seen in books. At the tombs of those where a death anniversary is observed at a place where pilgrimage is possible, there were some papers that were there verified by the descendant (*sāhib-i sajjāda*) and the attendants of the tomb. In the places where it was impossible to go, verification was conveyed and confirmed by disciples of the order of that Friend of God, or by residents of the place who were well-known and trustworthy men. Dates contained in the aforementioned *Book of Death Anniversaries* were retained without change or substitution. If something has been found to contradict that in the biographical books, it has been added, and displayed, as a means of salvation in both worlds. May God, in respect of the holy ones who are mentioned in this noble text, keep this rebellious and poorly armored sinner in the love of this lofty company, and make [me] die in their love, and resurrect [me] in the troop of their lovers and in the sanctuary of the Prophet and his noble Family.

On Fixing Death Anniversaries

2. The axis of the Friends of God, Shaykh Muhammad Chishtī (son of Shaykh Muhammad Hasan ibn Ahmad ibn Shaykh Nasīr ad-Dīn-i Thānī ibn Shaykh Badr ad-Dīn ibn Kamāl ad-Dīn, disciple and true nephew of the axis of axes, Shaykh Nasīr ad-Dīn Mahmūd Chirāgh-i Dihlī [757/1356]) has said in his writings, "Seeker of God, my dear, my beloved! You ought to observe the death anniversaries of the Friends of God Most High, for help comes to you from them. God Most High gives the capacity for this work to their descendants, from His own generosity. The author of the

Collection of Traditions (*Majmū' ar-riwāyāt*) has said, 'If one wishes to select the [time of the] feast, let him select it with awareness of the day of his death, and take care for the hour in which his spirit departed. For the spirits of the dead come every year in the days of the death anniversaries, in that place and in that hour. And it is fitting that one should take food and drink in that hour, for that makes the spirits glad. Indeed, there is an extraordinary [spiritual] influence in this. And if one wants edibles and beverages, they [the spirits] will be glad, and wish one well and not ill.' Thus if the aspirant, in pilgrimage to that place, regardless of conditions, regardless of where it is, regardless of anything whatever, makes an offering to the best of his ability—and if that hour is not known, then if the spirit has passed on during the day, he does this during the day, and if it has passed on during the night, he does it during the night. The holy master of the secret, Gīsū Darāz (826/1422), used to make a great offering to the spirit of the axis of axes, Shaykh Nasīr ad-Dīn Mahmūd Chirāgh-i Dihlī, during the night of the 18th of Ramadan, since the passing of his spirit had been on this night. But he also performed this during the day. And if it is not known with certainty whether it was by day or night, then one should perform it during the day and also do something at night." Such was the practice of the axis of the Friends of God.

Offerings to the Spirits of the Dead

3. "Know, seeker of God, that the perfectly guided ones, sincere disciples, and trustworthy adherents ought to present food to the spirits of their elders, their masters, and their guides, as much as possible without objection. Thus by their [the spirits'] blessing, the benefits and good fortune of both worlds are increased, and their [the disciples'] life and wealth grow, and they attain their desire and stand in need of nothing created; might and fortune become great, and since 'The [real] man is he who loves,' by their blessing, their final state becomes good if God Most High wills. This having become clear by experience, there is no success, unless [for] the possessor of fortune and happiness." If [celebrating] all of the death anniversaries causes difficulty, let him only do some and make an offering without sin to the spirits of all the prophets and Friends of God and all the people of the heart, in the month of Rajab.

Flexibility in Observing the Death Anniversary

4. Know that, if one does not perform it on the day and night of the death anniversary, but performs it on another day on account of business, it is good. "The perfection of deeds is in intentions." He [Muhammad Chishtī]

has also said, "One observes the death anniversaries of one's masters, as much as possible without objection, and in observing this, if one obtains the permission of the master both formally and spiritually, it is best. And if it is hard to give to anyone, let him give that which he owes to his family and children and people, and that which he eats [himself]; this shall be his intention. And if the death anniversary is on a day when it is hard [to perform all customary practices], he performs it on whatever day is easy. On the day of incurring expenses for the death anniversary, he does not become extravagant, but does whatever is without extravagance."

Distributing Food Offerings at the Death Anniversary

5. In the *Jalālian Treasury* it is written, "One of the conditions of the sincere is that, for the spirit of one to whom one wishes to offer food, he should distribute food for the dervishes at that subtle time in which that Friend of God has departed, for three days in succession. Whatever time he wishes is best." In the above-mentioned *Book of Death Anniversaries* it is written, "Making offerings on the day and night is a complete cycle, and the day of the death anniversary and the following night and the following day is the order of making offerings on the day of the death anniversary. And if the day is not known, nor the night, then it is performed in the [appropriate] month, but if the month is not known, it should be performed in the month of Rajab, especially on 'the night of wishes (*laylat ar-raghā'ib*)' or that day, the first Thursday that comes in the month of Rajab, which is called [the day of] 'the night of wishes.' They say that in this night or day, [or on the night of the Prophet's ascension,] if one performs it as much as possible for the souls of all the Friends of God and the people of faith, what happiness is [then] in the breasts of all! If one is a *faqīr* or dervish, whatever cooked food is in the house he dedicates to their spirits and eats it. And if it is a time of poverty, let him not forget the Fātiha [Qur'ān, 1]."

6. One of the offspring of the disciples of the axis of axes, Shaykh Muhammad Chishtī writes, "On the day of the death anniversary, or the night, one recites the Fātiha to his spirit and makes an offering of food. If one recites the Fātiha during the hour of the passing away of his spirit, it is better; otherwise, [one does it] at whatever hour and whatever day is easiest without objection. Let him recite the Fātiha over the food and drink. If he cannot [distribute food], indeed let him recite the Fātiha for their spirits and eat the food that has been cooked for his own meal and for his family." In attempting to observe one, two, or three death anni-

versaries of one's own masters, one ought to engage in music sessions, complete Qur'ān recitations, [distribution of] food, and similar things, and one ought to abstain from unlawful things. And if, in Rajab on "the night of wishes," until "the day of conquering," which is the 15th of Rajab, or the [27th] of the month, one distributes food dedicated to the spirits of the prophets, Friends of God, martyrs, and pious ones, they say that one will obtain much benefit.

Prayers for Deceased Relatives

7. In the *Guide of the Knowers of God (Dalīl al-'ārifīn)* it is written that the shaykh of shaykhs, Shaykh Husām ad-Dīn Mānikpūrī [852/1448], the disciple and successor of the axis of the world, Shaykh Nūr al-Haqq [813/1410], used to make a pilgrimage to [the tomb of] his parents after every Friday's prayers, and he did this without fail. Once he went [instead] to speak with his master's son after the Friday prayers. When he returned, the tomb was in the road. He, riding in his palanquin, stood and recited the Fātiha, and came home. On Saturday, after the morning prayers, he went out on pilgrimage. He said, "On Friday, and the first hours on Saturday, the spirits are present in the tombs, and one should perform pilgrimage." He also said, "If one recites eleven times Qur'ān 112, and Qur'ān 113–114 at the same time, and the Throne Verse [2:256], the people in the tombs are absolved." When he went to the tombs, he was near the tomb of his father. He greeted them, standing at the head [of the tomb], and recited the Fātiha and the Throne Verse, up to [the word] *eternally.* Eleven times he recited suras 112, and at the same time 113–114, and once 102. He went to the foot and kissed the top of the tomb. He performed the same pilgrimage to his mother, also kissing the top of the foot [of the tomb], and at the time of departure recited sura 94. He said, "If one holds one's hands on top of the tomb and ten times recites the word of unity and praise, the dead are absolved." He also said, "One should perform pilgrimage every day, though it is not easy. One should do it on Friday, for the dead expect it. It is of the same use to the mother and father." He also said, "My master, the axis of the world, Shaykh Nūr al-Haqq, every day after morning prayers used to perform pilgrimage to his father, Shaykh 'Alā' al-Haqq wa 'd-Dīn." He also said, "If someone once recites the Fātiha in a tomb, for forty days, the punishment will be removed from that tomb." The axis of axes, Shaykh Nasīr ad-Dīn Chirāgh-i Dihlī, says, "While standing at the head of someone's grave, one says the Fātiha once, the Throne Verse three times, sura 102 three times, and 112 many times."

Figure 7.   Main dome of the shrine of Nizām ad-Dīn Awliyā' in Delhi with devotees at the Friend's tomb. Photograph by Marcia Hermansen.

The Best Days for Pilgrimage and Prayer

8. In the *Jalālian Treasury* it is written, "'Pilgrimage to graves every week is [legally] approved,' and the best days for pilgrimage are four: Saturday, Monday, Thursday, and Friday. It is the same with the blessed and superior nights, such as 'the night of orders,'[2] and with blessed times, such as 10th Dhū 'l-Hijja, the two 'Īds,[3] and 'Āshūrā."[4] In the *Revival of Religious Sciences,* Imam Muhammad Ghazālī [505/1111] writes, "The superior days are seventeen: the first day is 'Arafa;[5] the second day is 'Āshūrā; the third day is 27 Rajab; the fourth day is 27 Ramadān; the fifth day is 15 Sha'bān; the sixth day is Friday; the seventh and eighth days are the two 'Īds; and the nine days of Dhū 'l-Hijja, from the first night of the moon until the ninth. The superior nights are fifteen: in the month of Ramadān, the 21st, 23rd, 25th, 27th, 29th, and 7th; the first night of the month of Muharram; the night of 'Āshūrā; the first night of the month of Rajab, and the 15th and 27th nights in Rajab; the 15th of Sha'bān; the night of 'Arafa; and the nights of the two 'Īds."

Efficacy of Prayer for the Dead

9. At the time when one is standing, facing the deceased, one says, "Peace be unto you, people of the houses, among those who submit and are faithful! May He have mercy on those who have come before us, and those who come after; God willing, we shall be joined with you. I shall ask God for you, and forgiveness will be yours." The Messenger of God spoke thus, then sat and said, "In the name of God, and for the community of the Messenger of God." One finds in Hadith that whenever one recites this by the tomb of someone, the inhabitant of the tomb will be spared the punishment, darkness, and straitness [of the tomb] for forty years. Then one says, "There is no god but God, He alone, Who has no partner; His is the kingdom, His is the praise; He gives life and death, while He is living and does not die; good comes by His hand, and He has power over everything." Then one recites the Fātiha, the Throne Verse, and gives the reward of that to the inhabitants of the tombs. After that, one recites sura 112 seven times, but if one recites it ten times, it is better. (See Figure 7.)

10. In the *Comprehensive Words (Jawāmi' al-kalīm)*, the discourses of Sayyid Gīsū Darāz, it is written that he said, "One day a great man passed through a graveyard, and he saw a commotion in the cemetery. He asked, 'What is this commotion?' In the midst of this, they [the dead] replied, 'It is a week since Habīb-i 'Ajamī [156/773] passed by us, and he had recited one Fātiha intended for us. The abundance and reward produced from that is being divided among us.'"

11. In the *Breezes of Intimacy,* in the account of Abū ar-Rabīʿ Malaqī, the disciple of Shaykh Abū 'l-ʿAbbās, it is written that it has come down in the Hadith of the Prophet with this meaning, that saying the phrase, "There is no god but God" 70,000 times for the salvation of the speaker or for the salvation of that person whom the speaker intends is completely efficacious. Shaykh Abū 'r-Rabīʿ has said, "I had said this chant (*dhikr*)[6] 70,000 times, but had not done it in the name of any particular person, until one day I was present with a group at someone's feast table. With them was a youth who had experienced [spiritual] unveilings. At the moment when that youth laid a hand on the food to eat, suddenly he wept. They asked him, 'Why do you weep?' He said, 'Right here I am witnessing hell, and I see my mother in it undergoing punishment.'" Shaykh Abū 'r-Rabīʿ said, "Secretly I prayed, 'God! You know that I have said "There is no god but God" 70,000 times. I have offered that [reward] for the sake of freeing the mother of this particular youth from hellfire.' When I had completed forming this intention internally, that youth laughed and became cheerful, saying, 'I see my mother freed from hellfire! Praise be to God!' Then he joined in eating food with the group."

Legitimacy of Pilgrimage

12. In the discourses of Sayyid Gīsū Darāz it is written that he said, "They asked Khwāja Naṣīr ad-Dīn Chirāgh-i Dihlī, 'Do you perform circumambulation around the tomb of Shaykh al-Islām Quṭb ad-Dīn [634/1236]? What is the [prophetic] basis of that?' He said, 'On "Pilgrimage to tombs," it is written, "Circumambulation around the tomb of a pious man is lawful."'" The collector of the above-mentioned discourses says, "He is a sincere lover who, at every new moon, circumambulates the hospice of his revered master with bare head and bare feet, saying, 'In this I find more than in pilgrimage to Mecca!'"

Spiritual Effects of Pilgrimage

13. In the *Ashrafian Subtleties,* the discourses of Sayyid Ashraf Jahāngīr Simnānī Chishtī [829/1425], it is written that he said, "After making pilgrimage to the Friends of God who are seated on the seat of guidance and the chair of dignity, one makes pilgrimage to the tombs of the Friends of God." He said, "One day I had sat in attendance on Shaykh Rukn ad-Dīn ʿAlāʾ ad-Dawla Simnānī [736/1336]. A dervish asked, 'Since in the tomb this body has no perception, and the acquired body (*badan-i muktasab*) is detached from it, together with the spirit, and since there is no veil in

the world of spirits, what need is there to visit tombs? Concentrating on the spirit of a Friend of God should be just as useful in any other place as at his tomb.' The shaykh said, 'It has many uses. One is that when one makes a pilgrimage to someone['s tomb], one's concentration increases as often as one goes. When one reaches the tomb and beholds it by sense perception, one's sense perception also becomes engaged with the tomb. He then becomes totally concentrated, and this has many uses. Another is that however much spirits lack a veil, and though the whole world is one to them, it keeps an eye on both the body with which it [the spirit] has been connected for seventy years and on its resurrection body that it will become after the resurrection, for ever and ever. Its [the spirit's] connection is greater here than in any other place. The benefits of making pilgrimage are great. If one concentrates here on the spirituality of that revered Mustafā [that is, the Prophet Muhammad], one obtains benefit. But if one goes to Medina, the spirituality of Mustafā is aware of one's traveling and the suffering of the road. When one reaches there, one sees by sense perception the pure shrine (*rawda*) of that revered one. One becomes totally concentrated. How can the latter benefit be compared to the former? The people of vision (*mushāhada*) realize this internal meaning (*ma'nā*).'"

The Friends of God Are Conscious

14. He [Ashraf Jahāngīr Simnānī] also said, "The dead are aware of the coming of a pilgrim and his concentration, for the spiritual world has a subtlety, specifically, that the spirits of the Friends of God take notice of even a little concentration of the pilgrim." He said that the Emperor of the Masters, Shaykh Nizām ad-Dīn Awliyā' [726/1325], had gone to make pilgrimage to the blessed tomb of the axis of axes, Khwāja Qutb ad-Dīn. In the midst of circumambulation, it occurred to him, "Is his spirituality yet aware of my concentration?" This incipient thought was not yet complete when from the luminous tomb a voice sprang up, with an eloquent expression, reciting this verse: "Think of me as living like yourself; I will come in spirit if you come in body. Do not think me lacking in companionship, for I see you even if you don't see me." He said, "Whenever one comes to a town, the first thing one ought to accomplish is to kiss the feet of the Friends of God who are full of life, and after that, the honor of pilgrimage to the tombs of Friends of God found there. If one's master's tomb is in that city, one first carries out the pilgrimage to him; otherwise one visits the tomb of every Friend of God shown him."

Controversy over Prostration

15. "There is a debate among the legal scholars about placing the forehead on the tombs of Friends of God, and they have not permitted it, though among the shaykhs there are differences of opinion. According to this *faqīr* [that is, Ashraf Jahāngīr Simnānī], just as in the world of travel many Friends of God are seen, who while living have been looked upon with respect (*taʿzīm*), so after death people look on them with the same respect. In the same way, the father and teacher and master and the like are worthy of respect. When my revered master [ʿAlāʾ ad-Dawla Simnānī] returned from congregational prayer, people placed their heads at his feet, and the heads that were not honored by his blessed feet they put on the ground and so prostrated themselves. One of the mullahs asked about the meaning of this, for it is unlawful that they should put their heads on the ground. He said, 'I have often forbidden them and restrained them, so that they do not come back.'"

16. In the *Lives of the Friends of God* it is written that one day in the assembly of the Emperor of the Masters, Shaykh Nizām ad-Dīn Awliyāʾ, there was talk about disciples coming to the revered master and placing their heads on the ground. The Emperor of the Masters said, "I wanted to forbid people, but since they have done this before my shaykh, I have not forbidden them." In sum, sincere friends and trustworthy aspirants involuntarily place their heads on the ground because of the form that they call vision in the mirror of the shaykh and the inner meaning (*maʿnā*) that they witness in the form of the shaykh. In the *Observer* (*Mirsād*) it is said that to place the head on the ground before the shaykh is not prostration; this is respect and honor for the light of the essence and attributes of the real object of worship [that is, God], for the shaykhs and Friends of God are illuminated with that light.

Rules and Prayers of Pilgrimage

17. He [Ashraf Jahāngīr Simnānī] also says that when one comes to make pilgrimage to tombs, from modesty (*hayāʾ*) he enters the tombs and circumambulates three or seven times. Then he puts his head at the foot of the grave, and turning his face toward the deceased, stands to the right of the grave and says, "Peace be unto you, people of 'There is no god but God,' from the people of 'There is no god but God'! How did you find his saying, 'There is no god but God'? God! [It was] by the truth of 'There is no god but God'! Resurrect us in the multitude of those who say, 'There is no god but God.' Forgive him who says, 'There is no god but God,' and do not deprive us of saying 'There is no god but God and Muhammad is

Figure 8.   *Dargāh* at Golrā Sharīf, Islamabad, Pakistan. Pilgrims engage in daily rituals of visitation. The wealthy shrine houses the graves of many recent *pīrs*, including Syed Ghulām Muhyuddīn Gīlānī (also known as Babujī, d. 1974) and, because of its proximity to Pakistan's capital, is often frequented by politicians eager to publicize their religious devotion. Copyrighted image by Jamal Elias.

the Messenger of God.'" Then he strews a rose or flower on the tomb and, sitting or standing, recites the Fātiha, the Throne verse, sura 99, 102 once, and 112 seven or ten times, and once recites this prayer: "There is no god but God, He alone, He has no partner; His is the kingdom and the praise; He gives life and death. He is the Living who never dies, full of beauty and generous with his right hand. He has power over everything. In the name of God, for the people of the Messenger of God." After that he says, "O God, I have recited this recitation, and I have made the reward for it as a gift for the spirit of so-and-so, son of so-and-so." One should not go to make pilgrimage to the shaykhs without sweets, roses, and flowers. If it is the tomb of his master, he makes an offering of gold there and then conveys [something] to the descendants of the master and also some alms—a bit of gold—to the people residing there. [See Figure 8.]

Benefits of Pilgrimage on Friday

18. In the commentary on *The Straight Path* (*Sirāt al-mustaqīm*) it is written, "On Friday the spirits of the faithful are near their tombs, near in a

real sense. The attachment is a spiritual connection; vision and contact are a connection that they have with their bodies. The pilgrims who come near the tombs realize this, though they always realize this, but on this day they realize it with a realization greater than the realization of the other days, from the point of view of being near the tombs. Undoubtedly the realization through nearness is better and stronger than the realization through distance." In some accounts it is said that realization at the beginning of the day is better than at the end, and therefore for this reason, pilgrimage to tombs at this time is preferred and customary in the holy shrines.

Rules and Prayers of Pilgrimage, Continued

19. In the *Comprehensive Words* it is written that if someone goes to make pilgrimage to the tombs of the shaykhs, when he reaches the door, he should say once or seven times, "Glory be to God," and so forth, and kissing the ground, recite the Fātiha once, pronouncing the name of God, the Throne Verse three times, sura 109 once, 102 seven times, 112 ten times, and praise of the Prophet (*durūd*) three times. According to the revered master Nizām ad-Dīn, [one recites] the Fātiha and the Throne Verse once, sura 112 twelve times, and praise of the Prophet ten times. After that one sits and recites what one has memorized from the Qur'ān. Rising, one circumambulates the tomb seven times and makes a petition for whatever concern one has; otherwise one kisses the ground. The feet are turned away, and one never shows one's back toward the revered one. At the time of pilgrimage, in coming and going, one is vigilant and expectant regarding who enters and leaves one's thoughts and who remains and what they did. From left and right, from before and behind, [one watches for] what they said, and what voice called out. In the *Syrian Subtleties* (*Latā'if-i shāmī*) it is written, "When from the garden one passes into the realm of the graves, the group who are honored by the happiness of [divine] protection, one faces them and says once, 'Peace be unto the people of the region, the faithful and submitting; may God have mercy on those who came before us and those who follow; God willing, I am with you who are attached [to God],' and once 'O God, make a reward for all these who are visited, O Most Merciful one!'"

Spiritual Presence of the Friends of God

20. In the *Treasury of Morals* (*Makhzan al-fawā'id*) it is written, "However much the spirit of the Friend of God departs from the body both in expressions and in relations, yet its influences nonetheless leave their mark on a place. Just as when musk is removed from a letter or tray, even

so his perfume continues to linger in the place to which he was related. Thus they have said (verse): 'When someone becomes dust after reaching perfection, / the dust of his feet replaces the elixir.'" In this manner, therefore, when the pilgrim presents himself in pilgrimage to the shrine with its miraculous influences, with firm faith, trustworthy belief, necessary good conduct, manners of sanctity, and good behavior, the beneficent spirit of the master of the tomb is present. The pilgrim may not be worthy of purity, but sincere belief in terms of the pilgrim's state obtains aid and assistance and brings about the production of happy fortune and the attainment of favors. If sometimes a kind of discrepancy appears in the order of necessary conduct, the pilgrim will be caught by the occasion for reproach. Such was the case when Sayyid ʿAlāʾ ad-Dīn Jīwarī one day went to make pilgrimage to Shaykh al-Islām, Khwāja Qutb ad-Dīn. He (disrespectfully) sat down near the tomb of the shaykh, and from within a voice cried out, saying, "Sayyid, you see me as dead; if I were living, could you sit in this way?" After only hearing these words, he arose from that place and sat down far away in good conduct.

21. It is written that when you walk over the graves of the Friends of God, ask their help and seek resolution (*himmat*), and entrust [yourself] to the Lord by the force of maintaining your conduct, so that you will never be able to recall the world's desire. A dervish walked on the earth over [the grave of] Abū ʾl-Hasan Fāshanjī and prayed to God Most High for the world. That night he saw Abū ʾl-Hasan in a dream, saying, "Dervish, when you come upon the earth over us, completely free yourself from both worlds, but if you want the world's goods, walk upon the ground over kings."

Respect for All the Dead

22. In the *Mirror of Consciences* (*Mirʾāt al-asrār*) it is written, "Since the state of the dead is concealed and hidden, thus it is not known who among them is wretched and who is happy, nor whether the deceased was learned, an ignoramus, or perfect. But it may be that his name is from the names of God and His Messenger. Thus, maintaining good conduct and respect for the deceased is necessary and required in all times for all people; so it is conveyed, and the rewards and benefits of the Fātiha are many and uncounted. May God aid us and you."

Conclusion

23. The goal of this arrangement and the purpose of the book contained here [is to show] each of the dates of the months of the whole year, for

perpetually enduring are the death anniversaries of these revered ones of lofty rank whose aid is sought, as also the generality of spirits of the noble Friends of God and great shaykhs. If one [wishes to know] the date of the passing away and death anniversary of one of God's Friends that is in accordance with past report, or is verified now or in the future, whether from a book or from a trustworthy tongue, and is authenticated by the agreement of books or transmitters, he should test it in this *Book of Death Anniversaries*, known as the *Treasury of Death Anniversaries*. Then by the blessing of the prophetic report "Whoever prescribes a good exemplary deed (*sanna sunna hasana*) has his reward and the reward of the one who performs it," may the author of this book also find a pleasure and share of the Last Day and its reward, with the help of God Most High. This noble and blessed text was collected and reached completion by the expansion of several authenticated texts, such as the *Book of Death Anniversaries*, by the previously mentioned Shaykh Sharaf ad-Dīn, which is from the sublime library of the exemplar of those united with God, the revered Shaykh Nizām ad-Dīn [Awrangābādī], which was transcribed the 24th of Rabīʿ I, 1128 Hijrī [17 March 1716], according to the direction of the revered shaykh. I later compared two texts from the blessed port of Surat and another text from Aurangabad, in the days when the lover of dervishes, the believer in their believers, Anwār ad-Dīn Khān Bahādur[7] was in the army of Nizām al-Mulk Bahādur Āsaf Jāh, on the 5th of Shawwal, in the 1,156th year since the prophetic emigration [18 November 1743]. Praise belongs to God, the Lord of creation, and blessings and peace be on our master and Prophet, Muhammad, the best of Messengers, and on the people of his house and all his Companions.

NOTES

1. An earlier version of this article, with full bibliographic details and historical context, was published in *Manifestations of Sainthood in Islam*, ed. Grace Martin Smith and Carl W. Ernst (Istanbul: Isis Press, 1993), 43–67; research for this article was supported by a Fulbright Islamic Civilization Research Fellowship. For a fuller account of Chishtī shrine pilgrimage, see Carl W. Ernst and Bruce B. Lawrence, *Sufi Martyrs of Love: Chishti Sufism in South Asia and Beyond* (New York: Palgrave Press, 2002), 85–104. This revised version is printed here with permission of the original publisher.

2. The "night of orders" (Ar. *laylat al-barāʾa*; Pers. *shab-i barāt*) is the night of the 14th of Shaʿbān, when all the decrees of Heaven are sent down to earth for the coming year and the dead are honored; see Jaʿfar Sharif, *Islam in India, or the Qanun-i-Islam*, trans. G.A. Herklots, ed. William Crooke (Oxford, 1921; repr., London: Curzon Press, 1972), 203–4.

3. 'Īd al-Adhā is the feast of Abrahamic sacrifice during the pilgrimage ritual in the month of Dhū 'l-Hijja, and 'Īd al-Fitr is the breaking of the fast at the end of Ramadan.

4. For Sunni Muslims, 'Āshūrā is the general day of repentance (cf. the Jewish Yom Kippur), observed on the 10th of Muharram, whereas Shī'īs on that date commemorate the martyrdom of Imam Husayn.

5. Standing on Mt. 'Arafa near Mecca on the 9th of Dhū 'l-Hijja and addressing God with the pilgrim's cry, "Here am I, Lord (*labbayk*)," is one of the high points of the Hajj pilgrimage.

6. From the general meaning of "remembrance," the term *dhikr* among Sufis took on by the sixth/twelfth century the technical significance of a repetitive chanting (silent or audible) of brief prayers and the names of God as a method of inducing ecstasy.

7. A prominent political leader and patron of Sufism who founded the kingdom of Arcot in southern India.

22 Sufi Autobiography in the Twentieth Century

The Worldly and Spiritual Journeys of Khwāja Hasan Nizāmī

Marcia Hermansen

Classical Sufis generally were eulogized by others in a range of biographical genres such as *tabaqāt* (books of ranks or classifications), *tadhkirāt* (memorials) and *malfūzat* collections (diary-like recordings of audiences with Sufi masters). A few exceptional examples of early Sufi autobiographies exist; for example, the *Deliverance from Error* of al-Ghazālī (505/1111) and the dream diaries of at-Tirmidhī (c. 285/898) and az-Zawawī (882/1477). Most of these Sufi autobiographies were composed to edify spiritual seekers and disciples and to confirm the authors' spiritual authority.

In the case of the Sufi figure Khwāja Hasan Nizāmī, a fourteenth/ twentieth-century Indian Muslim, we have an autobiography composed by a modern Sufi who was a well-known activist among his contemporaries and who was also acknowledged as a pioneering literary figure in the realm of Urdu prose. During his career, Nizāmī experimented with various biographical and autobiographical genres, most famously in his long-running diary known as the *Roznāmcha*. In this popular diary, which was serialized and published over a period of some forty years, he commented on well-known personalities and dramatic political events of his time, as well as on his own health and views. Nizāmī also composed travel accounts (*siyāhnāme*) in similar diary form, a number of which were published separately. One such book chronicles Nizāmī's travels just before World War I to Egypt, Syria, and the Hijaz. Late in life, during the 1370s/1950s, he traveled to Pakistan; a diary of this trip has also been published as a separate book. At a relatively early point in Nizāmī's career, in 1338/1919, when he was only forty-one years old, he composed an auto-biography, *Āp Bītī*, that has been declared a pioneering work in this genre of Urdu literature.[1] This work resembles Western models of a life story in that it begins with the author's formative childhood experiences and then

Figure 9. Qawwālī singers and musicians at the shrine of Nizām ad-Dīn Awliyā' in Delhi. Photograph by Marcia Hermansen.

moves to his youthful spiritual seeking and his gradual success as a journalist, writer, and Sufi guide with thousands of disciples. The final section of the work, on occasion issued as a separate small treatise, was termed by Nizāmī a "spiritual autobiography" (*Lāhūtī Āp Bītī*). This brief text seems to have been omitted from subsequent editions of this work and was later issued separately in expanded form. It represents a unique expression of a modern Sufi's ventures into the realm of the imagination.

KHWĀJA HASAN NIZĀMĪ

Nizāmī was born in 1295/1878 into the tight inner circle of families that were hereditary custodians of the shrine of the Sufi saint Nizām ad-Dīn Awliyā' (725/1325) in Delhi. (See Figure 9.) Nizāmī's parents and two sisters died before he was twelve, and he was raised by his older brother. Nizāmī received a traditional Islamic education in the area surrounding the tomb of Nizām ad-Dīn and later studied at Rashīd Ahmad Gangohī's madrasa for a year and a half.

Nizāmī spent the majority of his career pursuing literary and journalistic activities. He frequented intellectual and Muslim political circles and also initiated Sufi disciples numbering in the many thousands. The

1340s/1920s saw the most active political stage of his life for at this time Nizāmī initiated his own version of a Tablīgh movement, distinct from the Tablīgh-i Jamā'at movement of Muhammad Ilyās. Nizāmī, like Ilyās, confronted the challenge of identity politics at a time in India when populations whose Muslim identity had been rather fluid were being recruited to convert (or revert) to Hinduism by a large Hindu revivalist movement known as the Aryā Samāj. Nizāmī's counterstrategies included providing simple and basic education about Islam to Muslims, as well as engaging in literary projects designed to uplift and reform (*islāh*) the Muslim community both socially and morally. Accordingly, some of his works of this period treat subjects such as inculcating basic Islamic principles, reforming harmful social practices and customs, engaging in a range of trades and professions with a strong work ethic, and so on. In terms of institution building, Nizāmī did attempt to set up a school in Delhi, but this project seems to have failed shortly after its inception.

In the latter years of his life, Khwāja Hasan Nizāmī was afflicted with weakening health and loss of eyesight. He lived through the difficult times of Partition of the Indian Subcontinent, and in his old age seems to have felt embattled by the political and ideological conflicts raging around him.

Nizāmī excelled in self-promotion and had several colleagues write forewords to his autobiography, including his wife, Khwāja Bānū. She begins her foreword as follows:

> Thanks be to God that those things that we had only heard orally have now been collected in this book. Khwāja Sāhib's statement is absolutely correct that every person's life is a means of advice (*nasīha*) both for himself and for others if he reflects on it. This book is also written in the genre of counsel (*nasīha*).[2]

This twofold observation is noteworthy since it further contextualizes this "modern" Sufi autobiography as a work designed to impart lessons and give advice to readers. Khwāja Bānū later addresses her husband's female followers:

> Whoever reads this book should likewise reflect on her own life. I call upon whichever sisters God has blessed with resources to buy and distribute copies of this book to her poor sisters. To those sisters who are disciples of my spiritual guide (*pīr*) and husband, Khwāja Sāhib, I say that they should read this book aloud to other ladies so that they will also be able to take counsel from his life story.[3]

This appeal not only promotes sales of the book but also alludes to the position of many Indian Muslim women being reached at this time through new ideas and media.

In his preface to the book, "Mullā" Wāhidī, a close colleague of Nizāmī's, also comments on the virtues of the work as a literary production:

> I have gone over the autobiography of Khwāja Hasan Nizāmī in a cursory way. My opinion is that at minimum this is a completely new addition to Urdu literature. . . .
>
> People can derive moral edification from imaginary fables, and the world may be entertained and befitted through them. Would that we would become accustomed to being taught lessons from real life, since this is the greatest story and the best counsel. . . .
>
> Today the children of those who possess honor and prosperity are squandering the dignity and wealth of their forebears, despite thousands of attempts and efforts. However, Khwāja Hasan Nizāmī shows what an aptitude for advancement the children of poor families have, if only they are able to get education and instruction. As is his style, Khwāja Sāhib takes the smallest events of life and relates each one to some effect. Although the biography is composed of numerous small anecdotes from which lessons are drawn, it is still a compilation of integrated topics that can enlighten us on our life paths. It is at the same time an Urdu Gulistān,[4] the experiences of a life, a book of advice, and a self-improvement manual.[5]

TRANSLATION

In the Name of God, the Merciful, the Compassionate:

O' Allāh, grant me assistance. I am writing this book for those of Your bondservants who for the sake of Your love, seeking You, and in order to obtain the truth and spirituality of Your religion of Islam, have taken initiation at my hand. For this reason I am calling this book "Pīr Brother" [Fellow Disciple], since You are the spiritual guide of us all, and because we are all Your disciples, and thus we are all fellow disciples to one another. You are the Sought, we are the seekers. You are the Real, we are but the figurative (*majāzī*). You are the root and we are the branches. You are the light of the heavens and the earth, we are only your rays.

Clearly, when I initiate Your bondservants as disciples at my hand and take their oath of allegiance, in a spiritual sense Your hand is above my hand, and by placing Your hand on mine, it is You who accept their pledge of allegiance. As You stated in the Qur'ān, "The hand of God is over their hands" (48:10). . . .

O' Allāh, please accept this supplication. Amen. Please grant my intention and my wish that I may now explain things that will be beneficial to Your disciple servants and my Pīr brothers in this world and the hereafter.

[After giving a general description of his early life, physical features, and two marriages, Nizāmī continues:]

At the age of eleven years I accompanied my father to Tawnsa Sharīf in the district of Dera Ghāzī Khān in the Northwest Frontier Province. At the guidance of my esteemed father I took initiation into Sufism at the hand of Hazrat Allāh Bakhsh [Tawnsavī (1319/1901)]—all of my family, including my father, were his disciples. After the death of my father, I went to [the famous Sufi poet] Khwāja Ghulām Farīd [1319/1901], may Allāh have mercy on him, in the company of my brother Sayyid Hasan ʿAlī Shāh when I was at the age of sixteen. Khwāja Ghulām Farīd was the hereditary head (sajjāda)⁶ of the shrine of Chācharan Sharīf in the district of Bahawalpur. On my brother's advice I became his disciple. Each of these two initiations was not based on my own volition since I was not yet mature enough.

After that, at the shrine of Bābā Farīd Shakar Ganj [644/1265] at Pākpattan, District Montgomery, through a spiritual sign from Bābā Farīd I took initiation with Hazrat Mawlānā Pīr Sayyid Mehr ʿAlī Shāh [1356/1937], and this was based on my own well-considered decision. At this time I was twenty-four years of age, and through education, study, and spiritual exercises, I had built up a good background in the knowledge of Sufism.

I became a disciple with full engagement. Immediately after becoming his murīd, I began to make spiritual progress, while my worldly condition deteriorated so dramatically that I continually went hungry. My livelihood became settled after 1326/1908, eleven years ago. Ever since then my worldly advancement has steadily risen.

The urge to become a disciple had come from my own heart. I consider both Allāh Bakhsh and Ghulām Farīd to have been perfect spiritual masters; however, since they were no longer living, I needed to locate a living spiritual preceptor. For this reason I performed divination (istikhāra) repeatedly such that I would be guided to a spiritual master. One night I saw Hazrat Mahbūb-i Ilāhī [Nizām ad-Dīn Awliyāʾ] in a dream, and he asked me, "Whose disciple are you?" I replied, "I myself had wanted to ask you, whose disciple I should become?" He said, "Look at yourself."

I interpreted this as meaning that I should work on reforming my self, and in order to put this into practice, I spent a long time searching out spiritual exercises in books and performing them. After that it occurred to me that Mahbūb-i Ilāhī [the Beloved of Allāh, a title of Nizām ad-Dīn's] was not indicating something about my lineage, since I am from his lineage. "Look at yourself" could mean, "Look at the way that Hazrat himself acted." For this reason I made the intention that in the same way that Hazrat Mahbūb-i Ilāhī had gone by foot from Delhi to Pākpattan to meet his spiritual teacher Bābā Farīd Ganj-i Shakar, I myself would also go walking. However, I didn't have the strength to do that, so I went on foot from Manchanābād to Pākpattan, a distance of roughly twelve miles over a desert road.

I made this journey without any proper wherewithal. No one was with me, nor did I have a coin in my pocket or any food. Hungry and thirsty, I set off with enthusiasm and pleasure, and at twelve noon I reached the bank of the river. There was no ferry, I was not used to walking, and the road was not cleared. Due to the extreme heat and intensity of the sun I lost consciousness. I went and sat on the riverbank. My hunger had become so severe that my mind was half dazed. In the meantime a dervish traveler arrived and he had with him a heavy loaf of bread. He gave me a quarter of that and, smiling, said, "Eat this. Drink some water. You have to distribute bread [yourself in the future]! Now you are close to fainting." I ate that piece of bread and drank some of the river water. The ferry arrived and I boarded it and crossed, and by evening I had reached Pākpattan.

That night at the tomb of Bābā Sāhib, I submitted, "I have come in search of a shaykh." By morning my heart had become inclined on its own toward Pīr Mehr 'Alī Shāh, and at that time I went to him and took initiation.

Up to this point I have written the answer to every question according to the established template. I am now aware of the need to explain some personal circumstances so that future generations will derive benefit and get something out of my autobiography.

Some time ago I began to write a book under the title of "The Autobiography of Khwāja Hasan Nizāmī."[7] However, I abandoned the project because I had a feeling that it constituted self-promotion. Now I think that for the sake of the experience of my fellow disciples, it is appropriate for me to commit to writing all my good and bad experiences so that they would also know about the dark days of my life. I will try not to conceal any secret matter, and I will write about those things that in the eyes of some people are positive, while I will also discuss those things that are shameful, sinful, and against humanity.

If someone else were to write about me, he would select only the good things and conceal my shortcomings. The actual state of a person is what should be written about, and it is necessary not to deceive other persons but rather to write honestly, so that on learning all of the good and bad things about a person, others will have the ability to establish a true opinion in his regard.

It is also very necessary to disseminate my true state as I have many disciples and thousands of people have become my disciples without ever meeting me, since they have become disciples though correspondence and hundreds of thousands of persons have read my books and think well of me. Thus, if they are thinking of becoming disciples, they will easily be able to study this book and decide whether this person is worthy of being taken as a spiritual guide or not.[8]

Hasan Nizāmī's Birth and an Overview of his Life

Near the end of the thirteenth [Islamic] century, in 1296 AH, on the second of Muharram [26 December 1878], a Thursday night, at dawn, Hasan Nizāmī was born. Now it is Jumāda al-Awwal 1337 [November 1918], and his age is forty-one years. . . .

Education: Hasan Nizāmī at first studied the Qur'ān, then some general Persian books; after that, Arabic composition and grammar. He knows no English; at a more advanced age he tried to learn it with no success.

His first teacher was Hazrat Mawlānā Muhammad Ismā'īl Sāhib (deceased), who lived in Khandhala in the Muzaffarnagar district and who came to Delhi to be in the service of the Mughal court and lived near the Nizām ad-Dīn shrine all of his life, where he passed away and was buried. He taught Hasan Nizāmī the books *Sharh-i Tadhhīb* and the *Kanz ad-Daqā'iq.*

When Nizāmī was twelve years of age, both his parents passed away within a year of one another, so that his brother, Sayyid Hasan 'Alī Shāh, now deceased, brought him up and assisted in helping him continue his studies of Arabic. After finishing the works *Jalālayn* [Exegesis] and the *Mishkāt Sharīf*, he started studying the *Sunan Abī Dā'ūd* and *Sunan Tirmidhī* [Hadith].[9]

[Here Nizāmī describes his further education, his first marriage, and the struggle to establish himself. Then he turns to details about his Sufi affiliations:]

The Great Sufi Shaykhs Foundation

At the end of 1326/1908 Sayyid Muhammad Irtidā Sāhib, known as Muhammad al-Wāhidī, took initiation at the hand of Hasan Nizāmī and in cooperation with him founded the Great Sufi Shaykhs Foundation (*Halqa-i Nizām al-Mashā'ikh*) and the journal *Nizām al-Mashā'ikh.*

It should also be noted that during the time mentioned previously, Hazrat Mawlānā Pīr Mehr 'Alī Shāh gave Khwāja Hasan Nizāmī permission to initiate disciples. In the state of Alwar, Mawlvī 'Umar Darāz Nizāmī Dargāhī Shāh, together with a considerable group, took initiation at the hand of Khwāja Hasan Nizāmī. Not only in this way but also through correspondence, huge numbers of people were becoming disciples.

After the establishment of the Great Sufi Shaykhs Foundation, a new era of difficulties emerged. Some called the organization a childish game and made fun of it, and it is also true that initially those who joined the Circle [of Sufi Shaykhs Foundation] or worked for it were generally young people.

During this time a mountain of troubles fell on Nizāmī. His patient wife, Habīb Bānū, passed away, his two sons died, and the clan around the shrine started opposing him. Everyday at the *dargāh*[10] in front of those who were coming to visit the shrine, negative comments were made about Nizāmī, and all sorts of false rumors spread about him.

This clamor increased to the extent that once, at the time of the '*urs,* when thousands were gathered for the closing ceremony (*khatm*)[11], someone gave a severe speech against him, and the accusations made against him were supported by the closest people in his clan.

At the same time that this was happening, a report was given to the police that Hasan Nizāmī was stirring up trouble at the shrine. On the basis of this report the police surrounded Nizami and his inner circle. . . .[12]

After all of these tests and trials, Allāh inspired guidance into the heart of Hasan Nizāmī and he determined one goal for his life. This was to present and promote Islamic Sufism in a new form and a fresh way in his writings and speeches. In view of this project, the four objectives of the Circle of Sufi Shaykhs Foundation were laid out as follows:

(1)   to preserve and promote Sufism

(2)   to unite the Sufi shaykhs

(3)   to reform those practices at the shrines and '*urūs* [death anniversaries] that were outside the bounds of Sharia and Sufi practice (*tarīqa*)

(4)   to protect the political rights of the Sufi shaykhs[13]

In summary, from 1326/1908 to 1327/1919 the life of Khwāja Hasan Nizāmī was spent in writing articles, researching and composing books, and serving his disciples. By the grace of God, every year his efforts were rewarded by greater success, the number of his disciples reached 60,000, and his books and compositions to more than forty. Due to contracting his second marriage, his family life also entered a state of contentment and tranquility.

After World War I broke out, Hasan Nizāmī stopped participating in the nation's religious, educational, or political meetings and reduced his traveling and touring as well, since police surveillance had reached such an extent that he felt no peace or security anywhere. On the train the police would expect him at every junction as if he were a bandit or a terrible criminal, and sleep became a luxury because the police would wake him and question him if the train stopped at any station. If he stayed with anyone, that individual would also be in trouble, since the police would not cease to harass him.[14]

However, it will not be inappropriate to mention the regal courage of the Nizām Mīr 'Usmān 'Alī Khān Bahādur, the king of Hyderabad, Deccan, since he and his former prime minister, Sir Kishen Parshad Bahādur, demonstrated their complete fortitude on one occasion by treating Khwāja Hasan Nizāmī with respect. This is despite the fact that due to the negative indications of the British police and the English higher authorities [resident], Khwāja Hasan Nizāmī had to depart Hyderabad for Bombay in great haste.

The king of the Deccan sent a personal telegram calling Nizāmī back and invited him to stay as his personal guest for many days. He didn't care that the British administration suspected Khwāja Hasan Nizāmī of subversive designs.

This was a brief but comprehensive overview of the life of Khwāja Hasan Nizāmī. Now, the particular incidents of Khwāja Hasan Nizāmī's life will be recounted, one by one, in order to derive useful outcomes for the public so that his Pīr brothers may learn from them and [so that] these portions of the biography will be beneficial to them in situations that they may encounter in their own lives.

Detailed Stories from Nizāmī's Life

[The Influence of Mothers on Children]   I remember that when I was about three years old, I became very ill, even to the point of death. At that time there was a close relative of King Bahādur Shāh [Zafar, the last Mughal emperor], who was living in the *dargāh* as a dervish. My mother had me taken to him. He said some prayers and blew on me.[15] He sent for a small piece of silver foil and inscribed a diagram on it. Then this drawing was put around my neck, and my mother said, "This is the prayer of 'Alī (*nād-i 'Alī*) and the king of India has made it for you." On saying "the King of India" my mother's eyes filled with tears. I asked, "Mommy why are you weeping?" She replied, "Son, now that king is no more who gave you the prayer of 'Alī, and the Britishers have snatched away his kingdom." I think that this was the first time that I had heard of the King or the British.

This was the first seed of love for the House of Timur [the Mughals] that my mother planted in me.

From this story my fellow disciple may draw the moral that if the ladies of his household explain religion, faith, or even worldly aspirations in appealing ways before small children, the children will never forget them and from the start will become equipped with a virtue of strong fidelity.[16]

[A Lesson on Literacy and Self-Sufficiency]   My father knew the Qur'ān by heart, but he was unable to read or write Urdu. Once, my elder brother was away on a trip, and a letter came from him so that my father had it read out by a person who was an old enemy of our family. Although it had been a necessity, my father remained sorry about this for a long time thereafter. When I came home from school and detected his sorrow, I also made a sad face and sat beside him. At that time I was eight years old. Perhaps my father took my action well, and he began to smile and said, "You must quickly learn to read so that we will no longer need anyone else to read and write for us. Look how I didn't learn to read or write, with the result that today I had to show our long-standing enemy the letter from your brother." I asked, "Father, who is that enemy?" So my father told his name and then the names of all the members of his family, and said those people and their forefathers have been long-standing enemies of us and our ancestors. They have always had more money and more strength in numbers than us, while we have always maintained some distance from them.

I said, "My teacher [Mawlvī Sāhib] says that it is a sin to perpetuate resentment and enmity toward anyone." My father said, "Your teacher has spoken the truth. However, when some other person unnecessarily tries to harm you, then being intimidated and not responding to him is also a sin. Our forefathers were brave and a brave person can never be intimidated."

On hearing this pronouncement, I was primarily affected by two things. One, my desire to read and write increased even more. Second, animosity toward the persons that my father had named as enemies became imprinted on my heart as if etched in stone.

I need to speak frankly before my fellow disciples about this incident[, which indicates] that jealousy and enmity are very bad traits. Whatever advice my father had given me was the legacy of a family tradition that he passed on to me. I now see this from two aspects. The first is that thoughts of enmity toward any other person should be avoided and one should try only to safeguard himself from their attacks. In this manner, someday the enemies will automatically become friends. The second idea is that the lesson that can be derived from the wars in Europe and among great powers is that animosity can also make a people strong and alert, so as to instigate progress and instill the drive to attain glory. If the people of a country have no foes, they lose the essence of progress. Doubtless, the European War has taught the lesson that destiny and its Creator have complete control over human affairs and that, without the Divine will, worldly power will be of no avail, as we have observed and will see in the future. The fact is that extremely powerful and invincible nations were defeated and conquered. However, I think that other developments are still in process. Ultimately the nation that relies on God will be successful, and at the same time physical power must be rallied to contest the animosity of the opponent.[17]

Travel to the Hindu Pilgrimage Sites   In 1323/1905 and 1324/1906 Khāksār Sāhib's teachings instilled in me a desire to meet Hindu fakirs and visit the Hindu pilgrimage sites.[18] Leaving Delhi, I first went to Mathura and Brindavan and spent some time in the company of the fakirs who lived there. On this trip, my only baggage was a blanket, a bag, and a long colored shirt.

From Mathura I traveled to Ayodhya, Benares, Gaya, Bodhgaya, Hardwar, Rishikesh, and other sites. I visited their famous temples and met some fakirs.[19]

[Nizāmī then explains that he subsequently published only a few anecdotes about this lengthy trip, scattered in various publications. A full book about it that he wrote was never published because his opponents within the clan wanted to use his positive interest in Hinduism against him. Nizāmī did in fact publish a number of books explaining elements of Hinduism, including one on the story of Krishna and a few books about basic Hindu teachings. Nizāmī concludes his "worldly" autobiography with a reflection on the process of its composition.]

Whenever I write the daily account of my life, I feel as if I am also writing in a journal of self-knowledge, because when I review it, the account of income and expenditure comes into my mind. Thus this writing of my life story—and if I live longer, it will be continued—will disclose the accounts of my life. Readers can understand that in composing this book, I have knocked at the door of self-knowledge.[20]

[From the Spiritual Autobiography (Lāhūtī Āp Bītī)]   Listen carefully, O dweller in the human plane (*nāsūt*), trapped in the cage of perceptions and ideas, afflicted by sights, sounds, and smells. Listen to me, but do not look at me. You have just read, seen, heard, or been told about Khwāja Hasan

Nizāmī's autobiography, and you heard and understood this with the ear, understanding, and imagination of *nāsūt*.

This was Khwāja Hasan Nizāmī's description of the cage in which his spirit and senses are confined, in that he walked about in the world, ate, drank, laughed, cried, slept, awakened, and was seen. However, these events related to a puppet that walked about on the earth, a misperception at the human plane of sight and sound that imagines that it is the real Khwāja Hasan Nizāmī. However, Khwāja Hasan Nizāmī, and every other human being, is neither body nor spirit nor words nor states. He perceives by means of his body while he is absolutely distinct from it. . . .

Come to *lāhūt* [spiritual/divine reality], put on the glasses of *lāhūt*, and now listen to my autobiography. When I say that Khwāja Hasan Nizāmī was born, that he drank milk and cried, laughed, and lay unconscious, helpless in this mother's lap for a time, I am referring in a general way to the human (*nāsūtī*) plane and a form known as Khwāja Hasan Nizāmī [who] was born, and so on. However, from the perspective of the highest, divine plane (*lāhūt*), this is not Khwāja Hasan Nizāmī. Rather, Khwāja Hasan Nizāmī, and every other human being, is a ray from the divine essence, not in itself the very being of God—but after God, higher and more significant than every other thing. The divine essence comes first, followed by the spiritual essence of humanity, then the realm of spirits, then the world of physical bodies.[21]

[In this final brief section of his book, Nizāmī builds on the famous verses of the Sufi poet Rūmī:

I died as a mineral and became a plant,
I died as plant and rose to animal,
I died as animal and I was Man.
Why should I fear? When was I less by dying?
Yet once more I shall die as Man, to soar
With angels blest; but even from angelhood
I must pass on: all except God perishes.

Nizāmī therefore recounts his own imaginative journey through these five stages from the inanimate realm to the level of humanity. He depicts how the soul has always been present in spiritual form as it rises or even evolves to human stature. Even in human form the soul witnesses and somehow participates in the entire progression of human history from the earliest prophetic missions up to his own age of the First World War. After detailing his experiences in mineral and animal realms, he writes, for example, of human events:]

Who, other than I, was there during the fight between Cain and Abel?

It was I who was called Noah, and the creation was submerged by water before my own eyes. On the same day that I was Moses, I was also speaking with the tongue of Pharaoh, although I am something distinct from either of them.

Jesus was called "the breath of God" because I was Jesus, and I said with the tongue of Jesus, "Rise by the permission of God." It was I who brought the word "Recite" to be proclaimed in the cave of Hira', and it was I who recited, "*Iqra'*" (96:1). I defeated Abū Jahl at the battle of Badr, and my face was wounded by a stone at the battle of Uhud. . . . [22]

At Karbala' my parched throat was slit by a dagger. There also I was that dagger, and yet I was distinct from either one of them.

My name is Khālid, my name is Timur, and Nādir [Shāh],[23] I am both Mahmūd of Ghazna, and I am also called the idol at Somnath.[24] I am also Kaiser Wilhelm and Hindenburg—and King George and Lloyd George, and Marshall Foch is also my name! The ones you called Mr. Rowlatt and Mr. Gandhi were none other than me.[25]

[In his portrayal of the various forms the soul takes, Nizāmī claims that he is propounding a vision distinct from that of the transmigration of souls. We may rather see it as an autobiographical expression of the doctrine of the Unity of Existence (*wahdat al-wujūd*) espoused by Sufis who follow the teachings of Ibn 'Arabī. Everything is ultimately an extension of the divine emanated into existence. Through transcending the individual ego, one may contact this unity that underlies all things. This seems to be what Nizāmī is attempting to convey in the *Lāhūtī Āp Bītī*. He continues:]

The Coming Events

After a cursory hearing of the spiritual autobiography, you should also hear what will happen to Khwāja Hasan Nizāmī in the future. After observing the mineral, vegetable, and animal, and human stages and now passing through fire, sun, the twinkling of stars, and flashing of lightning, day by day, I climb higher. And I say: "I am the Sun, I am the Moon, I am Jupiter, I am Mars, I am the lightning." Then all of a sudden I will say, "Now I have transcended the worldly elements and I am an angel." Then I will pass through the degrees and ranks of the angelic host, and after many hundreds and thousands of years I will go higher and I will fly in the veils of secrecy. I will fly to the desert of Hūt, about which nothing is known, and if it were known, it would still be impossible to write about it, and if it were possible to write about it, it would be incomprehensible, and if it could be understood, the material world would become an impossibility.[26]

The Last Seal of the Material World   Look, look! I am that very worldly man who writes about happiness and sorrow and good and bad events. In a state of trance, I don't know what I have written or who has written it or why it was written. I now wish to give a final worldly imprint to a worldly book.

I, Khwāja Hasan Nizāmī, a Muslim, the son of a Muslim, age forty-one years, do hereby declare:

That death will come at an appointed time. The angels will come at God's command and take the person's life away. One day, the time of the Great Assembly[27] will come and I will say, "Myself, my self!"

I will run toward a king with the largest banner in his hand who is calling out, "My people, my people." I will be ashamed at my bad deeds, and I will fall at his feet crying, "I have wronged myself, O my Lord."

That one who is a mercy to the community will raise me up, clasp me to his breast, and grasping the leg of the Divine Throne, will say, "Our Lord, our Lord, this is your bondservant." Then a voice will come from the Throne: "I forgive my servant through the intercession of my Beloved and my Messenger [Muhammad]."

O my Lord, please cause all to enter Your Paradise, forgive all sins, overlook all faults.

This is that same place that we have been longing for on the human plane. In the idiom of the spiritual world it is called proximity (*qurb*); it has also been termed union (*wasl*), and in calling it annihilation in the divine essence, the speaker or writer falls silent.[28]

NOTES

1. Khwāja Hasan Nizāmī, *Āp Bītī* (Delhi: Halqa-yi Mashā'ikh, c. 1920), cited hereafter as *AB* with page numbers. The text of the "spiritual" autobiography, *Lāhūtī Āp Bītī*, is the one included in this Delhi edition of the *Āp Bītī*. In the following translation, the translator's comments appear in square brackets [ ].

2. *AB* iv.

3. *AB* iv–v.

4. The *Gulistān* (*Rose Garden*), a work by the classical Persian poet Saʻdī (see selection 6 in this anthology), consists of moral tales in poetic form.

5. *AB* vi–vii.

6. The successor of a Sufi is called the "one who sits on the prayer carpet" (*sajjāda nashīn*).

7. The term used for "autobiography" in the title of this work, *Āp Bītī*, is an Urdu coinage that literally means "what has happened to oneself."

8. *AB* 1–8.

9. *AB* 13–14.

10. *Dargāh* (lit., "court") here refers to a Sufi shrine.

11. *Khatm* means "sealing" or "closing," that is, concluding an *'urs* or *dhikr* ritual by invoking the names of the founders of the Sufi order.

12. *AB* 17–18.

13. *AB* 21.

14. *AB* 24.

15. The practice of "blowing" to communicate blessings or healing is based on the practice of the Prophet Muhammad.

16. *AB* 29.

17. *AB* 34–35.

18. Khāksār Sāhib was a colleague.

19. *AB* 60.

20. *AB* 134.

21. *AB* 135.

22. Here, rather boldly, Nizāmī identifies himself with episodes from the life of the Prophet Muhammad, such as the angel announcing to him the command "Recite!" and being wounded at the battle of Uhud. Abū Jahl was a Meccan enemy of the Prophet.

23. Khālid ibn Walīd was an early Islamic military leader and hero. *Timur* refers to Tamerlane, the conqueror. Nādir Shāh, the Persian ruler who sacked Delhi in 1739, is therefore a negative military example.

24. Mahmūd of Ghazna is known as an early Muslim conqueror of northern India. The temple of Somnath was destroyed by his troops; therefore this pairing again suggests contrasted experiences.

25. *AB* 140. "Mr. Rowlatt" refers to the British judge who drafted the notorious 1919 Rowlatt Act, designed to curb seditious activities in India. Gandhi is said to have launched his peaceful-resistance, *satyagraha* movement in response to this act.

26. *AB* 143.

27. An event in Islamic eschatology when the souls are gathered for judgment after the Resurrection.

28. *AB* 145.

23 Bonbībī, Protectress of the Forest
Sufia Mendez Uddin

Bonbībī is a saint of Muslim origins whose duty as a Friend of God is to protect the people who must risk their lives in the forest known as the Sundarban (Bengali, "beautiful forest"). The largest mangrove forest in the world, the Sundarban stretches from the southeastern region of West Bengal, India, to the Haringhata River in the east in Bangladesh. Mangroves are generally located in deltaic regions where rivers meet the ocean. The trees of the mangrove, which thrive in brackish water, protect the coastline by slowing the flow of water with sediment collected from the rivers. As a result of ocean tides and river flow, the geography of the region changes drastically over time. Mapping the region poses certain challenges. Islands vanish into the waters on one side while they expand on another side. This is a rich, fertile land with many natural resources. Fishermen rely on the bounty of the Sundarban waters for their livelihood. Others collect wood, honey, and wax from deep in the forest. Still others have reclaimed forestlands for rice cultivation and to meet the lumber demands of cities and towns outside the region. Although the forest is beautiful and provides many resources, it is also a dangerous place. Here the residents must contend with fierce storms and deadly predators.

Life in the Sundarban is simple, but it is in no way easy. The people who live on the edge of the forest live also on the economic margins. There is no electricity, roads are few, and even fresh water is becoming increasingly scarce. As in other parts of the world, fishermen here face dangerous storms. But along with honey collectors and woodcutters, the fishermen face additional dangers, including the most formidable predator—the Bengal tiger. Those courageous enough to enter the forest, do so in the hope that Bonbībī, the Lady of the Forest, will protect them.

Human habitation of the mangrove forest dates back to the eleventh/

seventeenth century. The forest was much larger then, reaching the out-skirts of the present-day city of Kolkata in the west. As more and more of the lands were reclaimed for cultivation and timber, the forest diminished in size. In the more recent past, population pressures and lack of jobs in other areas have also brought more people to the Sundarban, where they have sought to eke out a livelihood on the margins of society. Bonbībī is little known outside the Sundarban, while within the region her name is familiar to Muslim and Hindu alike. Bonbībī figures in the lives of the people because they consider her one of the more potent sources of protection.

Some of the better-known Muslim saints of Bengal include historical figures such as Khān Jahān Alī, Bāyazīd Bistāmī (who was never actually in the region), and Shah Jalāl, all of whom have *mazārs*, or tombs, within larger compounds that include mosques where people revere their memory. Among the many activities at these shrines, people make vows and seek the aid of the saint. In contrast to these other saints, Bonbībī has no *mazār*, though being a "mythic" figure is no bar to having a *mazār*. Villagers access her power via the *gunin* or fakir who accompanies working parties into the forest.[1] At his disposal are what he calls Arabic *mantras* that he recites and a number of rituals he performs.[2] Hindu venerators of Bonbībī also access her at *thaans*, or shrines. These house clay images of the saint and other characters associated with her story, including her brother, Shāh Jangali, who acts as her assistant, and Dukkhe, the first person she ever saved in the Sundarban. (See Figure 10.) Both Muslims and Hindus believe her to be a superhuman power in the forest, and therein lies her broad appeal. With her brother as her sidekick she slips easily into the form seen so frequently among the goddesses of Bengal, partially explaining her familiarity to Hindus, and in fact is often understood to function as, and is treated as if she were, a Muslim "goddess," without any sectarian uneasi-ness. Because Bonbībī is a figure of tremendous power, she is worshiped (with Bengali-style *puja*) in whatever conception is locally convenient.

Below is an excerpt of the birth episode of Bonbībī as rendered in *Jaharnāma (Tale of the Sublime Manifestation of Grace)*, Muhammad Khāter's 1889 narrative of the exploits of Bonbībī. Muhammad Khāter was a well-respected writer of *puthi* from the village of Govindapur in South 24 Parganas, West Bengal, with no fewer than thirteen of these books to his credit. *Puthi* is a genre popular in the thirteenth/nineteenth cen-tury, a form that was chapbook in size and thus easy to print in pages that were multiple of folds of paper (8, 16, 24, 32, etc.). Inexpensive and easily circulated, they were frequently reprinted with no indication of printing

Figure 10.   Shrine of Bonbībī, Southern Bangladesh. Bonbībī, with her brother Jangali (on her right), holds the hand of a young boy named Dukkhe (lit. "sorrow"), whom she has rescued from the forest. The bearded figure on the right is likely the villainous Dakkin Roy, who had threatened to harm Dukkhe. Photograph by Sufia Mendez Uddin.

dates. In the case of Khāter's *Jaharnāma*, I have been unable to locate a copy bearing the initial date of printing. Nearly all of the thirteenth/nineteenth-century *puthi* are in *payar* (rhymed couplets) and *tripadi* (rhymed triplets)—reminiscent of older manuscripts, but with a more colloquial and yet labored style that sought to introduce and Islamicize the Bengali language.[3] Although the language of *puthi* is sometimes called Dobhashi (Bilingual) Bangla, it is Bengali with an extensive use of Arabic, Persian, and Urdu. *Puthi* were directed to a Bengali Muslim audience, and the topic was always Islamic. Themes tended toward moral stories of basic Islamic instruction or retellings of Arabic and Persian hagiographies, including saints specific to Bengal such as Bonbībī in her *Jaharnāma*.

Muhammad Khāter's rendering of this story is one of the most important among the people of the Sundarban region of Bangladesh and India. Many people keep copies of the *Jaharnāma* in their homes, and during the annual Bonbībī festival, the *Jaharnāma* is recited aloud publicly. Below is the story of Bonbībī's birth and how she received her divine charge and arrived in the Sundarban. Bonbībī is not a saint who teaches individuals the Path to Allāh, but a saint whom God has asked to provide physical protection to those who seek it.

A brief summary of the events that preceded Bonbībī's birth provides context for the story that follows. Muhammad Khāter begins the story by introducing a Meccan couple, Berahim (Ibrāhīm) and Phulbībī, who wanted to have children but could not. One day Phulbībī suggested to her husband that he go to the Prophet's grave and pray for children. Berahim prayed at Muhammad's grave, and the Prophet came to him. Muhammad consulted Fātima, his daughter, and she in turn, consulted the eternal Qur'ān. The Prophet came back to Berahim and informed him that Fātima said he would have two children, a boy and girl, but only if he took a second wife. With that bittersweet news, Berahim returned to his home. Upon hearing the outcome, Berahim's wife was devastated. In the end she agreed to her husband taking a second wife, but in return she made him promise to fulfill some unspecified future wish. Although she had nothing particular in mind at the time, Berahim nonetheless agreed without condition. The translation picks up with the wedding of Berahim to his second wife, Golalbībī.

TRANSLATION

The Wedding between Berahim and Golalbībī

Happily, Fakir Jalīl Shāh assisted Berahim with his wedding regalia. Berahim invited all of the neighborhood people to accompany him to the wedding ceremony. Everyone sat together for the *majlis* [assembly] in which Berahim and Golal were joined in marriage. In order to ensure that the correct procedures were followed, one *ukil*[4] and two witnesses were sent to the bride. After getting Golal's consent, the happy couple appeared before the *majlis*. With the proposal from the *ukil*, the *kazi* (Ar. *qādī*)[5] married Berahim and Golal. The happy couple put their hands together and prayed.[6] Everyone in attendance gave their blessings to the bride and bridegroom and said their goodbyes. Berahim enjoyed having sex with his new bride in the home of his father-in-law.[7] They remained there enjoying each other's company for several days. After some time had passed, young Berahim took his new wife to his own home. Phulbībī was home when they arrived, and Berahim put Golal, his new bride, in Phulbībī's trust. Upon seeing her co-wife (*shatin*), Phulbībī became jealous. Her heart burned like the heat of the fire. The calm Berahim did not say a word, though he noticed Phulbībī's jealousy. Phulbībī soon grew silent, and Berahim passed his time keeping his two wives apart in their own rooms. Berahim enjoyed sexual relations with both of his wives. "Look, see how Allāh created fun!" [the poet exclaims to the audience].

Meanwhile, Bonbībī and Shāh Jangali were in heaven. God gave an order to the brother and sister. Allāh said, "In the name of Golal, wife of Berahim, go to her home and be born. Your glory and splendor will be in the low-lying region of the powerful Ray and Gazi. Listen, Bonbībī, at this time bow down." In reverence of Allāh, the sister and brother responded, "Hearing your command, we will go into the world. As brother and sister we will never suffer humiliation. Our full support comes from your word. Without you [God], no one can be saved." Bonbībī and Shah Jangali then departed for their mother's womb in order to be born into this world. On that night, Berahim was with Golalbībī and they happily had sex. The two of them [Bonbībī and Shāh Jangali] filled their father's head with air. In the form of a dot they entered their mother's womb. With Allāh's kindness and in the cloak of darkness, the brother and sister grew over time. One or two months were spent in this way. Then Golalbībī came to know of her condition. "Berahim, listen carefully with your heart. With Allāh's blessing, I think I may have become pregnant. Hearing this, Berahim was overjoyed and so he gave thanks to Allāh. The humble author says that in the mother's womb Bonbībī continues to grow day by day.

In the first month there was the dot in the water, and no one knew this. In the second month there was visible blood. Gradually a sign of the small lump developed. This is how they were created.

Then after three months there were veins, then generation of veins, bones, and flesh. And on the flesh, there appeared hands, legs, and backside. In the appropriate places there were arteries, fat, etcetera. In the fifth month the five senses came into being. Nothing remains to be done; nose, face, eyes, ears were made. Life came into this little body, but it cannot stay here much longer, the low-lying region calls. "Hū hū" is the sound it makes; no one can stop the birth.[8] It is the play of the sticky thing. In the sixth month, veins and bones come together. The body becomes pure. In the seventh month the gender becomes clear; the child is moving inside. The ninth month, the baby does not want to stay in darkness and wants to open his eyes. When it became the tenth month, it suffered a lot of pain in the womb. It said, "I don't want to stay here any longer. Now going out of the womb, opening my eyes, I see the way of the world." Humble Khāter says: at the feet of Bonbībī, who is Friend of God.

The Story of Golalbībī's Exile

In the womb of her mother, Bonbībī grew larger and larger everyday. The ninth month passed, and when the tenth month arrived, Phulbībī said to Berahim, "Listen, dear husband, I have something to tell you now. At the time of your wedding you gave me a pledge, now you must fulfill that pledge. Berahim said, "My darling wife, I'm listening; tell me what you want." Phulbībī said, "I want you to send Golalbībī into exile." Berahim was devastated. "Alas, what sufferings have come to me. My hands are tied in this terrible pledge. In deep sadness I got married at an old age, and my wife got pregnant with Allāh's blessing. I had a great desire to have children, so how can I send them into exile?" Berahim asked Phulbībī, "Bībī, how could you say these words? She is helpless and pregnant. How can I send her to the forest? Allāh will become unhappy with what you have asked of me. Ultimately, should I fulfill my promise, I will become a great sinner. Take back what you have said and Allāh will forgive me. Except for this, I will give you whatever you want." Phulbībī retorted, "Except for this, there is nothing else I want from you. Knowing that Allāh is present, you gave this pledge. For that reason, you must fulfill my pledge."

Hearing Phulbībī's reminder of his pledge, Berahim found himself at a loss. Berahim then began to wonder how he could fulfill his promise. How could he send pregnant Golalbībī into the forest? This is how he began to contemplate the sin he would commit. On his way to Golalbībī's room he began to cry. Tearfully, he embraced her and said to Golalbībī, "Your in-laws and sister-in-law are not here to nurse you. Let me take you to your father's home. At your father's home you will give birth to your children, and your mother will nurse you." Golalbībī was pleased to hear her husband's suggestion and rose up to go with her husband. They departed and Berahim's heart grew heavy as he walked ahead. After some distance they reached a forest, and by this time Golalbībī had become weak. Golalbībī asked her husband why they had left the road and come into this forest. Berahim replied, "I will tell you. There is a *mazār* of a *walī* here. I made a *manat* [vow] at the time of our wedding that if my wife gets pregnant, I will visit the shrine in the company of my wife.[9] I will make a visit to the grave of the blessed, and that is why I left the road to come into the forest."

Golalbībī accepted his response. After going some distance, she sat under a tree to take rest. Golalbībī said to her husband, "I can't walk anymore. The pain in my belly has grown more intense." She then spread her hand-kerchief on the ground. She said the name of God and the Prophet as she lay there. With the gentle breeze she began to feel comfortable and soon after fell asleep. Berahim saw that she was sleeping and began to scheme. He realized in the forest they were alone. He decided to leave her there and return home. But before doing so, he called out to his sleeping wife three times: "Get up, my wife, or else I'm leaving this place." She was in such a deep slumber, she did not hear her husband. Berahim then implored Allāh, "Dear God, you cannot blame me. I called my wife many times and she does not respond." At this moment all kindness in Berahim was lost, and he made up his mind to leave. Berahim returned home to Phulbībī, who happily took good care of him.

Meanwhile, in the forest, Golalbībī was lying down. After some time she awoke from her deep sleep to find Berahim gone. Golalbībī was at a complete loss as to what to do. In desperation, she cried out "Oh, no, no!" and hit her head, crying hysterically. She said "Alas, what danger has come to me? What will happen? Where will I go in this forest? My husband brought me here through deception and left me here alone in the forest. Is this what you had in mind, my Beloved? You pushed me into the fires of sorrow? Women are helpless. Worse, I am pregnant with no one to help me. How could you leave me in such a condition in the forest? I realize now that men's intentions are incomprehensible. When the time comes, you are merciless. And when a woman makes a mistake in difficult times, then she is alone. I have come to understand that everything in the world is a game of fate. In good times we have lots of friends, and in bad, we have none. In every condition I see that only Allāh is our friend and no one else. God looks after us in good times and bad. There is no one else who is as merciful as him." Saying this, she raised her hands to Allāh. With extreme sadness Golalbībī tearfully begged Allāh for mercy. "Oh Allāh, you are a sea of kindness. Except for you, there is no one in this forest. I have fallen into danger; bestow your mercy on me. Send me help to be rid of this danger." Golalbībī then became unconscious and fell to the ground. Allāh was merciful to Golalbībī. Allāh ordered four heavenly creatures to come down. The four stood around Golalbībī. She opened her eyes and saw the four female creatures standing around her. Golalbībī asked them, "Who are you? Where did you come from?" They replied, "We live in the forest and saw you alone and in need of help, so we came to help you. We will stay here together with you." They cared for Golalbībī and brought food from Heaven to feed her.

Ten months passed and the labor pains began. With the force of labor pains Golalbībī tossed and turned. The heavenly creatures reassured her by saying, "Don't be afraid. Allāh is kind to you. In a short time you will

give birth here." Soon after, Bonbībī was born. With Allāh's order she was
put on the soil. Everyone rejoiced. Slowly Shāh Jangali was born. At one
time, brother and sister had shared the same womb, and now with Allāh's
order the two were born. Golalbībī took one look at her newborn twins,
and her pain disappeared. She was absorbed with looking at them, during
which time the four heavenly creatures had returned to Heaven. When
Golalbībī raised her head, she realized the heavenly creatures were gone.
It was at that moment that Golalbībī realized that Allāh had helped her.
She took the two newborns in her lap and wondered, "Where will I go?"
Finally she decided she would leave her two infants in the forest. She said
her goodbyes and said, "Whatever God does will be their fate. At that
moment a doe arrived. Incredibly, the doe asked Golalbībī, "How can you
leave your children in the forest after carrying them in your womb? No
one is as cruel as you in this world. How could you behave in such a way?
My child was six months old when she died, and I carried her dead body
and I am just a beast of the jungle. I eat grass and leaves. I can't imagine
not seeing my dead child's face. How could you leave your children in the
forest? How can you be so cruel?" After saying these words, the doe did
not wait for response; she just went deeper into the forest.

Golalbībī pondered the doe's words. She wondered how she would raise
two children. She concluded it would be impossible, and so she would have
to leave the girl for the sake of the boy. Golalbībī was certain that she and
the boy would not survive long without food. Allāh is all the shelter they
have. Allāh chooses whom he wants to live and whom he wants to die. If
Allāh does not kill the infant girl and keeps her alive, surely he will send
the female child a helper. Golalbībī departed, leaving Bonbībī crying and
alone in the forest. Looking at her mother, Bonbībī said to herself, "Oh
mother, you have great fondness for the boy. You did not show any loving
kindness to your daughter, because she is a girl. In one womb brother
and sister were born. In one's fate there is kindness, and in the other's
there is none." In the end, Golalbībī left Bonbībī in the forest. Golalbībī
departed with Jangali, Bonbībī's brother, in her arms. She walked aimlessly through the forest. They soon became hungry and ate fruit and
leaves of the jungle. [The poet speaks directly to the audience:] See there
who is raising Bonbībī? When Bonbībī's mother cruelly left her in the forest, in tears, Bonbībī prayed to Allāh. "Oh Allāh, be merciful to me. You
sent me to this world, now with your mercy look after me." God was kind
to Bonbībī. He commanded all the deer in the forest, "Bonbībī is crying
in the forest, go all of you and raise her." With Allāh's command all of
the deer went to Bonbībī's side and fed her milk. This is how Shāh Jangali

and Bonbībī grew up separately in the forest. Muhammad Khāter says everyone shows kindness to those who are Friends of Allāh. In no place is there any need to pity Allāh's Friends. With Allāh's glory everything turns out well.

The Story of the Farewells of Bonbībī, Shāh Jangali, Their Mother, and Father and the Trip to Medina to Become Murīds

At God's command, the deer in the forest looked after Bonbībī. The heavenly creatures carried her around as a mother carries her child on her lap or in her arms. Whatever fruit they found in the forest, they would take and feed Bonbībī. Golalbībī and Shāh Jangali also lived in the forest. Whatever fruit they could find, the mother and son happily ate. Bonbībī and Shāh Jangali, brother and sister, separated at birth—the two were raised apart in the forest. They did not see or hear from each other for seven years. When the two became old enough, Allāh gave the following command, "Go to the city of the swamp forest."

[Poet speaks directly to the audience:] Now, all of you, listen to something I'm going to tell you about Berahim. One day he was remembering the two [his abandoned wife and unborn child]. Bitterly he said to Phulbībī, "Because of your desire I deserted Golalbībī in the forest. Without any wrongdoing on her part, I exiled her. So much time has passed, and I have never searched for them. I am a great sinner. How will I explain my behavior to Allāh on Judgment Day?" Angrily, he said, "You stay in your house, Phulbībī. I am going to search for them in the forest." With a heavy heart, Berahim left to search for Golalbībī. He went to the forest, and after some time he found Golalbībī. He saw her sitting under a tree with Jangali. They looked sad and in a poor state of health. Berahim cried and held her in his arms. He exclaimed, "My sin is great. What I did to you was my fate and God's commandment. Please forgive my sin and listen to me my darling. I have been searching for you for a long time and could not find you anywhere. What has happened cannot be changed. Please, get up, my dear wife; let us return home." Golalbībī asked, "Why do you tell lies? I have learned a lot about your mind. You are the kind of husband who abandons his wife in the forest and happily returns home. Now after so much time has passed since exiling your pregnant wife, you come and search for her?" Berahim pleaded, "Dear wife, I say to you, who can change the writings of Allāh? It was written in our fate, and so it happened this way. Now let us return to our home with our son." Golalbībī was satisfied with his answer, and with Jangali in Berahim's arms they departed the forest. [Poet speaks directly to the audience:] Look, who can understand Allāh's whim?

At the time, Bonbībī was still living inside that very same forest. Berahim, Jangali, and Golalbībī were nearing the area where Bonbībī lived when Bonbībī caught a glimpse of her brother and ran toward them. She shouted, "Where are you going, brother Shāh Jangali? We do not need the shelter of our parents anymore. We were together as brother and sister in Heaven. Our glory will be in the muddy, low-lying region. This is God's commandment to us now. Come on, let's go to the swamp forest." Hearing these words, Shāh Jangali leapt from his father's arms. It had been a long time since Bonbībī had seen her brother. They tried to make their parents understand, and besought them, "Leave the two of us and go home. It is Allāh's command that we should go to the swamp forest. For that reason we were born in your home. We will have a *murshid* for the sake of glory." Hearing this, Golalbībī's eyes soon flowed with tears. Crying hard, she said, "My child, my child, are you leaving me? I have given you shelter in my womb for ten months and ten days. In this world no one is as unfortunate as me. At the time of my death who will recite the *kalima* [*shahāda*, profession of faith]? At the time of my death who will give me my white cloth for my grave?" Berahim and Golalbībī cried at the thought of the separation from their children. Bonbībī tried to console them. She said to her parents, "Go home and don't cry anymore. If we forget our duty because of your love, how will we respond on the Day of Judgment?" Finally, mother and father understood and said their farewells. In order to become *murīds*, the two went to Medina. Both Berahim and Golal cried as they returned home.

Bonbībī took Shāh Jangali with her. After some time they reached Medina. They became *murīds* of Hasan's son.[10] Afterward, they went to Fātima's grave to offer their prayers. With tears in their eyes they said, "Dear mother, please pray for us. With your blessings, we will go to the low-lying region. Upon us, dear mother, give your blessing so that we do not suffer in the forest." At that moment a bodiless sound came from the grave, "Listen Bonbībī, I say to you, show respect to my master, then go to the muddy low-lying region. Allāh is great. Allāh has created 18,000 souls in the low-lying region. During their times of trouble, they will call out to you for help. They will call you mother. You will respond with kindness and rescue them." Bonbībī replied, "Dear mother, I give you my pledge I will do this. Please bestow your kindness upon me." After saying this at Blessed Fātima's grave, Bonbībī completed her *ziyārat* with great satisfaction. Bonbībī and Shāh Jangali departed for the city in the low-lying region.[11]

NOTES

1. *Gunin* is a Bengali term that may be translated as "skilled." It implies something akin to mystical learning. The other term often used is fakir (Arabic *faqīr*).

2. The fakirs of the Sundarban describe as Arabic mantras a set of Qur'ānic or Qur'ānically derived phrases they recite for protection. Like Sanskrit mantras, these formulas are short and are, fakirs believe, endowed with divine power to protect. For more on Arabic mantras, see Sufia Mendez Uddin, "Beyond National Borders and Religious Boundaries" in *Engaging South Asian Religions: Boundaries, Appropriations, and Resistances,* ed. Peter Gottschalk and Matthew Schmalz, (Albany: State University of New York Press, forthcoming).

3. For a discussion of the language of *puthi,* see Rafiuddin Ahmed's *The Bengal Muslims, 1871–1906: A Quest for Identity* (Delhi: Oxford University Press, 1981).

4. The lawful representative of Berahim for the purpose of marriage.

5. The *kazi* is the Muslim interpreter of law, usually a local judge.

6. This traditional prayer is for the soul of the Prophet Muhammad.

7. This sentence is a clear example of the entertainment value associated with this genre. Although the story deals with topics we would call religious, it does not mean that the text can't be fun at the same time. *Puthi* were intended for recitation and provided entertainment to villagers of all ages.

8. "Hū, Hū" (Arabic for "He, He") seems to allude to a common appellation for God.

9. Requesting the birth of a child is a common vow in South Asia.

10. Bengali *puthi* literature contains many Shī'ī influences, as evidenced here. Shī'ī especially show a great deal of reverence for Fātima and the other members of the Holy Five (members of the Shī'ī "family"). In addition, there is the fact that Bonbībī and her brother become *murīds* of the son of Hasan, the second Shī'ī imam).

11. I am grateful to Tony K. Stewart for all his advice on issues to consider in composing this translation.

24 The Tales of Mānik Pīr

Protector of Cows in Bengal

Tony K. Stewart

As early as the late seventh/thirteenth century, Sufi saints began to leave a permanent impression on the cultural landscape of Bengal, and by the eleventh/seventeenth century the stories of those saints and their miraculous powers populated every storyteller's repertoire. Not surprisingly, many stories are attached to historical figures, such as Shāh Jalāl and Badr Shāh Pīr, but an equally large number of tales narrate the exploits of the less historical, mythic *pīrs*. They are mythic only in the sense that their stories do not yield to the standards of positivist evidence that still seem to rule these classifications of history for many scholars of South Asia. Yet they are very real to the many millions who have heard and continue to circulate their tales. Like myths everywhere, they tell a truth, but that truth is conveyed in a simple narrative form.

These *pīrs* work for the people in their everyday lives, and in appreciation for their help, any number of devotees have undertaken charitable works—building a ghat, erecting a *masjid*, feeding the poor, or establishing a *dargā* (Persian *dargāh*, often locally called *samādhisthān*, especially in West Bengal) to honor the *pīr's* memory. *Dargās* quickly become pilgrimage sites, perpetuating the cult. Today one routinely hears fishermen extolling the powers of Khwāja Khizr, who aids those who make their living on the labyrinthine waters of the Sunderban's mangrove swamps or farther out to sea, fishing in the Bay of Bengal. One often hears of the exploits of Pāñc Pīr or Five Pīrs, who dispense a general aid to those in need, and of course the deeds of more marginal figures such as the Sunderban's Bonbībī, a powerful female figure who appears to protect woodcutters and honey-gatherers from tigers in the Sunderban, or Olābībī, who, residing deep in the forests, manages cholera and typhoid. All of these figures tend to be local or at best regional, but two mythic *pīrs* among this set seem unconstrained to specific locales and lay claim to the population at large: Mānik Pīr, protector of cows, and Satya Pīr, giver of wealth.

Judging from the size and extent of the literature that has circulated in manuscript and printed form, especially during the great efflorescence of printing in the mid- to late thirteenth/nineteenth century, Satya Pīr is easily counted most popular. Part of his broad appeal is that he is portrayed as a mendicant of uncertain provenance who wears a mixed garb, signaling an appeal to both Muslim and Hindu sensibilities. Appropriately enough, he is routinely called upon, if not worshiped directly, by people of all religious persuasions in a cross-sectarian allegiance, worship (i.e., Bengali-style *puja*) undertaken primarily for the attainment of wealth.[1]

Mānik Pīr is less well known and somewhat more specialized. He caters to cowherds and barren women while extending his power over healing and fertility. He appears in both image and function in the mold of a traditional Sufi saint: he is frequently depicted with a light "cloud-colored" complexion, hair long and curly, a full beard, staff in one hand, string of beads in the other. His garb varies, but generally he wears the patchwork cloak characteristic of Sufi mendicants, always with a simple cap that is, according to tradition, knitted by his own hand.[2] But for such a generic figure of Sufi piety, this mythic *pīr* has left an indelible imprint on the physical landscape.

Numerous tombs, or *dargās*, are dedicated to Mānik, which in form and function tend to conform to those of healing *pīrs* throughout northern and western India. Mānik shares the *dargā* of Badakhān Gājī both in Ghutiyāri and in Pātharādhāpur, as well as claiming more than a dozen discrete tombs throughout the mangrove swamps of West Bengal and Bangladesh.[3] The types of worship one finds in these *dargās*, each with presiding fakir, are again consonant with what one finds at tombs all over South Asia: small offerings of usually food, commonly *śirni* (rice flour, banana, sugar, milk), in exchange for the blessings of the *pīr*, especially the health and fecundity of cattle and family. Itinerant mendicants actively spread that same umbrella of protection to the families of Mānik's worshipers when they wander through the villages singing of his prowess. Typical was the visit of such a mendicant recorded by G. N. Dās: after singing of Mānik's exploits for alms, he tied a black thread around the wrist of each family member, wrote a verse in red ink on a piece of paper, dropped the paper into a glass of water, and then instructed the family members and all the domestic animals to drink, after which the paper itself was plastered on the sill of the house's front door, with promises of greater fortune and weal.[4] The physical instantiation of God's blessings through the ingestion of the

Qur'ānic verse dissolved in water is perfectly in accord with Mānik's powers as a dispenser of medicines and a healer.

Mānik's vocation as veterinarian is one of the most prominent features of his tales, and the singers are often themselves repositories of this practical veterinary knowledge, thereby extending the power of the *pīr*. The flavor and detail comes through in the following excerpt from a popular performance piece titled *Mānik Pīr Gān* by Satyen Rāy:

> Always remember the name of Mānik Jinda Pīr. He who, first thing in the morning, sweeps and cleanses his house, and then lights lamps at night for everyone's illumination, has a home where Lakṣmī, the goddess of fortune, resides. He who, in that same way, cleans his cowsheds in the morning, and in the evening lights lamps for his cattle, will never experience problems with his herd. Those who do not properly care for their cattle will discover them restless at night, lackadaisical in the morning, and often incapable of giving milk. . . . Courtesy of Mānik's intervention, sixty-four medicines are prescribed for cattle: sixty-four unique treatments targeting sixty-four different diseases. If Mānik is appeased and his guidelines followed, diseases can be avoided altogether. . . . Should a cow have a cut or bruise on its tongue, or a festering sore or wound on its neck, take salt in hand and rub it into the wound, massaging it thoroughly. In the rainy season, cows often suffer the painful itching and swelling from chilblain; to counter it, keep cattle in a dry place and administer phenol or carbolic disinfectant. When cows suffer dyspepsia and gas in the stomach, which often leads to excessive flatulence and even dysentery, feed them bamboo leaves mixed with the husks of paddy. When they suffer fever and tremble with chills, mix the raw *jhiṅgā* gourd with opium and make the cow chew it, then hold the mouth shut and blow the smoke up its nose. Not long will the cow be better and the fever dissipated.[5]

Additional cures are prescribed, as well as formulas for proper food mixtures according to local flora and the seasons, but punctuated always with the admonition, Look after your cows with love and affection and Allāh will be pleased with you.

The notion that cows were somehow special to God resonates strongly with the general Hindu esteem for cows, and in Bengal, *pīrs* are strongly associated with Vaishnavism, Satya Pīr even being incorporated as an *avatāra* of Krishna.[6] This is not to assert a kind of naïve syncretism; rather it suggests one more way that sectarian divisions taken for granted today in contemporary political rhetoric simply do not hold.[7] But it is probably safer to speculate that the connection is more indicative of the function of *pīr*s in the general spheres of healing and fertility, which in this context means cattle (the domestic animal par excellence) and women. Mānik Pīr joins Nāth *yogīs* (*jogīs*), *samnyāsīs, vairāgīs, gājīs,* and others in the itinerant world of holy men or saints, all of whom interact for the betterment of the general population. Consequently their exploits and even physical images are often conflated. In one cycle of tales reported by Shashibhushan Dasgupta, Mānik Pīr is even depicted to have learned the veterinary trade as the disciple of Goraksanāth (with a dubious etymology suggesting he was "protector" [*raks-*] of "cows" [*go*]).[8]

In a unique tale discovered by Asim Roy titled *Mānik Pīr Gān* by Shaikh Hābil, Mānik sought to accompany Īsā (Jesus) on a healing mission, but had first to demonstrate his power. So Mānik had the fever demon Jarāsur slay Īsā; then, aided by angels, he concocted an elixir retrieved from the liver of a boy whose parents had already lost seven other children, and with this he revived Īsā, then revived the boy.[9] While one might read Mānik's slaying and reviving of Īsā as a not-too-subtle commentary on the power of their respective traditions, the theme of human sacrifice, though subsequently reversed, suggests a certain ambivalence toward the power of the "healing" *pīr*. An equally ambivalent tale is the eighteenth-century *Mānik Pīr Pāñcālī* of Muhammad Fakīr.[10] Allāh specifically recruited Mānik from among all the *pīr*s of Mecca to join Haraj Ālī in bringing under control the many diseases endemic to the South Asian subcontinent. A cowherd named Dukhiyā stole Mānik's golden shoes as he was performing his prayers, and much of the remaining episode follows Mānik as he performs miracles of physical mastery and social engineering in order to get back his footwear. Consistent with the conflation of figures, and the interchangeable characters, Dukhiyā bears strong resemblance to the similarly named cowherd in the Bonbībī cycle.[11]

The most common trope in the Mānik cycle is the punishment and instruction meted out to a rich cowherd or his wife and family for failing to proffer milk or food to the begging *pīr*. Financial ruin and physical degradation invariably result, as in the story told below from the *Mānik Pīr Kecchā,* the primary target being first the mother of Kinu and Kānu and then the brothers themselves.[12] The trope is repeated in several *pīr* cycles, including Satya Pīr's destruction of the property of Dhanañjaya the cowherd in the cycle of Sandhyāvatī.[13] Likewise the story told below of Bādsā Kāle Śāhā, who, with the aid of the *pīr*, surreptitiously fathers a son who can spit pearls, is nearly identical to the *Motilāler Pālā* of Kinkara Dās in the Satya Pīr cycle, though the motivations for the actions diverge.[14] Stock stories, of course, are the hallmark of oral literatures that at the same time suggest certain features or personal characteristics every holy figure must possess. The descriptions often blur into generic images of Sufi piety and power. These routine acts of narrative appropriation signal a shared cosmology in which Muslims and Hindus of various sorts—but here especially Sufis, Vaishnavas, and Nāths—are accommodated and integrated through shared notions of how local power operates in the world, power available to all regardless of sectarian concerns.

Crystallized by the census of 1871, urban society has over the past century come to recognize sectarian affiliation as overt political identity, with Hindus and Muslims treated separately; but the narratives of the *pīr*, which still circulate today, suggest a different sensibility altogether. Nor is this simply an urban-versus-rural phenomenon, for the clients of the *pīr*s described in these narratives are not simple cultivators, but peripheral or semiurban owners of land and cattle, or the merchants who supply them. The *pīr*s operate within a prosperous pastoralist-settlement universe and have made the easy transition to the modern cosmopolis. Importantly, their stories were circulated and printed from urban presses soon after their introduction in Calcutta and Dhaka in the thirteenth/ nineteenth century. And these stories, many of which are simply reissues of thirteenth/nineteenth-century imprints, still circulate today among an urban population as well as those outside the urban setting. The narratives themselves and what we can reconstruct of their texts' circulation and consumption suggest that the stark divisions between Muslims and Hindus that are perpetrated by popular media and radicalizing political factions do not really reflect how many Bengali speakers see and inhabit their own social world, which is a much more sophisticated and integrated cosmos.

The two-part story that follows is a retelling and considerable abridgement of a much longer tale by Munsī Mohāmmad Pijiruddīn first published in the mid-1800s. The edition consulted bears no date on the title page, but does show the date of 1872 on the back-cover advertisement for another publication from the press, the prolific publishing house of Gāosiya Lāibrerī in Calcutta (today Kolkata). Truncated retellings of this tale can be found in Dinesh Chandra Sen's *The Folk-Literature of Bengal* and in Bengali in Girīndranāth Dās's *Bāmlār Pīr Sāhitya Kathā*.[15] A recent comic book version has appeared as the first number in the new Vivalok Comic series; it includes as a postscript an additional episode titled "Murād the Beggar." This is a story of a man who has to pawn his son to feed two fakirs, one of whom turns out to be Mānik, who subsequently rewards him for his sacrifice and generosity.[16]

For those unfamiliar with Bangla spellings, note that *j* is frequently pronounced like *z*, so *namāj* is *namāz*, *wajir* is *wazir*, and so forth; and *ch* is often pronounced like *s*, so Churat Bībī is Surat Bībī.

TRANSLATION

Kumāruddīn Sāhā was a prosperous man, and his wife, Dudhbībī, was, by any standard, a beauty of the highest order. By the grace of Allāh, Dudhbībī bore her husband twins, Gaja and Mānik, and they too were of uncommon beauty. When they were born, the attending servant, Hīrā, was astonished by their perfection; in her exclamations of joy and excitement, appropriately and without guile, she importuned Dudhbībī to give copious thanks to Allāh for blessing her with such a bounty of boys. They were in her eyes truly incomparable, and they glowed with an effulgence that could only have derived from the grace of God. But Dudhbībī's beauty was physical, for inside she was a vain and arrogant woman. She snippily retorted that the boys were indeed beautiful because she was herself beautiful: Do you not see how they are perfect copies of me? Allāh has nothing to do with it, you stupid wench. And should my husband and I live out a normal life, I fully expect to produce many more of equal or surpassing beauty. . . . Hīrā was aghast, speechless, but she thought that such blasphemy could only be borne of a hubris that exceeded her mistress's matchless beauty. While Dudhbībī boasted and Hīrā silently endured the shameless bragging aimed at her ears alone, Allāh did naturally overhear every single word. He was annoyed. His wrath welled at the thought that this ignorant woman arrogated to herself the power to produce such beauty, indeed even reproduce at all, without the divine intervention of Allāh. Her audacity was insolent in the extreme, and whether stupidity or her hubris was the greater, only God knew for sure. In an instant He decided to teach the wicked Dudhbībī a lesson, so he summoned Jibrīl to deliver a suitable punishment. Strangely enough, that very night, Dudhbībī succumbed to a wasting fever and soon drifted into a coma; and just as miraculously, that fever began to dry up the overabundance of milk that had oozed from her milkpotlike breasts, until they were like so much leather, wizened, withered, and cracked.

In the morning Dudhbībī's husband, Kumāruddīn discovered his wife's pitiable condition. Seeing her mistress's illness, Hīrā begged Kumāruddīn to pray to Allāh, to petition him so that He might send relief and see to her recovery. But Kumāruddīn was not unlike his wife and he swelled with a grief that was really more of an anger, and so he declared that he would cure Dudhbībī of the disease himself: What need of God? he asked the dumbfounded maidservant. We ourselves forge our futures, and without even the help of local physicians I will heal my wife myself! . . .

And so once again the ever-vigilant Allāh listened. With each word of Kumāruddīn's bombastic blasphemy, His anger swelled. He wasted no time in dispatching Jibrīl again: Deliver to Kumāruddīn a disease as debilitating as that delivered to his stupid and arrogant wife! . . . At Allāh's direct command, Jibrīl did just that; he graced the poor man with a boiling fever accompanied by equally excruciating migraines. And so it was that Kumāruddīn and his wife, Dudhbībī, found themselves soon perilously perched on the precipice of death.

As the gravity of the situation gradually fell upon them, Kumāruddīn finally sought the help of a physician, but it was Śaytān [Satan] himself who conveniently appeared to lead him astray. For two months they had endured all manner of suffering, and they were gradually regaining their strength, shaking off the illness in an excruciatingly slow recovery. Just as they thought to be getting back on their feet, albeit still vulnerable and weak in body and mind, who did appear but Śaytān? He coyly suggested that they needed a tonic to hasten their recovery and regain their strength: wine was just the cure! And so the still feeble couple, incapacitated, incapable of distinguishing right from wrong even at the best of times, found his suggestion good and reasonable. They began to drink, a little at first, but soon emboldened, they drank more regularly and in increasing quantity. Ever so subtly did Śaytān inveigle Kumāruddīn and his wife to drink more and more by constantly extolling the intoxicant's medicinal properties. But of course, rather than improve their health, the drink only exacerbated their already precarious condition, reversing what little progress they had made in recovery. Now totally addicted and thoroughly dissipated, they lost their rational faculties altogether and launched a spending spree to savor every imaginable indulgence. Their folly soon left them penniless, for they had managed to squander the full measure of their considerable wealth. They were broke.

Reduced to utter penury, all worldly possessions frittered away, the continually drunk and forlorn Kumāruddīn summoned Hīrā the maidservant and instructed her to take one of the boys to sell. Kumāruddīn justified this drastic action by reasoning there would not be enough milk in Dudhbībī's breasts to feed one, much less two; but the real reason was that they had no other resources—the boys were all they had to sell to survive. The maid reluctantly did as she was told, knowing that it was wrong. But she had to choose, so she chose Mānik. As she headed to town, she happened across the path of one Badarjinda Śāh, a merchant-ruler of no small stature. Badar instantly divined the maidservant's overtures and offered to buy the boy. Hapless, she sold him for the princely sum of ten rupees.

Meanwhile and some distance away, Badar Śāh took the young boy home to his wife, Churat Bībī. Churat Bībī had had no children of her own, so you can imagine her joy to receive the child, and such an extraordinarily handsome boy at that. She began to raise the child as her own. Not long after, Badarjinda Śāh begged leave of her to travel for trade through the countryside. For some twelve years did he roam, one region after another, amassing wealth. Somehow, and only God knows for sure, Badarjinda Śāh managed to forget completely about his foundling son. When he did finally return home, he found, much to his surprise, his wife sleeping beside a very handsome young man, whom he failed to recognize. In his wrath at being made the cuckold, he moved to kill Mānik. Mānik pleaded with him, but he would not be moved, finally forcing the young man into a wooden chest that he bound with steel straps and an equally strong hasp. Mānik prayed to Allāh, who reassured him: Do not fight it. Enter the coffin, and no matter what happens I will retrieve you in due time—and he dispatched Jibrīl to ensure that young Mānik was safe. Badar Śāh quickly slammed shut the lid of the chest and bolted it tight, doused it with oil, then set it afire; the wood was dry and thick and so it burned steadily for three full days. Witnessing this immolation, Churat Bībī fell swooned in her grief. But by the grace of Allāh and with Jibrīl's timely intervention, the fire turned into water when it entered the chest, and evaporated steadily, keeping Mānik cool and safe from the flames that consumed the outer skin of the chest.

When after three days Badar Pīr opened the chest, he found young Mānik completely unharmed. Mānik climbed out of the box, bowed to his father, who was more than a little nonplussed, and said: By the mercy of Allāh I am safe; please now release me. Badar quickly regained his wits and realized with a profound regret—and not a little fear—that he had made a terrible mistake, and begged forgiveness. Mānik gently replied: Though I am not your son, you raised me. I have known no other parents and feel for you the affection any child would. But after being punished unjustly when innocent by the very same man I called Father, I cannot remain any longer in this world. The Lord Allāh has seen me through my ordeal and Jibrīl showed the way. It is to God I am indebted and none other. . . . And with minimal ceremony, Mānik picked up a staff and pulled on the simple garment of a mendicant, bowed deeply to the feet of Badarjinda Śāh, and then to Churat Bībī. As he took his leave, he could be heard muttering the ninety-nine qualities of Allāh. Allāh was so pleased with the devotion of the young Mānik that he bestowed on him powers beyond compare.[17] Jibrīl came as Allāh bade him and delivered instruction and power to Mānik, after which he pointed him to the city of Derāg.

In Derāg, Mānik began to preach and bear witness to the greatness of God. Constantly guided by that unseen hand, Mānik eventually found his brother, Gaja, whom he had not known before. Gaja rejoiced and joined his brother, the two setting off as wandering fakirs: each with staff in hand, striped pajamas, patchwork mantle, and loose cloth wrapped like a turban around the head. By the grace of Allāh, Mānik located an abandoned and dilapidated dinghy, by which the two brothers managed to cross the seemingly endless expanse of the river. Soon they found themselves in front of the mansion of Kāle Śāhā in that handsome city of Derāg.

As merchant *bādśāh*s [kings] go, Kāle Śāhā was among the most powerful and influential. But Kāle Śāhā had no issue, an embarrassment that left him no peace. To accompany this unfortunate condition—or perhaps causing it—Kāle Śāhā likewise placed no faith whatsoever in Allāh. And so you might imagine he could not abide the sight of fakirs, Friends of God. It was to this *bādśāh*'s house Mānik and Gaja had come. Mānik Pīr announced himself at the entrance to Kāle Śāhā's compound, crying for alms: In the name of Allāh, O' Mother, please give some food to this poor wandering beggar who has just arrived at your door! The gift of but a single grain of rice will reap a thousand grains in return, for Allāh will shower you with the food of Heaven. Turn to the merciful Allāh and you will receive the boon of a son. . . .

A maidservant named Zuina informed Kāle Śāha's wife, Rañjanā Bībī, that two fakirs were standing before the house begging food. To get the beggars to leave, the *bībī* rather mindlessly sent five small coins in the name of the Pāñc Pīrs. Mānik, however, refused to accept the coins and asked to see the *bībī* herself. Rañjanā Bībī reluctantly came out to meet the fakir, and no sooner had Mānik laid eyes on her than he pronounced: You will soon bear a son. . . . The *bībī* placed no store in the prediction and, somewhat annoyed at his intrusion into her private affairs, retorted: "You look a madman; get out of my sight! A long time ago another one of you crazy fakirs came to me and told me much the same, but look at me! Do you see a son anywhere? I will honor you only if you can give me the identical prophesy, word for word; otherwise I will take for myself whatever is in your bag and have you thrown into prison . . . and so, once started, she continued her tirade unabated. She heaped such abuse on that *pīr* that Allāh Himself began to fume. Finally the *pīr* cursed her: If I am the *pīr* I claim, you have my word that you will languish in the barren stretches of forest and swamp for twelve years and six months, living like a wild animal with no fine clothes, no prepared foods, not even a roof over your head. Time and again you will have to flee for your life, like a bird escaping a hunter. . . . When she heard this, the *bībī* was outraged and ordered her maidservant Zuina to beat the two fakirs and send them away, or better yet, just kill them on the spot. The maidservant followed her orders, but when she raised her sword to strike them, the sword would not comply. Swinging a second time, the sword magically changed course, turned wildly back on her, and sliced her to ribbons. One of the other maidservants witnessed the event and scurried off to report to the *bībī*, who was understandably afraid—but more afraid of her husband, the *bād-śāh*, than of the power of the *pīrs*. She ordered her maidservant: If you are indeed loyal to me, do not breathe a word of this to the *bādśāh*.

After meeting with his ministers and other advisers all morning, the *bādśāh* returned to his private chambers. He bowed to the feet of his mother, paying his respects, then explained to her that it was imperative for him to undertake a commercial trading voyage. He instructed his mother to look after his wife, but he said: Should she in any way bring dishonor on you or our clan, you must banish her to the forest. . . . Then Kāle Śāhā left his palace in the care of his guards . . . and the rest of his story we will hear in due time.

. . . Shortly thereafter, as Mānik Pīr was finishing the obligatory prayers of *namāj*, he prayed for the merciful guidance of Allāh. Hearing his prayer, Allāh sent his messenger Jibrīl to guide Mānik in the city of Virāta. And so it was that Mānik Pīr and Gaja Pīr soon found themselves at the house of the prosperous Kinu and Kānu Ghosh. The Ghosh brothers were exceedingly wealthy and their house was a palace, a large portion of which was dedicated as a cowshed, filled with the finest cattle imaginable. Every day they were awash in milk and cream and curd. And to comple-ment that wealth, they each had produced a beautiful young son.

The *pīrs* stood at the entrance to the compound and called out to the mistress of the house, reciting the *kalimā* in praise of Allāh. The mis-tress instructed her maid to check who was calling her so insistently. The maidservant found Mānik and his brother at the door and asked what they wanted. Mānik replied: It has been seven long days since either of us has had food or drink. Please give these two poor fakirs some milk and curd, and Allāh will show you his favor. . . . Now the woman was a maid of long standing and savvy to the ways of swindlers and all manner of riffraff that happened by her wealthy employer's house, so she knew how to react and told him: We have no milk to give, not even a drop; and with no milk, how could we provide you with alms? . . . Mānik quickly retorted: Do not lie to me! I know you have ten large measures of curd and double that amount of milk from this day's milking alone. . . . But the milkmaid paid him scant heed and reported back to her mistress. The old woman had seen a lot in her time, and she reasoned loudly to herself in the way that bombasts always seek an audience, anyone within earshot: If these *pīrs* know so much, if they can see inside houses without looking, if they can gauge wealth without counting, indeed if they can know everything there is to know—why do these self-important seers have to live by begging, clad in their stinking filthy rags? . . . Mānik overheard the insult and challenged her: Why do you pretend you have no milk and curd when we know you do? . . . Now irritated and feeling a little mischievous, she showed him a barren cow and offered him its milk: O fakir, prove your great powers! Milk this old cow and drink as much as you want from her withered dugs. . . .

At this point the *pīr* realized he was going to be tested to the limit, so he prayed to Allāh: This cow has no calves. How can I get her to produce milk? . . . At the direct command of Allāh, the messenger Jibrīl soon arrived, remaining invisible to all but Mānik and Gaja. To the old cow he led a young calf of great beauty and charm, named Manurāya, which instantly prompted her to lactate. Mānik then instructed the old lady to bring some milk pots. As Mānik tweaked and pulled the teats of the cow, two gushed creamy milk and two leaked a rich thick butter. As if by magic the *pīr* managed to fill seven large pots in quick succession, each spilling over with a thick cream, and pots of butter, too. Realizing the worth of this rich produce, the old woman had the jugs quickly hauled indoors and drove the *pīr* away. (See Figure 11.)

Sanakā, the daughter-in-law of this mean old woman—she was married to Kinu—was completely puzzled by her mother-in-law's behavior: Why did you not give food to those two beggar fakirs? Yet you steal away the very milk they conjured by their miraculous powers! . . . The old woman looked askance at her too-soft daughter-in-law and scoffed: Miracle? Miracle? You call what they did a miracle? You don't know anything, young lady; they didn't work magic, they played a trick, bringing the milk from some other place, only pretending to milk the dried up cow. Have you ever heard of a barren cow yielding such rich milk and butter? These two aren't fakirs; they are fakers. . . . And so the diatribe continued. But Sanakā would not relent: Whether they brought it from their own home or some other source, does not the milk belong to them? How can you take it away? . . . The old woman was adamant and would not back down. Though secretly she worried that these two *pīrs* may indeed know some powerful magic, her greed got the best of her.

On her own, and certainly against the wishes of her mother-in-law, Sanakā gave a small portion of her own allotment of milk to the *pīr* (see

Figure 11. The old milkmaid chases Mānik Pīr out after he has miraculously produced jugs of rich milk and butter. From *Mānik Pīr Kecchā,* courtesy of the Trustees of the British Museum. (Asia 1955. 10–8. 095.) Acquired with the support of the Art Fund.

Figure 12. Sanakā gives some of her own milk to Mānik Pīr. From *Mānik Pīr Kecchā,* courtesy of the Trustees of the British Museum. (Asia 1955. 10–8. 095.) Acquired with the support of the Art Fund.

Figure 13. After Kānu and Kinu chase Mānik Pīr away, a gold coin fallen from the *pīr's* turban turns into a cobra and bites Kinu. From *Mānik Pīr Kecchā,* courtesy of the Trustees of the British Museum. (Asia 1955. 10–8. 095.) Acquired with the support of the Art Fund.

Figure 12), and Mānik responded with a blessing: May you ever remain with your husband. . . . As he pronounced this blessing, he placed his hand on her head. The old milkmaid, who had been secretly watching, saw him touch the head of Sanakā. Off she flew to her sons Kānu and Kinu, loudly complaining that two crazy fakirs were joking and carrying on with his dear wife, Sanakā, with an intimacy that was in bad taste, if not flagrantly provocative. Given to the same outbursts as their mother, the Ghosh brothers erupted like a match set to dry tinder. They rushed outside, and Kinu wasted no time in swinging at Mānik's head, but before his punch had fully connected, the *pīr* and his brother vanished. No sooner had Mānik dematerialized than a single gold *mohar* [coin] fell from his turban. Just as greedy as his mother, Kinu paused and bent down to pick it up. Right then the *mohar* transformed into an irritated black serpent, a cobra. (See

Figure 13.) It sank its poisoned fangs into the leg of the hapless Kinu, who fell unconscious and was just as quickly dead. Everyone screamed. But, always with her wits about her, Sanakā instead turned her heart and mind toward God. She prayed, and Allāh, ever merciful to his loving followers, heard her prayer with his uncommon grace.

Meanwhile, Mānik had put on the guise of a Brahmin and just happened to find his way to the home of Kinu and Kānu. The old milkmaid was desperate for help, and when she saw the Brahmin, she latched on, begging him: O' my good young man, if you can restore the life of my son, I will give you half of all the wealth I possess! . . . In his Brahmin guise, Mānik pretended to be a healer, a master of snake bite and antidotes. So he quietly took the name of Allāh, bent over, and blew gently across the bite on the leg of Kinu, and the poison seeped out like so much water. Kinu was restored to life and sat up in a daze. The old woman's joy was short-lived, for she suddenly realized that she might have to make good on her promise to give the Brahmin half her wealth. In her distress—for it was clear by now what she valued most—she feigned to faint. Mānik, still in his guise as a Brahmin, meditated on Allāh to administer justice. Later that night, the old woman died in her sleep, and the entire herd of cattle housed in the expansive Ghosh cowsheds was consumed in a magnificent conflagration. (See Figure 14.) The calves, the heifers, the cows, and their bull all died, so many in fact that it is impossible to enumerate. (See Figure 15.) Yet again, understanding the nature of religious power and unruffled, Sanakā sought to fetch the *pīr*, Mānik, in the hope of reversing this disastrous fortune.

The young Sanakā then related to Kinu how his mother, the old milkmaid had shamefully insulted the *pīr* and then spirited away his miraculously produced milk, curd, and butter. Though a greedy and irritable young man, Kinu was not without his intellectual accomplishments, and in her words he recognized the clear pattern of cause and effect in these events. So he sent Sanakā to find and fetch the *pīr*. When Sanakā found him, however, Mānik made her wait for seven full days and seven full nights before he would entertain her petition. Sanakā submitted her request in a most respectful manner, assuming nothing, holding his ankles as she made her plea. (See Figure 16.) When Mānik was persuaded of her sincerity, he agreed to accompany her back to the house. Once there he began to pray, invoking the name and mercy of Allāh. Slowly, bit by bit, the wealth of the house was reassembled and restored. (See Figure 17.) Even more miraculously, so too did he bring back to life the cows and calves and heifers, one by one. Eventually the entire herd was restored and

Figure 14. At Mānik Pīr's prayer, the cowsheds of the Ghos family burn down. From *Mānik Pīr Kecchā,* courtesy of the Trustees of the British Museum. (Asia 1955. 10–8. 095.) Acquired with the support of the Art Fund.

Figure 15. The countless cows that died in the fire. From *Mānik Pīr Kecchā,* courtesy ofthe Trustees of the British Museum. (Asia 195 5. 10–8. 095.) Acquired with the support of the Art Fund.

Figure 16. Sanakā beseeches Mānik Pīr for help. From *Mānik Pīr Kecchā,* courtesy of the Trustees of the British Museum. (Asia 1955. 10–8. 095.) Acquired with the support of the Art Fund.

Figure 17. Sanakā's household restored upon Mānik Pīr's intervention. From *Mānik Pīr Kecchā,* courtesy of the Trustees of the British Museum. (Asia 1955. 10–8. 095.) Acquired with the support of the Art Fund.

the cowshed was overflowing with the milk-producing livestock, which immediately began to yield their bounty. (See Figure 18.)

Deeply appreciative of the restoration of his wealth, Kinu had brought and then offered Mānik the entire day's milking, ten large measures. But he was not satisfied to limit himself to such a small gift, so he pre-

Figure 18.   Mānik Pīr with
the cows resurrected through
his prayer. From *Mānik Pīr
Kecchā*, courtesy of the Trustees
of the British Museum. (Asia
1955. 10–8. 095.) Acquired with
the support of the Art Fund.

sented Mānik with the best cow from the herd and ten full *bighas*—about
three acres—of land. Mānik accepted the gifts with humility, but in turn
vouchsafed them to Kinu and instructed him to hold them in reserve:
For the general weal, when you milk your first cow with calf each day,
offer the first stream to the land in the name of Allāh. Be prosperous and
spread this message far and wide. . . . Then Mānik returned whence he
had come.[18]

. . . While Mānik and Gaja had suffered through this misadventure,
Bādśā Kāle Śāhā had made considerable progress in his trading journey
south.[19] He had reached the banks of the Āmīrāvāda River, where he had
moored his vessels. Suddenly Mānik Pīr and Gaja Pīr materialized before
the sleeping Bādśā. Mānik revealed to the somewhat befuddled man that
this particular night was a rare opportunity, for a special configuration of
the planets and stars bestowed an extraordinary power: were he to make
love to his wife that very night, she would bear him a noble son who would
in due time increase his wealth beyond measure, for every time he would
laugh in pleasure, he would spit up lustrous pink pearls of inestimable
value. . . .

Later that night, Mānik transformed himself into a majestic creature,
part swan, part horse—a flying animal. With Kāle Śāhā perched com-
fortably on his back, he flew to the private quarters of the *bādśāh*'s wife,
Rañjanā Bībī. Because he had his own key, the *bādśāh* naturally let himself in without waking anyone; he then passed the night making love to
his understandably surprised wife. As dawn approached, he mounted the
waiting swanlike creature, who winged them back to the just-waking fleet.
As he set the *bādśāh* down, Mānik reassured him that there was nothing
about which he should worry: Just go ahead with your business voyage,
and you will amass wealth sufficient to keep you comfortable for the rest
of your days; now go in the name of God and remember Him always. . . .
And so a few hours later that morning, Kāle Śāhā set sail with his crew.

Back at Derāg, Kāle Śāhā's mother, Āyemāna Bībī, got up as usual and dispatched her maidservant to check on Rañjanā Bībī, who was normally up by then performing her morning tasks. The maidservant rushed back breathless and could barely stammer the news to Āyemāna Bībī that the lock on Rañjanā Bībī's door was tripped, the door itself wide open, and inside she had found Rañjanā Bībī dead to the world, sprawled on her bed, the bed clothes rumpled, her garments disheveled, her normally smoothly combed hair a tangled mess, and looking altogether ravished. Āyemāna Bībī went to inspect for herself and confronted Rañjanā Bībī: It is clear that you have entertained a man in your private chambers last night. You, my daughter-in-law, have brought shame and dishonor on our family. . . . And so the angry, humiliated woman ordered her maidservant to strip Rañjanā Bībī of her jewelry, strip off her fine garments, and give her nothing more than a coarse jute rug to cover her modesty. Then the old woman turned her daughter-in-law out into the forest of Āmīrā to fend for herself.

Rañjanā's delicate complexion and the supple golden color of her skin quickly faded to a dusty, dingy black as she roamed through the thickets and dense undergrowth of the forest. Overwhelmed by her misfortune, she was given to uncontrollable fits of weeping, punctuated only by her remembrance of Allāh. She wandered aimlessly and alone for nine months, growing ever more weary. Then one day she stumbled onto the hut of Dīnu Fakīr. Rañjanā Bībī soon shared with him everything that had transpired, and Dīnu recognized in her story the ring of truth. His compassion aroused, he granted her shelter and protection. Shortly thereafter, when Dīnu Fakīr had gone to the village to beg, Rañjanā finally gave birth to a beautiful boy. When Dīnu returned, he was stunned, indeed smitten, by the lustrous pink of this baby boy, who was the image of the effulgent moon. He affectionately dubbed him Lālcānd, though his formal name was Lāl Mānik. To assist Rañjanā Bībī, Dīnu called a midwife who hurried over and who, after examining the child, declared it to be anemic and sickly. Rañjanā and Dīnu both were shocked and then alarmed. The midwife strongly advised the fakir to take the child to Śāhā Habīb in the city of Kamīnā, the only man she knew who could cure the child's afflictions. The naturally alarmed fakir picked up the child and scurried off to said Śāhā Habīb, who prescribed medicines that, as far as the fakir accepted on trust, were appropriate to whatever ailed the child. The fakir quickly returned the child Lāl Mānik to his mother and paid the midwife. Meanwhile Śāhā Habīb called privately on the local *wajir* [minister] and asked him to kidnap the son of Dīnu in exchange for a tidy sum. Aided by the "medicines" already prescribed by Śāhā Habīb, the *wajir* and the midwife contrived to dope the mother and steal the baby, and do this they did. The baby was promptly but scrumptiously delivered to Habīb, who raised him as his own son.

For twelve long years did Rañjanā Bībī search in vain for her Lāl Mānik. Then one day another fakir—this one named Mānik Pīr—arrived at the door of Dīnu's hut and introduced himself. Always compelled to honor those Friends of God, Bībī Rañjanā fell at his feet. The *pīr* was gracious toward her and listened carefully to her long and woeful tale. Contemplating her plight, Mānik then advised her to go to the king's durbar to lodge a formal complaint and make public her accusations of wrongdoing. She did as advised, but found herself summarily thrown out of the court because the king was not a particularly intelligent or caring ruler, a stupid man who assumed that the poor were always wrong and the wealthy right. Rañjanā Bībī was, he opined, a liar out to extort money or child or both from Habīb. At wits' end, all she could do was sit in the dust of the road and weep.

Now each day along that road the young boy Lāl Mānik used to walk to school. And on this particular day he saw a poor woman, squatting in the dust, shedding bitter tears. As soon as the woman looked up, she recognized him as her son and began to wail uncontrollably, emitting eerie groans that unnerved the young boy. Sensing something important, he gathered his wits and found the courage to query her: Why are you crying so? . . . Rañjanā Bībī then composed herself and between sobs managed to make the boy understand that Śāhā Habīb had abducted him at birth. Just as Dīnu had recognized the truth of the mother's tale, the boy, too, instinctively knew the truth of it, and his heart melted as he contemplated what it all meant. Seeing her pathetic condition, and realizing that she was weak from hunger, he tried to give her a bit of food. Bībī Rañjanā recoiled instantly and cried out: If you are my son, how can I possibly take food from your hand? . . . Lāl Mānik was more convinced than ever of his mother's claim.

Now harboring suspicions about Habīb, the young but intelligent Lāl Mānik decided to test his erstwhile father: Listen, Father, I need to tell you something very important, but first you must place your hand on my head by way of surety. . . . Śāhā Habīb did not hesitate, placing his hand firmly on the head of Lāl Mānik. Lāl Mānik's suspicions grew. He thought to himself: If that man were truly my father, he would never have placed his hand on my head for fear of endangering me, for no parent ever takes an oath on the head of his or her own child, lest bad luck or the evil eye fall. And so his doubts continued to grow.

Not long after that encounter, Mānik Pīr personally shepherded Rañjanā Bībī back to the court of the king, and in that royal durbar he explained in no uncertain detail precisely what had transpired at the birth of Lāl Mānik. Because of the manifest stature of Mānik Pīr, the king had no choice but to listen seriously, and though reluctantly, he had to summon Habīb to account. When Habīb appeared in the durbar, he simply countered the charge with his own assertion: The boy is my son. . . . The king, not being terribly bright, was flummoxed and could see no way through the impasse. But Mānik Pīr offered a reasonable solution in the form of a test of maternity. Always eager to escape making any decision of his own, the king listened and agreed. The boy was brought forward, and at Mānik Pīr's instruction, the guards in the court placed seven double-thick layers of cloth over the boy's mouth. Then the mothers were challenged to squirt milk from their breasts in sufficient quantity to soak through the cloth and nourish the boy. The reason? Only a mother's love could generate such spontaneous lactation, especially when the mother had not breastfed the boy for years. The woman who managed to produce enough milk to soak the cloth sufficient to fill the boy's mouth would be proved the mother. Habīb's maidservant, who had all those years after the theft been named the mother, tried to get the milk to rise, kneading her breasts black and blue in the process. She finally gave up when she failed to muster a single drop. Rañjanā Bībī was a different story. She effortlessly produced a bounty of sweet milk that shot thick streams across the room that splattered onto the cloth in large dollops; they nearly choked the boy as he tried hard to swallow it. The king could do nothing but recognize her as the mother and so awarded her custody of her son. They left the durbar reunited, leaving the stupid king to deal with Habīb.

As they parted ways outside the court, Rañjanā Bībī and her son bowed to Mānik Pīr, grateful for his aid. Then she asked him where he would have her and her son go since neither really had a home. Mānik advised her to proceed to the bank of the River Āmīrāvāda. They did as they were told, and miraculously the first person Lāl Mānik met was none other than Rañjanā Bībī's husband and his father, Kāle Śāhā, who was only then returning from his trading voyage after more than twelve long years. Lāl Mānik had no trouble recognizing Kāle Śāhā as his father. Having been coached by Mānik Pīr, he accosted him, loudly making a claim on his wealth for having abandoned him. The father could retain his wealth, said Lāl Mānik, only if he accompanied him to the local king's durbar and explained his absence. Nonplussed at being addressed so aggressively by these strange people, Kāle Śāhā was unsure how to proceed; but out of anxiety, and no doubt fueled by his fear of the fakir aiding Lāl Mānik, he reluctantly agreed. Off to court they went.

In the durbar, Kāle Śāhā protested his innocence and ignorance of the claims, but Lāl Mānik countered with his own pitiful story, directing his words to Kāle Śāhā: My mother has for more than twelve years been wandering in the forests bereft of husband and son, and I too have since birth searched in vain for my father. My mother, Rañjanā, came from the city of Derāg. Speak frankly, do you know who she is? Does she mean anything at all to you? . . . Then it finally dawned on Kāle Śāhā just who these people were, and he took Lālcānd to his lap and hugged him, smothering him with kisses. When he called him by name, Lālcānd laughed in pleasure and involuntarily spat up luminous pink pearls. Kāle Śāhā looked upon his long-lost wife and his only son and wept from grief and joy. Lālcānd then observed: It was only by the grace of Mānik Pīr that we are alive; without him, my mother would have perished. . . . The connection sank in, and Kāle Śāhā became very anxious to meet with Mānik Pīr again and pay his proper respects.

Mānik, who had already slipped away, heard from afar the man's earnest appeal and miraculously materialized in his presence. Though startled that he had conjured Mānik Pīr so easily, Śāhā Kāle recovered his wits and greeted him with the promise: I shall give you everything you want. . . . Mānik graciously replied: I want nothing. Just go back to your own country in the name of Allāh. . . . But Kāle Śāhā was adamant and refused, promising to go but not before he had made an appropriate donation to charity in the name of Mānik Pīr. And so Kāle Śāhā began a pattern of systematic donations of wealth, cattle, gold, and silver, whatever was needed or appropriate to each locale he visited, and all in the name of Mānik Pīr. Eventually he wended his way back to his own land, prosperous and joined by his long-lost family. In the name of Allāh, he never forgot to heap praise on the grace and mercy of Mānik Pīr, nor should any of you who hear this tale.

NOTES

1. For the literature regarding Satya Pīr, see Tony K. Stewart, *Fabulous Females and Peerless Pīrs: Tales of Mad Adventure in Old Bengal,* translations with introduction (New York: Oxford University Press, 2004); Stewart, "Satya Pīr: Muslim Holy Man and Hindu God," in *The Religions of India in Practice,* ed. Donald S. Lopez Jr. (Princeton, NJ: Princeton University Press, 1995), 578–97; Stewart, "Alternate Structures of Authority: Satya Pīr on the Frontiers of Bengal," in *Beyond Turk and Hindu: Rethinking Religious Iden-*

tities in Islamicate South Asia, ed. David Gilmartin and Bruce B. Lawrence (Gainesville: University of Florida Press, 2000; repr., Delhi: Indian Research Press, 2002), 21–54; Stewart, "Surprising Bedfellows: Vaishnava and Shi'i Alliance in Kavi Ariph's 'Tale of Lālamon,'" *International Journal of Hindu Studies* 3, no. 3 (1999): 265–98, anthologized in *Surprising Bedfellows: Hindus and Muslims in Medieval Early Modern India* (New York: Lexington Press of Rowman and Littlefield, 2003), 55–88.

2. Girīndranāth Dās, *Bāmlā Pīr Sāhityer Kathā* (Kājīpādā, Bārāsat, Cabbiś Parganā: Śahid Lāibrerī), 1383 BS [1976], 418.

3. Ibid., 419.

4. Ibid., 419–20.

5. *Mānik Pīr Gān* by Satyen Rāy, quoted in ibid., 420–21. I have been unable to locate a copy of this text, but Dās includes a transcription of this complete passage.

6. Stewart, "Satya Pīr." More than 150 authors made this claim from the sixteenth to the twentieth century.

7. For the most useful illustration of the problematic concept of syncretism, see Asim Roy, *The Islamic Syncretistic Traditions of Bengal* (Princeton, NJ: Princeton University Press, 1983); for a trenchant critique of syncretism, see Stewart, "In Search of Equivalence: Conceiving Muslim-Hindu Encounter through Translation Theory," *History of Religions* 40, no. 3 (Winter 2001): 261–88, anthologized in *India's Islamic Traditions, 711–1750,* ed. Richard M. Eaton (Delhi: Oxford University Press, 2003), 363–92; see also Tony K. Stewart and Carl W. Ernst, "Syncretism," *South Asian Folklore: An Encyclopedia,* ed. Margaret A. Mills and Peter J. Claus (London and New York: Routledge, 2003).

8. Shashibhusan Dasgupta, *Obscure Religious Cults,* 3rd ed. (Calcutta: Firma KLM, 1969), 371; this is also cited in Roy, *Islamic Syncretistic Traditions,* 212.

9. Roy gives a lengthy summary; see Roy, *Islamic Syncretistic Traditions,* 245–48.

10. The story is summarized in Āhmad Śariph, *Bāmlā o Bāmlā Sāhitya,* pt. 2 (Dhaka, Bangladesh: Bāmlā Ekādemī, 1983), 842–45, and repeated in slightly different form in Dās, *Bāmlā Pīr Sāhityer Kathā,* 437–41, who considers it a degeneration of the cycle.

11. *Bonbībī Jahurā Nāmā: Nāryānīr Janga o Dhonā Dukher Pālā* (Kolkata: Nuruddīn Āhmād at Gāosiya Lāibrerī, 1394 BS [1986]).

12. D. C. Sen cites two other versions, that of Mālati Kusum Mālā by an anonymous Muslim author and an unnamed story by Daksināraṇjan Mitra Majumdār. See Dinesh Chandra Sen, *The Folk-Literature of Bengal* (Calcutta: Calcutta University, 1920), 117.

13. Krsnahari Dās, *Bada Satya Pīr o Sandhyāvatī Kanyār Punthi* (Kolkata: Nuruddīn Āhmād at Gāosiya Lāibrerī, n.d.), 214–16; for a summary of that story, see Stewart, "Alternate Structures of Authority," 41–43.

14. For a complete translation of the Satya Pīr version, see Stewart, "The

Mother's Son Who Spat Up Pearls," in *Fabulous Females and Peerless Pīrs,* 120–48.

15. Sen, *Folk-Literature of Bengal,* 13–23; Dās, *Bāmlā Pīr Sāhityer Kathā,* 424–35. Importantly, T. Richard Blurton, curator in the Department of Asia, has identified this tale in several registers of one of the most extraordinary Bengali scroll paintings of the eighteenth or nineteenth centuries; see T. Richard Blurton, *Bengali Myths* (London: British Museum Press, 2006). The scroll itself is more than forty-two feet long and contains fifty-four distinct registers, but is incomplete on both ends. Half of the scroll illustrates the story of Mānik, the other half Gāzi Pīr. At the time of this writing, the entire scroll can be viewed online at www.thebritishmuseum.ac.uk/bengal/gazi/gazi_scroll. html. The story of Gāji and Mānik and information about the scroll can be found on pp. 67–72. The eight sequential illustrations of the Kinu and Kānu story that accompany this article are from that scroll, published with the kind permission of the British Museum.

16. *The Sunderbans: Folk Tales from India,* Vivalok Comics, vol. 1 (New Delhi: Viveka Foundation, 2002), 7–19.

17. G. N. Dās indicates that Allāh then instructed Jibrīl to visit Mānik again and entrust to him the responsibility of the sixty-four Vedas, probably a scribal error confusing Veda with *vidhi,* referring to the sixty-four formulas or treatments for ailments that afflict cattle, as noted in the introduction.

18. D. C. Sen ends his text here.

19. A version of this same story can be found in the Satya Pīr cycle; for a complete translation, see Stewart, *Fabulous Females and Peerless Pīrs,* 120–48.

PART VI

Southeast and East Asia

.   .   .   .   .

Southeast Asia includes the mainland nations of Burma (Myanmar), Vietnam, Laos, Cambodia, Thailand, and all but two of the states of Malaysia; as well as the island nation of Indonesia and two Malaysian states on the north of Borneo, with the tiny Muslim sultanate of Brunei tucked between them. There are small communities of Muslims in Cambodia and Thailand, but the largest Muslim populations are found in Malaysia and Indonesia. The following selections offer samples of hagiography, in premodern Malay language, of the early Shīʿī figure Muhammad al-Hanafīya, as well as a twentieth-century account, written in modern Indonesian, of one of the most important of the Wali Songo (Nine Friends of God). Significant communities of Muslims have developed in western China since, according to traditional reckoning, the mid-first/seventh century. A remarkable early modern Chinese hagiography offers an unusual look at a distinctively Chinese interpretation of exemplary religious figures.

25 The Malay Story of Muhammad al-Hanafīya

Lode F. Brakel

Muhammad (ibn) al-Hanafīya played an unusual role in the first/seventh-century Shī'ī story of the martyrdom of Husayn at Karbalā' (in southern Iraq) in 61/680 and the unfolding subsequent events. He was the last surviving son of 'Alī by a woman of the Banū Hanīfa tribe, and thus also an indirect descendant of the Prophet. Shortly after the martyrdom, this Muhammad emerged as a contender for leadership of the Prophet's family. Although he could not truly claim legitimate descent from the Prophet, his supporters considered his descent from 'Alī sufficient legitimacy. Muhammad al-Hanafīya himself remained politically aloof and refused to challenge the caliph Yazīd after the disaster of Karbalā'. In 66/685, after Yazīd's successor Marwān died, 'Abd Allāh ibn az-Zubayr (whose father had rebelled against 'Alī in 656) led a revolt to take the Caliphate. Ibn az-Zubayr faced stiff resistance from the caliph's son 'Abd al-Mālik as well as from the Shī'ī supporters of al-Mukhtār, who claimed prophetic status. Mukhtār based his claims on his support of Muhammad al-Hanafīya as the *mahdī* (the "guided one" who would lead the community to victory), even though Muhammad himself disavowed any connection to Mukhtār. Ibn az-Zubayr attacked Mecca and took Muhammad and his family hostage, however, and Muhammad reluctantly sought help from Mukhtār, who then freed the captives.

Muhammad took refuge in at-Tā'if, near Mecca, and opted for neutrality in the struggle. After both Mukhtār and Ibn az-Zubayr had disappeared from the scene in 73/692, Muhammad acknowledged 'Abd al-Mālik as caliph. He remained politically inactive until his death in Medina in 81/700. Husayn's son Zayn al-'Ābidīn, the only other then-living Shī'ī survivor of Karbalā' and contender for power, died in 94/712. Despite Muhammad al-Hanafīya's historically insignificant part in the story, he nonetheless became the hero of a popular romance that enjoyed great popularity in Southeast Asia during the early years of Islamization.

Shī'ī Islam's early years were embroiled in political protest, and its adherents grew to be focused on the suffering of its leaders. By 65/684, pilgrimages to Karbalā' had become increasingly important in Shī'ī thought and practice. Husayn's story made its way into a book attributed to an Abū Mikhnaf, the two parts of which covered reports of the martyrdom of Husayn and Mukhtār's revenge. Part one was particularly influential on later Shī'ī literature. Muhammad al-Hanafīya achieved exalted importance because, in the story, Mukhtār had declared him the *mahdī*. He became a focal point of a subsect of the Kaysanīya during the second/eighth century, who regarded Muhammad as alive and hiding in the mountains, biding his time before reappearing as the *mahdī*.

A Malay version of Muhammad (ibn) al-Hanafīya's story, written around 917/1511, is based on a Persian original probably written in the eighth/fourteenth century. The much embellished story translated here is excerpted from that Malay text and describes the events following the hero's capture in a battle with troops of the caliph Yazīd and his subsequent release to fight again. Relating an encounter that never actually happened, the tale is a fine example of how one relatively minor religious figure gained stature as his story traveled eastward.[1]

TRANSLATION

Chapter 21

After Muhammad Hanafīya had been taken captive, the brothers assembled on the battlefield to deliberate. Someone stood up and suggested that it would be better to go home and cease fighting, because without a commandeer it was beyond their ability to continue the war any longer. However, Masib Kaka opposed this suggestion. He pointed out that the army, except for Muhammad Hanafīya, was still intact, so that actually it was simply a question of appointing a new commander. Then they would be capable of attacking Damascus and killing Yazīd; if anyone were to die, he would achieve martyrdom; the promise to God and the house of the Prophet should be kept. Tughan Turk and Mughan Turk suggested that Masib Kaka himself be appointed commander. The latter declared, however, that the sons of 'Alī must have preference and that 'Umar 'Alī should therefore be considered for this function.

All were in agreement with this. At that moment a messenger reached them from one of Yazīd's men who was named Mahajana and was secretly on the side of the Family [of the Prophet—i.e., the Shīʿa]. He sent a letter wherein he informed them that Yazīd had agreed with his ministers to burn Muhammad Hanafīya on the slopes of the hill of Lezah, on Saturday toward midday. However, if they would stay hidden in the woods there, then as soon as smoke arose from the fire, they could undertake a surprise attack on the enemy, throw them into confusion, and free Muhammad Hanafīya. After reading this letter, they were all overjoyed, and Masib Kaka offered to go to the hill of Lezah and undertake a rescue attempt. However, Ibrāhīm Astar was thoroughly familiar with the terrain and therefore preferred to go himself.

He set out together with Hārith and, upon arriving at the place, hid himself and his army. Meanwhile, the main army, under ʿUmar ʿAlī's command, went to Damascus and halted at the place where Muhammad Hanafīya had fought. The next morning, ʿUmar ʿAlī had the war drums sounded. Yazīd was upset when he saw that the sons of ʿAlī had returned. Marwān advised him to send the army out against them and at the same time to attempt to burn Muhammad Hanafīya as quickly as possible. Dalmal Zanggi offered to fight. He was extraordinarily valiant, large in stature, dark-faced, inflexible of heart, and thirty ells tall. He mounted a war elephant. Upon arriving on the battlefield, he shouted: "Sons of ʿAlī! I shall cut off your hands! I shall kill you all! But if you desire to stay alive, then come here and I shall take you to King Yazīd, so that he might grant you pardon! For Muhammad Hanafīya is no longer to be found among the living!"

Tālib ʿAlī became enraged and brought his horse right opposite the Negro.[2] The latter cut the legs of Tālib ʿAlī's horse with his sword, so that he fell to the ground. However, he got up quickly and dealt with Dalmal's elephant in the same manner. Dalmal fell to the ground but stood up quickly. Then they seized each other by the belt, until Tālib ʿAlī succeeded in flinging his opponent to the ground. As soon as he attempted to get up, Arkas cleft his chest with his sword so that he died. Upon seeing this, Yazīd cried out, enraged: "No one is capable of taking on the sons of ʿAlī! First let me burn Muhammad quickly and then take them all captive!" He had the drums of retreat sounded and both armies went back to their own camps.

On the following morning, Muhammad Hanafīya was taken from the prison to the place of execution on the slopes of the hill of Lezah. He was brought to the stake, and from all sides wood was piled on the fire. As soon as Ibrāhīm Astar saw the smoke rising, he attacked with his 30,000-man army and his son Hārith. Yazīd was aghast and took to flight while crying,

"Woe! Whence comes this disaster? Has this army descended from Heaven or arisen from the earth?" Meanwhile, Ibrāhīm Astar freed Muhammad Hanafīya and paid respectful homage to him. He brought him back to the brothers in a palanquin. All were in extraordinarily high spirits when they saw that their commander was still alive, and they fell down at his feet.

They continued fighting, day and night. Muhammad Hanafīya, meanwhile, was sad and weepingly implored God to enable him to reach his goal: to free the Family, make Zayn al-ʿĀbidīn[3] king and kill Yazīd. At night he dreamed that the Prophet came to him and asked why he was so sad. He replied: "Oh Envoy of God! The Family of the Prophet is still in prison, without me being able to free them, because one of my arms has been cut off!" Thereupon the Prophet advised him to have his arm searched for and to fasten it to his shoulder with the help of the Prophet's seal, should it be found. With the aid of the prayer "Dhū 'l-Akbar" ("The Supreme One") and God's will, it would assuredly be completely healed.

After waking up, Muhammad Hanafīya prepared a sacrificial meal for the spirit of the Prophet. He related his dream to his brothers, who became overjoyed and cried out: "Surely your dream is veracious!" Masib Kaka volunteered first to look for the arm, but Ibrāhīm Astar pointed out that he was more familiar with the arm, since it had rested so often on his shoulders. He found the dried-out arm on the battlefield. He wound it in his headcloth and, carrying it above his head, brought it back to Muhammad Hanafīya. Muhammad Hanafīya recognized his arm; the brothers placed it against his shoulder and put the seal of the Prophet upon it. They recited the prayer "Dhū 'l-Akbar," raised their hands up high, and said "Amen!" At God's command the arm was completely healed. Muhammad Hanafīya uttered thousands of prayers of thanksgiving and blessings upon his Prophet. The brothers were overjoyed and had the drums of rejoicing sounded.

The next day Muhammad Hanafīya equipped himself for battle and told the army to bring along firewood in order to fill in the moat surrounding Damascus. They marched against the city and filled in the moat. Hereupon they jumped across and approached the city gate. It was battered until it collapsed. They marched into the city and continued the battle within its walls, killing many of the enemy. Many of the enemy died. Yazīd fled to the palace that he had just recently built. Muhammad Hanafīya ordered his men to take him captive, but no matter where they searched, they could not find a trace of him. At God's command a cloud made of light appeared in the firmament. In that cloud was the spirit of amir Husayn, the martyr of Karbalāʾ. The cloud went to Yazīd's hiding place. A voice rang out from the cloud: "Yazīd, you hypocrite! Where have you fled and where are you hiding?" Yazīd was exceedingly terrified at hearing that voice and fell into a pit under the palace. This was the pit he had ordered to be dug and filled with the Family's bodies. His bones were crushed and God flung him into Hell, where he was burned up into ashes.

Thereupon a meeting took place between Muhammad Hanafīya and the cloud. Muhammad Hanafīya spoke: "O' you who have taken on the shape of a cloud; in the name of Him Who has created both of us, tell me who you are!" A voice rang out: "I am the spirit of amir Husayn, the martyr of Karbalā'! I have burnt Yazīd at God's command! Brothers, behold Yazīd in the pit under the palace where he has burnt up into ashes!" Hereupon Muhammad Hanafīya burst into tears. They found the ashes of Yazīd in the pit. Muhammad Hanafīya went to the prison where the Family was languishing. He demanded the key from the guard, but the latter claimed that he did not have it in his possession, because Yazīd himself kept it with him. Hereupon Muhammad Hanafīya cleft the door with his club and stepped inside.

Umm Salamah cried out to Zayn al-'Ābidīn that he must stand up because his uncle had arrived. However, the boy fell down because of his shackles and chains. He kissed and embraced him and freed all the prisoners. He bathed and rubbed him with fragrant spices. He placed a crown of emeralds upon his head, presented him and all the members and relatives of the Family with robes of honor, and seated him upon the throne. On Friday he had the *khutba* [mosque sermon] read in his name. Thenceforth, Zayn al-'Ābidīn ruled as king.

One day, however, Muhammad Hanafīya and his brothers longed intensely for their relatives who had been left behind. Muhammad Hanafīya suggested that they return to their own countries. He himself wanted to remain in order to further aid Zayn al-'Ābidīn in governing the country. At first the brothers would not hear of parting, but in the end they yielded to Muhammad Hanafīya's entreaties. On the eve of their departure Zayn al-'Ābidīn held a banquet for them. The next day they said an emotional farewell to each other. Thereupon each one set out for his own country.

Chapter 22

After the departure of his brothers, Muhammad Hanafīya devoted himself to the instruction of Zayn al-'Ābidīn, whom he assisted in governing the country. The name of the Caliph became renowned far and wide, while the followers of Yazīd were wiped out by Muhammad Hanafīya. A number of them were able to escape and fled into a cave. This was reported to Zayn al-ʿĀbidīn. When the news reached Muhammad Hanafīya's ears, he went to his pupil and stated his determination to march against the enemy. Zayn al-ʿĀbidīn agreed. As soon as he had arrived at the cave, Muhammad Hanafīya drew his sword and plunged amidst the enemy. A countless number met their deaths, and their blood flowed like a river that floods its banks. Suddenly a voice was heard that asked Muhammad Hanafīya if he was not ashamed of the slaughter he had caused. Muhammad Hanafīya ignored the voice and continued the bloodbath. Only when the voice had sounded for the third time did he throw away his sword and fall down. At God's command the gate of the cavern fell shut, because He disposes of all His servants as he alone sees fit.

[With Muhammad Hanafīya's disappearance into the cave, the account comes to an end, leaving ambiguity sufficient for the myth of Muhammad Hanafīya's anticipated eventual return to flourish.]

NOTES

1. Editor's introduction, based on the late Lode F. Brakel's commentary in his *The Story of Muhammad Hanafiyyah: A Medieval Muslim Romance* (The Hague: Martinus Nijhoff, 1977). The translation is excerpted, with permission of the Royal Netherlands Institute of Southeast Asian and Caribbean Studies, from pages 74–77 of that volume. Reprinted in recognition of Professor Brakel's outstanding contributions to the study of Southeast Asian Islamic texts.

2. I.e., Dalmal Zanggi. Epic tales often depict large, fearsome foes as black skinned to heighten the sense of otherness and threat.

3. Zayn al-ʿĀbidīn (Ornament of the Servants of God) was a title of Husayn's son ʿAlī (95/712), who became the Fourth Imam.

26 Sunan Ampel of the Javanese Wali Songo

Anna M. Gade

The Wali Songo are the "Nine Saints" of Java, understood to have first spread Islam in the region during the ninth/fifteenth century. They are associated with major sites along the north coast of Java, where their tombs remain important pilgrimage sites today. Although the classical hagiography of the saints is in the Javanese language, today these figures are the focus of a resurgence of popularity in a variety of media in the Indonesian language. Some of these Friends of God are known for their asceticism or esotericism, while others are known more as teachers of normative Islam. Many of the stories of the Wali Songo relate to royal dynasties, particularly the establishment of the first Muslim states. Some others address the doctrinal issues discussed across the Muslim world in the ninth/fifteenth century, such as the esoteric concept of the Unity of Existence associated elsewhere with the figure of Ibn 'Arabī. On Java, the period of the coming of Islam in the ninth/fifteenth century nearly coincides with the coming of European interests to the region in about the tenth/sixteenth century. (See Figure 19.)

Sunan Ampel (804/1401–883/1478), whose story appears below, is one of the earlier *wali*; in fact, he is the progenitor and teacher of several others. He is said to have had a father who came from Samarkand, Central Asia, whereas his mother was a princess from Champa, a kingdom once located in what is now Cambodia and Vietnam. Sunan Ampel's parentage thus represents the transregional character of Islam in maritime Southeast Asia. In addition, there are possible Shī'ī connotations to his heritage, also supported by the origin in Champa. Within Southeast Asia, Sunan Ampel is known especially for having established religious schools; his paternal heritage in "Bukhara" is often noted with respect to his learning in religious sciences such as Hadith. Among the tales of the Javanese Wali Songo,

Figure 19.　There are other indigenous Indonesian Friends of God as well.
Here Prince Selarasa pays homage to Kiai Nur Saiyid, who has lived apart in
the wilderness so long that he seems to be inextricably entwined in it. Courtesy
of the Trustees of the British Museum, BL MSS c12243–0. MSS Jav.28ff.7v-8r.

his story emphasizes his special style and effectiveness in preaching and teaching the faith of Islam. In this version of his biography, Sunan Ampel is presented as a defender of "Sharia-mindedness," which this modern text portrays as a complement to other qualities of the saints of Java.

The following text is a revised and abridged translation of a popular book on Sunan Ampel in the Indonesian language, entitled *Sunan Ampel Took Great Care in Spreading the Religion of Islam*. It is one of a series, "Perjuangan Wali Songo" ("The Struggle of the Wali Songo"). The author, A. Setiawati, writes that he compiled the account from a number of popular and scholarly sources.[1]

TRANSLATION

The lineage (*silsila*) of Sunan Ampel is from ʿAlī and not directly from the Prophet Muhammad. His father was Shaykh Ibrahim al-Ghazālī, or Ibrahim Asmarakandi [Arabic As-Samarkandī]. He was the brother of Shaykh Barebat Zainul Alam, also known as Jamāl ad-Dīn Kubrā, who lived in Bukhara. Ibrahim Asmarakandi, the father of Sunan Ampel, was able to associate with great figures of his age. Coming to mainland Southeast Asia, he was married by the king of Champa to the king's daughter, Dewi Candrawulan. With his marriage to Dewi Candrawulan, God blessed Ibrahim Asmarakandi with two sons. The older of them was named Sayyid Ali Rahmatullah, who was born in the year 804/1401 in Champa, Cambodia. Sayyid Ali Rahmatullah was someday to become known as Sunan Ampel. In his youth, he was called Raden Rahmat (Prince Rahmat) because he was from the royal line of Champa through his mother, and because of his later connections to the royal line of Majapahit on Java.

Dewi Candrawulan, the wife of Ibrahim Asmarakandi and the mother of Raden Rahmat, had a younger sister who was called Dewi Dwarawati. Dewi Dwarawati was married to the king of the kingdom of Majapahit on the island of Java, Prabu Brawijaya V (also known as Prabu Kertabumi). The king loved his new queen deeply. And with this, Sayyid Ali Rahmatullah (or Raden Rahmat), and his brother, Sayyid Ali Murthado, became the nephews of the king of Majapahit, Prabu Brawijaya.

At that time, the kingdom of Majapahit was suffering an irreversible decline. This had begun when the great king Prabu Hayamwuruk and his general Gajah Mada passed away. The kingdom had been unstable and breaking apart due to civil wars, and many small states had formed. A large portion of the taxes collected from the people did not reach the coffers of the state. With this, hunger began to spread across the land of Majapahit. As a result of famine, there arose bands of youths who wanted to do as they pleased without having to work. Many soldiers and those who joined the palace guard were leaders in such gangs. They wanted to gain power and prestige with this social status only in order to plunder the wealth of the people. Because of this, the hearts of the people were anxiously haunted by the shadow of a death that could come upon them swiftly and at any moment.

The king was gravely concerned about the growing crisis in his kingdom. He viewed it as a moral and spiritual problem, stemming from a lack of knowledge and respect for religion among his people. The new queen, Ratu Dwarawati, suggested that they invite her nephew, Ali Rahmatullah, to come from Champa to help. With the coming of Islam, the kingdom of Champa had overcome similar problems, she told him, and in fact it was flourishing. This "Raden Rahmat" had already become well known for his religious teachings there. And so with the blessings of the king and queen of Champa, and filled with his own great eagerness to spread Islam and to assist the nobles of Majapahit, Raden Rahmat set out for Java. He traveled along with his father and his brother. Sadly, his father, Shaykh Ibrahim Asmarakandi, passed away in Tuban soon after their arrival. Not long after this, Sayyid Ali Murthado asked permission from his brother Raden Rahmat to spread Islam outside of Java. The brothers parted ways with heavy hearts, since they had always been very close.

When Sayyid Rahmatullah arrived in Majapahit, he first met with his aunt, Ratu Dwarawati. He then went to see the king. The king asked Sayyid Rahmatullah to bring moral teachings to the people. Sayyid Rahmatullah accepted this charge, and the king then granted him permission to come and go as he pleased, and especially to work in the region of Surabaya [in eastern Java]. With the arrival of Raden Rahmat in the palace of Majapahit, there were immediate changes. The spreading light of his noble character was apparent for all to see, and the wish to follow the right path was felt once more. Raden Rahmat was married to Dewi Candruwati, who was also known as Nyai Ageng Manila.

On an appointed day, the entourage of Raden Rahmat departed for the region of Surabaya. All along the way, Raden Rahmat carried out *dakwah* [Ar. *da'wa,* Islamic preaching]. The distinctive manner through which he spread Islam was unique and extraordinary. As he traveled, he thought to himself that for the people to accept a new belief, they must be approached through media they already enjoy. While on his way to Surabaya, he thought it would suit the people who lived in this area best if he were to make some rattan fans for them. Only, his fans would not be like everyday fans. As he looked at the trees around him, he chose one from which to fashion fans. Because his work was aided by his own gifts and blessings, he carried it out rapidly and skillfully.

While still continuing along his journey, Raden Rahmat started to hand out his fans to people whom he met along the road. The fans were given out for free, just as long as the words of the *shahāda* were said in exchange. Because the fans were so nice and pleasing, the people gathered around to receive them. And when they did, with sincerity they uttered the words of the *shahāda*. For these residents of the region, Raden Rahmat explained basic knowledge about Islam. And for those who wanted to continue to study with more depth, he offered them the opportunity to learn more. The people always listened to the advice and admonition of Raden Rahmat. Their hearts were thus opened to Islam without any hardship placed upon them and with no compulsion to convert. The people praised Raden Rahmat far and wide, and his influence spread easily among the people.

There was an amazing quality to the fans that Raden Rahmat had made out of rattan. They were said to be able to cure fever and cough. Perhaps this was a blessing that Raden Rahmat had channeled from God into the fans that he made. The miraculous powers of the fans that he made were the source of wonderment among the people. As the influence of Islam seeped further into the hearts of the people, their wicked deeds also became less and less frequent. All of these were signs that Raden Rahmat was a *wali*. The hopes and the prayers of God's Friends are always heard by Allāh.

Raden Rahmat and his entourage arrived in the district of Kembang-kuning. All around Kembangkuning at that time there was still jungle with trees, great and small. There were also many marshes filled with water. What is today the capital of the district of Kembangkuning was still just a swamp, never having been touched by humans. Raden Rahmat quickly toured the area. He asked God to permit him to build a center of Islam in that place. The next day, they cleared the land quickly thanks to the help of God. As soon as the land was cleared, they constructed a simple place for meeting and for prayer. Today this is the site of a big and beautiful mosque. In this area, Raden Rahmat quickly gained two followers of influence, Ki Wira Sarojo and Ki Bang Kuning, who embraced Islam along with their families. They helped Raden Rahmat to get further acquainted with the people.

With Raden Rahmat's teaching, the people came to know how to distinguish right from wrong. The doctrine of Islam was never mixed with other beliefs, and nothing was ever preached that could ever lead people to stray from the straight path. In Raden Rahmat's preaching, the purity of Islam was always supported by the Qurʾān and the Hadith. With great concern and compassion, Raden Rahmat instructed the hearts of the people. He was careful to impart to them the teachings of Islam, whether glorified or essential, which could actually be grasped by them at that time. The people came to love the teachings of Islam. It was not long before they began to refer to themselves as "Muslims" in great numbers. And with this, the area of Kembangkuning became a center for Islamic activity.

Raden Rahmat came to reside in a village called Ampel Denta. Here he was to become known as a *wali*, addressed by the title "Sunan Ampel Denta." ["Sunan" is a respectful term of address for a great teacher.] After he felt that his *dakwah* had been successful, he began to construct a religious boarding school (*pesantren*). The site had formerly been used to teach the nobles of the kingdom of Majapahit, along with others who wished to study to become teachers. Although many of those who followed Sunan Ampel came from among the sons of the lords and aristocrats of Majapahit, Raden Rahmat never distinguished social class among his students. With pleasure he would teach the religious knowledge that makes life rewarding (*selamat*) in this world and the next to people from all walks of life.

In Ampel, Sunan Ampel instructed his followers about the foundations of becoming a person with good character. He taught them how to perform acts of worship properly and correctly, in accord with Islam and following the Qurʾān and Hadith [Sunna]. The teachings of Sunan Ampel for which he became the most well known were five. These are that it is not permitted to do the following five things: (1) do not gamble; (2) do not drink alcohol; (3) do not steal; (4) do not smoke opium or *ganja* [marijuana]; (5) do not engage in illicit sex. As Sunan Ampel imparted these five teachings to his students, he also provided compelling reasons for them. He explained in detail the degradation and corruption caused by these five actions. Thus, his students could take these teachings fully to heart. It is not surprising, then, that many from among Sunan Ampel's students would someday themselves become saints on the same level of the original nine Wali Songo.

Prabu Brawijaya V, also known as Prabu Kertabumi, was very pleased with the accomplishments of Raden Ali Rahmatullah in improving the moral character of his people. The king himself came to realize that the teachings of Islam are the most exalted of all moral teachings. When Raden Rahmat, now known as Sunan Ampel, invited Prabu Brawijaya V (who was in fact his uncle) to covert to Islam, however, the king politely declined. The reason that Prabu Brawijaya V gave was that he wanted to be remembered as having been the last of the Buddhist kings of Majapahit.

When the great teacher Maulana Ibrahim passed away in Gresik in the year 822/1419, Sunan Ampel was already himself ranked in spiritual status among the *wali*. At that time Sunan Ampel became the mufti, or leader of the religion of Islam, for the entire land of Java. Later, when Raden Patah of Demak was to achieve the rank of the other Wali Songo, their number was fixed at nine. According to most, they are said to be the following figures: (1) Sunan Ampel; (2) Sunan Giri; (3) Sunan Bonang; (4) Sunan Drajat; (5) Sunan Kalijaga; (6) Sunan Muria; (7) Sunan Kota, also known as Raden Patah; (8) Sunan Kudus; and (9) Sunan Gunungjati. According to legend, there were also many other *wali* on the island of Java at that time, not to mention all of the other *wali* who were outside of Java. However, the Wali Songo represent the leaders of all of these other *wali* who were active during the same period. Each of the nine Wali Songo had a special task in accord with his own individual gifts and expertise.

Sunan Ampel had the talent of a special style of *dakwah,* and so he is known especially for his teaching and doctrine. An example of his *dakwah* is the following story. One day when Sunan Ampel was still alive, he was sitting under a shady tree on the banks of the River Brantas. He had just begun a tour of itinerant preaching in the district of Trowulan. Even as he was at rest, Sunan Ampel never once stopped praising the greatness of Allāh, who had created the entire world and everything that is in it.

As Sunan Ampel sat along the riverbank gazing far into the distance, suddenly a strange sight captured his attention. Sunan Ampel saw an old man who was trying to walk on top of the water. After two or three steps the man would fall in, then he would repeat. And thus it went on until the man was worn out and had to stop to rest. His efforts having failed over and over again, the old man finally sat down, utterly exhausted, and watched the current of the River Brantas with an empty stare. "When will I be able to walk on water? It has already been decades that I have been attempting this feat, but still up until now I have not had any results," he grumbled softly.

Sunan Ampel had already guessed in an instant what the old man was up to. However, just as any wise person would do, he wanted to hear the explanation directly from the man himself. Sunan Ampel approached the old man, who was sitting and resting under the shade of a tree. But Sunan Ampel was soon startled when all of a sudden the old man jumped into the river water and went back to what he had been doing. After the man had returned to the riverbank, once more panting and out of breath, Sunan Ampel addressed him respectfully.

"How long has it been that Grandfather has been making this attempt to walk on the water?" inquired Sunan Ampel. The old man answered with a long face, "Forty years!" As he said this, he looked out at the waters of the River Brantas that had so long been the object of his efforts. Upon hearing this reply, Sunan Ampel was taken aback. "Astaghfir Allāh al-Azīm!" ["I ask forgiveness from God the Magnificent"], he exclaimed, placing his hand on his chest. "That length of time, and this all for the sake of something utterly useless!"

Hearing these words from Sunan Ampel, a man who was much younger than he, the old man was offended. He considered his own attempt to be utterly exceptional. The old man's face turned red as he tried to contain his anger. He growled, "Young man, you may not just speak up any way you please! An effort such as this, when it is successful, will surpass the level of what is merely a human power (*kesaktian*)."

"Just for the sake of crossing the river, is it really necessary to practice for dozens of years? What a waste of time! Wouldn't it be more efficient just to cross the river on a raft or a rowboat? It seems to me that by such means we would also be able to get over to the other side, and much more easily," mused Sunan Ampel.

The words of Sunan Ampel were so funny to the old man that he began to laugh heartily out loud. Sunan Ampel stayed silent, but he was smiling too. "Anybody can cross on a raft or a rowboat! I want to do that which no one else is able to achieve," the old man clarified, still laughing. "So then, Grandfather wishes to be greater than others?" Sunan Ampel asked. "That's right! I want to have expertise that no one else possesses. I desire to be seen as a sign of miracles in the eyes of others," retorted the old man with pride.

With this, Sunan Ampel was at a loss. At first he had thought that the old man had only wished to hear others praising him, since at his advanced age he would soon be approaching the edge of the grave. But with a person as arrogant as this, it is very hard to find any accommodation or compromise. So without any further ado, Sunan Ampel simply walked away from the old man, who was still standing by the river's edge.

After a while, Sunan Ampel wished to cross over the river to continue along his journey. His way was obstructed because at that time there was no still bridge. There was no sign of a boat or even a little raft. At last he was forced to rely upon his own spiritual powers (*kesaktian*). With ease Sunan Ampel glided across the river. He did this without causing as much as a ripple in the water, just as if he had been walking along a path on dry land. It just so happened that the old man saw what Sunan Ampel was doing.

The old man watched with a wide, unblinking stare. He almost did not believe what he was witnessing with his very own eyes. When he was sure that what he was seeing was actually real, he stood up at last. The old man realized that this younger man, who was walking across the waters of the River Brantas, was no ordinary person. He bowed at the feet of Sunan Ampel, asked for his forgiveness, and requested that he might become his teacher. The end of the story is that the old man became a devoted student of Sunan Ampel. Of course, Sunan Ampel really crossed the water as he did so that the arrogant man could see his own cherished desire realized, and in this way Sunan Ampel could capture his attention. In this way, Sunan Ampel's teachings could reach an arrogant person indirectly yet effectively, and without hurting his feelings or causing him offense.

Among the many students of Sunan Ampel was a student called Mbah Bolang, whose real name was Sonhaji. Once day, at about the time that the construction of the mosque at Ampel was being completed, Sonhaji began to chip away at the wall of the prayer niche, hollowing it out. When the companions of Sonhaji peered into the hole he had made in the wall of the *mihrāb,* there appeared an image of the Kaʿba in Mecca! The companions of Sonhaji felt as though they themselves were alongside the Kaʿba too, since the pilgrims performing *tawāf* [circumambulating it] were so clearly visible. With this, the students of the school at Ampel gave Sonhaji the title "Mbah Bolang." They called him that because Sonhaji had carved out a hole in the wall (*lubang*) of the *mihrāb* in order to view the Kaʿba. With their teacher, being Sunan Ampel, who was a *wali* possessing great spiritual gifts, it is to be expected that his students could also have the ability to acquire similar powers as well. Naturally, however, not every student would demonstrate such powers, since these are special gifts given only by God.

There is another story about the special powers of another student of Sunan Ampel. Naturally, his powers are inexorably linked to those of his teacher, Sunan Ampel. His story goes as follows. When Sunan Ampel was still alive, he had a student named Mbah Soleh. Mbah Soleh was responsible for sweeping up the mosque at Ampel, and he also served as the custodian of its grounds. His work was so thorough that there was hardly ever a speck of dust to be seen at all in the mosque, it was so neat and tidy all the time.

The worshipers who came to pray in Sunan Ampel's mosque were happy with the job Mbah Soleh did. They praised Mbah Soleh, but with humility he would always answer them, "All praises are due to Allāh, who created the world and all that is in it." Mbah Soleh was never satisfied if there was the smallest speck of dirt in the place of worship, even if it was just one atom of dust. Not only did the people praise his work in the mosque, but people all around were struck when they would see the face of Mbah Soleh himself, which was always shining with clarity and light.

When Mbah Soleh passed away, he was buried in the yard of the mosque. The students of Sunan Ampel, and even he himself, had lost a great help upon which everyone had depended all of the time. The students of Sunan Ampel now tried to fill the shoes of Mbah Soleh, acting as the sweepers and custodians of Sunan Ampel's mosque. However, all their efforts could not match, much less rival, what Mbah Soleh could accomplish in just one day.

Mbah Soleh had passed away only a few days before when there was already a change apparent inside and outside of the mosque. The atmosphere of the mosque started to seem dark and gloomy because of the dirt that was building up, no matter how hard the students tried to clean it up. The worshipers who came to pray in Ampel's *masjid* [mosque] began to feel uneasy, because the floor of the mosque began to seem dirty as a result of the dust that was clinging to it. They started to complain about the dirt in the mosque and the untidiness of the garden around it. As they did this, they sighed and looked out at Mbah Soleh's tombstone, forlorn.

The unkempt conditions of the mosque came to the attention of Sunan Ampel. When he saw the dirt that was building up in the mosque, he pronounced the words: "If Mbah Soleh lives, let him come and clean up the *masjid!*" Sunan Ampel had barely uttered these words when suddenly Mbah Soleh appeared, sweeping up the floor under the place of the imam [prayer leader]. Of course this extraordinary event occurred by the will of Allāh, consistent with His great favor for Sunan Ampel.

In no time this amazing happening had become the talk of the town. News of a resurrection from the dead spread across the area. And with the return of Mbah Soleh, the mosque now appeared clean all the time, just as it had been before. The students and the congregants who prayed in Sunan Ampel's mosque were relieved and happy once more. This state of affairs did not continue for long, however. After only a couple of months, Mbah Soleh passed away again. His body was buried just to the east of the site where his first grave had been.

Right after Mbah Soleh died for the second time, the mosque and the yard around it became dirty again. The followers of Mbah Soleh regretted losing him once more. The students tried all over again to do Mbah Soleh's job, but they could not perform the task as well as he had. With all of their strength and effort the students tried to clean the mosque just like Mbah

Soleh used to clean it, but their results were very different from his. There was still a film of dust all over the mosque, and a layer of sticky grime clung to the floor. The students now grumbled again as they stared at the pair of two graves.

When Sunan Ampel saw that the mosque was getting dirty once again, he did exactly the same thing he had done before, saying: "If Mbah Soleh lives, the condition of the mosque must always be clean!" By the permission of Allāh, as enacted by the blessings of Sunan Ampel, Mbah Soleh came to life again as his former self. Then he swept up the mosque just as usual. And the condition of the mosque and the yard around it was clean once more. The students and those who came to pray observed *salat* [daily ritual prayer] in the mosque with contentment once again. The mosque was clean and tidy and looked after well. But a few months after this, Mbah Soleh died once more, and the mosque and its yard became dirty all over again. The students started to complain again.

Sunan Ampel spoke the words just as he did before, and Mbah Soleh revived in order to perform his task, which was to sweep up the mosque. This amazing occurrence was repeated over and over again several times. When Mbah Soleh had been brought back to life for the eighth time, Sunan Ampel himself passed away. Sunan Ampel's body was buried on the west side of Masjid Ampel. The students knew that the death of their teacher could mean that Mbah Soleh would disappear in time as well. And indeed, when Mbah Soleh passed away the ninth time, this would prove to be his last and final death.

With what they surmised to be their final opportunity to be with him on his eighth life, the students studied with sincerity from Mbah Soleh how to clean the mosque. It turned out that with five men at work they could clean up the mosque almost as well as him. Mbah Soleh instructed them with his knowledge of how to perform this task so that the mosque was clean and pleasing. A few months later, Mbah Soleh died for the ninth time. After this ninth death, Mbah Soleh did not come back to life because his medium of regeneration, Sunan Ampel, had himself passed away. The body of Mbah Soleh was reburied for the eighth time. And since that time the graves of Mbah Soleh line up in a row of nine. This row of graves belonging to Mbah Soleh lies on the east side of Sunan Ampel's mosque today.

When teaching his pupils, Sunan Ampel was always exceedingly patient and understanding. He was not averse to repeating many times over instruction and lessons that were not yet fully learned by his students. He would always say to his pupils, whoever does not yet understand this or that may ask about it some more so that they may fully understand. As an example of this, Sunan Ampel had a pupil who was named Abū Hurayrah. This particular student was less than fluent (*fasīh*) and correct when he would recite the Arabic words of the Qur'ān. Even though he tried very hard to improve his pronunciation, it was still very poor whenever he would try to read out loud.

One day, as was his custom, Sunan Ampel was drilling his pupils in the memorization of the Ninety-Nine Most Beautiful Names of Allāh (*al-asmā' al-husnā*). None of the pupils in the class, not to mention any of the other students who happened to be there, had any problem repeating what Sunan Ampel demonstrated to them. Their pronunciation was fluent and correct. Then it came to be Abū Hurayra's turn. Sunan Ampel called on Abū Hurayra to recite the words *Yā Hayyu, Yā Qayyūmu*, which are expressions for the Names of God that mean "O' Living One, O Self-Sustaining One!" "Now, would you please repeat what I just said?" requested Sunan Ampel. Abū Hurayra hesitated to recite, however, because he felt he could not pronounce the words of the Qur'ān properly.

"Come on, speak up, Abū Hurayra!" Sunan Ampel asked Abū Hurayra once more. "Ya . . . ya . . . ya kayuku, ya kayumu!" uttered Abu Hurayra while bowing his head.[2] The other pupils tried to stifle a laugh. However, there were those who could not manage to do this, and they were forced to laugh out loud, try as they might to keep quiet. Hearing that there were some in the class who seemed to be making fun of Abū Hurayra, Sunan Ampel addressed them immediately.

"You do not need to laugh in ridicule of your classmate. Allāh created 'His Umma,' that is, all of humanity, so that there are those who are greater in ability and those who have less ability. This situation may be food for thought for all of us. Since beings are created in this way, some having more capability and some with less, we may always give thanks to God for whatever gifts that He showers upon us. With this as well, it is assured that each of us will have to confront our own shortcoming in certain areas of learning and knowledge. So if you hear or see such an area for development in a person, well then, instruct him or her so that he can do better in the future. There is no action done by a human being that escapes the awareness of Allāh," Sunan Ampel instructed his students.

Not one of the students dared to raise his head. Those who had giggled before now asked sincerely for forgiveness from Sunan Ampel. He told them that they should not do what they had done again. Sunan Ampel then turned to Abū Hurayra. "That is not correct," he said gently. "Yā Hayyu! Yā Qayyūm!" Abū Hurayra once more repeated after Sunan Ampel, "Ya kayuku, ya kayumu." Sunan Ampel smiled. He knew that Abū Hurayra's tongue would never be able to shape the words that he uttered. Even after it was repeated many times, Abū Hurayra still could not do it as he heard. Sunan Ampel understood. Then he explained the meaning of the expressions in their own native language. The pupils all repeated what Sunan Ampel said, including Abū Hurayra.

Then Abū Hurayra spoke up to ask his teacher, "Kanjeng [Respected] Sunan, I am not able to pronounce Arabic just as Sunan Ampel does. However, *inshā'Allāh* [God willing], I am able to understand and comprehend its meaning. Is this acceptable, Kanjeng Sunan?" Sunan Ampel smiled. He was touched by the frankness of Abū Hurayra. "Of course it is all right! God will always recognize and understand your situation," replied Sunan Ampel, full of wisdom and compassion. Abū Hurayra was in fact able to absorb every lesson offered by Sunan Ampel with deep sincerity. All the knowledge that was imparted to him by Sunan Ampel he studied with profound patience and purity of heart. Thanks to his diligence, perseverance, and enduring will, Abū Hurayra was able to reach a high level of achievement. Abū Hurayra joined the ranks of the Friends of God (*wali*) and attained his own spiritual blessings (*keramah*). And from then on, the name *Abū Hurayra* was changed to *Sunan Kapasan*, [and Sunan Kapasan] became a *wali* on the same level as the original Wali Songo.

The great works of Sunan Ampel were not just in the area of spreading Islam through *dakwah*, but in his teaching he also made major contributions in the areas of language and learning. He developed the Arabic-derived script (*huruf pegon*) used for writing the Javanese language. Thanks to this alphabet, he could impart the teachings of Islam to his students. Using the languages and dialects of Java made it much easier for students to absorb and understand these lessons, since for the most part they were Javanese. They were able to study with facility, and this made them enjoy learning all the more as the teachings became firmly grounded in their knowledge. Up even until today this writing system for local languages that relies on Arabic letters is still used in religious boarding schools (*pesantren*).

The essential teachings of Sunan Ampel were also applied in advanced study. If these principles could be summarized in a list, they would be *dzatul wujudi* [essential being], a quality that can be seen manifest only at the moment or death or extinction (*sarakatul maut*); *tawhīd* [divine unity], a teaching that makes humanity uphold the certainty that all existence is owing to Allāh, and unto Him we shall return; and, *marifat* [spiritual knowledge], a characteristic of a person that is the result of having mastered both *dzatul wujudi* and *tawhīd*.

At the time that Sunan Ampel was carrying out these great works, his wives were also performing many great works of their own. The wives of Sunan Ampel who were the most active in this way were Nyai Ageng Manila, also known as Dewi Candruwati, and Nyai Ageng Bela. Nyai Ageng Manila bore the following children: the sons, (1) Maulana Makdum Ibrahim, also known as Sunan Bonang (one of the Wali Songo); (2) Raden Qasim, also known as Sunan Drajat (one of the Wali Songo); and (3) Maulana Ahmad, also known as Sunan Lamongan; and the daughters, (4) Siti Mutmainah; (5) Siti Alwaiyah; and (6) Siti Ashikah, who was married to Raden Patah (one of the Wali Songo). In addition, there were also children born to Sunan Ampel and Nyai Karimah, who was the daughter of Ki Ageng Bungkul. These children were (1) Dewi Murtasiah, who was married to Sunan Giri (one of the Wali Songo); and (2) Dewi Mursimah, who was married to Sunan Kalijaga (one of the Wali Songo). The followers and descendants of Sunan Ampel spread Islam far and wide, across the land of Java to the east and then outside of Java as far as Ternate. Sunan Ampel's brother, Sayyid Ali Murthado (who had come with him from Cambodia), is said to have gone to the island of Madura and then on to Bima, where he had close connections to the royal line there; eventually he died in Gresik.

Sunan Ampel was convinced that a Muslim people needed to have a king who followed Islam. To establish such a polity, however, he knew that it must have a strong foundation. Sunan Ampel therefore instructed his students to go to a place called Glagah Wangi, or Bintoro, to start such a center at which Islam could take root. A follower of his was Raden Patah (also known as Raden Hasan), the son of the king of Majapahit through a Chinese princess named Kian. He was thus a prince, although he had grown up off the island of Java since his mother was remarried when Prabu Brawijaya became devoted to his new wife from Champa. Raden Patah was asked to lead the new community at Glagah Wangi. Raden Patah was destined to become the first Muslim king there and someday himself to become one of the Wali Songo.

At first Raden Patah wanted to refuse Sunan Ampel's invitation, since the area of Glagah Wangi was short of water and it was known to be extremely barren and dry. Sunan Ampel and the other *wali* promised to help to overcome the problem of the water supply, however. They prayed to God to bring enough water to meet the needs of the new Muslim community. Then as they dug for a well, a water supply was found that was deep and never ran dry, even long after the end of the rainy season. This was a blessing from the *wali*. And with this, the area became arable for cultivation.

Raden Patah established a religious boarding school and madrasa in the area. The construction began in the year 880/1475. The effort was undertaken with seriousness and sincerity, and soon people from all over the empire of Majapahit, and even from outside Majapahit, were coming to study with Raden Patah. Glagah Wangi or Bintoro thus became a major center for the study of Islam, a popular place for Muslims to visit from far and wide, thanks especially to the trade connections of its students. And with this, the religion of Islam also became stronger among the local people.

After a while, Glagah Wangi or Bintoro became known as Demak, from the Arabic words *dhī mā'in,* meaning "having water." At the time that the great historic mosque at Demak was being constructed, in the year 882/1477, Sunan Ampel was directly involved. To remember and also to remind others of this and also his many other great works, one of the four main support pillars of the mosque at Demak is named *Sunan Ampel.*

As the *pesantren* at Demak became even more renowned among those who wanted to study Islam, the *wali* made a suggestion to Raden Patah. They had the idea that Demak could become a *kadipaten* [regency] of Majapahit. So Raden Patah went to the palace of Majapahit to meet with his father, who was the king of Majapahit, Prabu Brawijaya V. Prabu Brawijaya V granted permission for Demak Bintoro to be recognized as a *kadipaten,* and he appointed Raden Patah, who was now also known as Sunan Kota, as its *adipati* [regent or governor].

No sooner had Demak been inaugurated as *kadipaten* when some of the younger of the Wali Songo began to think further ahead. They suggested that Raden Patah might now seize power from Prabu Brawijaya V in order to rule as a Muslim king. Sunan Ampel was still the leader of the Wali Songo at that time, however. Having had a great deal of experience in such matters, Sunan Ampel took a longer and wiser view of the kingdom of Majapahit, whose influence was on the wane. According to him, Majapahit would inevitably fall in time. It would not be necessary for Demak to attack it in order to bring this about. And at the time that Majapahit fell, power would come next into the hands of an *adipati* who had once had good associations with Prabu Brawijaya V. Sunan Ampel knew this not only from his own astute reasoning but also from his ability actually to see firsthand what was going on inside the palace of Majapahit with his own spiritual vision. Thanks to the help of Allāh, he had special insight into unseen matters. Many of the other *wali,* including Raden Patah himself, agreed with the views of Sunan Ampel.

However, there was still a group of *wali* who respectfully disagreed.

They held the opinion that Sunan Ampel could be overly partial to Majapahit, since he himself had originally come to Java as an agent of Prabu Brawijaya V and he was after all a prince of the realm himself through kinship and marriage. According to them, Sunan Ampel was a wise leader, but he was also too sympathetic to the interests of Majapahit.

They noted also that Sunan Ampel had a different attitude than the other *wali* in matters of religion. The type of Islam that flourished among the younger *wali*, such as Sunan Bonang, Sunan Kalijaga, Sunan Muria, Sunan Gunungjati, and Sunan Kudus, was more flexible with respect to matters of religion. Sunan Kalijaga and Sunan Kudus, for example, were two of the Wali Songo who were especially ingenious at harmonizing the teaching of Islam with the local customs of Java, such as the entertainments of shadow puppet theater (*wayang kulit*) and *gamelan* musical orchestras. In the views of Sunan Kalijaga and Sunan Kudus, a people that may still depend on the support of old customs can more easily accept the religion of monotheism, that is, Islam. They held that when people do not feel challenged in their old habits, the elements of Islamic doctrine can seep in slowly and surely.

In contrast, Sunan Ampel, Sunan Giri, and Sunan Drajat were all committed to spreading the teachings of Islam just as the Prophet Muhammad had done. They never compromised in matters pertaining to the established customs or revealed laws of Islam. The preaching of Sunan Ampel and his followers excelled in teaching the people to be acutely aware in the observance of the requirements of Islam. This is so that they would not stray from the true path in accord with the Qur'an and the Hadith. The people considered this an essential support for religion, one that was also connected to the world outside Indonesia. In this way, Islamic doctrine could be imparted completely free from any innovation that could cause deviation from the essence of true religion. This teaching of Sunan Ampel proved to be a great contribution to the development of Islamic law among the Muslim people. Just like the teachings of all the other Wali Songo, the teachings of Islam that were imparted by Sunan Ampel represent a true reality that could be accepted with certainty.

With this, it can be seen that styles of *dakwah* among the *wali* differed. However, these were just two different paths leading to the same destination. That single goal is nothing other than to achieve the favor of Allāh. The teachings that were spread by Sunan Ampel became known as Pure [White/Putihan] Islam. Whereas, the teachings imparted by figures like Sunan Kalijaga and his followers are known as Folk [Red/Abangan] Islam."

At the time of the discussions about the future of Demak, Sunan Ampel held the view that it was best to be patient and to spread Islam to the center of the palace of Majapahit in a peaceful manner. He noted that the king had always had a favorable stance toward Muslims. Even more, the king had granted freedom to all of the *wali* to spread Islam throughout the land of Java, never forbidding them to perform their *dakwah*. This showed that he was truly a friend of religion. Given this, it would not be right for Raden Patah, who was in any case the son of the king, to attack Majapahit, according to Sunan Ampel. He asked, How would it be later if people would say that Raden Patah, student of Sunan Ampel, had attacked his very own father?

Nevertheless, the group of *wali* who seemed to be led by Sunan Kalijaga was not satisfied with this answer. Although the difference of opinion never caused a great division among the *wali,* some still wanted to attack Majapahit by force. In 883/1478, Sunan Ampel passed away. With this, the Wali Songo needed to appoint a new leader. Sunan Giri was named the new leader, and he became the *muftī* of the land of Java. Even though he had the same orientation to doctrine as Sunan Ampel, he had another point of view on the current political state of affairs. Right away he supported the position that had been held by Sunan Kalijaga and issued a *fatwā* [authoritative ruling] that Raden Patah ought to attack Majapahit. How could it be that Sunan Giri would have such a different approach than Sunan Ampel? The answer is that several important events had occurred all at once.

The kingdom of Majapahit was attacked by Prabu Grindrawardhana from the Kadipaten of Kediri, also known as Keling, in 883/1478. Starting at that time, the king of Majapahit was no longer actually Prabu Brawijaya V, the father of Raden Patah. So now Raden Patah had the right to defend his right to succession from Prabu Grindrawardhana, who had recently taken on the title "Prabu Brawijaya VI." This was because Raden Patah was the last blood descendant of the throne of Majapahit. Just when Raden Patah was ready to attack Majapahit, however, in the year 904/1498, Prabu Grindrawardhana was killed in an attack by Prabu Udara. Prabu Udara, who had now become the king of Majapahit, felt threatened by the power of Raden Patah at Demak Bintoro. He knew that an attack on him was imminent, and so he asked the Portuguese, who were in Melaka on the southern tip of the Malaysian peninsula, for help in defending his kingdom.[3]

In 923/1517, Demak attacked Majapahit, which was now led by its new king, Prabu Udara. Before hardly anyone had been lost in battle, however, the kingdom had already fallen easily into the hands of Raden Patah, or Sunan Kota. Had it not been the case that Demak had attacked Majapahit immediately at that time, there is a great likelihood that the Portuguese could have colonized the land of Java even before the Dutch attempted to do so.

After Majapahit fell, all of the regalia of state were relocated to Demak Bintoro in order to be in the possession of the rightful heir to the throne, who was Raden Patah. With the passing of Majapahit to the hands of Raden Patah, even more power was his to command. This fall of the kingdom of Majapahit meant that the first Islamic state on Java, that is, Demak, was established, with its king being Raden Patah, also known as the *wali* Sunan Kota. All of the *wali* gave thanks to God, because the religion of Islam now had a great influence and also a base from which to spread further. This would be the first great victory of Islam in Java. It was made possible by the great *dakwah* and the profound teaching and example of Sunan Ampel of the Wali Songo, who had first come to Java from Champa so many years before.

NOTES

1. A. Setiawati, *Sunan Ampel Sangat Hati-Hati Menyiarkan Agama Islam* (Jakarta: Penerbit TALISAM, 1997). Special thanks to James Hoesterey for locating this text in Indonesia. [For the sake of consistency through the volume, the editor has inserted Hijrī dates. (Ed.)]

2. In an Indonesian language the phrase could sound as though it meant "O' my chunk of wood, O' your chunk of wood!"

3. Melaka had fallen to the Portuguese in 1511; Batavia (Jakarta) was established on the coast of Java in 1536 by the Dutch.

27 Lan Zixi's "Epitaphs of the Real Humans"

Sachiko Murata

In 1268/1851 a Muslim scholar from Wuchang in Hubei Province, Lan Zixi (1197/1782–1274/1857), wrote a book titled *The True Learning of the Heavenly Direction* (i.e., of Islam) (*Tianfang zhengxue*), which was published ten years later.[1] It consists of a preface, an introduction, and seven chapters—altogether about 90,000 characters (247 pages). In the introduction, Lan says that the book belongs to the *Han Qitabu*. As he explains, *Qitabu* (a transliteration of *Kitāb*) refers to the classics of Islam, and *Han Qitabu* designates the translations of these classics into Chinese. This seems to be the first instance of the use of this expression (usually *Han Kitab* in the secondary literature) to refer to the school of Chinese-language Islamic writing that flourished from the mid-seventeenth through the nineteenth century.[2] At the beginning of the book, Lan explains that his book is a simplified version of the teachings of the *Han Kitab* as presented in the writings of Wang Daiyu (c. 1068/1657), the father of Chinese-language Islam, and Liu Zhi (after 1137/1724), who is probably the more influential author.[3] In the first chapter, six diagrams outline the teachings of Islam, including a depiction of the chain of prophets. Chapter 2 has six sections explaining the twenty-eight letters of the Arabic alphabet, not only in terms of script and pronunciation but also in terms of cosmological symbolism. In chapter 3, Lan deals with the meaning of the *shahāda* in twenty-nine sections. Chapter 4 clarifies "Nature and Mandate" (*xingming*), that is, the spiritual and cosmological roots of the cosmos. Chapter 5 dedicates twenty-four sections to the concealment of the Real One. Chapter 6 has thirty-eight sections explaining "the essential purport of the Real Commentary," that is, Wang Daiyu's major work, *The Real Commentary on the True Teaching* (*Zhengjiao zhenquan*), published in 1052/1642.

This brings us to chapter 7, titled "Epitaphs of the Real Humans" (*zhenren mouzhi*).[4] It consists of fifty-two sections that describe fifty-one prophets and Friends of God; Arabic names are usually provided in the margin. Forty-nine of the sections were written by Lan, and one of the sections has a subdivision, giving a total of fifty. Two more sections, one on Lan and one on his mother, were added to the printed text by two of Lan's disciples.

The term *zhen*, or "real," plays an important role in Chinese Islam, not least because, certainly from the time of Wang Daiyu if not before, Chinese Muslims referred to Islam as "the pure and real teaching" (*qing-zhen jiao*), an expression that can also be translated as "the teaching of purity and reality" or "of purity and truth." "Real" has a long history in Chinese thought, as do most of the terms employed by Muslims, but unlike most, *zhen* is closely associated with Daoism. In translating texts from Persian, Muslims often used it to render *haqq*. Thus Liu Zhi translates *wujūd-i haqq* as *zhenyu*, "real being."[5] In any case, by "real humans" Lan clearly has in mind those who have lived up to their human role in the cosmos—that is, the prophets and Friends, or the "perfect human beings" (*insān kāmil*) of the Sufi tradition.

The figures mentioned by Lan as leading up to Muhammad are Adam, Eve, Seth, Noah, Fu Xi (Japheth), Shen Nong, Abraham, Ishmael, Isaac, Jacob, Moses, Lot, David, Joseph, Solomon, Idris, Jonah, Yuhala, Jesus, and 'Abdallāh and Āmina (Muhammad's parents). Most are called "great sages" (*tasheng*); Eve is a "great lady" (*taitai*), and Yuhala is called both "real human" and "pure woman" (*nüjing*). 'Abd Allāh is called "father of the sage" and Āmina "mother of the sage." The Prophet himself is called "the Utmost Sage" (*zhisheng*) and, in Arabic script, "Muhammad Mustafā." (See Figure 20.)

Fu Xi and Shen Nong are legendary sage-emperors, and much of what Lan says about them is mentioned in the *Great Treatise of the Yijing* (2.2.1–5).[6] In Lan's account, Fu Xi was Japheth, son of Noah, who was the emperor of Tianfang, "the heavenly direction," that is, Arabia, or the country of the Western prophets. Fu Xi came to China at the command of his father. By gazing upward in contemplation and downward in observation, he was able to draw the eight trigrams and sixty-four hexagrams of the *Yijing*. By examining the alteration and transformation of yin and yang, he penetrated the virtue of spiritual clarity and came to know the good fortune and misfortune of the hard and the soft.

Shen Nong was also a man of Tianfang. At Noah's command he came to China with Fu Xi and served as his attendant. He taught people how to cultivate the five grains, which he had brought from Tianfang. Fu Xi

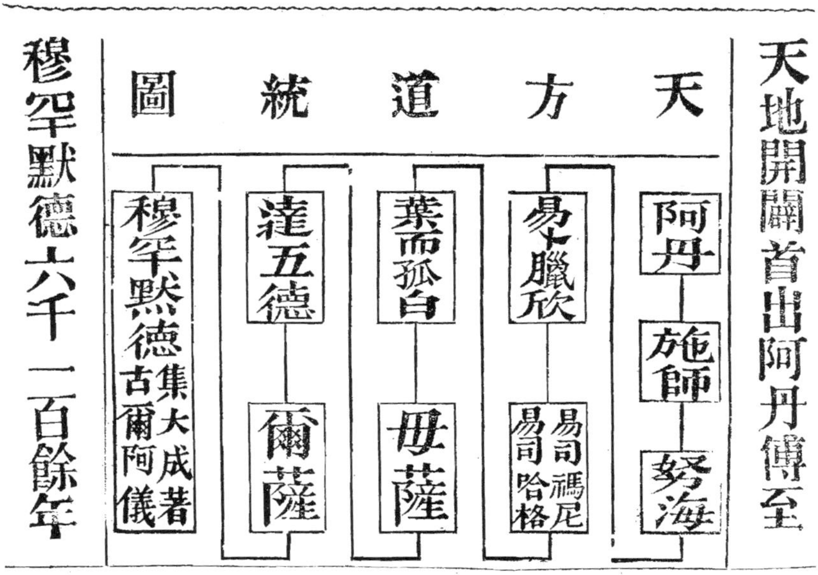

Figure 20. Lan Zixi, *Epitaphs of the Real Humans,* chart of individuals described in text, which reads as follows:

Top-center panel: Diagram of the Succession of the Tianfang Dao [or, the Dao of Islam]

Right-hand column: When heaven and earth split open, first Adan (Adam) emerged; then the transmission reached

Left-hand column: Muhanmeide (Muhammad), taking 6,100 and some years.

Beginning with first box on the upper right and following the line to the left: Adam—Shishi (Seth)—Nuhei (Nūh)—Yibulaxin (Ibrāhīm)—Yisimani/Yisihage (Ismāʻīl/Ishāq)—Yeergubo (Yaʻqūb)—Mūsā (Moses)—Dawude (Dāwūd)—Ersa (ʻĪsā)—Muhanmeide, The Great Compiler of the Perfect and Revealed Guerayi (Qurʼān).

appointed him as the spirit or god (*shen*) of agriculture, which is why his title became *Shen*.

The identity of Yuhala, who is given the Arabic name *Zahrā*, is not clear. She is said to have been born in Tianfang and to have died in Kunlun, the great mountain range in China and Tibet that is said to be the location of the Taoist paradise (and also Shambhala and "Shangri-La"). In the account of Noah, Lan tells us that Kunlun is the ancestral mountain of the 10,000 countries and that Tianfang is located at the center of those countries. When Noah was emperor, he commanded his son Ham to take twenty-four statesmen and officials to rule over Ouluoba (Europe), which is located 120,000 *li* to the west of Kunlun; and he commanded his son Fu Xi to take twenty-four statesmen and officials to rule over China, located 120,000 *li* to the east of Kunlun. Besides Noah and Yuhala, Lan names several others as having their tombs in Kunlun: Adam, Ishmael, Isaac, Jacob, David, Joseph, and Uways al-Qaranī.

Most likely, Yuhala is the Virgin Mary, not least because the list is chronological and she is mentioned right before Jesus. She is said to have spent her time meditating—perhaps a reference to the Qur'ānic verse that tells us Zakarīya would find her in the *"miḥrāb"* (3:37). If Yuhala is Mary, however, it is strange that Lan would not mention that she was the mother of Jesus.

When we turn to the Islamic period, the Chinese orientation of the book is evident in the list of names. Most of the figures after Muhammad are central to the early tradition; fifteen, however, are Chinese, and few can be identified easily. The first Muslim to be mentioned after Muhammad would be surprising anywhere outside China: Waqqās, who alone of the forty-nine figures is called a great human (*taren*). This is Saʿd ibn Abī Waqqās, a kinsman of the Prophet who played an important role as a military commander. The Arabic histories tell us that he was for a time governor of Kufa, but the caliph ʿUthmān removed him from that position. He returned to his home near Medina, where he died in the year 55/674. As far as the Muslim community in China is concerned, however, Waqqās was sent by the Prophet as an emissary to China in 11/628 and was received by the emperor, as can be seen in the account below.[7]

After Waqqās, Lan mentions Uways al-Qaranī, who alone in the list is not called by any title. The fact that he is mentioned, however, points to the strong presence of Sufism in Chinese Islam.[8] Next in the list are the four Rightly Guided Caliphs, who are called great worthies (*taixian*). Worthies, as contrasted with sages, were much discussed in Confucianism and Daoism. Confucian authors often say that Confucius was a sage and Mencius a worthy. One well-known Daoist scholar, Wang Bi (249), tells us that Confucius was a sage and Laozi and Zhuangzi, the greatest of the Daoist masters, were worthies.[9] In any case, the Chinese Muslims adopted the terms to make the distinction between *nabī* and *walī*, prophet and Friend.

Next in the list is Fāṭimat az-Zahrā'—like Eve, called a "great lady." Then come Hasan and Husayn, called "real humans." Next are the four imams of the Sunni *madhhab*s (schools of religious law)—Shāfiʿī, Mālik, Ahmad (ibn Hanbal), and Abū Ḥanīfa—who are given the transliterated title *Imamu* preceded by the adjective *great* (*da*). In the margin the Arabic for Abū Hanīfa is preceded by the title *A'zam* (supreme), presumably because most Chinese Muslims are Hanafīs.

From here on we have the fifteen Chinese Friends, some of whom are given Arabic as well as Chinese names. Fourteen are called "real humans," and one "the ancestral teacher." As far as I know, despite the growing interest of Chinese scholars in the history of Chinese Islam, no one has yet tried to sort out the historical identities of these figures.

.   .   .   .   .

In what follows I have translated six entries: those for Yuhala, Jesus, Waqqās, Uways, Wang Daiyu, and Ma Minglung. Wang Daiyu, as already mentioned, is the author of *The Real Commentary on the True Teaching* and a few other, short works. Ma Minglung (1006/1597–1090/1679) has left us with a single fifteen-folio treatise called *To Know Oneself Is to Awaken (Senzhi xingwu)*, clearly a commentary on the Hadith "He who knows himself knows his Lord." Dated 1661, it may not have been published until 1735. The book uses five- or seven-word stanzas, apparently the first example of this style in Islamic texts.[10]

All of Lan's accounts end with mention of the tomb of the real human in question. Each has a puzzling five-character phrase—*gutubu aoshi*—that seems unintelligible as pure Chinese. One of the only scholars who has discussed this text, Tazaka Kōdō, suggests that the first three characters, *gutubu*, are a transliteration of Arabic *qutb*, "pole or axis," and that *aoshi* can be understood to mean "landmark."[11] In Sufi teachings, of course, the Pole often designates the greatest saint of an age, around whom circle the affairs of the spiritual realm; for Ibn 'Arabī, there are many sorts of Poles, each of which is the axis of a specific domain. We can read the expression to mean something like the holy person who became the reference point and landmark in the area in which he or she was buried, implying that the tomb is a regional center of pilgrimage. The passages that include this expression usually also mention that the person in question passed away during one of the twenty-four periods into which the year is divided.

Notes on Lan's text following the entry on Adam, perhaps written by Lan's student, explain *gutubu* as the subtle body of the real human, attended by the "heavenly immortals" (*tianxian*, a Taoist expression that Muslims used to translate *angels*).[12] *Aoshi*, then, refers to the ground in which the real body of the real human is buried, a ground preserved from all calamity. The commentary goes on to say that there have been more than 100,000 real humans, all of whom have traveled the Way (*Dao*).

Those who became the *gutubu* of the season became the great immortals of the Great Way. It is worth noting that the entry on Muhammad adds the adjective *great* (*da*) to the two words, so he is the Great Pole of the Great Landmarks.

TRANSLATION

Epitaph of the Real Human Yuhala (Zahrā), a Pure Woman

Her Dao name is *Yuhala*, and she was a person of Tianfang. From a young age she loved the Dao. She was unlettered, and she used to sit quietly in a dark room clarifying her heart and gazing upon Nature. The Dao Nature was shining brightly, illuminating all things in the 10,000 directions. At the time of returning to the Real, her body issued forth the real fragrance, in contrast to ordinary days. Her tomb is at Kunlun. She became *qutb* of the landmarks. It was the end of autumn, and she was attended by the heavenly immortals.

Epitaph of the Great Sage Ersa ('Īsā)

The Dao name of this great sage is *Ersa*. He was a fifty-second-generation descendent of Adam. He was more than ten feet tall. His sagely countenance was a white face with black beard, elongated eyes, and long eyebrows. He was dwelling in the Pure and Clear Chamber, yet his body traveled to every country.[13] He followed the continuity of the Dao lineage of the teaching of Tianfang. The Heavenly Classic that he received from the Real Lord had the *ayati* of ten paths (*dao*).[14] He taught and transformed the students of the Western learning so that they became loyal and faithful scholars. His exhortations reached every country, and the people made progress and became students of the Western learning.

As for the country of Tudusi,[15] he exhorted the people, but they did not become transformed, and he came to know that he could not transform them. Finally he declined to act and, holding to the steps, he ascended. Mounted on a cloud, he moved around in the Pure and Clear Chamber. The people of the Tudusi country saw that the great sage went up to Heaven, so they designated him as the Heavenly Lord. Thereafter, the people of this country started to respect and have faith in him, and this itself was designated as the teaching of the Heavenly Lord.

The great sage was not able to make the people of this country his disciples, for they had not yet received the transmission. Therefore their actions in the way were still perplexed. The teachings of the Heavenly Lord had not yet been transmitted, so the students of the Western learning did not obtain the Dao. So, as long as the lineage of the Dao-teaching does not obtain the [right] person, there will be no transmission.

The great sage predicted that after six hundred years, Muhammad, the Utmost Sage, would emerge. The Utmost Sage would have knowledge from birth and would not wait for transmission to continue the teaching.

The great sage clarified his heart and saw Nature. His Dao Nature illuminates brightly with true greatness. At the time of going home to the Real, his body issued forth the real fragrance. His grave is in the vicinity of the Ka'ba. He became *qutb* of the landmarks, at the beginning of winter, being attended by the heavenly immortals.

Epitaph of Wuweisi Gaileni (Uways Qaranī)

Wuweisi Gaileni was a man of Tianfang, a wise sage who had knowledge from birth. He used to sit quietly in a cave at Kunlun, clarifying his heart and gazing upon Nature. The Great Dao was shining brilliantly, and everything in the 10,000 directions was illuminated.

Musidefa [Mustafā] said that between heaven and earth is a position upon which is seated an elder of the Dao, who is Uways. At the time when Musidefa was going back to the Real, he commanded the Four Great Worthies to confer a patched garment on Wuweisi Gaileni, whose body was revealed and whose substance was united, so as to continue the succession of the Sage. The Four Great Worthies said to him, "Our Sage did not meet you face to face. How did you come to know and love each other?"

He said, "Although I never met your sage face to face, I was never apart from him for a single moment. You saw your sage's face on the surface—his beard and his eyebrows—but you did not see his original face."

The Four Great Worthies prostrated themselves in submission. They said, "Inadvertently we became perplexed and deluded. We forgot the Sage's original face, which was known primordially.[16] Please give us teachings on how to turn away from our perplexity, so that we may not betray the primordial teaching and nurturing of the Sage. When we see you, sir, we also see the original face of the Sage. We know that you and our Sage are not only one in the turbid body but also one in the pure substance—you are one in level and position. By means of this patched garment, the succession of the Dao teaching is conferred. As for us, we still have dependence and reliance."

Thirty years after this, the succession of the Dao teaching was transmitted to Hasan [ibn 'Alī].

When the sage went back to the Real, his body issued forth the real fragrance. His tomb is in Kunlun. He became the *qutb* of the landmarks, in the middle of the winter, attended by heavenly immortals.

Epitaph of the Great Human Wangeshi (Waqqās)

The Dao name of this great human is *Wangeshi*. He was a man of Tianfang and the maternal uncle of the Utmost Sage of the West. He received an order to escort the Heavenly Classic to China in the Tang Era in the year 11/632. He traveled and arrived at the [capital city] Changan. The Tang emperor Dai Zong saw that he was a man of luminosity and greatness and that he had solid learning in expounding the Classic and explaining the Dao. He again and again retained and kept him in Changan, and then he gave him an imperial edict to erect the great temple of the Pure and Real. He welcomed the edict and obeyed it, and subsequently he dwelled there.

The Great Human wrote many chapters to expound the canon of the Classics. He urged everyone to transform their country, and his followers increased daily like teeth. The emperor Dai Zong gave an imperial edict to erect another, branch temple of the Pure and Real in Chianning [Nanking], in the province of Canton.

Later, when the Great Human was one hundred years old, he boarded an ocean-going vessel on the sea of Canton and set sail for the West. When he arrived at Chingshi,[17] he thought in humility that, although he had gone to China at the command of the Sage, he had not yet received a command to return. How then could he return to his native country? Hence he turned back again to the sea of Canton.

The Great Human went back to the Mandate and returned home to the Real while on the vessel. His body greatly issued forth the real fragrance. His tomb is outside the city of the province of Canton. He became the *qutb* of the landmarks. The time was at the beginning of winter, at the time of pleasing God.

The graveyard is on the dragon's pulse coming originally from the West. His tomb is on the dragon's neck and is locally called the echoing mound. It is said that there was an echoing sound from the middle of the tomb and that it could be heard from a distance of ten *li*. From the midst of the tomb there was the sound of the recitation of the Classic, which could also be heard as far as ten *lis'* distance. The tomb's beauty is beyond description.

·   ·   ·   ·   ·

The sincere and devout who visited his tomb saw that the Great Human was seated on a green sedan chair, emerging with a rush and entering with a rush. The middle gate was opening in a flash and then closing again to be united with the other gates.

Once there was a man carrying manure, and he rested his shoulders outside the tomb's courtyard. Then he saw two golden dragons at the head of the gates, guarding the many layers on the outside of the enclosing wall. It was clear to the man that his foulness would not be allowed to pass there.

Once forty people went home to the Real at once. Their tombs are next to the Great Human's tomb, and they also became the *qutb* of the landmarks.

Epitaph of the Real Human Daiyu

This Real Human's family name is Wang, his given name *Dai*, and his honorific *Daiyu*. At the time of the Ming, he was commended as a worthy scholar of Chinling [Nanjing]. For a while he traveled to Peking. He spent many years accumulating the learning of the Dao of the Pure and Real. He wrote *The Real Commentary on the True Teaching, The True Answers of the Very Real,* and *The Great Learning of the Pure and Real.* His translations of the Western Classics are evidence that his learning is of the utmost truth and his principles of the utmost clarity. His explanations of the rich and deep content of the Western Classics are refined, unmixed, extensive, and elegant. He penetrated thoroughly everything from ancient times to the present. Those who read him will surely sigh deeply and say, "The learning of this Real Human is not easy to obtain. The learning of the Western Classics is refined, unmixed, extensive, and elegant, and never has there been such a person! How rare is the learning of the Real Human! Not easy is it to obtain!"

The Western Classics have deep purport. While listening to the recitation of the text, the quick-witted hear spiritual penetration in the sound. Their hearts become still and their intentions satisfied; they repent of previous transgressions and advance straight to the Root Origin. But, if someone who is not quick-witted listens, he will be as if he has never heard it before. Those who have penetrated the books of Confucianism but have not penetrated the Western Classics do not understand the language nor what the talk is about. When people know that there are sages and worthies in Confucianism but do not know about the sages and worthies of the West, how will they recognize the sages and worthies?

There are some who can recite but cannot expound; there are some who can expound but cannot penetrate to the essence. There are many who can neither recite nor expound, and there are many who have penetrated the books of Confucianism but are not acquainted with the Western Classics. This Real Human penetrated the Confucian books as well as the Western Classics. He was refined, unmixed, extensive, and accomplished—this is indeed not easy to obtain, so people sigh deeply. This Real Human cultivated the Real Principle and Nature and, with genuine Nature, he went home to the Real. His tomb is in Sanlihe, outside the Fuzheng gate of Peking, where he became the *qutb* of the landmarks.

Epitaph of the Real Human of Wuchang (Muhammad Sāhib)

The family name of this Real Human is *Ma*. He was from Jiangxia and lived at the time of the Ming. He was a great scholar and became an *imamu* at Wuchang. He obtained real transmission of the Dao of the learning of the Western Classics and became a leader of the Hui teaching. As a person he cultivated his virtue so much that the light of glory was seen in his nature. He used to sit quietly in a cave, and day by day, more people longed for his virtue.

The governor-general of Hugan requested him to enter the public chamber and opened up the public gates in the three directions. He saw him walking on a three-feet-long white cloud and entering the middle gate. They looked at each other, and [the governor-general] said, "The Real Human's endeavor has been perfected. Please do not venture to speak much. I request that you return to the cloud and sit quietly. Spiritual clarity has become great."

On the twelfth day of the winter month [December 1678] he went home to the Real, while the fragrance of the real body was issuing forth. He left a will saying that the thirty books[18] of the Heavenly Classic should be placed upon his breast when he was buried. His followers built his tomb in the province of Wuchang in the graveyard of the Ma family, twenty *li* east of the city, where he became *qutb* of the landmarks. An octagonal tower was built at the tomb for the veneration of the family.

About this time the Real Human welcomed his son on the road in Hunan, where he was passing by the riverbank in the central part. The son saw his father in the midst of the road, and the Classics were emerging from his breast. He instructed his son, saying, "The household is waiting for these thirty books of the Perfect Classic. You must return home at once." When he received this command, he took the Classics and went back.

At this time, there were seven books of the Perfect Classic,[19] so everyone was inquiring about the thirty books. Once his son arrived home, holding the classics, he came to know that his father had gone home to the Real. The teacher of the people took the thirty books, which are the Perfect Classic.

Afterwards someone said that the Real Human Ma is still in the world and that they should desire to find him and seek the Dao from him. The people divided and took the five roads, each group searching for him. One group arrived at the border of Chou and heard that he had left by the gate of Yang. They hurried to reach the gate, but on inquiring, they heard that he had left for the state of Yang. They hurried toward the state of Yang. Before arriving at the prefectural city, there was a mountain road. They reached a temple of the Pure and Real in the midst of the mountain. They entered it and saw that everyone was performing the Friday ritual. There were two bottles of pure water, and two of them immediately performed the minor purification and hurried to join the Friday worship. They saw that the Real Human was at the head, leading the worship. The two said to themselves that they had obtained the seeing of the Real Human. They made the prostration, but then they saw that they were in a field of weeds in the wild mountains. There was no temple, people, or bottles of water. They came to know that the Real Human was in the realm of the immortals. There was only that one gathering, and it was not possible to search for him and visit him. Humbly they reflected upon themselves and awakened to self-cultivation—*that* could be done.

NOTES

1. Lan Zixi, *Tianfang zhenxue* (Wuchang, 1862; repr., Beijing: Qingzhen Shubao, 1925).

2. Zvi Ben-Dor Benite, *The Dao of Muhammad* (Cambridge, MA: Harvard University Press, 2005), 160.

3. On the importance of the two, see Benite, *Dao*, 134–53; Sachiko Murata, *Chinese Gleams of Sufi Light: Wang Tai-yü's Great Learning of the Pure and Real and Liu Chih's Displaying the Concealment of the Real Realm* (Albany: State University of New York Press, 2000).

4. The Chinese expression, which literally means "tombstone-inscription," and it is clearly used in a figurative sense to mean something like "memorial" (e.g., Arabic *tadhkira*). Benite says that most of the biographies of the Chinese Muslims are "from Lan's time and region," but he does not provide any evidence other than the literal meaning of the name of the chapter: "Most of the information in the biographies [of the Chinese Muslims] was recovered from tombstones [that Lan] examined" (*Dao*, 48).

5. See Murata, *Chinese Gleams*, 123.

6. See, for example, R. Wilhelm, *The I Ching or Book of Changes* (London: Routledge and Kegan Paul, 1951), 328–32.

7. For the secondary literature on the Waqqās in China, see D. D. Leslie, Yang Daye, and Ahmed Youssef, *Islam in Traditional China: A Bibliographical Guide* (Sankt Augustin, Germany: Monumenta Serica Monograph Series, 2006), 144.

8. The role Uways al-Qaranī plays in Central Asia has been highlighted by Julian Baldick, *Imaginary Muslims: The Uwaysi Sufis of Central Asia* (New York: New York University Press, 1993).

9. Fung Yu-lan, *History of Chinese Philosophy* (Princeton, NJ: Princeton University Press, 1952–53), 2:170.

10. Tazaka Kōdō, *Chugoku ni okeru kaikyō no denrai to sono gutsū* (Tokyo: Tōyō Bunko, 1961), 1412.

11. Ibid., 1428n.16.

12. In twenty-nine of the accounts, the real human is explicitly said to have been accompanied by the heavenly immortals after death. Eighteen of these are pre-Islamic, and the rest are Muhammad, his parents, his family (Fātima, Hasan, and Husayn), the Four Caliphs, and Uways.

13. "The Pure and Clear Chamber" refers to the heavenly realm. Presumably, Jesus is singled out for dwelling there while also in the world because he is God's "spirit," as the Koran puts it, and was born not of a human father but of the spirit "blown into Mary."

14. *Ayati* is a transliteration of *āyāt*, "verses, signs." Lan tells us in other entries that several prophets received *ayati* of a specific number of paths: Adam, 16; Noah, 5; Abraham, 5; Idrīs, 4; and Muhammad, 24,000—a total of 24,040.

15. This seems to be a transliteration of *Qudus*, Jerusalem.

16. Perhaps a reference to the Hadīth "I was a prophet when Adam was between water and clay." The concept of the Muhammadan Reality as origin of all things was well-known to Liu Zhi and other Muslim scholars.

17. A marginal note says that this is in the west of the West Ocean, still eighteen stages from the Ka'ba.

18. A reference to the traditional division of the Qur'ān into thirty sections (*juz'*, *ajzā'*).

19. That is, only a partial copy of the Qur'ān.

Appendix

COMPARATIVE/SYNOPTIC CHART LISTED BY ORDER IN TABLE OF CONTENTS

	Main Figure			Text					
Name	*Dates*	*Places Birth/life*	*Influence/stature*	*Title*	*Author*	*Dates*	*Language*	*Place*	*Genre*
1. Abū Bakr	c. 570–16/634	Mecca, Medina	Global	1A. *Sahīh Muslim* (Authentic Hadīths of Muslim)	Muslim ibn al-Hajjāj	d. 262/875 wc 257/870	Arabic	Nishapur, NE Persia, Central Asia	Hadith collection, section on *Fadā'il* of Companions
				1B. *Kitāb al-lumaʿ* (Book of Light Flashes)	Abū Nasr as-Sarrāj	d. 378/988	Arabic	Tūs, NE Persia, Central Asia	*Fadā'il* (encomium, account of virtues)
				1C. *Kashf al-mahjūb* (Revealing Things Veiled)	ʿAlī ibn ʿUthmān Hujwīrī	d. 475/1072 w.c. 1068–72	Persian	Lahore, South Asia	*Tabaqāt* (spiritual attainments (*ahwāl*=*fadā'il*))
				1D. *Hilyat al-awliyāʾ* (Ornament of God's Friends)	Abū Nuʿaym al-Isfahānī	d. 430/1038 w. 422/1031	Arabic	Isfahān, SW Iran	*Tabaqāt* (generations)
2: Abū Yaʿzā Yallanūr ad-Dukkālī	c. 572/1177 Al-Moravid	Middle Atlas Mtns, near Fez	Regional	*Al-Mustafād* (Beneficial Account)	Abū ʿAbd Allāh Muhammad at-Tamīmī	d. 603/1207 wc 1200	Arabic	Fez, Morocco	*Manāqib* (feats, marvels)
3: [Thematic text: Miracles, Various Friends]		Middle East		*Nashr al-mahāsin al-ghāliya* (Diffusion of Perfumed Merits)	ʿAbd Allāh ibn Asʿad al-Yāfiʿī	Mid-8th/14th cent.	Arabic	Hijāz (NW Arabian Peninsula)	*Fatwā/radd* (legal advisory/response to inquiry)

Note: b. = birth date; c. = circa; cent. = century; d. = death date; w. = date of written work; wc = approximate date of written work; F = Fulfulde; H = Hausa

4: Muhammad Wafaʾ	d. 765/1363	Mamlūk Egypt	Regional	*Al-Minah al-ilāhiya (Divine Gifts)*	Abū 'l-Laṭāʾif	Early 9th/15th cent.	Arabic	Egypt	*Manāqib*
5: Abū 'l-Qāsim al-Junayd	d. 297/910	b. Persia a. Iraq	Global	*5A. Hilyat al-awliyāʾ*	Abū Nuʿaym al-Isfahānī	d. 430/1038 w. 422/1031	Arabic	Isfahān, sw Persia	*Tabaqāt* (generations)
				5B. Nafaḥāt al-uns (Breaths of Intimacy)	ʿAbd ar-Raḥmān Jāmī	d. 898/1492 w. 881/1476	Persian	Herat, E. Persia, now Afghanistan	*Tabaqāt* (generations)
6. Various Friends of God	Most 3rd/9th/ 5th/11th cent.	Middle East	Regional/ transregional/global	*Gulistān (Rose Garden); Bustān (Orchard)*	Muslih ad-Din Saʿdi	d. 692/1292 w.	Persian	Shīrāz, sw Persia Iran	"wisdom literature," hybrid of prose and poetry
7. Ostad Elahi 1895–1974 and Hajji Niʿmat	Iran	Transregional		*Āthār al-ḥaqq (Traces of the Truth)*	Ostad Elahi	1895–1974, w. 1978	Persian, some Kurdish	Iran	*Malfūzāt* (tradition, autobiographical reflections)
8. Najm ad-Dīn Akhūndzāda, aka the Mulla of Hadda	late 19th cent. Afghanistan d. 1903	Regional		Miracles of the Mulla of Hadda	(Oral Tradition)	13th/19th cent. on	Pashtu	Afghanistan	*Manāqib* style
9. Sulaymān, aka Hakim Ata	Prob. Ear. 7th/13th cent.	Central Asia/ Khwarazm	Regional	*Hakim Ata kitabi (Book of Hakim Ata)*	Anonymous	10th/16th or 11th/17th cent.	Chaghatay Turkic	C.Asia/ Khwarazm (Uzbekistan)	*Manāqib* style, called *hikāyat* in some mss.
10. Sarı Saltık	660s/1260s	Anatolia/ Rumelia (Balkans)	Regional/ transregional	*Saltuknāme (Book of Saltuk)*	Ebu 'l-Hayr-i Rūmī	wc 878/ 1473–885/	Turkish	Turkey	Epic romance with features of *manāqib*

(continued)

COMPARATIVE/SYNOPTIC CHART LISTED BY ORDER IN TABLE OF CONTENTS (continued)

	Main Figure			Text					
Name	Dates	Places Birth/life	Influence/stature	Title	Author	Dates	Language	Place	Genre
11. Sarı İsmail	fl. c. mid-8th/14th cent.	Anatolia	Regional	Vilāyetnāme (Spiritual Biography)	Anonymous?	c. early 9th/15th cent.	Turkish	Turkey	Manāqib style
12. Yūnus Emre	d. c. 720/1321	Anatolia	Trans-regional	12A. Vilāyetnāme (Spiritual Biography)	Anonymous?	c. early 9th/15th cent.	Turkish	Turkey	Manāqib style
				12B. Dertli Dolap (Woeful Waterwheel)	Nezihe Araz	b. 1992 w. 1961	Modern Turkish	Turkey	(Hagiographical) Novel
13. Members of the Tijāniyya order	18th–20th cent.	West Africa	Regional/transregional	Téeré buy tektalé dëgg (Book That Recommends the Truth)	Shaykh ʿAbbās Sall	d. 1990 w. 1966	Wolof	Senegal (w. in Abidjan, Ivory Coast)	Panegyric poem
14A. Usman dan Fodiyo	Mid-13th/19th cent.	Nigeria	Trans-regional	14A. Filitago (F) Wa'kar Gewaye (H) (The Journey)	Nana Asma'u bint Usman dan Fodiyo	d. 1281/1864 w. 1839, 1865	Fulfulde, Hausa (separate versions)	Nigeria	Panegyric poem
14B. Prophet Muhammad	d. 11/632	Mecca, Medina	Global	14B. Begore (Yearning [for the Prophet])	Nana Asma'u	w. date unknown	Hausa	Nigeria	Panegyric poem
14C. Various Sufi Women	3rd/9th–12th/19th cent.	Middle East, Nigeria	Transregional/global	14C. Tindinore Labne (F), Tawassuli Ga Mata Masu Albarka (Sufi Women) (H)	Nana Asma'u	w. 1836	Fulfulde, Hausa (same year)	Nigeria	Panegyric poem

15. Job's Wife and Prophet Job	Pre-Islamic	Middle East	Global	*Utendi wa Ayubu (Epic of Job)*	Unknown	w. early 13th/19th cent.	Swahili	East Africa	*Tendi* verse form (used for Swahili epic narrative)
16. Shaykh Uways ibn Muhammad al-Barawī	1847–1909	Somalia (East Africa)	Regional	From *Jalāʾ al-ʿAynayn fi manāqib ash-shaykayn* "The Death of Shaykh Uways"	Shaykh Qāsim al-Barawī	wc 1917	Arabic	Somalia	*Manāqib*
17. Sadr ad-Dīn Sadri Jahān	921/1515	Punjab (Pakistan)	Regional	*Bāgh Anbiyāʾ Punjab (Garden of the Saints of Punjab)*	Sufi Muhammad Ismail	w. 1995	Urdu	India	*Tadhkira*
18. Ahmad Sirhindī	1034/1624	Punjab (Pakistan)	Trans-regional	*Zubdat al-Maqāmāt (Cream of Spiritual Stations) Hadarat al-Quds (Spiritual Presences)* plus excerpts	Badakhshānī, Badr ad-Dīn Sirhindī	11th/17th to 14th/20th	Urdu, Persian, Arabic	Indo-Pakistan, Syria	*Tadhkira* (apologetics. "auto/biography")
19. Various, ambiguous	Not specific	Sind (Pakistan)	Regional, NW South Asia	*Dīwān-i Khwāja Farīd* selected lyric poems	Khwāja Ghulām Farīd	1319/1901	Siraiki	Sind, Pakistan	*Naʿt*, panegyric
20. Pir Sadr ad-Dīn	a. mid-14th, early 15th cent. d. c. 819/1416	Gujarat, west-central India	Trans-regional (b. Iran, a. Sind, Punjab)	*Nūr am-mubīn (The Clear Light)*	ʿAli Muhammad Chunārā	1936	Gujarati	West-central India	*Tadhkira*
21. Thematic text (ziyārat)	N/A	Central India, various	N/A	*Makhzan-i aʿrās (Treasury of Death Anniversaries)*	Muhammad Najīb Qādirī Nāgawrī Ajmerī	1155–56/1742–43	Persian	Awrangabad, India	Treatise, manual
22. Khwāja Hasan Nizāmī	1878–1955	Northern India	Regional	*Āp Bītī Khwāja Hasan Nizāmī (Autobiography of Khwāja Hasan Nizāmī)*	Wc mid-14th/20th cent.		Urdu	India	Autobiography

(continued)

COMPARATIVE/SYNOPTIC CHART LISTED BY ORDER IN TABLE OF CONTENTS (continued)

	Main Figure			Text					
Name	Dates	Places Birth/life	Influence/ stature	Title	Author	Dates	Language	Place	Genre
23. Bonbibī	Mythic	Story set in Arabia, "active" Bangladesh	Regional, Sundarbans India/ W. Bengal, Bangladesh	Jahārnāma Bonbibī (Tale of Bonbibī's Sublime Manifestation)	Muhammad Khāter	Late 13th/19th cent.	Bengali	West Bengal	Puthi (Bengali literary form)
24. Mānik Pīr	Mythic	Bangladesh	Regional	Mānik Pīr Keccha (Tales of Mānik Pīr)	Munsi Muhammad Pijir ad-Din Sāhib	w. early–mid-13th/19th cent.	Bengali	Bangladesh	Katha (narrative/tale; Bengali literary/ hagiog. form
25. Muhammad ibn al-Hanafiya	1st/7th cent.	Central Middle East	Transregional, global	Hikāyat Muhammad Hanafiya (Narrative of Muhammad Hanafiya)	Abū Mikhnaf (Arabic?); anon. Persian	Persian wc 8th/14th cent. Malay 917/ 1511	Malay added details to Persian	Malaysia	Narrative, features of maqtal (martyrology)
26. Sunan Ampel, Wali Songo	9th/15th– 10th/16th cent.	Indonesia	Regional	Sunan Ampel Sangat Haithati Menyiarkan Agama Islam ("Sunan Ampel of the Wali Songo")	A. Setiawati	w. 1997	Indonesian	Indonesia	Popular print lit. based on classical Javanese hagiography
27. Various prophets and Friends	Pre-Islamic/ medieval	Middle East/ East Asia	Global, regional, transregional	Tianfang zhengxue (True Learning of the Heavenly Direction)	Lan Zixi	w. 1861	Chinese	China	Tadhkira (?)

Glossary

Terms are Arabic unless indicated otherwise by the following abbreviations: B = Berber; Bg = Bengali; C = Chinese; H = Hindi; I/J = Indonesian/Javanese; K = Kurdish; P = Persian; Pk = Pakhtun; T = Turkish; U = Urdu; W = Wolof. Unless otherwise noted, whole words in ( ) are Arabic "broken" plurals, suffixes in parentheses (e.g., -āt) are simple plurals, and (a) indicates the feminine form of the term.

'abd	servant (of God), godservant, believer and spiritual seeker
'abīd ('ubbād)	devotee, worshipper
abdāl (sg. badal)	substitutes (40), personalities inhabiting the upper realm of the cosmos
abrār (sg. barr)	devout or dutiful ones (7); a rank among awliyā'
adab (ādāb)	conduct, behavior; etiquette in discipline or devotional ritual
adab az-ziyāra	guidelines for ritual propriety on visitation
'adat	etiquette toward a holy person
addiya (W)	gift offered by disciple to his marabout on recurring basis
afrād (sg. fard)	unique ones, incomparables; low in hierarchy of Friends of God
agurram (B)	common Moroccan term for Friend of God
ahl al-ighātha	people of assistance; intercessory Friends of God
akhyār	chosen ones (300) among Friends of God; a rank within Sufi orders

amīn	controller or financial officer of a Friend's shrine/tomb
amghār (B)	elder, leader; roughly synonymous with *shaykh*
ʿamūd	column or pillar; sometimes an inscribed tomb monument stone
anāshīd (sg. *inshād*)	recitation of mystical poetry in Sufi ritual settings; spiritual songs
āp bītī (U)	type of autobiographical account
aqwiyāʾ	strongest ones; Tirmidhī's term for high rank among Friends of God
arkān (sg. *rukn*)	pillars or supports; structural element in Sufi cosmology
aṣḥāb an-nawba	masters of time's wheel; rank in saintly hierarchy (unique to Shaʿrānī)
āsitāne (T)	central residential facility of a Turkish order
āstān (P)	entrance to shrine, threshold of Friend's residence
āstānbusī (P)	threshold kissing; part of ritual etiquette of *ziyāra*
ʿatabāt	technical term for Shīʿī sacred sites in Iraq
athar (āthār)	trace, vestige; esp. relics of Friends; material remains, ruins, monuments
awliyāʾ (sg. *walī*)	Friends (of God), saints
awtād (sg. *watad*)	tent-pegs, fulcrums, anchors (4), at cardinal points in Sufi cosmic hierarchy
babad (J)	Javanese historical chronicle; one source of hagiographical material
baraka	blessing, spiritual power, charisma communicated by Friends of God
kalīd baridār (P)	keeper or the key of a Friend's *dargāh*
bidʿa	novelty, innovation; deviation from acceptable teaching and practice
buqʿa	place; Sufi residential facility or tomb
buzurg (P)	great person; sometimes used of Friends of God
dafālī (H)	caste of Indian Muslim and Untouchable musicians, esp. connected with disseminating lore about Gāzī Miyān or the Five Pīrs

dakwah (I)	Ar. da'wa, invitation; missionary activity, proselytizing
dam (P)	breath; holy person's breathing scriptural words over sick person
darbār-i awliyā' (P)	royal court of Friends (of God); gathering to honor a saint
dargāh (P)	door-place; Sufi institution such as residence or tomb-shrine
dede (T)	elder; honorific given to spiritual guide; synonym for shaykh
dhikr	recollection, invocation; both individual and communal prayer ceremony
du'ā'	supplication, invocation, personal prayer
durūd	prayer recited during some dhikr ceremonies
dūst (P)	friend; synonymous with lover of God, or God Himself as Beloved
eren(-ler) (T)	"one who has attained" the goal of the spiritual quest; Friend of God
faḍīla (faḍā'il)	excellence, noble qualities, virtue (of either persons or cities)
fahrasa	genre used in hagiography; listing of one's teachers
faqīr (fuqarā')	poor person, mendicant; generic term for seeker of God
faqr	poverty, whether actual or spiritual
fard (afrād)	"singular" one from the lowest rank of Friends of God
fatā (fityān)	youth, courtly gentleman; synonym for seeker of altruistic values; associated with futūwa institutions and values
fayḍ	overflowing, superabundance; grace bestowed by a holy person
firāsa	power of spiritual perspicacity; a type of clairvoyance, "mind-reading"
futūwat-khāna (A/P)	principle institutional venue of chivalric organizations
ghawth	help, assistance; figure at top of cosmic hierarchy (syn. quṭb)

ghāzī	raider, warrior on the frontiers; name given to some Friends associated with combat for the faith
ghayb	unseen realm, home of cosmic hierarchy
ghusl	ritual for cleansing tombs of Friends of God during *'urs* ceremonies
ginān (Sindhi)	poetic/song form popular among Ismā'īlīs
gongbei (C)	tombs of Sufi founders and leaders, esp. in Northwest China
gutubu aoshi (A/C)	possibly "landmark axis/pole"
ḥaḍra	gathering with invocation and ritual dance; presence of the Prophet
haft tanān (P)	the seven figures, mysterious members of saintly hierarchy
haftawāna (K)	seven powers, members of saintly hierarchy beneath *haft tanān*
ḥakīm	wise one, sage, teacher of spiritual or metaphysical wisdom
ḥawlīya	turn of the year; Friend of God's death anniversary
ḥawma	section, cluster of tombs in a cemetery
ḥawsh	a walled enclosure, as in that which surrounds a grave cluster
ḥikāya	narrative; one of many hagiographical genres
'īdgāh (P)	place for festal celebration, e.g., shrine or tomb of Friend
ijāzat at-tabarruk	license conferring authority of the *shaykh* of an order
ikhlāṣ	sincerity, spiritual uprightness
imāmbāra (P)	Indian facility for Shī'ī gatherings to commemorate imams
imāmzāda (P)	descendant of imam; common name for saint's tomb
'imāra	structure; often referring to Sufi residential facility
insān al-kāmil, al-	complete person; image of spiritual perfection
'ishratīyān (A/P)	those who see unity in multiplicity; class of saints, esp. Naqshbandī

isrā'	Night Journey of Muhammad, prior to Ascension
istidrāj	deceiving by degrees; apparent miracle, result of evil forces, including sorcery or magic
jabarūt	cosmological realm of absolute divine power, between *mulk* and *malakūt*
jadhb(a)	attraction; God's drawing the mystic to God-self
jam'	union; joining with God, spiritual focus
jaman kuwalen (J)	epoch of the Friends of God, following pre-Islamic period in Indonesia
jaras	bell; term used for Pole Friend at peak of hierarchy
jawsaq (jawāsiq)	resting place, venue for assembled devotees in cemeteries or shrine areas
jeballu (W)	disciple's oath of faithfulness to the *shaykh* of an order
karāma(āt)	gratuitous marvels, wonders; saintly, as distinct from prophetic, miracles
keccha (Bg)	tale, story; Bengali equivalent of Arabic *qiṣṣa*
khādim	attendant, steward, assistant *shaykh* with special duties within an order; resident attendant at a Friend's *dargāh*, superintendent of a *ribāṭ*
khādim al-muṣḥaf	assistant charged with distributing Qur'ān texts for recitation
khādim ar-rub'a ash-sharīfa	assistant for the performance of communal prayer rituals
khādim as-sajjāda	assistant charged with maintaining prayer rugs for a community
khalīfa	successor; chosen as heir to a *shakyh*'s authority over an order
khalwat dar anjumān	solitude in the midst of a throng; Naqsh-bandī retreat in everyday life
khānaqāh (P)	major type of Sufi residential facility, often linked with other functions
kharq al-'āda	contravention of custom, as in a saintly marvel or prophetic miracle
khatm al-anbiyā'	Seal of the prophets; Muhammad

khatm al-awliyā'	seal of the Friend of God; term given to certain leading saints
khāṭir (khawāṭir)	passing inclinations, movements of soul
khulla	intimacy; friendship with God, esp. of Abraham
khwāja	sir, master; honorific title of great teacher; term for some Naqshbandīs
kibrīt al-aḥmar, al-	red sulphur; alchemical power; metaphor for spiritual transformation
kramat (J)	Indonesian term for holy place, grave (from Ar. *karāmāt*)
kudi terantang (J)	small axe, weapon of Friends of God in Javanese lore
kunnāsh (kanānīsh)	a type of journal or diary, often hagiographical
kyai (J)	elder, senior, venerated teacher; sometimes in names of *wali*s
lāhūt	cosmological realm of divinity itself
lāhūtī (U)	divinely inspired (referring to a type of Urdu autobiography)
langar khāna (P)	free kitchen part of Sufi institutional complexes or *dargāh*s
magal (W)	magnification, yearly pilgrimage to tomb of Amadou Bamba (Senegal)
mahfil	gathering, assembly of participants in *dhikr*, musicians
mahfil khāna (A/P)	temporary facility constructed near Friend's tomb for musical concert
majdhūb	one who is drawn by God; mystic who advances without personal effort; name given to some solitary, itinerant mystics
majhūl	unknown; referring to Friends of God whose status only God knows
majlis	session, assembly; spiritual gathering; also collection of saint's sayings
makhdūm	one who is served; honorific of major *shaykh*, member of family of shrine custodians
makhfī	hidden; referring to Friends of God whose status has not been made public

malang (?)	Southeast Asian term for *qalandar;* dervish at Sehwan shrine in Sind; individual, unaffiliated itinerants who sometimes take up residence in service of a shrine's saint as his disciple
malakūt	cosmological realm of lordly dominion, of angels and pure spirits
malfūz (-āt)	utterance(s); collected (originally) oral discourses of Sufi *shaykh*s
manām	dreaming; important vehicle of divine disclosure requiring interpretation
manāqib (sg. *manqaba*)	virtue, wondrous feats, legendary deeds; type of hagiographical account; in singular form, usually refers to a hagiographic work on an individual Friend of God
manāsik	ascetical rituals (pl. of *mansik*), pilgrimage rites, including those associated with shrines and tombs of Shī'ī imams
mansik	place where one engages in asceticism; hermitage, ascetic's cell
maqbara	mausoleum, tomb-shrine, funerary structure
marabout (marbūṭ)	French/colloquial form, Maghribī: bound, attached, confined to a *ribāṭ*
marthīya	lament, threnody; usually poetry honoring a martyred saint or imam
mashāyikh az-ziyāra	guides for pilgrims engaged in visitation to Friends' tombs
mashhad	witness-place; martyrium, burial place of a martyr; funeral procession
mashhad ar-ru'ya	vision-shrine, i.e., one constructed on instructions via a vision
ma'ṣūm	impeccable, beyond reproach; quality of Prophet, Friends, imams
mawlānā	our master; honorific title given to some outstanding religious figures
mawlid (mawālīd)	birthday; celebration for the Prophet Muhammad or Friend of God
mawsim	season, annual agricultural observance, or feast of death of holy person
mawzun (Pk)	successor to a *pīr*, authorized to teach arcane/mystical traditions

mazār(-āt)	place of visitation; shrine, goal of pilgrimage, esp. saint's tomb
mi'rāj	ascension; Muhammad's guided tour of the heavens to the Throne of God
misbāḥa	praise device; the rosary, made of up 33 or 99 beads for names of God
mīangul (P)	"flower of the saints"; Afghan title of line of Akhūnd of Swat
mudhakkir	one who makes mention; reminder, storyteller
mufrad	unique one; Tirmidhī term for highest-ranking Friend of God
mujaddid	renewer, reformer expected at beginning of each new lunar century
mujāhadat an-nafs	struggle against the ego-soul; engaging in battle with the inner enemy
mujāwar	residing at a saint's tomb as an act of devotional piety
mujāw/vir	neighbor; custodian who maintains a Friend's shrine or tomb
mu'jiza	evidentiary or apologetic miracle; power manifested through prophets
munājāt	intimate prayers; brief, at times paradox-laced form of discourse with God
munāqara	contest; hagiographic topos with Friends competing in miracle power
munfarid	singular one; early term for highest-ranking Friend of God
munshid	singer of poetic verses; provides sung prayers at formal rituals
muqaddam(a)	deputy; group leader, representative of *shaykh*, with authority to initiate; assistant at Friend's shrine
murābiṭ	one who takes up residence in a *ribāṭ*
murshid	one who directs; a spiritual guide; synonym for *shaykh*
musāfir	guest; itinerant Sufi who seeks hospitality on his travels
musāfirān (P)	sojourners; itinerant Sufis unattached to specific institutions/orders

mutawallī	custodian or administrator of a *waqf*, pious endowment of an institution
muwallah	driven to distraction, ecstatic, enraptured, spiritually crazed; in state of *walah*
muzamzim	chanter; performer of musical texts in Sufi ritual
nā'ib	deputy *shaykh* in some orders, to whom *muqaddam*s reported
najīb (nujabā')	preeminent, noble one; Friends in cosmic hierarchy (the seven regions of the cosmos)
naqīb (nuqabā')	chief; custodian of liturgy or overseer of aspirants in some orders
nāsūt	cosmological realm of humanity
na't	description, attribute; poetic genre extolling exemplary one's virtues
nawbat khāna (A/P)	music hall; important ritual facility at major Friends' shrines
nawgaza (P)	nine yards tall; "giant" Friends of God in ancient times
nazrāna (P)	monetary donation to a Friend of God at a *dhikr* or *samā'*
nerccas	Malayali (Kerala) term (to vow) for public celebrations in honor of Friends, Muslim adaptation of pre-Muslim observances
niyaz penceresi (T)	mausoleum window allowing passersby to salute the deceased
nüjing (C)	"pure woman"; title of Mary mother of Jesus
nujabā' (sg. *najīb*)	preeminent ones; (3) Friends of God near top of cosmic hierarchy
nuṣaḥā' (sg. naṣīḥ)	sincere ones, early term for a rank in the saintly hierarchy
panj pīr (P)	Five Elders; group of antinomian Friends in Northern India
panj tan (P)	Five Persons; Shī'ī family (Muhammad, 'Alī, Ḥasan, Ḥusayn, Fāṭima)
parsā (P)	an individual noted for devotion and piety
pīr (P)	elder; spiritual director; synonym for *shaykh* and for Friend of God
pīrī-murīdī (P)	system of traditional relationships between seekers and guides (India)

pīr parastī (P)	worship of the *pīr,* condemned as excessive
pīrzāda (P)	descendant of a Friend of God; member of an order or organization
pundhen (J)	Indonesian term for spirit abode, sometimes falsely identified as a Friend's tomb
puthi (Bg)	genre of story sometimes used for hagiographical tales
qabr (qubūr)	tomb, grave, burial place
qalandar (P)	rough block of wood; antinomian dervish; member of a class of itinerant mendicants
qaṣīda	ode; medium-length mono-rhyming poem often panegyric in tone
qāṣṣ (quṣṣāṣ)	professional storyteller, entertaining with edifying tales
qawwāl/ī	chanter of popular devotional music, esp. in South Asia
qawwūm	subsistent one; title given to highest figure in some saintly hierarchies
qiṣṣa (qiṣaṣ)	tale, story; literary and oral hagiography, esp. "Tales of Prophets"
qubba	cupola, dome; type of structure for tombs of holy persons
qudwa	example, paragon, or model of Sufis and potential Friends of God
quṭb	pole, axis; (one of) top figure(s) in Sufi cosmic hierarchy
rābiṭa	hermitage; local or regional Sufi residence instituted by one *shaykh;* replaced by *zāwiya* in Maghribī parlance during ninth/fifteenth century
rāhraw (P)	wayfarer; one who travels the mystic path and actual roads
rāhbar (P)	way-shower, a spiritual guide
raqṣ	dancing; ritual paraliturgical movement of various kinds
rātib	assigned prayer often associated with set times in the day
ribāṭ	frontier stronghold; Sufi residential facility
riḥla	travel, journey; often referring to pilgrimage and visitation
riyāḍāt	spiritual exercises, disciplines

ru'yat al-qalb	vision of the heart, inward vision of angelic realm
ru'yā ṣāliḥa	correct vision, often called a "veridical dream"; 1/46th of prophecy
ṣadr	center of one's being; an aspect of the human heart
ṣāḥib-i sajjāda (A/P)	holder of the prayer rug; heir to authority in a Friend's tomb-shrine
ṣāliḥ (ṣulaḥā')	upright; noted for holiness and serenity; esp. in Maghribī accounts, saint
sālik	wayfarer; seeker who progresses through hard work, opp. of *majdhūb*
sulūk	wayfaring; mystical progress or path
sāqī	cupbearer; poetic metaphor for one who supplies mystical intoxication
sarishtadār (P)	registrar of pilgrims at a *dargāh*
sëriñ (W)	saintly individual, spiritual guide (esp. in Senegal)
shadd ar-riḥla	saddle cinching; i.e., embarking on journey for visitation
shafā'a	intercession; much-discussed attribute of some prophets or Friends
shāh (P)	king; common South Indian term for Friend of God
shahīd	martyr; one who sacrifices self to the "death" of mystical love
shāhid	witness; term for one endowed with mystical experience
shajara	tree; chart of one's Sufi spiritual lineage or genealogy
sharīf	noble, descendent of Prophet; title given to *shaykhs* in some orders
shen (C)	Sage, common term for Prophet, as distinct from *xian* (Friend)
shuṭṭār (sg. *shāṭir*)	couriers; rank in the hierarchy of Friends of God
siddīq	authentic; person of unassailable veracity and sincerity
silsila	chain of spiritual succession, Sufi genealogy

sīra (sīyar)	life story; hagiographical genre, esp. of Prophet Muhammad
sunan (J)	abbrev. of *susuhunan* (highly esteemed); honorific title of the Wali Songo
ṭabaqa (ṭibaq)	dervish cell; part of Sufi residential facilities
ṭabaqāt	generations; successive groups of Sufis; major hagiographic genre
tābūt	cenotaph, ceremonial coffin for processional use
tadhkira	remembrance, memorial; major hagiographic genre
taitai (C)	great lady, hagiographical term applied to Mary
taixian (C)	"Great Worthy," title of the Rightly Guided Caliphs
tanazzul	descent of the *majdhūb* from divine reality to created nature
taqashshuf	asceticism, mortification, self-denial, simplicity of life
taraqqin	ascent of the *sālik* from created nature to the divine presence
taren (C)	great human, Chinese hagiographical term
ṭarīqa	Sufi "path," "order"
tasheng (C)	"great sages," common term for prophets
tawaṣṣul	entreaty, pleading; seeking "access/means" to God via saintly intercession
thaan (Bq)	small shrine huts in the Sunderban
türbe/turba (T/A)	tomb, mausoleum; lit. "earth, soil, dust"
ūlū 'l-albāb	possessors of hearts, a synonym for spiritually advanced seekers
umanā' (sg. *amīn*)	trustworthy ones; early term for an upper rank in saintly hierarchy
uns	familiarity, intimacy; quality of divine-human relationship
'urs	wedding; holy person's death, hence meeting with Beloved/God
'uzla	seclusion, withdrawal, lesser retreat
'uzlatīyān (A/P)	seekers of seclusion, withdrawal; class of saints

waḥdat ash-shuhūd	unity of experience/witnessing; experiential unity with God
waḥdat al-wujūd	Unity of Being/Existence; ontological oneness of all things
wahm	suspicion, conjecture, mistaken notion, opinion
waḥy	divine revelation given to prophets only
walāya	status of a Friend of God; one enjoying divine patronage; see *wilāya*
walī	Friend of God; connotation of "patron" or "protector" when referring to God
Wali Songo (J)	Nine Friends of God, chief group of Indonesian saints
waqf	pious endowment; support in perpetuity for religious institutions
waqfa	standing, staying; an aspect of ecstatic experience
wāqif	one who experiences "standing" before God
wārid(-āt)	spiritual on-coming; form of mystical enlightenment
waṣīla	mediation; term used by some critics of Friend veneration as more acceptable than *shafā'a*
waṣīya (waṣāya)	testament; *shaykh*'s final instructions to students or successor
watad	anchor; used syn. with *ṣāliḥ* in Morocco; sg. of *awtād*
wazīfa (waẓā'if)	daily office prescribed for *murīd* by *shaykh*
wilāya	spiritual office or authority to rule, often used syn. with *walāya*
wilāyāt	saintly domains, provinces of authority
wirātha	spiritual heritage or legacy
wird (awrād)	litanies, often unique to an order, bestowed at initiation
wisāṭa	intervention, mediation by a holy person
xian (C)	"worthy"; common term for Friend of God, as distinct from *shen*
yār (P)	friend, whether human or divine; Abū Bakr was called "Friend of the Cave"
zāhid (zuhhād)	one who practices asceticism, renunciation

zaʿīm	leader, guide; honorific given to some North African national heroes
zaʾir (zuwwār)	visitor, devotee at tombs of holy persons
zāwiya (zawāyā)	corner; cell, small residence of a *shaykh,* superseded by larger institutions
zhanxian (C)	writing saintly lineages on dead person's burial clothes
zhenren (C)	"real beings" (i.e., Prophets/Friends) who have fulfilled their purpose in cosmos
zhisheng (C)	"Utmost Sage"; title of Muhammad
ziyāra(-āt)	visitation; regional or local pilgrimage to holy person's tomb
zuhd	asceticism; self-discipline after the model of the Prophet

About the Contributors

J. W. T. ALLEN (d. 1979) was educated at Oxford and the School of Oriental and African Studies and spent many years in East Africa where he did extensive research in Swahili religious literature. His publications include *The Swahili and Arabic Manuscripts and Tapes in the Library of the University College, Dar es Salaam: A Catalogue* (1970); *Tendi: Six Examples of a Swahili Classical Verse Form* (1971); and *A Poem Concerning the Death of the Prophet Muhammad: Utendi wa kutawafu Nabii, a Traditional Swahili Epic* (1991).

ALI S. ASANI is Professor of Indo-Muslim Cultures and Islamic Civilizations at Harvard University. He is a specialist in the Muslim literatures of South Asia, particularly Shiʻi and Sufi devotional literatures in Sindhi, Gujarati, and Urdu. His publications include *Ecstasy and Enlightenment: Ismaili Devotional Literatures of South Asia* and *Let's Study Urdu: An Introductory Course*.

ANNA BIGELOW joined the faculty in Philosophy and Religion at North Carolina State University in fall 2004 as Assistant Professor. She received her MA from Columbia University and PhD in Religious Studies from the University of California, Santa Barbara, where she focused on South Asian Islam. Her dissertation, "Sharing Saints, Shrines, and Stories: Practicing Pluralism in North India," won an award for best dissertation from the Department of Religious Studies at UCSB. Her current research focuses on the interreligious dynamics of contested and cooperatively patronized multiconfessional sacred sites.

LODE F. BRAKEL (d. 1981) was Professor of Southeast Asian Languages and Literatures in the Department of Indonesian and Oceanic Studies at the University of Hamburg during the last years of his life. He published several works on Malay literature, on the origins of the Malay *hikāyat* form, on the poetry of the mystic Hamza Fansūrī, and most notably for present purposes, on the Malay version of the story of Muhammad al-Hanafīya.

ARTHUR BUEHLER, a graduate of Harvard University's History of Religions Program, teaches at Victoria University, Wellington, New Zealand. He has published two monographs dealing with the Indian Naqshbandiyya, *Sufi Heirs of the Prophet* (1998) and *Analytical Indexes for the Collected Letters of Ahmad Sirhindi* (in Persian). His forthcoming *Sirhindi* will be a selected translation of Ahmad Sirhindī's *Collected Letters*.

DEVIN DEWEESE is Professor of Central Eurasian Studies at Indiana University. He studies the history of Islam in Central and Inner Asia, with a special focus on problems of Islamization and the history of Sufi communities in the region. He is the author of *Islamization and Native Religion in the Golden Horde* (1994) and numerous articles. His current work is focused on a history of the Yasavī Sufi tradition, a study (authored with Ashirbek Muminov) of a fourteenth-century narrative of Islamization in Central Asia, and a critical analysis of western studies of Islam in contemporary Central Asia.

SOULEYMANE BACHIR DIAGNE (PhD Sorbonne, 1988) has taught philosophy at Cheikh Anta Diop University, Dakar, Senegal, for twenty years. He is currently Professor of Romance Philology and Philosophy at Columbia University, with research interests in Islamic philosophy and African philosophy. His publications include *Boole, l'oiseau de nuit en plein jour* (1989); a translation and presentation in French of Boole's *Laws of Thought* (1992); and *Islam et société ouverte, la fidélité et le mouvement dans la pensée de Muhammad Iqbal* (2001). His latest publication is *Léopold Sédar Senghor: l'art africain comme philosophie* (2007).

DAVID EDWARDS is Carl W. Vogt '58 Professor of Anthropology at Williams College. His publications include *Before Taliban: Genealogies of the Afghan Jihad* (2002) and *Heroes of the Age: Moral Fault Lines on the Afghan Frontier* (1996). He also codirected and produced the film *Kabul Transit* (www.kabul-transit.net), released in 2007.

JAMAL J. ELIAS is the author of a number of books and articles on a wide range of subjects dealing with Islamic cultural and intellectual history in West, Central, and South Asia, including *Death before Dying*, an edition and translation of the Punjabi Sufi poems of Sultan Bahu (1998). He is the editor of *Keywords for the Study of Islam* (2009) and the author of a forthcoming book on religion, culture, and truck decoration in Pakistan. Elias is Professor and Chair of Religious Studies at the University of Pennsylvania, where he holds the Class of 1965 Term Professorship in the School of Arts and Sciences.

CARL W. ERNST is a specialist in Islamic studies, with a focus on West and South Asia. His most recent book, *Following Muhammad: Rethinking Islam in the Contemporary World* (2003), received several international awards. He studied comparative religion at Stanford University (AB 1973) and Harvard University (PhD 1981). He is now William R. Kenan Jr. Distinguished Professor of Religious Studies and Director of the Carolina Center for the

Study of the Middle East and Muslim Civilizations at the University of North Carolina at Chapel Hill.

ANNA M. GADE is a historian of religions who specializes in Islam and religious systems of Southeast Asia. Her work focuses on trends in contemporary Muslim revitalization across mainland, peninsular, and island Southeast Asia, especially Cambodia and Indonesia. She is the author of *Perfection Makes Practice: Learning, Emotion, and the Recited Quran in Indonesia* (2004). She now teaches in the Religious Studies Programme, Victoria University, Wellington, New Zealand.

MARCIA HERMANSEN (PhD University of Chicago, Arabic and Islamic Studies) is Professor of Theology and Director of the Islamic World Studies program at Loyola University, Chicago. With extensive experience in Egypt, Jordan, India, Iran, Turkey, and Pakistan, she conducts research in Arabic, Persian, Urdu, and Turkish. Her publications on Islamic thought, Sufism, Islam and Muslims in South Asia, Muslims in America, and women and gender in Islam include *The Conclusive Argument from God* (1996), a study and translation (from Arabic) of Shāh Walī Allāh of Delhi's *Hujjat Allāh al-Bāligha*. She also coedited the *Encyclopedia of Islam and the Muslim World* (2003).

KENNETH HONERKAMP, Associate Professor in the Department of Religion at the University of Georgia, Athens, is a graduate of the Qarawiyīn University of Morocco and the University of Aix-en-Provence, France. Extensive experience in Pakistan, Afghanistan, and Morocco facilitated his study of traditional institutions, Sufi orders, and manuscripts in Fes and Marrakesh. He edited and translated several previously unpublished works of Abū Abd ar-Rahmān as-Sulamī (d. 412/1021), and his critical edition of the *Rasā'il al-kubrā* of Ibn Abbād of Ronda (d. 792/1390) was published in 2005.

AHMET T. KARAMUSTAFA (PhD McGill University, 1987) is Professor of History and Religious Studies at Washington University in St. Louis. He is the author of *God's Unruly Friends* (1994), a book on ascetic movements in medieval Islam, and *Sufism: The Formative Period* (2007), a comprehensive historical overview of early Islamic mysticism. He also helped edit, and wrote several articles for, *Cartography in the Traditional Islamic and South Asian Societies* (1992). He is currently working on a book project titled "Islamic Perspectives on Religion."

FATEMEH KESHAVARZ (PhD SOAS, London) is Professor of Persian and Comparative Literature, and Chair of the Asian and Near Eastern Languages and Literatures Department, at Washington University in St. Louis. Her major publications include *Reading Mystical Lyric: The Case of Jalāl al-Dīn Rūmī* (1998); *Recite in the Name of the Red Rose: Poetic Sacred Making in Twentieth Century Iran* (2006), and *Jasmine and Stars: Reading More Than Lolita in Tehran* (2007).

NURTEN KILIC-SCHUBEL is Assistant Professor of History and Religious Studies at Kenyon College. A specialist on Central Asian history, she is the author of numerous articles on Central Asian culture and history. Prof. Kilic-Schubel is currently finishing a book on the political culture of the Shibanid-Uzbek dynasty.

BEVERLY B. MACK is Professor of African Studies at the University of Kansas, where she teaches courses in women in Islam and Islamic literature. She has done fieldwork among Muslim women in northern Nigeria and Morocco. Her publications include *Muslim Women Sing: Hausa Popular Song; One Woman's Jihad: Nana Asma'u, Scholar and Scribe* (with Jean Boyd); *The Collected Works of Nana Asma'u bint Shehu Usman dan Fodio (1793–1864)* (with Jean Boyd); and *Hausa Women in the Twentieth Century* (with Catherine Coles).

RICHARD MCGREGOR graduated from McGill University's Institute of Islamic Studies in 2001 and spent the following two years at the Institut Français d'Archéologie Orientale in Cairo. He is the author of *Sanctity and Mysticism in Medieval Egypt: The Wafā' Sufi Order and the Legacy of Ibn 'Arabī* (2004), and his latest project will take up the problem of aesthetics in the medieval Islamic mystical tradition. Appointed Assistant Professor of Religion at Vanderbilt University, he recently edited *The Development of Sufism in Mamluk Egypt* (2006).

JAWID MOJADDEDI is currently Associate Professor of Religion and Director of the Center for Middle Eastern Studies at Rutgers University. His most recent book is his verse translation of Rumi's *Masnavi*. The first volume, published in 2004, was awarded the Lois Roth Prize by the American Institute of Iranian Studies. The second volume was released in July 2007. His previous books include *The Biographical Tradition in Sufism* (2001) and (coedited with N. Calder and A. Rippin) *Classical Islam: A Sourcebook of Religious Literature* (2003).

JAMES W. MORRIS is currently Professor in the Department of Theology at Boston College. He has written and taught in many areas of spirituality and religious thought, including the Islamic humanities, Islamic philosophy, Sufism, and cinema in spiritual teaching. His most recent books include *The Reflective Heart: Discovering Spiritual Intelligence in Ibn 'Arabī's 'Meccan Illuminations'* (2005); *Orientations: Islamic Thought in a World Civilisation* (2004); *Knowing the Spirit* (2006); and *Ibn 'Arabī: The Meccan Revelations* (2002).

SACHIKO MURATA is professor of Religious Studies in the Department of Asian and Asian American Studies, State University of New York, Stony Brook. Her publications include *The Tao of Islam: A Sourcebook on Gender Relationships in Islamic Thought* (1992), *The Vision of Islam* (with W. Chittick; 1994), and *Chinese Gleams of Sufi Light: Wang Tai-yü's Great*

Learning of the Pure and Real and Liu Chih's Displaying the Concealment of the Real Realm (2000).

ERIK S. OHLANDER is Assistant Professor of Religious Studies in the Department of Philosophy at Indiana University–Purdue University, Fort Wayne. A specialist in the social, cultural, and intellectual history of Islam during the medieval and early modern periods, he is currently working on issues related to the history of Sufism and Sufi institutions in the central and eastern regions of the Islamic world between the twelfth and fifteenth centuries C.E.

SCOTT REESE is an Associate Professor of History at Northern Arizona University. He has published numerous articles on Sufism and reformist discourse in Northeast Africa during the colonial period and is the editor of *The Transmission of Learning in Islamic Africa* (2004). He published *Renewers of the Age: Holy Men and Social Discourse in Colonial Benaadir* in 2008.

JOHN RENARD (Ph.D. Harvard, NELC, 1978) is Professor of Theological Studies at Saint Louis University. Earlier publications include *Seven Doors to Islam* (1996) and *Windows on the House of Islam* (1998). More recently he has authored *Knowledge of God in Classical Sufism* (2004), *A Historical Dictionary of Sufism* (2005), and this volume's companion monograph, *Friends of God: Islamic Models of Piety, Commitment, and Servanthood* (2008).

VERNON JAMES SCHUBEL is Professor of Religious Studies at Kenyon College. He is the author of *Religious Performance in Contemporary Islam: Shi'i Devotional Ritual in South Asia* and numerous articles on Islam. He has conducted research in Pakistan, Uzbekistan, and Turkey. His most recent research has been on the religious worldview of the Alevi-Bektaşi community in Turkey. He is currently finishing a book on traditions of humanism in vernacular Islam.

MARK SOILEAU is Assistant Professor of Religious Studies at Albion College, where he teaches courses related to Islam. His research interests include Sufism in Turkey, particularly the Bektashi order, ritual and performance, collective memory, and nationalism. His PhD dissertation, "Humanist Mystics: Nationalism and the Commemoration of Saints in Turkey" (University of California, Santa Barbara, 2006), examines the ways mystics such as Rumi, Hajī Bektash, and Yūnus Emre have been commemorated in modern Turkey.

TONY K. STEWART, Professor of South Asian Religions and Literatures at North Carolina State University, specializes in the premodern religious literatures of the Bengali-speaking regions of India and Bangladesh, focusing on Hindu-Muslim interaction. His recent works include *Fabulous Females and Peerless Pirs: Tales of Mad Adventure in Old Bengal* (2004) and translations of Tagore's Vaisnava poetry, with poet Chase Twichell, *The Lover of God* (2003). He has just completed a monograph on the literary practices of the Gaudiya

Vaisnavas tentatively titled *The Final Word: The "Caitanya Caritamrta" and the Grammar of Religious Tradition* (forthcoming).

SUFIA MENDEZ UDDIN currently teaches at Connecticut College in the Department of Religious Studies. Her main interest is Islam in Bengal and the religious life of Muslims and Hindus in West Bengal and Bangladesh. Her recent publications include *Constructing Bangladesh: Religion, Ethnicity, and Language in an Islamic Nation* (2006), and "Beyond National Borders and Religious Boundaries: Muslim and Hindu Veneration of Bonbībī" in *Engaging South Asian Religions: Boundaries, Appropriations, and Resistances,* edited by Peter Gottschalk and Matthew Schmalz (forthcoming).

Index of Names

Index of Concepts, Themes, Places, and Book Titles

Qur'an Index

The index lists both actual quotations and generic references to specific texts.

Text: 10/13 Aldus
Display: Aldus
Compositor: BookMatters, Berkeley
Printer and binder: Sheridan Books, Inc.